MY RACE TO FREEDOM

MY RACE
to
FREEDOM

A Life in the Civil Rights Movement

GWENDOLYN PATTON

FOREWORD BY BOB MOSES

NEWSOUTH BOOKS

Montgomery

NewSouth Books
105 S. Court Street
Montgomery, AL 36104

Library of Congress Cataloging-in-Publication Data

Names: Patton, Gwendolyn M., 1943- author. | Moses, Robert Parris, writer
of foreword.
Title: My race to freedom / Gwendolyn Patton ; foreword by Bob Moses.
Description: Montgomery : NewSouth Books, [2020]
Identifiers: LCCN 2020018820 (print) | LCCN 2020018821 (ebook) |
ISBN 9781603064507 (trade paperback) | ISBN 9781603064514 (epub)
Subjects: LCSH: Patton, Gwendolyn M., 1943- | Patton, Gwendolyn M.,
1943—Family. | African American women civil rights workers—Alabama—
Montgomery—Biography. | African American civil rights workers—Alabama—
Montgomery—Biography. | Civil rights workers—Alabama—Montgomery—
Biography. | Montgomery (Ala.)—Social conditions—20th century. | Detroit
(Mich.)—Social conditions—20th century. | Montgomery (Ala.)—Biography. |
Detroit (Mich.)—Biography. | Patton family.
Classification: LCC F334.M753 P393 2019 (print) | LCC F334.M753 (ebook)
| DDC 323.092 [B]--dc23
LC record available at https://lccn.loc.gov/2020018820
LC ebook record available at https://lccn.loc.gov/2020018821

Printed in the United States of America

To my mother (1922–1958), who, in our too brief earthly time together, taught me resilience

To my father (1923–2000), who nurtured me for fifty-seven years and taught me perseverance

To my maternal grandmother (1904–1980), who taught me endurance

To my paternal grandmother (1903–1983), who taught me that God will take care of me

To my paternal grandfather (1900–1979), the embodiment of solemn piety, who taught me to prayerfully keep the faith

To my brother, Bob: may our sibling love deepen like that of our father's and his sister, our Aunt Samella

Contents

Foreword

By Bob Moses

Welcome to a complex portrait of a complex life. Gwen Patton reflects on her life surrounded by all kinds of family, intertwined with a caste system that knew no shame, whiplashed by civil rights organizing and movement events large and small. A life which, on the verge of coming into its own at Tuskegee Institute, deteriorates into an unanticipated, unexpected infliction: tuberculosis.

From January 1, 1963, to January 1, 1964, young Gwen leaves Tuskegee Institute to stay in the Batson Memorial Sanatorium for tuberculosis patients. Isolated from the known world, incarcerated into forlorn, decrepit segregated rooms of the Sanatorium, Gwen refashions a life replete with accurate empathy for her fellow patients, courage to confront hospital administrators, and a deep, deep self-regard.

When Gwen returns to and graduates from Tuskegee Institute, she decides that "movement work was legitimate work and that it should be within the mainstream to carry the message for fundamental social change if America was to live up to its creed of participatory democracy."

One such message demanded that the National Student Association (NSA), pay reparations to an affiliated student group, the National Association of Black Students (NABS). Although this and other accounts from those "Black Power" years are informative, even riveting, in the end the central story line is Gwen herself through the life she exercises with dedication, principle, and an unbending devotion to justice, equality, and the well-being of all people.

Editor's Note

The memoir that is *My Race to Freedom* began two decades ago with journal entries, recollected vignettes, and an extended narrative through Gwen Patton's colorful life as a student, activist, and national organizer. The original manuscript she brought to me around 2007 was almost 2,000 pages long. We decided to split it in half, concluding with her return to Montgomery in 1978, with a brief epilogue telling what had become of many of the family members, friends, and fellow activists she describes in Volume 1. I worked with Gwen on her manuscript for thirteen years, rewriting, smoothing, and tightening her text—as much as possible. Finally, in late 2016, she finished proofreading and correcting the final chapters and the epilogue.

Sadly, she did not live to see the book in print. She became ill and was hospitalized in the spring of 2017 and died on May 11 of that year. NewSouth still had considerable work to do in copyediting, designing, and producing the book, but without a living author we set the project aside until 2020, when Bob Moses agreed to write a foreword, and we were able to work with Gwen's executor to publish the book.

Gwen's was a unique life, split in her early years between Detroit, where she was born, and Montgomery, where her roots were and she spent summers with her grandparents. In many respects, she grew up as a typical teenager. But by her teens, she was caught up in the Montgomery Bus Boycott, and as a college student leader she dove into the civil rights protests around the Selma-to-Montgomery March. She went on to a career as an organizer and teacher. Her story is worthwhile.

— RANDALL WILLIAMS

Preface

The following pages narrate my sojourn to seek freedom as a Black child/ teenager/adult in America. It begins with my family ethos before I was born, and when I entered this world how their racial pride and quest for freedom shaped and informed me and my generation to "race to freedom."

Perhaps, some of my readers of all races and ethnicities will see parallels of their stories in mine. Hopefully, we can bond together as Americans to help make this world a better place for all of us to live, work, and play.

ACKNOWLEDGMENTS

Foremost, I want to thank Jesus, the Christ, who promised not to leave me alone. During the fifteen years of writing my memoir and having it edited and published by Randall Williams, an excellent and empathetic editor, and New-South Books, I have had serious bouts of frustration, impatience and doubts. Thanks be to God . . . He tempered my anxieties with His grace. Among many of God's revelatory blessings, a synopsis of my memoir was published in the 2011 best selling anthology, *Student Nonviolent Coordinating Committee Women: Hands on the Freedom Plow*. For this I am grateful to my SNCC sisters and editors of love, Martha Prescod Norman Noonan and Faith Holsaert.

I especially want to thank my family, many who have gone to dance with my ancestors since I began writing this memoir. My father (1923–2000) was my first content editor. He read with delight my initial narrative outline, fleshing out the myriad details of his family upbringing, his southern and northern experiences. He often visited with me for the expressed purpose to help me hone my manuscript. Though he recognized my maturity, admired and through the years supported my Movement commitment, I was still "Daddy's Little Girl."

Flora Elmore Moore Andry (1929–2007), my maternal second cousin, was elevated in my eyesight as my "big sister" when I came to live with her, her sons, Lloyd and Arthur, and mother, Aunt Chick, in Montgomery at the tender age of sixteen. She guided me into lady hood. Though she considered my Movement enthusiastic commitment over the top, she never smirked at my seriousness. Her descriptions of train-men's labor and what it was like for Negroes to ride the train during Jim Crow Montgomery were invaluable.

Despite my painful, teenage encounters by the hands of my step-mother after the passing of my mother, her sister, my Aunt Frances and her children, Betty Jane Wells, Johnny and Judy Whitaker, refreshed my memories of my childhood community—Inkster, Michigan. Aunt Frances provided recollections of what Inkster was like in its early development as a hamlet and how my father, her husband, Uncle Herman Smith and others in the 1950s mounted a community movement to transform our hamlet into a city-representative government, which still exists to this day. Betty Jane and her son, Michael, who is a member of Inkster Historical Society, forwarded historical documents that confirmed the transformation. Judy visited, telephoned and emailed me about the factory process of spray-painting a car on the assembly line, a job my father once performed when he worked in the factory. The Smith Family proved and instilled in me that family relations can arise above personal adversity. Though we are in-laws, ex-laws and out-laws, we are all family and should always manifest our love for one another. For this lesson in unconditioned love, I will always be grateful to the Smith Family.

For my dear friends, Marty Jezer (d. 2005), author of *Abbie Hoffman: American Rebel*; Edith Chevat, author of *Love Lessons*; and, Donald P. Stone, author of *Fallen Prince: William James Edwards—Black Education and the Quest for Afro American Nationality*, I thank them for their reading of my initial narrative outline and for offering their suggestions to flesh out and tighten my manuscript outline. Donald wanted to publish the outline "as is" as a short Movement biography. Edith went the extra mile of proof-reading my unedited manuscript. I will always appreciate their strong words of encouragement that I had a memoir worthy of sharing and their instructive criticisms to make my memoir more readable.

My half-sister, Sandy, whom my mother raised me to love as my sister minus the biological description, was an ardent listener as I read passages and chapters in my manuscripts. It mattered less that she was telephoning me from Bern, Switzerland. She had resided in Bern since 1992 as a vocal professor at the Swiss School of Jazz. Her acceptance of my critical analysis of my relationship with her mother meant much to me. After all, we were both "Daddy's Girls."

It was always a joy when my Uncle Sam "Junior" Patton Jr. called to share his childhood memories about my father and the Patton family. Junior continues to be a fountain of hope eternal.

My beloved Aunt Samella "Tee" Patton Davis Richardson (1922–2011) truly loved my father, her "big brother," though she was the eldest of her seven siblings. Their enduring love for each other is the idyllic model for sister-brother relationships for all generations, past, present and future.

Her weekly telephone calls to me from Las Vegas for more than 30 years were an unending source of strength to break through my frustrating walls will forever be my mantra . . . "just keep on living."

Carole Watson and her mother, Frances Webb, my next-door neighbors in Inkster until I moved to Montgomery in 1960 and my Delta Sigma Theta sorority sister and Delta Dear, provided vital details about my public school days. Tina Strozier and her mother, Hazel, also Inkster neighbors, searched through hundreds of personal photos for me to include in my memoir.

When I heard my name called in the Atlanta airport, I turned around to see who was the caller. There stood statuesque Sharon Thompson Sullivan. I had not seen my Inkster High School friend and co-cheerleader Sharon in forty years. My visits with her in Augusta, Georgia and Minneapolis, Minnesota were delights as we pored over her Inkster High School yearbooks, waxing nostalgic about those 1950s "happy days."

No matter what hour, and oft-times in the wee hours in the morning, my SNCC sisters Mae Jackson and Efia Nwangaza were always on the ready. They roused from their deep sleep to listen to my reading of entire draft chapters. They offered suggestions as to how I could make my memoir come more alive. We often laughed heartily when we recounted our sisterly experiences. I am most thankful for their humor in our times of struggle for freedom.

Lastly, I want to thank the many people, especially my colleagues at H. Councill Trenholm State Technical College, my Sunday School sisters and my Church Family of six generations, currently under the pastorate of Reverend Doctor G. W. C. Richardson, for their encouragement and confidence that my race to freedom was a good fight.

My Race to Freedom

1

Roots

I came into the world in 1943 in Detroit, Michigan, but my roots were in the deepest South, in Montgomery, Alabama. My mother was of the Foster family, and my father was a Patton. These were proud, independent black families, and their blended heritage shaped my outlook and my personality. It is no wonder that according to a family anecdote I helped push myself out of the womb, kicking eagerly backwards with my infant feet. In fact, a family tragedy may have precipitated my mother's early labor, but in any case the story remains that after the doctor cut the umbilical cord and the nurse cleaned me and placed me in my mother's arms, the nurse asked, "What is her name?"

"Gwendolyn Marie," my mother replied. "She will be a free child."

The nurse took me from my mother's caressing arms and carried me to the hospital nursery. My father, waiting outside the window, beamed with loving joy as the nurse placed me in the designated Patton bassinet. My father had saved every penny from his moonlighting job as a Detroit city bus driver. A few days later, he collected my mother and me and we left Henry Ford Hospital not owing the white establishment one red cent.

That, too, was typical of my heritage.

MY GRANDFATHER, SAM PATTON, was a quiet, soft-spoken man whose demeanor betrayed his strict and disciplined nature. He was a tall man of 6'4", slim with a straight-arrow posture and always clean-shaven. With a fourth-grade education, he was a master carpenter-builder and a Biblical scholar. The Pattons lived next door to our family church, Hutchinson Street Missionary Baptist. My grandfather had remodeled and bricked the church, one of the largest and most beautiful churches in Montgomery in the 1940s. The church and community held him in high esteem. Deacon Sam Patton never smoked or cursed and was said never to have had a drink of whiskey in his life.

He had served in every leadership capacity from Sunday School superintendent to chair of the trustee board and president emeritus of the deacon board. When Deacon Patton spoke, everyone listened and abided, whether it was in the home, on the job, or in the church.

The Patton family was considered "well-to-do" and had been driving their own car since the 1920s, changing models every three years. The home, located on the east side of town and within walking distance of the Negro Alabama State Teachers College, was a spacious dwelling with an inside bathroom, a radio that received signals from England, a Victrola, and two telephones. The house had five bedrooms to accommodate the first set of four children. By 1935, two more children had been added.

The backyard garden yielded pole beans, tomatoes, greens, peas, okra, and corn. A section was cordoned off to house the chickens, turkeys, and ducks. Plum, apple, peach, and pomegranate trees graced the yard. The Pattons never felt the harsh sting of the Great Depression. My grandfather insisted that his family be self-sufficient and self-sustaining—his strategy to avoid dependence on unpredictable whites as much as possible. My grandmother, Mary Jane, called "MaDear," handled the books for the construction business. Later, she became a midwife, delivering hundreds of Negro babies throughout Montgomery County. She served as president of the church's nurses' guild and deacons' wives, and sang in the choir.

MY FATHER, ROBERT Patton, was the second child and the only son. Within the family, he was called "Brother." His sisters Samella, Beatrice, and Edith Mae adored him. They kept his shirts and handkerchiefs starched and pressed. They pressed his undershirts and shorts. They polished his shoes until they could see their faces in the shine. Brother likewise adored his sisters and protected them. They had prestige in their school, Booker T. Washington, because they were Brother's sisters. Fellows were polite and respectful toward the Patton girls. They did not care to tangle with Brother.

Social life for the Patton children was restricted to church teas and outings and very limited school activities. Brother was a charmer, chased by girls in and outside the church. He would often leave church activities to experience his own ideas of social life. He received many chastisements for his outings outside the church. Nonetheless, he was industrious and had worked since his early teens, first throwing papers for the *Montgomery Journal* in the Negro community, and then as a delivery boy for the Jewish-owned E. J. neighborhood grocery.

Sam Patton had bought his son a bicycle, and this transportation made my father employable. On weekends he worked for a downtown drug store and delivered medications to "old money" whites in the posh Cloverdale neighborhood.

Persuading his father to buy him a bicycle had been a stroke of genius. Between deliveries, Robert would visit girls. While downtown, he stopped by the white hotels and conversed with the bellhops—always Negroes, some with college degrees—and learned how to gamble and heard about the wiles of rapacious white men.

Occasionally, Robert worked with his father. Sam Patton had up to forty workers on his payroll in the peak seasons of spring, summer, and fall, building homes and commercial buildings. Through the years, I heard stories like this one:

"Brother, I need you to work with me tomorrow," Grandfather would say. "Tell Mr. E. J. you're not coming in. We have to be at the bank by 9 in the morning. We're leaving at 8."

My father hated for his father to call the white grocer "Mr. E. J.," especially since E. J. was not present. More than hating to hear his father say "Mr. E. J.," he hated going to the bank. And to leave at 8 in the morning, when his father was a fast driver, meant that they would have to sit in the car in complete silence for fifty minutes before the bank opened. My grandfather always carried my father to business meetings that involved finances. My father was known for his mathematical acumen. He could add and subtract columns of numbers and factor percentages in his head.

When the bank doors opened, my grandfather and father got out of the car, taking off their hats prior to entering the bank. After some time, the clerk ushered them into the bank president's office.

"Good morning, Mr. President," my grandfather said, his hat still in his hand. My father said nothing, following behind.

"What do you want, Sam?" the president asked.

"I need a line of credit to buy supplies. I have contracts to build two houses, one in Madison Park and the other on Hall Street, and a private business school on West Jeff Davis Avenue."

"Why don't you use your savings? You have a nice account here."

"This is a business venture. Our savings are for our family. Of course, we'll put the savings up for collateral," my father piped in. If the bank president had known that my father was only seventeen, he would have considered this remark impudent. For a Negro to know anything about business, he had to be old, no matter how young he might look.

"You're certain you're doing just niggah work in building houses and schools?"

"Yes, suh." My father shifted his weight from one foot to the other, and then he stood firmly. He camouflaged his rage with a slight smile. Though my father detested the humiliation, he knew deep down inside that my grandfather's disciplined life was a buffer to stem the violent whims of racists who had absolute control over Negro lives, especially in financial matters.

"Okay, boys. I'll approve the loan."

All during the negotiations, the bank president never got out of his chair behind his grand desk, nor offered my grandfather and father seats in his luxurious suite.

Driving home, my father broke the silence. "Daddy, I want to leave Montgomery when I graduate from high school in May."

"I knew this day was coming. Son, where will you go? And, who's going to take over the business if you leave?"

"They are hiring factory workers in the automobile industry in Detroit. I can stay with Samella and her husband until I get a job and land on my feet. If I stay in Montgomery, I'll probably kill a white man or he may kill me."

My grandfather said nothing as they drove home in silence.

Detroit had another pull for Robert: his future wife, who would be my mother, was there.

THE FOSTERS, MY maternal family, were "well-to-do Negroes" on the west side of Montgomery. Leonard Foster Jr., my great-grandfather, raised horses and was a professional jockey on the chariot and trotting race circuits. Mary, my great-grandmother, was a housewife who tended to the backyard garden and the grandchildren, who called her "Big Mama." They lived in a large two-story frame house with six bedrooms to accommodate the nine children.

By 1943, four of the Foster children had died, and three others—two sons and a daughter, the baby, had moved to Philadelphia; Dayton, Ohio; and Pittsburgh. When Big Mama died in 1945, the youngest daughter, by then a school teacher and a professional seamstress, moved back from Pittsburgh to live in the family home with her husband, Tom Thomas, a house painter.

Juanita, my grandmother, was the seventh of the Foster children. She was nicknamed "Coot" and eventually would be called "Mommy" by her three grandchildren. At age sixteen, she married Nathaniel Bolden, a laborer, and Leonard Foster built a home for his daughter's wedding present, as he had done when his oldest daughter, Nathia Lee, married Eugene Elmore. The Elmores with their two children lived next door to the Foster family home, while the Boldens lived with their three children three blocks south.

My grandmother did not fare well in marriage. Nathaniel drank too much for her taste and the couple separated; for all intents and purposes, she considered it a divorce. Nathaniel accepted her terms to leave with visitation rights as long as he did not come to the home drunk. She did not demand child support for their three children—Jeanetta (Dot), Nathia Lee, and Nathaniel Jr. Coincidentally, Nathaniel Jr. was also called "Brother" within the Foster/Bolden family; Nathia Lee was called "Sister."

Juanita Bolden—Mommy—was twenty-one years old when she asked her husband to leave. It was uncommon in 1929 for a wife, who was reared to "serve" her spouse, to stand up to a man and demand respect for a whole-some family life. But Mommy did not accept the notion that "a piece of man is better than no man."

As a single mother with children ages five, four, and two, she became a day-worker for white families. Her aim was to achieve the highest position she could in what was a fundamentally demeaning occupation for Negro women—serving white women and their families at the expense of the nurturing of one's own children. Because she was a nursing mother at the time, Mommy landed the "prestigious" job of "nanny" for a rich white family. She nursed her son on one breast and the white baby on the other,

As a nanny, she never washed windows, dishes, floors, or the white family's clothes. Other hired help performed those chores. When the white family traveled, she traveled with them to tend to the child, a boy, Paddy. She always brought souvenirs home to her children. Mommy also babysat when the white family had dinner parties, and she would bring home leftover choice cuts of meat and fancy dishes. On her days off, she hosted tea parties for her children and their friends with the fancy leftovers. The tradition of "Mommy's tea parties" has spanned five generations in her honor, particularly by me, her granddaughter.

Mommy taught her two daughters to create hors d'oeuvres trays of finger sandwiches, cheese straws, fancy-cut pickles and radishes, cheese-filled celery stalks, and deviled eggs garnished with paprika, parsley flakes, and pimento. The trays would be adorned with sprigs of parsley, mint leaves, and pitted olives, green and black. The punch bowl was the shell of a watermelon. It was important to purchase a round, not oblong, watermelon that could sit on its bottom. The sweet meat was scooped out in perfect miniature balls the size of marbles with one of Mommy's kitchen gadgets. The watermelon balls, along with cherries and crushed pineapples, were put back into the shell, now ornately carved into a vertical, zigzag pattern at the top. Ginger ale was poured into the delightful concoction.

This was before refrigeration. I remember hearing stories of how the ice man's truck rattled through the neighborhood. "Brother, here's twenty cents. Buy two five pounds of block ice," Mommy would instruct. After emptying the water pan, Mommy placed one block of ice in the compartment in the icebox. Brother crushed the other block with a hammer, and placed it on the rack right below the ice compartment.

"No one is to go into the icebox until I say so!" Mommy warned. And no one dared to open the ice-box for fear of getting a whipping with an ironing cord.

After tea party guests arrived and it was time for the repast, Mommy would retrieve the crushed ice and pour it into the sweet punch mixture. Sometimes she would add mint leaves picked from the back yard. Her children were always dressed in their Sunday best to receive their neighborhood guests at the tea parties.

Mommy was called "Coot" by her family because she was considered eccentric. She had a deeper perspective on life and her role in it. Though she was considered "weird," her friends and neighbors would gather on their front porches to see Mommy leave her home for work. She was a dashing sight in her white uniform, stockings, and shoes, with her navy nurse's cape draped about her shoulders. Though she was considered different, she was admired for her determination and independence, especially by young wives and mothers struggling to maintain wholesome families.

MY FATHER FIRST met my mother by chance in 1940 at the annual Loveless High School Dance. He noticed her, demure and petite, with long hair—a treasure in the Negro culture. It was a fleeting glance with the intent to follow up with a possible courting call later. He asked for her address and then turned his attention to his immediate agenda. He was looking for a girl adventurous enough to leave with him rather than staying to dance in the school's multi-purpose room that served as a cafeteria, gym, and space for extracurricular activities like plays and dances.

Later, while on a bicycle errand to deliver medicine to a patron in the white community, my father decided to pedal further west to the Negro community. He reached my mother's home. My grandmother, Mommy, was in the backyard tending to her herb garden of mint, oregano, basil, and parsley.

"Mrs. Bolden, is Dot home?" my father asked as he dismounted his bike. "My name is Robert Patton."

"I know who you are, young man." My grandmother studied my father's countenance, assessing whether he was a worthy suitor for her daughter. The Pattons had garnered a respectful reputation on both sides of town in the Negro communities, as well as in the white community. "Dot is in Detroit attending Lewis Business College for Women."

Mommy was determined that her girls get an education and be independent. After sending my mother to settle with relatives in Detroit and paying first-year tuition at the business college, she now was saving to send her other daughter, Sister, to Alabama A&M College in Huntsville to become a school teacher.

"Oh, I didn't know she was away in college," my father said as he mounted his bike and rode away.

IT WAS ALMOST two more years before my father got to Detroit; his marriage there to my mother followed in 1942. First, he had to convince Sam Patton to let him go.

The year he met my mother, Robert—Brother—was sixteen years old, soon to be seventeen on August 22, 1940. He would be entering his senior year in high school that fall. There was plenty of construction work during the summer, but the highlight was that his father taught him how to drive. This rite of passage from the bicycle to the automobile lifted his spirits. After a hard day's work from 5 a.m. to 5 p.m., my grandfather would let his son use the Plymouth to drive his friends around the city until sundown. At the end of summer, my father passed the driver's test and received his license.

With the privilege of driving his father's car to special school events, and sometimes slipping out at night and driving the car without permission to less than respectful events, he was considered the "most popular student" by his classmates. They elected him student treasurer because of his knack for raising money, sometimes from craps winnings during his late-night excursions.

Graduation for my father came in May 1941. Though his beloved sister, Samella, had been in the 1940 graduating class at Booker T. Washington High School—the first year the state board of education had instituted a full high school program for Negro youth in Montgomery—it was a special celebration for my father, a young Negro man, to graduate. Many Negro youth quit school after the tenth grade, brainwashed with the racist school board policy that Negroes needed only ten years of schooling,

In the Patton home after my father's graduation, with family and church friends in attendance, Sam made the announcement: "Brother, I'm turning the business over to you as president to handle the books and to bid on contracts. I'll continue to oversee construction."

My father's heart sank. Though his family was prominent and prosperous in Montgomery within the restricted opportunities for Negroes, this announcement left my father feeling trapped. His rambunctious spirit could never soar in Montgomery. Couldn't his father see that he would bring shame on the family by either killing a white man or being killed by one of them if he remained in Montgomery?

"Brother, you'll work part-time with me this summer," his father continued. "I also want you to enroll in Alabama State Teachers College."

"Daddy, I do not want to be a schoolteacher. I want to go to Detroit," my father said, knowing that he had dampened his graduation party with what was considered "sassing" by talking back to his father.

Sam did not respond. He had already stated his decision for his son.

One morning soon after, returning from the bank after what seemed the umpteenth time of having to swallow their pride to obtain a line of credit, instead of driving home his father drove them to the college campus, announcing that he had made an appointment with President H. Councill Trenholm to register Robert for summer school.

My father was bewildered. He had heard that factory workers in Detroit made ten times more money than teachers in Montgomery. And what he heard about the night life, the "sporting life," also suited him. But he dared not sass Sam Patton about this decision. He followed his father into the president's reception office. Dr. Trenholm was there to greet and invite them into his private office, where he offered them seats at a round table, soft drinks on coasters at each seat.

My father had never experienced this level of courtesy and respect in the secular, professional world. Though he was impressed, it was not enough to change his mind about going to Detroit where he would be in full charge of his own life. He wanted to be respected on his own terms and on his own merits, not by someone doing a kind gesture for him. Now, he felt, he would not only be beholden to his father, but also to Dr. Trenholm.

Nonetheless, once enrolled, my father excelled in his classes. He also worked hard with his father, becoming an expert house painter and concrete pourer as well as the business manager for his father's construction company. He loved going to college and being a business manager, but he hated living in restrictive Montgomery. Going to Detroit was the answer to his dreams of becoming "a man in his own right," without bowing and scraping for a white man's approval, despite his financial standing that elevated his status in the Negro community. My father consciously was willing to commit class suicide by abandoning the legacy of his father's business. He knew that this would hurt his father. But, then there was Junior, his baby brother at age seven already demonstrating an inclination to go into the construction business. Every day during the summer Junior climbed into the bed of his father's truck, tagged behind him, begging to measure and to saw a piece of lumber or to watch with focused attention an electrician wire a construction project. Junior could continue the business.

"Daddy, I'm eighteen years old. If you don't give me permission to go to Detroit, I plan to join the Army." Sam said nothing as he continued to drive home from the construction site. "Daddy, I've saved enough money to go to Detroit and to stand on my own two feet until I get a job."

"Son, I don't want you to go to the Army. This country has not done right by our people. Why would you want to fight for white men's privileges? Our race continues to suffer indignities of slavery to this very day of Jim Crow laws. I know the humiliation." This quiet assessment shook my father. His father was a race man after all, full of pride and militancy in his own quiet manner.

"What do you want me to do, Daddy?'

"Let me study this for a while, son."

"A while" took until late 1941. Meanwhile, my father continued college and the handling of his father's business.

THANKSGIVING WAS A festive time in Montgomery. It was the holiday season when black Montgomerians from around the country returned for Homecoming to be with family and to attend the annual "Turkey Day" parade and football classic between rivals Tuskegee Institute and Alabama State Teachers College. Tuskegee was the famed college founded by Lewis Adams that reached national acclaim under the presidency of Booker T. Washington; State was considered by the premiere educator John Dewey as one of the best teacher-training colleges in the country.

Though they had been loyal Alabama State fans since 1923, when the classic was initiated with its grand parade from downtown Montgomery to the college's football stadium, the Pattons celebrated the season more in a religious manner than with a "sporting good time."

The day began at 5 a.m. with my father's mother, MaDear, pulling the string to switch on the light in the hallway between the two bedrooms for the girls. "Girls, it's time to get up!" MaDear announced. Then she called out to the adjacent bedrooms, "Brother, Junior, it's time to get up."

It was still pitch-black night but the children did not grumble. They knew it was time for family prayers on this Thanksgiving morning, a Patton tradition for giving thanks to God for keeping the family together thus far. As delicious smells of liver and onions, grits, and homemade biscuits permeated the home, the children sleepily assembled in the living room and dropped to their knees before chairs and sofas for family prayer led by my grandfather.

"God, thank you for keeping us together. None of my children are dead or in prison. This is because of Your grace. We thank You. Lord, it's not easy being colored down here. But, we thank you, for we are a blessed family. Please look on my son, Brother. Wrap him in Your grace. He, like my daughter, Samella, who has married and moved to Detroit, wants to leave the nest. God, I ask You: Who will continue the business? He's my oldest son. I await and will abide by your answer." My grandfather continued to pray. It was his custom to pray long on these special occasions. "Lord, we thank You for Your Son, who was crucified and died upon the cross so we, Your children, can enter Your Kingdom with everlasting life. On the third day, He arose from the grave with all power in his hands. To God be the glory!" The children, knowing that the last sentence in the supplication was the end, reverently said in unison, "Amen."

Rising from their knees, the Patton family reassembled at the kitchen table on the closed-in back porch behind the kitchen. Again, Sam gave a blessing for the morning meal, followed by the children saying Bible verses. My father's favorite came from Exodus 20:12: "Honor thy father and mother that thy days may be long upon the land which the Lord thy God giveth thee."

Junior seemed glued to the picture window in the living room. He wanted to be first to see his big sister, Samella, and her husband, Jesse "Black" Davis, drive up. Finally, he exclaimed, "They're here!" From every direction in the large, rambling home, family members rushed to the front porch as Samella and Black stepped out of their long, shiny car. My grandparents remained on the front porch as the children scampered down the steps to assist with suitcases and boxes, sure to be loaded with gifts from Detroit.

My grandparents did not approve of Black. He was "too sporty," though MaDear had softened as she rode with the newlyweds to Detroit and spent two weeks with the couple as they settled in a two-family flat on what was to be their honeymoon. Still, she had her doubts, deepened by the long, shiny car. My father, on the other hand, was impressed with the sleek car and its white-wall tires, running board, and windshield visor. He had never seen anything like it.

As the children mounted the porch, my grandfather again thanked God for bringing his daughter and son-in-law safely back home and that the family was once more united. "To God be the glory!" he concluded. The family said, "Amen."

That afternoon, my father, his sisters, Bea, Edith Mae, and Samella and her husband, Black, went to the football game. The younger children, Carrie and Sam Junior, stayed at home with their parents. Again, Junior was glued to the picture window in the living room, waiting on his big brother and sisters to come home from the game.

MaDear and her daughters cooked and baked all week leading up to Thanksgiving. The spread was an incredible feast of turkey with giblet gravy, possum meat baked with sweet potatoes and honey, coon meat spiced with whole garlic, collard greens seasoned with ham hocks, snap beans with Irish potatoes, stewed okra, onions and tomatoes, rice, oyster dressing, cranberry sauce, deviled eggs, pickles and olives, candied yams, homemade rolls and cornbread, sweet potato and pecan pies, peach and apple cobblers, lemon-pound cake, and homemade ice cream, hand-cranked by the children in a churn surrounded by crushed ice and rock salt to harden the stove-cooked egg custard into ice cream. Whiskey was never served in the Patton home, but there was an assortment of non-alcoholic beverages.

All of the vegetables, including the cucumbers which were pickled and canned, came from the family garden. The turkey was raised and fattened from the Pattons' barnyard. The eggs came from the henhouse. Though the yams and sweet potatoes were purchased at the farmers' market, the pecans were shaken and the fruits were picked from the backyard orchard by the Patton children.

Three tables and fifteen or more chairs were set up in the expansive dining and adjacent living rooms for relatives, friends and church members who celebrated with the Pattons. The Pattons sat at the main dining room table of eight: my father and his five siblings, with his father and mother at the respective heads of the table. An extra chair was pulled up at the dining room table for brother-in-law Black to sit next to his wife, Samella, my father's oldest sister.

Later that evening, after the meal had been eaten, the game replayed, family and community news rehashed, politics discussed, and the dishes finally cleared, my father pulled his sister aside. "Sammie, Daddy wants me to stay home to take over the business. I can't stay. Please do what you can to get me out of here! I want to go to Detroit!"

2

Freedom Bound

My father's full name was Clarence Robert Patton, but he hated the name "Clarence" and preferred to be called "Bob." My mother, Jeanetta Bolden Patton, was the only one who could get away with calling him "Robert." And she was affectionately called "Dot" because of her petite size. Robert and Dot were not yet courting in 1941, but Dot was already in Detroit attending school. By December of that year, Grandfather Patton had relented and given permission for Robert to join his sister Samella and her husband

Black there. Family lore has it that he announced his decision during the family Christmas dinner:

"Brother, I've prayed over this matter. Your Christmas present is a train ticket to Detroit. I hope the city lights will not corrupt your spirit of love for our Savior Jesus Christ, which is the source of strengthening our love for our family. When you get to Detroit, I want you to right away find a church family you like and then join it."

Over the next few days, the Patton home was abuzz with preparations for my father's departure. His three younger sisters ironed and packed their brother's clothes, and MaDear fried chicken, boiled eggs, and baked a pound cake to pack into a shoebox, along with cans of Vienna sausages, and a supply of napkins; each item was tightly wrapped in waxed paper and bound with rubber bands.

Five days after Christmas 1941, my father left his family home, Jim Crow laws, and the Cradle of the Confederacy to go to Detroit, the purported land of freedom and opportunity, particularly in the automobile industry. He abandoned his place in Montgomery's upper middle-class black community to become his own man in the unknown urban world.

He had a ticket on the 5:30 a.m. Humming Bird, one of the lines of the Louisville and Nashville Railroad. The entire family loaded up to see him off. My father's sisters and baby brother sat quietly on the back seat. His father was at the wheel, with MaDear sitting snugly in the middle between her husband and son. When they turned onto Jackson Street, my father could make out the shapes of buildings in the early dawn. There was the grocery store owned by the Jew, E. J., who gave him his first job, and Hiawatha's shoe shop, to which he would slip away in the wee hours of the night to shoot craps in the back room. At Jackson and High streets, my father could see to one side the Negro movie house, a special courting place for his dates, and to the other side the commercial building that he had helped his father build as a mini-shopping center for the Negro community, housing a clothing shop, a barber shop, and a beauty parlor. And there was the pool hall where my father learned how to shoot pool and bet with the neighborhood hustlers. Across the street was Grayson's Candy Store, where candies were made on the premises.

They drove on into downtown, past the bank and the whites-only, Whitley Hotel, where Negro bellhops with college degrees fetched Negro prostitutes to serve white conventioneers. Here, my father learned the "procurement" business, and the complicated science of betting on sports.

At last, his father parked the car at the end of Montgomery's ornate, Gothic train depot, Union Station. His train ticket was already in hand. Having ticket in hand at least a day before departure minimized the guaranteed humiliation encountered at the one ticket window for Negroes, where the clerk was always slow and surly. On many days of departure, Negroes standing in the long line would get to the window only to find that the train was departing and that they would have to purchase a ticket for a later departure or for the next day. This caused extreme hardships for Negroes, especially for those who traveled—often in broke-down, second-hand cars—fifty or more miles from the surrounding rural Black Belt counties. Many of these Negroes were sharecroppers or tenant farmers on former plantations, who never managed to get out of debt to the heirs of the former slave owners.

Having missed a train, most unfortunates had to remain in the dingy so-called "colored" waiting room. They simply could not afford the gasoline for a second round trip to the train station. Rural travelers knew to bring extra shoeboxes of fried chicken, white bread, and pickles just in case of a racist-caused delay. But it was far better to have one's ticket already in hand, and Sam Patton was not one to let his son risk missing a train.

The Patton family sat briefly in their car, lost in their thoughts. Finally, Sam Patton spoke a prayer for the safekeeping of his son, to which the family said in unison, "Amen." Then Sam helped Robert lift the suitcase and heavy footlocker out of the trunk. Junior and Carrie carried the suitcase. Father and son each took an end of the footlocker, and everyone walked briskly through the colored entrance, past the colored waiting room, directly up to the colored ticket window.

My father slid his train ticket under the cage and checked the footlocker and the suitcase to Detroit, Michigan. The Pattons then elected to wait on the platform rather than in the colored waiting room. They joined other Negroes huddled at the front of the train. Whites congregated at the rear.

Train station sounds fascinated my father. An amplified Southern drawl that announced destinations, trains, and track numbers seemed to be coming from a hollow chamber. Clouds of steam billowed from under the train, wafting warmth across the waiting bodies. Blue-suited train men were everywhere. One was swinging a lantern as he walked up and down the platform. Others were in wide blue and white vertical striped work clothes with matching soft caps with bibs. Redcaps were loading the train's baggage car. My father idly wondered if they separated Negro luggage from white luggage.

The amplified voice announced my father's train for boarding. A conductor, walking along the train from back to front, shouted, "All aboard! All aboard!" The Pattons hugged my father, tears cascading down their cheeks. Edith Mae handed her brother his shoebox of goodies. MaDear said, "Brother, I packed your overcoat on top in your suitcase. Make certain you take it out when you get to Michigan. It is very cold up there. Probably snowing." She draped a blanket over his shoulders. "I forgot the pillow, but you can rent one on the train."

My father boarded and found a window seat next to the platform. (He might have mused about the absurdity that Negroes had to ride in the back of segregated buses, but in the front of segregated trains, the reason being that the cars at the front of the train were nearest to the coal-driven engine and thus the dirtiest and least desirable.) He looked out at his family, all waving and blowing kisses. He was sad about leaving his family, yet glad about leaving Jim Crow. He knew then that he would never return to Montgomery to live. His father also knew it.

As the train slowly pulled out of the station, the Pattons walked along the platform as far as they could. Edith Mae blew another kiss to Robert and mouthed, "I'll see you soon." Sam watched this, knowing she would be the next to leave the Patton's nest.

DAWN GAVE WAY to a sunny morning as the train rolled northward across Alabama's rural countryside to the "Magic City," Birmingham, Alabama. Some Negroes here fared better with low-level jobs in the steel mills. These Negroes had fought—sometimes with guns—to join the union, the Congress of Industrial Organizations (CIO). My father had contemplated a move to

Birmingham, but even in Alabama's largest city, Jim Crow still ruled with a vengeance.

The Humming Bird had left Montgomery at 5:35 a.m. It would arrive in Cincinnati at 9:15 p.m. As the train sped toward freedom, my father settled in his window seat in the "colored" section and watched the countryside pass by between stations. One stop was at the Decatur, Huntsville and Scottsboro depot on the Tennessee River. The area was internationally notorious for the famous 1931 Scottsboro Boys case in which a group of Negro teens were wrongly convicted of raping two white women on a freight train.

Most of the young men were sentenced to death in Alabama's electric chair, morbidly nicknamed "yellow mama." One youth escaped to New York and the governor refused to extradite him to Alabama. Young Negro men were told over and over again by their fathers, preachers, and buddies the deadly story of Scottsboro and admonished to stay away from white women, even if it meant crossing the street if you saw one approaching on a sidewalk.

As the train rolled on, my father was occupied with thoughts of the Scottsboros that he was leaving behind, by copies of *Jet* and *Ebony* magazines, by conversations with his fellow passengers, and with frequent snacks from MaDear's shoebox of food. He bought a Nehi orange soda from the Negro porter and tipped him well, knowing that the porter probably reaped nothing from the exorbitant, inflated price. My father had learned the art of tipping by watching white businessmen at the Whitley Hotel in Montgomery. He knew a good tip would be discussed with the other porters, who would then go out of their way to make his trip more comfortable. But at the same time, he was a Race Man—conspiratorially in league with Negro men everywhere, seeking manhood with dignity and respect in a white man's world—and he asked the porter not to make a fuss over him.

The porter asked his name.

"Bob Patton," he replied, startling himself at the announcement. All of his life he was known as "Brother" by family and friends, as "Clarence" by school officials, and as "Sam Patton's boy" by Montgomery whites. "Yes, my name is Bob Patton."

His transformation was beginning. He would henceforth be known as

"Bob Patton," usually being called by both names as one.

He retrieved a can of Vienna sausages and crackers from his survival kit to go with his soft drink.

BEFORE CINCINNATI, THE train would leave Covington, Kentucky, and cross the high bridge over the Ohio River. As it did, it would also cross the Mason-Dixon Line, the famous surveyor's line which historically divided the free North from the slave South and which in the hundred years after slavery marked the point beyond which segregation of the races was mostly not legally mandated. In other words, Jim Crow law ruled south of the line, but did not restrict black men's behavior north of the line. My father knew this intellectually, but he had yet to experience it for himself.

While he waited, he continued to read his magazines. Most of the stories centered around World War II and the Japanese bombing of Pearl Harbor that had taken place just a few weeks earlier on December 7, 1941. *Ebony, Jet*, and the Negro newspapers were full of stories about the valor of black soldiers shipping out to keep democracy safe for the world. The big news was the training of 992 Negro military pilots at the famed Tuskegee Institute. These were the first black pilots in U.S. military history, and the pioneering airmen overcame prejudice and official and unofficial discrimination every step of the way as they became known as the "Tuskegee Airmen." Glory awaited them in Europe, but the United States had just entered the war and they were still training at Tuskegee in 1941.

My father admired these Negro men who did not flinch at being called "black" at a time when the term was considered derogatory in the Negro community. "If you're white, you're all right; yellow, you're mellow; brown, stick around; black, stay back," went the saying that carried divisive weight in the Negro community, even within families. As he studied the photographs in the magazines, he couldn't help noticing that some of the Negro airmen were "bright-skinned, damned near white."

Musing on race and skin color, he thought with a smile of his Uncle Charlie Minor, brother to his maternal grandmother, who had joined the Army as a cook at the start of World War I in 1914. His sister, Carrie, was as black as coal but Uncle Charlie was known as the "whitest black boy" in north Montgomery. The neighborhood children, hearing grown-up whispers, nicknamed him the "milk-man's bastard." Uncle Charlie had a light complexion, a keen nose, full lips, and wavy hair. While in Europe, he had his hair "processed," the experimental vogue for Negro men at the time. The texture of his hair required minimum relaxer to make his hair as straight as that of any white man.

While stationed in London, he met, fell in love with and married a white woman. They had three children, Walter, William, and Esther. After the war, Charlie stayed in England with his family, reasoning that he could easily land a job even if the wages were lower than the average Englishman. But as the post-war years passed, England turned its attention to tightening its grips on Ireland. American soldiers, Negro and white, were too demanding for the British culture. The Brits employed poor British women and children to work at slave wages in their factories and sweatshops. American ex-soldiers were neither needed nor wanted.

Uncle Charlie decided that his family should go to the states. His children were now ten, nine, and eight years old. His wife refused to come with him, but insisted that he take the children. Uncle Charlie knew not what would be in store for his children in the Deep South, but he found comfort knowing that his family had land and a farm in north Montgomery, Alabama. North Montgomery at this time was a Negro community. It once was a vast plantation with hundreds of Negro slaves. Many of the ex-slaves demanded the promised "forty acres and a mule" after the Civil War. With family and friends, Uncle Charlie knew he could easily build a home there for himself and his children. After all, he had a nephew, Sam Patton, who was a carpenter and had his own construction company.

Family lore provides few details of how the Minors—a light-skinned Negro man with three white-appearing children with strong British accents—reached New York City on a cargo ship and then arrived at the train station in Montgomery. But there were many Uncle Charlie stories for my father to recall. He remembered how Uncle Charlie would drive his children to Montgomery's white movie houses as a chauffeur, jitney hat atop his now wavy hair, and his children in tow in the back seat, masquerading as privileged white kids.

He would leave the driver's seat and open the back door as his children exited and went to the ticket booth. In his strongest British accent, the oldest, Walter, would purchase three children tickets and one adult ticket for the "chauffeur," pointing to his father. "He will see the movie from the Negro balcony," Walter explained.

But the white community soon knew that the Minor children were "colored" and they were banned from the white movie houses. These and other experiences took a sad toll on the children. Walter, like his father, looking white as ever, became a proud Negro and married the darkest woman he could find. He moved to Atlanta to work with his Uncle Jack, a successful businessman. William left Montgomery, "passed" for a white man, and totally disappeared from the family. Ester remained in north Montgomery until her death (in 2001), claiming that she was a white woman who was kidnapped by a Negro, never acknowledging that Uncle Charlie was her father. She, presumably like her mother, for whatever reasons, preferred black men and married one. She became close to her black in-laws, and later embraced the Minor-Humphrey-Patton families as friends, not as relatives.

At Cincinnati, Bob Patton left the Humming Bird and entered the cavernous Cincinnati Terminal Union station. He had crossed the Mason-Dixon Line. He had a two-hour layover and went in search of his first desegregated restaurant meal. He was amazed that a white waitress came to his table to ask for his order. This was his first experience where a white person waited on him and not vice versa.

When he boarded the Cincinnatian Number 58 for an 11:45 p.m. departure continuing on to Detroit, the conductor told him to sit where he wanted—"If you go left, you'll be closer to the dining car."

He chose the car before the dining car. The car was not yet full, but he saw Negroes and whites, mainly sitting with their own race. He thought, "Yes, the train is desegregated, but by choice Negroes and whites decided where they want to sit, and with whom." He claimed an empty two-passenger seat as the car continued to fill. Soon a white man sat next to my father.

My father was shocked and speechless but the man said, "Good evening," shook his hand, and introduced himself as "Bob Simone," pronouncing his last name, with an accent, as "'Cee-mone.' I'm French."

Simone turned out to be a Detroit resident who worked for the United Automobile Workers (UAW) union. The two Bobs talked, went to the dining car and ate, and slept sitting next to each other as the train rolled on toward Detroit. At breakfast, they again dined together. My father bowed his head to give grace. Simone followed suit. When my father raised his head, he had a broad smile on his face that matched his smile in his heart.

"Yes, indeedy, Simone," my father said with obvious happiness. "The North is going to suit me just fine."

"I know, Bob. Please call me. If you land a job in the factory, you'll be an asset to the UAW union. Thousands of southern Negroes are coming North to stake their futures in the automobile industry. Our union makes certain that they are not discriminated against and that they are given skills-training with fair promotions and salaries. Call me."

3

Freedom Land

My father always enjoyed telling how when he stepped off the train in Detroit on New Year's Eve 1941, the first thing he heard was a familiar voice calling, "Brother! Brother!"

Samella had taken the train from Detroit to Montgomery and back several times and knew just where to wait for him on the platform. Big sister and little brother affectionately embraced and then picked their way through the crowd of redcaps and passengers and into a long, somewhat dank tunnel which soon opened into the massive train station with its vaulted ceiling, Roman columns, marbled walls and ornate chandeliers. My father must have felt like a king in a castle.

It was cold in Detroit and there was snow on the ground, an unfamiliar sight for young Bob Patton from Alabama. After a redcap brought his trunk, he opened it and took out his overcoat that MaDear had carefully packed on top. Then he and the redcap followed my aunt to her car in the parking lot.

Surprised not to see his brother-in-law waiting at the car, he blurted, "Sammie, you can drive?! Where is Black?"

"Oh, Brother, everybody drives in Detroit, even teenagers," my aunt said, the knowing twinkle in her eyes a tease of my father about his unauthorized escapades in Montgomery. "Black is at work. He works the midnight shift but he's working overtime this morning. He gets time and an half for overtime."

Bob thought about that as he settled into the passenger seat and admired as his sister expertly manipulated the clutch and gears of the shiny, fancy car as they drove toward her and Black's home.

When Black first arrived in Detroit, he worked in the foundry, pouring fiery molten steel into molds. The hell-hot, smoke-filled foundry was the most dangerous and dirtiest section in the General Motors plant. The soot was so thick that after a while you couldn't tell the Negro workers from the white workers. Despite the harsh conditions, Black could steady the long-handled ladle and pour the hot steel into the molds without spilling a drop. His precision soon landed him a position on the assembly line, which would soon be converting to produce military aircraft.

The start of 1942 was both a good and a bad time for Negroes in Detroit. As the "Motor City" transitioned into the "Arsenal of Democracy," its booming job market absorbed thousands of emigrants from the Deep South and Appalachia. But decent housing for black families was almost impossible to find. Neighborhoods were strictly segregated, and the Negro housing stock was bursting at its seams as two or more families moved into single-family flats. The public schools could not handle the influx of Negro children. And recreational facilities were scarce.

Perhaps my father could read these worries on the faces of Negroes he saw on the streets as my aunt sped pass the new Sojourner Truth Housing Project which was scheduled to open in early 1942 to provide sorely needed apartments for Negro families. However, whites protested, and the government flip-flopped, even declaring for a time that the complex would be restricted to whites—no matter that it was named for a famous black abolitionist. During the first six months after my father's arrival in Detroit, the Sojourner Truth Project would be the site of protests, counter-protests, and white mob violence so severe that the National Guard had to be called out to protect the black families who eventually moved in.

Detroit was seething with racial tensions in 1941. White women factory workers constantly protested that they had to share restrooms with Negro women. White men balked that they had to work under Negroes who had been promoted to foreman on the assembly lines. A violent uprising on June 20, 1943, was fueled by rumors that white men threw a Negro mother and her baby off the Belle Isle Bridge and that Negro men raped and murdered a white woman in the same place. The Detroit Race Riot lasted thirty-six hours as Negroes beat a white doctor to death and whites beat a Negro to death at a bus stop. The riot claimed thirty-four lives, twenty-five of them Negroes. More than eighteen hundred persons, the majority Negroes, were arrested for looting and other infractions.

Even as late as 1943, housing for Negroes was still a problem. However, my aunt and uncle were fortunate when they arrived in Detroit two years earlier, and by extension so was my father. Black and Samella rented one of a pair of two-family flats owned by Alabama acquaintances, the Smarts.

In Montgomery, the Smarts had owned the Twilight Inn and Social Lounge. The Smarts were prominent, tithing members of Hutchinson Missionary Baptist Church, where my grandfather was president of the deacon board and served on the trustee board. Though my grandfather had built the Twilight Inn, he did not approve when the Smarts expanded it into a social lounge. My father, however, had frequented the lounge, and particularly the inn, which rented rooms by the day and the hour. My grandfather prayed about that last part; my father presumably took advantage of it.

The Smarts sold the Twilight Inn in 1939 and moved to Detroit, hoping to take advantage of the lucrative opportunities as thousands of black families migrated to the industrial north. The patriarch Smart was a smart businessman; he knew the relocated Negroes would need housing and social outlets.

WHEN SAMMIE AND Black arrived in Detroit in the spring of 1941, they went straight to 18000 Northfield, one of the duplexes owned by the Smarts. Sammie and Black rented one side of the two-story building. The basement had been converted into additional living space, and it became my father's first home in Detroit. The furnishings were pleasant enough, but the basement apartment seemed dark and damp compared to the airy, open home he had grown up in.

Most houses in Montgomery had expansive front yards that became beds for colorful arrays of flowers and flowering bushes and hedges. Many backyards were even more expansive, often with a variety of fruit trees, vegetable gardens, and at least one pecan tree. Picking fruit, shaking the pecan trees and picking the nuts off the ground afterwards were recreational and fun activities for children and their way to contribute to their families' well-being.

Few Montgomery homes had basements, although the ever-enterprising Sam Patton had built a basement in the second Patton family home. In fact, it was a huge basement with ten dormitory rooms, five showers and toilets, and a central kitchen. The Patton Girls' Dormitory was registered with the housing department at Alabama State Teachers' College for Negroes, two blocks south. As many as twenty coeds routinely lived there.

Now, however, my father was settling into a dark basement that had not been expansively constructed by Sam Patton nor designed as a residence. On the plus side, the basement stairs led to a landing that opened into Samella's kitchen, where the delicious smells of greens, ham hocks, peas with salt pork, and crackling cornbread kept him from being homesick.

SAMMIE AND BLACK also lost no time in introducing my father to Detroit night life. He arrived on New Year's Eve 1941, and that very night they took him to see Cab Calloway at "the Million Dollar Theater on Woodward." My father found it curious that Detroiters didn't add "street or avenue" to the names of the thoroughfares.

The Million Dollar Theater, living up to its moniker, was luxuriously spectacular. Almost as many whites as Negroes had turned out to hear the "Hi De Ho Man" and his famous orchestra. This was the first time my father had been at an integrated social event.

The crowd counted down the seconds to midnight and then burst into "Auld Lang Syne." Father Time was on stage, directing the audience while the orchestra played the tune with an upbeat tempo.

And then Cab Calloway returned to the stage, bedecked in a white tuxedo with tails, zoot-style pants, satin-gold shirt the color of his smooth skin, white bow-tie, white shoes with gold spats. His wavy, black hair was slicked back. As he raised his baton to lead the orchestra, women swooned and screamed and men whistled and roared with pleasure.

"Yeah, Detroit suits me fine," my father told Sammie and Black.

As they were leaving the theater, my father caught a glimpse of a familiar face. He shouted, "Dot! Dot Bolden!"

Her head turned, her long hair flipping over her shoulder as she searched the crowd to locate the caller of her name. My father caught her glance and weaved his way through the crowd. He was struck by her petite beauty and she was struck by his handsome build, square-jawed good looks, and exquisite dress. As she recalled later, he looked like a million dollars.

"Bob Patton," he reminded her. "You called me 'Clarence' in Montgomery. I went to Booker T. Washington High. Class of 1941."

"Oh, glad to see you, again. You're here on a visit?'

They quickly caught up with one another and she gave him her phone number. He called later that afternoon, and by the end of the day their courtship had officially begun.

MY FATHER TOOK a test and was selected to train as a welder in the General Motors plant where Black worked. He was the only Negro in a class of fifty trainees. Welding was a prestigious, high-paying job, and Bob Patton seemed off to a good start in his new career in his new city.

Though my father enjoyed learning the welding trade, he told his family that he could not tolerate the ignorant racism of the white workers. He had left Montgomery because he feared he might kill a white man. Now, in Detroit, he sometimes felt certain that he would kill one.

One difference between race relations in Montgomery was that a Southern Negro had to go through extreme measures to avoid an arrogant racist. But in Detroit, the Negro could refuse to budge when confronted by a racist. The racist knew without a doubt that his punch would be met with a counter-punch. My father knew that racial tensions in Detroit had erupted into violence during the summer of 1941. The stories about Negroes organizing and arming themselves to protect their communities from invading youth gangs of white thugs had fascinated him. At each telling, his pride in his race grew stronger: the Negro in the North did not seek trouble, but he did not run from it either.

Finishing the welding course, my father was placed in the Cadillac engine section of the plant. He liked the work, yet he desired to work in an area where there were more Negroes. Ford Motor Company was making a special effort to hire Negro workers. The company had a bad reputation during the 1920s and 1930s of working its workers to death. But now Ford promised better working conditions and pay. Ford advertised for workers in the Negro newspapers not only in Detroit, but throughout the South.

When my father received notice that he had passed the test and could fill a position as a spray-painter at Ford Motor Company's River Rouge plant, he left General Motors without hesitation.

MY PARENTS' COURTSHIP developed into an engagement and then marriage on February 19, 1943. The wedding was at my cousin Bertha Faulkner's home, where my mother was living while attending Lewis Business College for Women. My great-Aunt Chick— Nathia Lee Foster-Elmore, the namesake of my mother's younger sister— and her teenage daughter, Flora, came up from Montgomery as representatives of the Foster-McCall Family. Aunt Chick was special to Dot and Robert. She was Mommy's oldest sister. She had been a school teacher since the early 1920s in the Montgomery public school system. Her husband, Eugene, was a stower with the Louisville and Nashville Railroad Company and thus had rail passes which allowed Aunt Chick and Flora to travel to Detroit for the wedding. Dot was Aunt Chick's favorite niece.

Aunt Samella and Uncle Black as best man represented the Patton family. The wedding was well attended by family and friends who had migrated to Detroit and by my mother's business college classmates. The occasion was the talk of the town among Montgomery transplants and was written up in the Negro weekly, the *Michigan Chronicle*.

The newlyweds moved into my father's basement apartment while he searched the housing sections of the daily newspapers. The government and industry were quickly building factory towns to accommodate the ever-expanding Negro workforce. Despite long lines at bus stops, grocery stores, and everywhere else because of population growth and rationing, people had plenty of money in their pockets. The war-time economy was booming.

My father had bought a Chevrolet while working at the General Motors plant, but the commute from Detroit to River Rouge was too much for him. Inkster, Michigan, a small all-Negro hamlet west of Detroit and near River Rouge, was becoming a "Ford Factory Town" with government financed housing for Negroes. There were three different community layouts. For lower-paying workers, there was a "card-board city" of prefabricated housing that was assembled like a child's doll house—and practically of the same materials. For middle-income workers, there were two-story duplexes that resembled the two-family flats in Detroit. For upper-income workers, there was a mixture of two-family flats and single bungalow homes with front and back yards. All the project communities had paved streets and winding sidewalks.

The compact community was between Carlysle Avenue on the south, Middlebelt Road on the west, Inkster Road on the east, and railroad tracks on the north. Local businesses, mainly owned by Negroes, were located on the major thoroughfares. However, across the railroad tracks was Michigan Avenue, the major (and white-owned) business district. Michigan Avenue ran through Dearborn to the downtown Detroit business district. Negroes were prohibited by covenants and custom from living in the posh Dearborn community, though not as plush as Cloverdale in Montgomery. Adjacent to the Inkster community was a section of individual homes owned by Negroes. Many of these were imposing brick homes with grand wraparound porches. This community was called "Old Inkster," and its residents considered themselves as Inkster's elite; most were proprietors of the businesses in the Negro community.

Inkster would become incorporated, first as a village in the 1950s, and then in 1964 as a city, with the help of my father and my uncle Herman Smith and cousin George "Shorty" Hamilton Jr. Several of my family members remained active in Inkster city government. As of 2010, my cousin

Wanda Harris Foster was mayor *pro tem*, and my cousin Teline Strozier was a city employee.

MY FATHER SECURED a single-family bungalow and he and my now-pregnant mother moved to Inkster's Ludington Street.

The back door of Dot and Bob Patton's bungalow served as the main entrance into the home. To the sides of the back porch were the coal chute on the left and the milk chute on the right. The coal chute opened into the utility room, where the huge coal furnace was located in the home. My father used a small shovel to scoop brick-sized chunks of coal into the roaring furnace that heated the two-bedroom bungalow. The milk chute opened onto on a window-high ledge in the kitchen. My mother would place empty pint milk bottles in a metal rack in the chute; the milkman would exchange the empty rack for a fresh one with filled bottles. My parents paid the milkman by the month.

Linoleum covered the floor of kitchen, which housed the kitchen table, the gas stove, refrigerator, a double-sink, top and bottom cabinets, The living room contained an American signature couch and two matching over-stuffed chairs and an ottoman, upholstered with a navy-blue, rather coarse, fabric. The ornate coffee table with its inset glass covering to protect a wood-carved, embossed image of a peacock in a grassy setting was my mother's pride and joy and was never covered with magazines and books. There were end tables with lamps and a floor lamp. Light blue carpet covered the floor. A magazine rack with *Jet, Ebony, Saturday Evening Post,* and *Life* magazines was in one corner and the telephone table was in another corner.

To the right of the living room was a short hallway with two closets. The hallway quickly turned right, becoming an L-shaped passageway. The guest bedroom (later the bedroom shared by me and my brother), the bathroom, and my parents' bedroom lined this part of the hallway.

Wanting to maximize space in the small bungalow, my mother supervised the construction of a pantry, storage closets, and a washing and ironing area in the utility room. She moved the kitchen table into the utility room, and my father bought a Duncan Phyfe dining table with folding leaves and matching chairs for the kitchen. This purchase was too large and grand for the small bungalow, but my parents did not intend to stay in the projects for long.

SHORTLY BEFORE I was born in the fall of 1943, there occurred one of the darkest incidents in my family history.

Nathaniel Bolden Jr., my mother's baby brother—like my father, called "Brother" within his immediate family—had graduated from Montgomery's Loveless High School that previous May 1943. The school was named after Mr. H. S. Loveless, a prosperous Negro undertaker who had donated the land. Brother was a carpenter by trade and had intermittent work in the public sector. The work was not enough to sustain his independence, nor did it shield him from the rage-inducing torment of Jim Crow segregation at the hands of racist Southern whites and institutions.

To make matters worse, he had received his draft notice, and he told my grandmother that he had no intention of responding to it. Filled with the pride of his race and the heat of youth, he told Mommy, "Mama, I'm not going to fight and die in a white man's Army for a country who treats me worse than its pet dog."

In the family lore, she recalls advising him that the Army could be a way out of the white supremacist South. But he would not hear it, responding that if he had to gamble with death, he would rather do it another way.

He told her he was running away to Los Angeles. She suggested he go to Detroit instead, where my parents were. Brother replied that he feared he would only cause trouble for Dot and Bob, besides which he didn't like the cold in Detroit; Los Angeles better suited his ambitions and taste.

Mommy said this talk ripped her heart with pain, but he had always been headstrong. Whippings had never deterred him. And when other black nannies took their toddlers to the job where there were white charges of the same age, they played together, but not Brother. It was as if he hated the white boy she looked after, as if at even the age of a toddler he consciously refused to be a living toy. When the white child attempted to order Brother around, Brother looked at the child as if he were crazy. Brother would run to Mommy and spend his entire day clutching her around her knees.

MY PARENTS WERE at home in Inkster on October 9, 1943, when the phone

call came from my mother's younger sister, Nathia Lee—"Sister" within the
family—a schoolteacher in Huntsville, Alabama.

Brother was dead, shot and killed by the Montgomery police.

My mother was hugely pregnant and her feet and legs were so swollen
that her doctor had ordered complete bed rest. A trip to Alabama for her
brother's funeral was out of the question.

Nathaniel Bolden Jr., age eighteen, was buried on October 12, 1943.

In a telephone call afterwards, Aunt Chick gave my father additional
details. Brother's classmates had attended his funeral in great numbers and
the principal at Loveless had given permission for current students to be
there. Thus there was an overflow of mourners, which was a great comfort
to the family. Mommy, she reported, had taken the death very hard but had
not shed a tear at the funeral.

The "what" of Brother's death was straightforward. Aunt Chick said that
he and another youth apparently had determined to rob the neighborhood
Jewish-owned grocery to obtain money to buy a used car to drive to Los
Angeles to avoid the draft. The store owner, sleeping in the back, heard
prowlers and called the police. When the police arrived, they shot Brother
twice, first in the head and then in the chest. They shot Brother's friend, too.
Both died instantly. Brother and his friend were unarmed, but the police
report declared their shootings to be "justifiable homicide."

The "why" is more speculative.

Nathaniel Bolden Jr. was from a respected Montgomery family. He
was a high school graduate, popular, and had a trade. He was as angry as
the next young black man, but he was not a thug and had committed no
previous criminal acts.

He rejected military service for a government that expected him to fight
overseas for freedoms he did not have at home. There was even an anecdotal
story about one of his friends who had been killed while in the Army by a
white serviceman who thought he was "too uppity."

Those are factors but not explanations for why a member of our family
was killed in the course of a crime. Whatever else may have been motivating
my late uncle can never be known.

4

Upbringing

I was born in Henry Ford Hospital on October 14, 1943. My brother Bob, Clarence Robert Patton Jr., was born only fourteen months later on December 29, 1944, after which my mother had her fallopian tubes tied to prevent future pregnancies.

Sometime in 1945, my mother's sister, Nathia Lee Bolden Smith, pregnant with her own firstborn and with her husband off at war in Europe, came to Inkster to help my mother with her babies. My cousin Emmett Alfonso Smith was born in Inkster on March 21, 1945, giving the Patton household three infants. After three months, my aunt returned to Montgomery with "Cousin-Brother Al" to reunite with her husband who had received a furlough to see his newborn son.

My early childhood memories are when I was about four years old. I remember a television set in our living room. My father worked a lot, and when he was home, he was always resting on the couch with pillows under his head looking at television. My mother had mastered the cooking of midwest chili, loaded with hamburger and red beans. The family's treat—with my brother and I lying on the floor, my father on the couch, and my mother in the side chair with the ottoman—was watching Milton "Uncle Milty" Berle on the television, now called "the TV" or "the tube."

TV cartoons delighted my father, my brother, and me. We loved the antics of "Farmer Brown" and his war on the rats that overran his ramshackle farm. Another favorite was the "Howdy Doody" show, with the mute clown Clarabelle who communicated with a squeeze horn, the fussy cuss Phineas T. Bluster, and Princess Summer-Fall-Winter-Spring who looked like a Native American.

After lunch and playtime, Bob and I took our naps in our bedroom furnished with exquisite twin beds and matching maple dressers and a secretary, with a leaf that folded out into a study desk. Our naps started at 2 p.m. At precisely 3:50, Mother would wake us and we would make a beeline to watch "Howdy Doody" and to join the TV "peanut gallery" in the theme song, "It's Howdy Doody Time."

Other TV shows we watched were the "Untouchables," my father's favorite; "Boston Blackie" with his furious rooftop chases of criminals; and shoot-em up westerns with good guys in white hats and bad guys in black hats. At 11 p.m. the programs ended with a humming sound and a black and white circle with a striped cross in the middle as the closing image. Many nights my tired father fell asleep on the couch with the humming sign-off of the TV; broadcasting resumed at 6 a.m.

MY BROTHER AND I had a carefree childhood. After breakfast and a few chores, we were free to go outside and to play wherever we wanted in the neighborhood.

My favorite fun was making sturdy dirt cakes—not mud pies. I would crack colored glass into slivers to sprinkle on my cakes as icing. I took my tea set out of my play bag and made make-believe tea. My brother and his boy friends, along with my girl friends, sitting in a circle on the side-walk, would pretend to eat my cake and sip my tea while we chattered about whatever children talked about. After the tea party, the boys would be off to play their games, mainly marbles. My brother, though quiet and reserved, always seemed to be the leader of the pack. While the boys were doing their "manly" things, we girls cooked make-believe collard greens out of weeds and made beautiful table settings of dandelions and Queen Anne's lace.

Soon my brother and I would hear the yodel-like echo of our mother calling us home. If we were deep in the neighborhood and did not hear the summons, the "call" was relayed by neighbors, "Your mother is calling you to come home." Hurriedly packing my play bag, we beat a path back to our bungalow for lunch. I always said the blessing.

My play after lunch was with my paper dolls. My brother spent his down-time playing with his miniature horses, cowboys, and Indians. Then it was nap-time.

I ENTERED KINDERGARTEN in September 1948 at a school in the Inkster Recreation Center, on the other side of our neighborhood park of swings, slides, and merry-go-rounds. For a month, Mother and Bob accompanied me on the ten-minute walk to school, but I assured my mother that I could walk with my classmates and on my fifth birthday, she said okay and afterwards I walked to school by myself.

My teacher, Mrs. Young, lived in a two-family flat diagonally across the street from our home. Mrs. Young's sister, also a school teacher, lived on the other side of the flat.

I loved school and would stay late to help Mrs. Young put away the school supplies. The school day was from 9 a.m. to noon. When I stayed late, Mrs. Young called my mother to tell her that she would give me lunch at school. One Friday in the spring of 1949, I stayed after school to help Mrs. Young and then walked home alone through the park. One of my classmates, a neighbor boy, was lying in wait. He leaped out of nowhere, tussled me to the ground on my back and climbed on top of me. Somehow, I managed to wriggle free and ran home as fast as my little legs would carry me. I was so mad I couldn't even cry. I told my brother what the boy had done.

A few minutes later, my mother and I heard shouting and screaming outside. We ran to the back door. Bob was beating the boy as hard as a four-year-old can beat a five-year-old. The boy's mother came outside as my mother was breaking up the fight. The fight happened in their yard, so she accused my brother of starting the fight. When Bob told her what the boy had done to me in the park, the boy received an even worse whipping from his mother.

When our father came home from work, mother told him what the boy had done to me and what Bob Jr. had done to him. My father beamed with pride. "Son, you must always protect your sister. It's called honor."

From that day forward, my brother no longer wore short pants. He was four years old and had yet to go to school, but he had proved himself to be a "little man." My father took him everywhere with him. They were known as "Big Bob" and "Little Bob" throughout Inkster, in the barber shops, at River Rouge Ford Plant, in the United Auto Workers (UAW) Local 600, and at craps games.

GOING SHOPPING FOR first-grade outfits with my mother was as exciting as shopping for Christmas and Easter. I was thrilled when she led me to the school supplies section and let me choose my book satchel without her assistance. I chose a light green-blue-yellow plaid accordion style with special inside pockets for crayons, pencils, notebook, and ruler. The cover flap was fastened with leather straps, buckles, and had a suitcase handle. I was a big girl now.

George Washington Carver Elementary School was a cinder block building newly erected to accommodate the growing population of Negro children. The school sat cater-cornered from my kindergarten. I don't remember much about Carver except that my wondrous classroom had individual desks and chairs, unlike the round tables where five pupils sat together in kindergarten. The teacher, small and petite like my mother, called the roll by last names, and we sat in rows accordingly. I landed up front in the third row.

MY FATHER WAS now the UAW shop steward for his painting section in Ford's River Rouge Plant. I know from listening to him over the years that he had a close relationship with his union-elected committee man, Joey, an Italian who had an office and did not work on the line. If there were worker grievances in my father's part of the shop, he would take the list to Joey.

I liked hearing about my father's job at Ford, both his work on the assembly line and his role with the union and the other workers. Though I was too young to understand it, my first introduction to organizing was listening to him talk about the interplay between the workers and the bosses. I remember one riveting incident when the assembly line workers staged a slow-down after an unpopular foreman, a Pole who had less seniority than the majority of Negroes on the line, moved to fire a man. A group of my father's co-workers cornered the foreman in the locker room, and then had to restrain the aggrieved worker who had triggered his paint gun with the intent to spray paint in the foreman's eyes. "Brothers, let's not do this," my father said quietly, quelling the anger. "I'll take care of this."

The foreman was moved to another section of the plant, presumably through union grievances. Naturally, he was replaced with another white man, this time an Irishman, but my father observed that at least the new man understood that if he wanted to make his production quotas, he couldn't treat his workers like he was running a plantation.

After five years in Ford's paint section, my father had been promoted to paint inspector. After the car bodies and frames were riveted together and primed, four workers wearing blue, lint-free coveralls, blue hair nets, white air masks, and goggles sprayed each car with enamel paint. There were 140 workers in a section, painting 35 cars an hour. After the cars were painted, they moved on the assembly line to a heated oven to dry and harden the paint. From there, the cars were washed, rinsed, and inspected. My father's responsibility was to make certain that there were no nicks, scratches, or unpainted areas.

Cars that passed inspection moved on down the famous Ford assembly line. The trim workers installed carpet, ashtrays, mirrors, windows, steering wheels, head and tail lights and electrical harnesses, and door handles, and then sealed inside doors and dashboards. Meanwhile the chassis department was installing motors, brakes, carburetors, batteries, exhaust pipes, and mufflers and connecting all the wiring.

My father hoped eventually to be promoted to final-line inspector. This inspector earned more money and reviewed only seven cars per hour with a check-off list for painting and installation before going on to the tire section and then ultimately to the testing and accountability section, where there were no Negro inspectors. However, even in his present position, Bob Patton had a responsible, good-paying industrial job. Our family, like thousands of Negro families who had left the completely segregated Deep South for the only partially segregated North, was making progress toward the American Dream.

It was ironic then, that I came home from school one day to find my mother and her friends packing our belongings in boxes—the Pattons were moving out of the projects. The irony was that our move to a nicer house in a nicer neighborhood was made possible not by my father's hard work but by luck.

In addition to my father being the union shop steward who collected assembly-line workers' grievances against the company-picked foreman, the workers also brought him money and slips of paper with their numbers for placing bets.

Gambling, or the numbers, was just as prevalent inside Detroit auto plants as it was on the streets. The numbers game was an illegal lottery in which players picked a series of numbers to be compared to the unpredictable results of horse races at various tracks throughout the country. The odds were astronomical that your three numbers would match the first-place winners of the first three races.

A lot of work was involved in the numbers racket. On a typical day, my father and Joey, the committee man, would collect hundreds of bets from workers. They would tally the bettors' names, bets and their numbers on a list, issue receipts from a numbers pad, then call in the amount of the take to a point man, who would bet the sum at the track before the 1:30 p.m. race.

My father got a percentage of the daily betting totals, as did Joey. On every level, from the runners in the plant to the track bookies, money was skimmed off the top. The numbers business also had lucrative auxiliary enterprises, from selling green tip sheets that outlined horses' pedigrees and records, to compiling "dream books" for bettors who were inclined to believe in both superstitions and luck.

Joey and my father not only ran the numbers, they often bet them, too. On one particular day, my father returned from his lunch break to the underground news quietly murmuring throughout the plant: "Bob Patton hit the numbers for $30,000!" (That would be about $240,000 in 2015.)

THUS THE PATTONS moved out of the projects to 3115 Henry Street. Our new block was an eclectic array of homes. The eight three-story wood-frame homes on my family's side of the street were built in the 1930s. There was also a shotgun house where an integrated couple, a stout white woman and a stocky Negro man, lived with their children. The last three houses were bricked and built by the home owners.

Across the street on the corner was a wood-frame house with an expanse of front, side and back yards enclosed by a fence. It was a mysterious house. We never saw the owners. They cared for five foster-care boys. At a set time of day the boys came outside and played along the sidewalk, never stepping beyond the fence. No children in the neighborhood ventured to play with them.

Adjacent to the mystery house was the neighborhood "victory" garden—about three lots owned by Mr. and Mrs. Robert Harris Sr. The entire vegetable garden was planted and cultivated by Mr. Harris. It contained corn, tomato vines, cucumbers, okra, pole and snap beans, and other vegetables. Neighbors would pick the vegetables pay Mr. Harris for them on the honor system according to the costs he placed on stakes by the rows of the various crops.

The Harrises' commodious three-story brick home was a work in perpetual progress. The Harrises occupied the completed basement while Mr. Harris completed the interior of the main and upstairs floors, working in his spare time.

God only knows how Mr. Harris had any spare time. He was a tool and die worker at the Ford plant. He gardened. He built his house. And he owned a Ford pick-up and a bicycle which he used to collect scrap. At specific times in the week he rode his bicycle throughout the neighborhood, calling out, "Rags, newspapers, old iron!" Neighbors gladly deposited their discards into the large baskets on the front and back of Mr. Harris's bicycle.

Mrs. Harris, whom we affectionately called "Mama Joe," served as the neighborhood counselor. Mr. and Mrs. Harris had children the ages of my parents, who in turn had children the ages of my brother and me. "Mama Joe" counseled both generations. Much of her advice was rooted in Christian ethics, which she and Mr. Harris practiced at their beloved Second Baptist Church around the corner. The church was a formidable yellow-brick edifice built under the supervision of Mr. Harris.

The Harrises' oldest daughter, Mrs. Bernice Harris Glover, became my mother's best friend. The four Glover sons became my and my brother's childhood friends. As we grew older, both sets of parents tried to matchmake me with Joe, the eldest son.

By coincidence, Mr. and Mrs. Robert Harrises' next-door neighbors had the same last name, though they were not kin. Willie and Eva Harris lived in an avocado green wood-frame home. Their daughter, Hazel Strozier, lived across the street. Hazel, too, became a close friend to my mother, and her daughter, Tina, became mine and especially my brother's friend; he and Tina were the same age.

This Harris home had a large front porch with a swinging glider, like you saw on front porches in the South, and other yard furniture. The front yard was a prize-worthy flower garden. Next to Willie and Eva Harris lived the Rileys, in a rambling unfinished, white wood-framed home resembling a long house trailer. Next to this home was a vacant lot, which served as the neighborhood playground and softball field.

This was my world from age six to age sixteen.

MY DEAREST FRIEND on our block was my next-door neighbor, Carole Chapman. She was exactly my age and her mother was my sixth-grade teacher. Mrs. Chapman was a divorced single mother who eventually married three more times. Around 1950 she bought a Volkswagen Beetle. This German-manufactured car had an impact on my father. In 1949, he had wanted to buy a Cadillac but was told that he had to sign a waiting list. It was a quota system, which restricted the number of Negroes who could purchase USA's premiere automobile.

My father thought about purchasing a Volkswagen as a protest, but could not bring himself to contribute one red cent to the Germans who characterized Negro soldiers as monkeys. My father opted to buy a Buick with the Dynaflow transmission, the famous four portholes on the fenders behind the front wheels, a windshield visor, and running boards at the bottom of both sides of the four-door sedan. My father called his sleek car, "Black Beauty."

Later, my father bought a Ford Fairlane to show loyalty to his place of employment though he no longer worked in the factory. When my mother finally learned how to shift a manual transmission, my father bought her a convertible Chevrolet Bel Air so we could "see the USA" in the open air. (My father's last car was a Cadillac brougham. He called it "Black Beauty," too.)

THE EXTERIOR OF our new Henry Street home was covered in the front with Italian marble-like stone and on the sides with green and white siding. All the windows had awnings.

My parents brought their Southern sensibilities with them. Though there was central heating, it could not replace the warmth of a fireplace in the living room. My father without discussion accommodated my mother's desire to build a fireplace with a mantel and an overhead inset for a large mirror. The fireplace was a replica without a flue or chimney, but its gas logs radiated warmth and ambiance, especially during Christmas.

When we moved in, the main floor was empty except for the bed in my parents' room. Workmen were painting the living room a deep chinaberry red with gray trim, the kitchen two-tones of yellow at top and apple green at bottom, and the bedrooms soft blues. All ceilings were painted egg-shell white. The bathroom was covered from floor to ceiling in petite tiles and ceramic stones of black and white.

Gray Mohawk carpet was laid throughout the main floor except for the kitchen, which had squares of yellow tile with apple green accents. Though the kitchen had an expansive yellow table that could seat six, my mother wanted a dining room. So the kitchen was opened up with an arch that led into a formal dining room built to my mother's request. It, too, was painted chinaberry red with gray trim. The dining room seated sixteen people with space for extra tables and chairs during special gatherings of family and friends.

A huge picture window graced the west wall of the dining room. It was always a thrill to see the Christmas tree with trimmings and hundreds of colorful lights glistening through that window. French doors on the east wall opened into our new den. To my chagrin, Mother furnished the den with modern furniture of sofa and tent chairs, a TV and record player on stands, and my piano as the center attraction. It looked like an "I Love Lucy" television set. Yet when I was older, the den became my cocoon where I practiced piano, entertained my friends with records on our hi-fi, or watched television.

Mother furnished the living room with a Duncan Phyfe sofa, chairs, and center and end tables with slue-footed legs to complement the embossed peacock coffee table. Tiffany-style lamps adorned the end tables and the ornate round table in front of the picture window. A huge television console with radio and record-player was in the corner, and wherever you sat, you had a TV view.

The guest bedroom, which later became my bedroom, had Queen Anne furniture, including a poster-bed, high-mirrored vanity, and a ten-drawer dresser with a special compartment for jewelry.

When we first moved to Henry Street, Bob and I were still sharing a bedroom. Our twin-bedroom set occupied a room on the upper floor. A door behind the stairs led to a large play area and a closed attic where our toys were stored. We had loads of fun in our quarters with our friends, shooting marbles on the carpet and jumping up and down on our twin beds (breaking slats under the bed springs). Soon our bookcase was filled with a set of the *World Book Encyclopedia* and our friends visited our quarters as if it were the neighborhood library.

Knotty-pine paneling covered the concrete walls in the basement. My father had a wet bar and counter with stools installed on the right side of the basement. In this area card tables and chairs were set. On the left side of the basement were a stove, refrigerator, freezer, washer, and dryer. To the right of this area was the utility room, which soon became my father's business office.

Outdoors, our backyard had a double-car garage with automatic doors opening from the front of the long driveway and from the back that led to the alley. My father mounted a basketball goal above the garage door.

My father kept our yard manicured. It had Bermuda grass and fir trees, which became outdoor Christmas trees when we draped colorful lights around them. Behind the house, we had a concrete patio and a fenced dog run within the fenced backyard. My brother and I didn't need swings and slides. Our next-door friend Carole had them, and our daily routine was to play with her in her backyard.

WE HAD SEVERAL dogs throughout my childhood and teen years. The big dogs—German Shepherd, collie, Great Dane, Boxer and Doberman Pinscher, all registered and sent to obedience schools—were under my brother's watch. The small house dogs, Cocker Spaniels and a dachshund, were under my care. When our twin blond Cocker Spaniels died of distemper, I was distraught. Father bought me a black Cocker Spaniel puppy and I nurtured him for seven years. He became blind and one day while I was walking him,

I became engrossed in conversation with a neighborhood friend and dropped his leash. When I looked around, Blackie was gone. I ran home to tell my brother. Bob and Father got in the car and drove around the neighborhood looking for Blackie. After what seemed like an eternity, they came home with a dachshund and no Blackie. I named the new puppy "Duchess"; Bob called her "Hot Dog."

Much time passed before I learned that Blackie was run over and killed by a car. By this time, I was devoted to Duchess. She slept with me and sat at the kitchen table while I fed her meats and vegetables during our family meals. I made clothes for her slinky black and brown body to keep her warm during the winters. Some of the happiest times with Duchess were watching her walk on her front legs while dragging her hind legs and the rest of her body on the floor. I was convinced she understood television, especially when we watched "Lassie," "Rin-Tin-Tin," and later "Beagle," a Basset Hound that could be a first-cousin to a dachshund. Duchess would bark whenever Beagle came on the screen.

We also had pet rabbits, but Bob and I did not want them to be caged all the time. However, when they hopped all over the basement, it was a chore to clean up behind them. We were soon through with rabbits as pets. One day Bob brought home a wounded bird. We put it in a cage in the basement and nursed it back to health then set it free.

We learned much, as our father wanted us to, caring for our pets. Other kids marveled as our big dog met us at the close of a school day and walked us home. Smaller kids would mount our Great Dane like he was a Shetland pony. Mother no longer had to stand on the porch to call Bob and me home from play in our new and larger neighborhood. She simply instructed our big dog, "Go find Gwen and Little Bob and bring them home for dinner."

BEFORE LONG, MY brother and I were too big and too old to share a bedroom. So one night after dinner, Mother and I moved my belongings from upstairs to the Queen Anne room. The move was exhilarating for me and for Bob.

Gradually, various rooms in our home became personal spaces for different family members. Father was king of the living room and basement, where he had regular gambling parties. Mother was queen of the kitchen and the formal dining room. My brother absolutely controlled his upstairs bedroom and the extended playroom. He had become leader of his pack and he and his buddies planned their exploits in his upstairs domain. I was princess of my Queen Anne room, where no one dared to enter without my permission, and the den, where I practiced piano daily.

The basketball rack atop the garage and the wide concrete driveway became the neighborhood basketball court. With our father's permission, our basement became the community center, where our friends were invited to our dancing parties. Many afternoons, our classmates would come straight to our home after school to listen to music and to learn how to dance the "bop" we saw on Dick Clark's "American Bandstand"; the "social," which was a two-step or a complicated three-step foxtrot with girls swinging out and twirling and then back into the arms of the boys, similar to Fred Astaire and Ginger Rogers on the popular television dance revue movies; the Latin "cha-cha-cha"; the "hulley gulley," a fast dance on the style of our childhood "hokey-pokey" round dance; and the "chicken," which required a weird twisting and stamping of the feet.

I loved to dance, and was considered one of the best dancers in Inkster. The "big boys" always wanted to dance with me. Because I was petite, they would throw me up in the air, catch me coming down, and then I would fall back in a graceful lean in their arms. This dance was akin to ballet. Sometimes on the dance floor of the school's gym or at grand ballrooms where concerts were held, other couples would stop dancing and form a circle around my partner and me as I twirled, gracefully stepped on tip-toes and swayed to my partner's lead. I will always remember sharing the center of attention with one of my partners, Titus, a "big boy" known for his ballroom agility, while Ray Charles was in concert at the Greystone Ballroom, or with another "big boy" partner, Debussy, known for his cool social dance techniques at UAW Local 600 Union Hall while Smokey Robinson and the Miracles crooned the love songs of the day.

I became the dance teacher for my male classmates and for my brother and his pack. Our living room, den, and basement became dance studios as our friends flocked to our home after school to learn the new dance steps. Our father was a close friend to the owner of Inkster's only record shop and this guaranteed that we had the latest hit records. Nothing pleased us more when 78s reformatted into vinyl 45s. No more dropping and thus breaking into pieces the glass-like 78s.

A memorable part of my youth was being one of the girls in the "Flip Jips." We were in the same grade and cheerleaders. I served as road manager, which meant I only placed the 45s on the turntable, while my girlfriends, Audrey, Lenora, Julie, Marilyn, and Sharon, pantomimed with instruments the smash hit, "Tequila." They were stunning in their white Bermuda shorts, red blazers, Mexican blouses, and crazy straw hats designed by Audrey. Lenora was our transportation leader. Her parents gave her a 1950 black Chevrolet, which we affectionately called, "shove-a-leg" because of the many break-downs we experienced on our way to gigs at Dairy Workers' Hall and the Urban League's Latin Quarters. But, oh my, when we finally arrived, we were greeted with thunderous applause from awaiting fans! We became known in greater Detroit's black bourgeois circles as "Inkster's chic hicks, chicks with class."

The other favorite pastime of my youth was roller-skating. I could never master skating, and soon gave up lacing up the magnificent boots. Nevertheless, I frequently visited roller rinks and marveled at the skaters' graceful manipulation of the roller wheels while they skated in pairs, trios, foursomes and lone line, sometimes tipping on the front wheels, then twirling around and skating backwards.

THOUGH OUR NEIGHBORHOOD had paved sidewalks, green street signs and red four-way stop signs, there were no street lights and the streets were unpaved. During the thawing and rainy spring season, the dirt streets were rivers of mud, trapping many cars in the deep ruts.

After driving once too many times out of his paved driveway only to get stuck in the muddy street and then placing a wooden plank under the tires and gunning the motor to get out of the rut, my father had had enough.

He met with the hamlet president and received no satisfaction. He then met with the "Black Mafia," some of whom were considered "first families" of Inkster. They controlled the numbers racket, the gambling joints, and brothels, as well as other legitimate business like cleaners, candy stores, and some restaurants. Their businesses were mainly on Harrison Road, which was paved. In fact, all the business thoroughfares were paved. Only the neighborhood streets were unpaved, and the "Black Mafia" was not interested in "neighborhood beautification."

My father was not to be deterred. He met with the Wayne County commissioner whose district included Inkster.

I don't know all that transpired or how long it took, but soon workers with bulldozers were in the neighborhoods smoothing out the dirt streets, installing storm drains, and paving the streets. My father insisted that young black men be hired as part of the construction crew. To the consternation of the "Black Mafia," he was becoming "godfather" of Inkster. Soon he would become even more a thorn in their sides when he took a leave of absence from his factory job and started his own numbers business. Many neighborhood folks began playing their numbers with my father and his "maverick crew" rather than with the "Black Mafia." His old UAW acquaintance, Bob Simone, arranged for numbers-running in the plants to come under my father's bank. My father expanded his territory in Inkster to include Jones Sub, a predominantly black community in the adjacent city of Wayne.

Meanwhile, my father, along with my Uncle Herman Smith, Cousin George "Shorty" Hamilton Jr., and other civic leaders, mounted a community movement to change the governance structure of the Village of Inkster. The minority-white community across Michigan Avenue supported this effort.

As a result in December 1952, the Village of Inkster established an elected council/manager structure to work with the president of the village. For the first time, local leadership controlled the police, fire, sanitation, parks, and recreation positions.

Some suggested that my father run for public office, but he had no interest in being a politician. He had me read some of the governmental documents. Though I did not understand the details of forming a city government, I fully understood the concept that government should be "of the people, for the people and by the people."

MEANWHILE, MY EXTENDED Patton-Bolden family was growing and changing. Aunt Samella divorced Black and moved to Los Angeles. Mae, the sister who adored my father, had married, divorced, and remarried and moved to Detroit with her daughter, Deborah, her new husband, Paul Caldwell, and his daughter, Paulette—on some Sundays my family drove the twenty-five miles from Inkster to Detroit to visit with them. On special occasions, my mother hosted elaborate family dinners in her formal dining room.

Most astonishing, at least to my father, Grandfather and Grandmother Patton had had two more sons, Marion, a year older than I, and Earnest, the same age as my brother. My father was floored that his parents were having more children at the same time he was having children.

We were soon to have considerably more family around.

Uncle Junior had joined the Army, but Aunt Carrie had divorced her husband and wanted to leave Montgomery. In fact, she wanted to come to Detroit to be near her brother Bob and her sister Mae. So she did, and she came to live with us. Aunt Carrie's daughter, Zenobia, was sent to Los Angeles to stay with Aunt Samella until Aunt Carrie got on her feet in Detroit; then she would send for her.

Carrie's coming to our home in Inkster was a disruption for Bob and me. Carrie and I needed the twin beds which were in his upstairs domain, so he had to switch rooms with me; my Queen Anne furnishings were much too sissy for his taste.

The move was short-lived as Carrie soon wedded her second husband. He bought her a home and they sent for Zenobia to live with them. My mother gave them several pieces of our living room set as she redecorated our living room.

A little later, my father's first cousin, Jack, came up from Montgomery to live with us. He shared my brother's upstairs domain. Working for my father, he soon earned a salary that made it possible for him to get his own apartment.

Before we could blink an eye, my mother's cousin, Bobbie, came to live with us. She was a student at Wayne State University, majoring in library science. Ironically, much of her college costs were paid by the State of Alabama. To minimize legal challenges to the farce of separate-but-equal higher education, Alabama and other Southern states would pay the out-of-state college expenses for black students who sought majors or professional degrees not offered at Alabama's black colleges. Library science was one such field.

This time, my brother refused to trade rooms. This meant that I had to share my bed with Bobbie. At first I did not mind, but after two years, I did. I could not understand why she couldn't stay with her brother, Cousin George "Shorty" Hamilton Jr., and his family who lived in walking distance from our home on the next street. In Bobbie's junior year, she moved into an university apartment.

Relatives coming to live with us instilled in me the importance of the extended family in standing in the "gap" when a family member needed a haven to plan the next life-move towards personal independence.

As INKSTER GREW, housing stock improved. "Card-board city" projects were demolished and replaced with brick structures. Families in the bungalow projects purchased these modest abodes for a nominal price, and then renovated them into fabulous homes. A new subdivision, Annapolis Park, with its brick homes, gas lights in every yard and wide paved boulevards was considered a spectacular neighborhood.

My elementary school, a corrugated metal structure named after President Abraham Lincoln, was torn down and a brick structure was erected in the old space. Lincoln School had an auditorium, but no cafeteria. Our hot lunches were served in the basement of Smith Chapel CME Church, across the street.

Smith Chapel was one of the two oldest churches in Inkster. The other was First Baptist Church, whose minister was the Reverend J. H. Johnson, brother of the Reverend H. H. Johnson of Hutchinson Street Missionary Baptist Church in Montgomery, which had been my father's family church for three generations. Naturally, my family joined First Baptist, but we also attended Smith Chapel, for my mother was a Methodist.

I remember getting our sugar-cube polio vaccinations at Smith Chapel. We received other vaccination shots, one of which was injected in the upper arm and was very painful to me. Nevertheless, I suffered with measles and chicken pox, but never the mumps.

Our district spelling bees were held in the church basement. I shall never forget losing in the finals as a third grader when I spelled "debri" for "debris." My father, who took the lead in helping Bob and me with homework, pronounced the word as "deb'-ris" when we practiced my spelling list. I soon learned that the word was French, and that "s" and other consonants at the end of words were not pronounced in that language. From that day forward, I correctly pronounced and spelled "Illinois," "Louisville," "St. Louis," and, with great satisfaction, "rendezvous."

MY ELEMENTARY SCHOOL days were quality learning experiences. If pupils needed paddling—always boys—they were taken to the cloak room or to the principal's office and disciplined out of sight of the other children. However, I remember my second-grade teacher washing the faces, ears, arms and legs of pupils in front of the class. This disturbed me and I complained to my father. Thereafter, wash-ups were done in the cloak room.

My third-grade teacher carried a thin leather strap across her shoulder. As she walked up and down the classroom rows to check assignments, she would lash the hands and knuckles of pupils if their work was incorrect. If pupils were talking without her permission, she lashed them across their backs. I never was lashed, but her idea of discipline angered me. I again complained to my father who met with the principal, and soon afterwards the teacher instituted a "demerit system," though she continued to carry her leather strap across her shoulder.

My fourth-grade teacher, Mrs. Virgil Reid, was an intellect. She and her husband owned a commodious home on Michigan Avenue, the divide between black and white Inkster. Michigan Avenue was also the corridor that connected one township to another through several counties, from Ann Arbor to Detroit. Behind the Reids' home was a greenhouse that I often visited. Mr. Reid, a horticulturalist, explained the art of growing exotic flowers. In my later years, when I became an avid reader of Nero Wolfe mystery novels, I often recalled my lessons in the Reids' greenhouse—Wolfe was a master grower of orchids.

Adlai Stevenson of Illinois won the 1952 Democratic presidential nomination to run against the Republican nominee, General Dwight D. Eisenhower. Mrs. Reid was interested in the political opinions of her pupils. Though I could not discern who Mrs. Reid favored, I made it clear that I supported Adlai Stevenson. First, his unusual name connoted intelligence to me. Second, he was labeled an "egghead," which was really the shape of his balding head. Mrs. Reid explained to the class that "egghead" was a derisive term applied to extraordinarily smart people. She stressed the importance for children to learn about political affairs and to urge their parents to vote. Mrs. Reid deepened my budding understanding of politics, lawmaking, and the shaping of public policies.

Discussing politics in my family with my father leading the conversations was a mainstay activity, especially when he read the morning *Detroit Free Press* and the weekly black *Detroit Chronicle* at the table. My father had no influence with the sheriff, who was elected by all of the townships in Wayne County, but he had helped to elect Inkster city officials and his strategy was for them to influence county government and its politics.

My fifth-grade experience was laced with fun. My teacher, Mrs. Lorraine Patterson, orchestrated and encouraged her pupils to engage in extracurricular activities such as the school newspaper. As advisor, Mrs. Patterson taught her pupils how to gather news on school and community activities and then how to lay out this news with graphics in a newsletter format. She typed the stencils, but her pupils mimeographed the pages and stapled the newsletter into its final form. The mimeograph machine spewed ink all over the place if the stencil flew off the drum. And, the manual cranking of the drum rivaled any exercise to build muscles in the forearm. But what a joy it was to distribute our newsletter to schoolmates, parents, and the community at large.

Then Mrs. Patterson decided her pupils should produce a musical and invite the community to the performance. I cannot remember what the boys did, but the girls had a dance routine while singing "Glow Little Glow-worm, Glimmer, Glimmer."

This was not enough for Mrs. Patterson. She now embarked on acting out the long poem by Henry Wadsworth Longfellow, "Hiawatha." She truncated the poem into a play. I recited portions of the poem while Jauanna, my Creole classmate with naturally straight, silky black hair plaited into a French braid that reached her waist, acted out the role of the Indian maiden. The lightest boy in our class played the missionary. Roger played Hiawatha and with his incredible voice that ranged from tenor to first soprano sang "Trees" and "Mother McCrea."

My sixth-grade teacher, Mrs. Frances Tyler, was more contemplative. She and her daughter Carole Chapman—my best friend—and her mother, Mrs. Gordon, lived next door to my family. Carole's family hailed from New York City but had roots in New Orleans; they, too, were Creoles.

Carole seldom visited in my home, probably because her mother took exception to my father's numbers business. Nevertheless, my brother and I were welcome to visit with Carole every day. We played "spin and freeze" in her backyard and had great fun on her swing set. Carole had her own bedroom, living room, and bathroom in her family's basement. Carole and I spent many, many hours there playing Scrabble. We each had Corona typewriters and taught each other how to type. Carole read the teen novels about "Nurse Clara Barton," and I read the novels of the "Bobbsey Twins" and their vacation adventures. We made weekly treks to the public library on Michigan Avenue to borrow books and spent time at the next-door drugstore fountain, drinking cherry Cokes or savoring banana splits.

In sixth grade, Mrs. Tyler instilled in me the thirst to travel and to see the world. Her geography classes came alive as we studied not only the terrain but also the people, culture, dress, and food of a place.

Negro history was taught throughout the year, not just in the second week of February during "Negro History Week," sandwiched between the birthdays of President Abraham Lincoln, the "emancipator," and Frederick Douglass, the famed scholar, orator, and abolitionist. Every month our bulletin boards displayed photos and biographies of famous Negroes and their achievements in fields from medicine to sports. Pupils knew in detail the works of Carter G. Woodson, Paul Lawrence Dunbar, Mary McLeod Bethune, Charles Drew, and other Negroes who excelled despite prejudice and bias, the common terms in the 1950s to describe institutional racism. Mrs. Tyler impressed upon her pupils that it was okay to be smart and to over-achieve, and that if persistent in our studies we too would achieve success, even greatness.

Mrs. Tyler required her pupils to write research papers on famous Negroes. My subject was Dr. George Washington Carver, the famed and

humble scientist at Tuskegee Institute, who discovered wondrous uses of
the peanut and sweet potato. Mrs. Tyler submitted my paper to the district
science fair. At age twelve, I delivered my first scholarly paper to a panel of
refereed judges.

MY INKSTER, A little larger than six square miles and almost totally Negro on
the south side of Michigan Avenue, had a small professional class of teachers,
mostly women, who taught in our five elementary, one junior high, and
one high schools; male school principals; two male medical doctors who
owned a five-bed clinic, mainly for the delivery of babies; one male dentist;
one newspaper publisher (of the *Inkster Ledger*); and two male pharmacists.
There were no lawyers (my father's dream was for me to fill this void). This
professional class was a close-knit group with their sorority and fraternity
functions, often traveling downtown to Detroit to social events.

My father fell in the business class. Mostly men, they owned and managed
retail and service shops including drugstores, restaurants, auto and TV repair
shops, clothing stores, nightclubs, beer gardens and candy stores as venues
for gambling, and one motel. We had one Negro-owned grocery store (one
white-owned grocery store also catered to our Negro community). Inkster's
business class lived within the working-class culture, which was served by a
Veterans of Foreign Wars post and an Elks Club.

Several families had tremendous numbers of children—up to twenty-
three in one family. The Myles family, with ten children, lived down the street
from us. This family owned the White and Black Cab Company. Two of the
older Myles daughters were our babysitters and my mother's housekeepers.
Mr. Myles was hired by my father on many early mornings to bring home
brown bags of money from his winnings at all-night crap games.

Some families on the rural outskirts farmed large tracts and sold their
produce to the local Negro-owned grocery store.

The predominant religious denomination was Baptist, though Smith
Chapel CME was the preeminent church for Inkster's elite. There was St.
Stephens Episcopal Church, which was the site for youth activities and our
piano recitals, but I knew no one in our community who attended it. Inkster
had a modest, practically plebian-looking Catholic Church. I attended one

service with my neighborhood Creole friend, Millicent, cousin to Jauanna. I was mystified with some of the service in Latin, the swinging of tiny, incense-filled urns on long chains by the priest, and the kneeling on rafters that were released by hand from the low backs of immediate front pews.

Inkster also had Pentecostal denominations. I could never figure out the differences or the hierarchy. Nevertheless, I attended a tent revival with my neighborhood friends, Norma Jean and her sister Verdi, and was completely awed when everyone prayed individual prayers aloud, and some were taken over by the spirit to pray in "tongues." When Norma Jean and Verdi visited in my home, we did not play rock and roll records or even watch television. We would go to the den where I played church hymns on my piano or we would go outside to play jacks. Norma Jean was a phenomenal jacks player. After I had mastered the rudiments, Norma Jean taught me the ultimate step of picking up jacks with one hand, tossing them in the air, in "the flying clouds," and catching them in the other hand. We spent hours playing jacks and our other favorite, "Mary Mack," a clapping and rhyming game.

I had another set of friends who were Seventh Day Adventist. I was fascinated with their Saturday worship services that started out with members washing each other's feet. My father noticed my curiosity about various religious denominations and entreated a Jehovah's Witness and the Muslim family down the street to teach Bob and me the tenets of their faiths.

With this appreciation of diversity, I became a firm Baptist and have remained loyal to my father's family church, Hutchinson Missionary Baptist Church in Montgomery, Alabama, where I am a fourth generation tither.

ON THE OTHER end of the spectrum, Inkster had its community "stills." The father of one of my dearest friends was a moonshiner. Their home was really a hallway in a rented dwelling. You entered into the kitchen after climbing up rickety outdoor steps. After walking through the kitchen, you entered into the parents' bedroom with a small bathroom off to the side, and then directly into a bedroom shared by my friend and her older sister. The rooms were separated by two curtains.

It was an exciting nature exploration to walk behind my friends' humble abode through the thick trees and brush and come to a small clearing where the stills were located. A hot wood fire burned beneath three copper drums. Inside the drums was a concoction of fermented corn mash, yeast, and water. The mixture boiled and roared like the witches' brew in *Macbeth*. Copper pipes extended from each of the covered drums into a large covered wooden barrel. It was a lengthy process, and many nights my friend's father and his friends stayed up all night tending to the fire, cleaning out the drums, preparing another fermented corn mash, and pouring the new batch into the copper drums. I understood the chemistry of making corn liquor, called "white lightning." However, it mystified me how the distilled, colorless liquor was pumped through the pipes to the wooden barrel.

When the barrel was full, the moonshiner used a dipper, not wasting a drop, and poured the white liquor into jugs. If a customer wanted moonshine to resemble gin, nothing was added. If a customer wanted the liquor to resemble bourbon, the moonshiner placed peeled, baked apples into the colorless liquor. In a few days, it turned brown. The moonshiner carefully transferred the liquor from jugs to pint and quart bottles. My friends' father had a never-ending waiting list of customers.

"Gwen, Little Bob, Colored is on television!" my father would shout from his living room domain. Wherever we were, we would run to the living room and plop down on the carpet before the television.

The all-Negro cast of *Amos and Andy*, with Kingfish's schemes and his wife, Sapphire, as his foil, and the *Jack Benny Program* with the Negro butler, Roscoe, giving indirect counsel to disentangle Benny from embarrassing predicaments, were television staples for my family. Later the *Nat "King" Cole Show* was added to our required television viewing.

But the *Ed Sullivan Show* on Sunday nights was the premiere show for our family. When Negroes were on this television program, they crossed over to the mainstream and were watched by white audiences.

"He's sooo typical," my cousin Bobbie, a library science major at Wayne State University, would say in disgust as we watched Louis Armstrong master his golden trumpet on the *Sullivan* show. Bobbie's disgust registered when Armstrong, affectionately called "Satchmo," would constantly wipe his sweaty, dark face with a white handkerchief and flash his ever-present grin of incredible teeth that shone pearly white on a black and white television screen.

"People have to do what they have to do," my father responded. "You can't deny his talent. Negroes should not scorn Negroes." My father had every album that Satchmo recorded.

This principle constantly expressed by my father indelibly impacted how I understand people. It is why I cannot hate anyone. There are reasons why people behave the way they do. The secret to getting along with people, even if they are your nemeses, is to find out why they do what they do. Everyone comes from a set of circumstances as they enter the journey of life and it molds their outlooks on life in their travels, and what their relationship may be to you.

Growing up, my father's example allowed me to move more freely within and between social groups than many of my friends and classmates. Though Inkster was overwhelmingly working class, with most of her citizens working in automobile factories, there still existed a class-layered society of cliques, even among the youth. I tried to interact within all of the cliques. I also tried to be sensitive to others' emotional needs. I remember especially a classmate I invited once to the movies because it had upset me how he was taunted by other kids.

Going to the movies was a regular Saturday activity for Bob and me. Father would pay a teenager to take us and would give him extra money to buy all the junk food we could eat while we watched the silly antics of Abbot and Costello or the Three Stooges, the never-ending serials of Flash Gordon, and the now-spectacular cartoons in color, all of which preceded the feature.

This classmate, John, and his sister, Mary, had moved from Detroit to stay with their maternal grandparents in Inkster. John was constantly in schoolyard fights and was considered a bully. Wanting to know why, I learned, probably from my father, that John's father had brutally killed John's mother and was in prison. As that fact became known, other schoolmates, always boys, taunted John. Of course, he had no redress but to fight back, beating to a pulp every boy who aggravated his pain. Making matters worse, the execution date for John's father and the grisly details of the murder and dismemberment of the body were reported in *Jet* magazine, which was read in practically every Negro home.

Over dinner one night, I told my mother that I wanted to invite John to the movies. Mama, tapping into my feelings for someone who was emotionally tortured and was being physically tortured by others in the wake of his deadly loss of his mother and father, responded that I should go alone with John to the movies.

The next day, I told John that I would like to take him to the movies after church on Sunday. He looked at me as if I were from outer space, but accepted. Mother and I picked up John and she came back to the theater at 5 p.m. to pick us up, then we went to our home for dinner and afterwards returned him to his grandparents' home.

I remember telling John that he should not feel ashamed, that he was not responsible, and that I understood his terrible empty feeling of his losing his mother and father. As I walked him to his grandparents' door, I hugged him and told him that I was his friend and that he could always call me and my family whenever he needed to and for whatever reason.

This was my first date. I was eleven years old. I don't recall the name of the movie.

THE TRANSITION FROM my neighborhood all-Negro elementary school to Ford Junior High School (named for the automobile magnate, Henry Ford Sr.) required my classmates and me to cross a set of railroad tracks each morning and afternoon.

At Ford, we sat for the first time in classrooms with white students who had come from their all-white elementary schools on their side of Michigan Avenue. I don't recall discord among the students. However, when it rained and we were outside, my Negro classmates would comment that our white classmates smelled like wet dogs. I soon learned that this smell was the result of permanents in the white girls' hair. Negro girls in the rain soon smelled like wet dogs, too, as they began to perm their hair in the quest to have the "fly away" hair white girls had when the wind was blowing.

As seventh graders, we all felt grown up with the changing of classes every hour, having different teachers for each class, and walking up and down the staircase—Ford was the only two-story school in Inkster. Strangely, I cannot recall the names of any of my teachers, most of whom were white. My favorite class was language arts. Nothing was more fascinating to me than learning the parts and uses of speech, conjugating verbs and diagramming long sentences on the blackboard, a long way from the simple, simple sentences of "See Jane. See Dick. See Spot."

The highlight of my day was stopping at the McClarens' sweet shop, Do Drop In, with my classmates on our way home. The jukebox was the centerpiece of the shop as we danced to the beat of the music. The hot records at the time were Clyde McFadden's "Gum Drops" and Chuck Berry's "School Day." Berry's lyrics—"Up in the morning and off to school, the teacher is teaching the Golden Rule"—were fun to listen to but also encouraged attendance and doing well in school. My father would play the Berry record and the Coasters' "Yakety yak (don't talk back)" full blast on our living room record player when he wanted to send a message to my brother and me.)

Mr. McClaren was in the same business as my father. He was old enough to be my father's father and was one of the founding members of Inkster's "Black Mafia." When a dispute arose about the expanding turf of the numbers business. Mr. McClaren and some other old-timers realigned their businesses with that of my father, whom they adopted as a son. They were impressed with his commitment to improve Inkster.

Mrs. McClaren formed the "Inkster Uplift Club" for children whose fathers were in the numbers business; there were about ten of us. In weekly Thursday after-school meetings in her home, she taught us the importance of caring for one another and for poor people, standing up for one another, and helping one another with our homework. Civic pride was another cornerstone in her teachings. We were taught to care about the cleanliness of our neighborhoods and the community at large, especially to keep our Inkster Park litter-free. Going to school and doing well in our subjects were her constant admonishments. Our weekly dues were fifty cents of which half went to the "sinking fund" to buy cards and fruits when one of our members or a kid in our neighborhood became sick.

At the close of our meetings, while we ate her homemade cookies and drank lemonade, Mrs. McClaren always posed a question for us to research in our community library. One intriguing question was "how do televisions work?" My cousin, George, whose father worked with mine, knew all the answers. Today, he is an electrical engineer working with satellite transmittal of sound and images.

Our childhoods are filled with memories, some joyful and warm that draw us back into those carefree times, but others that are terrible markers of the dividing line between youthful innocence and adult awareness of the grim realities of life. One such searing memory for me involves the tragic death of one of my classmates.

Walking to and from Ford Junior High each morning and afternoon meant not only crossing Michigan Avenue but also the parallel railroad tracks. If a long train was on the tracks at the time, you had to wait and wait. Some daring children, if the train was moving slowly enough, would crouch down and dart beneath the passing freight cars. They would time their dashes to start as soon as the front wheels of a car passed them and they would scamper out the other side before the back wheels reached them. This spared them the inconvenience of waiting, and it was exciting, a dangerous thrill.

One day a group of us approached the tracks as a long train lumbered along. A boy named Tyrone, the shortest boy in our class, crouched down and made a sprint under the slow-rolling train across the tracks to the other side. The crowd cheered.

"Dorothy, it's your turn," someone called out in a dare. "Don't do it," some cried out. "You can do it! Go ahead," others urged her on.

Dorothy crouched down. I do not recall whether she tripped or her clothing got caught or she was simply too slow, but she did not make it. We watched in mute horror as the squealing wheels severed her body, sending her legs one way and her arms another.

Afterwards, we stood frozen, wailing, with tears rolling down our faces until the train stopped and three police cars arrived with sirens blasting. Our parents began to arrive soon after. Crying with uncontrollable pain, my brother, classmates, and I piled into the cars and were taken home.

No doubt our parents discussed this juvenile escapade among themselves.

Perhaps my classmates did so as well, but I was too distraught. I angrily told my father, as if he were at fault, that no kid should have to cross a train track to go to school.

The following year, Fellrath Junior High School was constructed and opened in the heart of our Negro community. Whether white students who did not have to cross train tracks continued their educations at Ford Junior High, I do not know. I was simply relieved that my Negro classmates and I no longer had to cross a deadly barrier to enjoy our right to learn.

5

Walking for Freedom

As was common in the 1950s with Negro families who had moved North, children were often sent back South in the summers to be with grandparents, cousins, and other members of the extended family. In 1956, I was especially looking forward to spending the summer with my relatives in Montgomery, Alabama.

One reason was that I needed to find inner peace after the horrific death of my schoolmate, Dorothy. Another reason was that I was just at the age of becoming aware of news, politics, and current events, and a really big event—if you were Negro—was unfolding in my parents' hometown. All during the past year, my family in Detroit had kept abreast of the Montgomery Bus Boycott by calling relatives in Alabama and by reading the headline stories in the Negro press and the outstanding articles by Negro journalist Ted Poston in the *New York Post*. My father and his associates sent money to support the boycott and even shoes to replace those that blacks in Montgomery were wearing out by walking everywhere instead of riding the bus.

I was only twelve years old, but I think I understood quite well the significance of the boycott, and I thrilled to the courage of Rosa Parks and the eloquent leadership of Reverend King. It is not that racism didn't exist in the

North, but segregation in the Deep South at that time was so pervasive that you couldn't escape it, and it was so humiliating that you never forgot it.

Even small children were not spared. I well remember an incident in Montgomery when I was eight years old. On many Sunday afternoons, after church and a light snack, my maternal grandmother, Mommy, would stand with me, my brother, and our cousin on the corner of Holt and Early streets and wait for the bus to arrive so we children could ride downtown. When the bus came, while we waited by the back door, Mommy climbed the front steps of the bus and deposited coins in the fare box. Then she stepped back down off the bus and came to the back door. That was the procedure for Negroes.

As she ushered us onto the bus, if the very back seat was empty, she would remind us, again, to go straight to the "fun seat." What was the fun seat? Well, that was one of those many fictions that Negro adults told small children to spare them as much as possible from the constant belittlements of their race. In Mommy's case, she always told us, "The long, back seat and looking out the large window to see the scenery going backwards, is the best seat on the bus," thus distracting us from any ideas of wanting to ride in the front of the bus.

On this particular Sunday, we eagerly climbed the steps and walked briskly to the back seat, climbed up and balanced ourselves on our knees, and looked out the back window and waved to Mommy as the bus pulled away. At the town square, we got off the bus and went into Liggett's Drug Store to buy ice cream cones. Before we ordered, I asked the soda-fountain jerk if I could have a cup of water.

"That'll be three cents for the cup," she responded.

As I gave her my three pennies and she handed me the paper cup, I sat down on one of the stools to drink my water.

"Pickaninny! Get off the stool!" the soda jerk screamed at me.

We left without our ice cream cones. When we got home, Mommy was on her front porch swing, waiting for our arrival. I ran across the street with tears in my eyes to Mommy's loving arms and blurted, "Mommy, she called me a 'pickaninny'! What's a 'pickaninny'?"

After I told Mommy what happened to me, she hugged me tightly and said, "You are the most beautiful little girl in the world. When God made you, he made you very special."

THAT WAS IN 1952. In my Alabama summer four years later, I threw myself into whatever my elders told me to do to help with the bus boycott. It was a glorious time to be in Montgomery. The unity and love among Negroes was thicker than Alaga syrup and a hundredfold sweeter.

People everywhere in the community were offering assistance to each other, from providing rides through the "people's transportation system" spearheaded by Coach Rufus A. Lewis to the delivery of medicines to homebound patients coordinated by pharmacist Richard Harris.

On weekends neighbors with cars visited or called neighbors without cars to get their grocery lists to purchase their weekly staples. My responsibility was to jot down the lists as my Aunts Chick and Mary and Cousin Flora handed the phone over to me. When I went grocery shopping with my relatives, I had a separate grocery cart to load food items from our neighbors' lists.

Mommy took me to weekly Monday night mass meetings in support of the boycott. These rotated among the larger Negro churches in the community. These were often commodious and resplendent edifices, with stained-glass windows, pipe organs, ornate pulpits, and high ceilings with balconies that could seat the hundreds of people regularly attending the mass meetings.

I had no doubt that God was listening as church choirs movingly raised our petition in song for our race to freedom. Inspirational messages of hope at the mass meetings were delivered by Dr. Martin Luther King Jr. and the Reverends Solomon S. Seay Sr., Ralph D. Abernathy, W. J. Powell, A. W. Wilson, H. H. Hubbard, H. H. Johnson, and W. F. Alford, among others. When these ministers rose to preach, we knew that the Holy Ghost was present, and the Spirit emanating from these ordained men of God set our souls on fire.

On occasion, after begging my paternal grandfather, I accompanied him to Thursday night business meetings of the Montgomery Improvement Association (MIA). Grandfather had built the first and only black hotel in Montgomery, the Ben Moore Hotel. Mr. Moore, my grandfather, and other businessmen were part of this group. Most times, I was the only child present. Here, I had the opportunity to see up close our ministers and lay leaders, men and women, in deliberative action. Mrs. Hazel Gregory, secretary of the MIA, could write faster than anybody I knew. Mrs. Erna Dungee was firm in making sure that income and expenditures were accounted for with receipts. Alabama State College (ASC) Professor JoAnn Robinson was brilliant in her assessment of the past week's activities as the baseline to plan next week's strategies. She was extremely detailed and wanted it carefully written down who was to do what. She was adamant that boycott plan should run smoothly.

ASC Coach Rufus A. Lewis served as chair of the MIA's pivotal transportation system, the finely tuned engine of the boycott that used, in part, a fleet of church station wagons as substitutes for the city buses that Negroes had vowed to boycott until segregated seating ended.

Lewis was also chair of the voter registration committee, and that was his work of passion. Though Lewis himself had been turned down for military service because of problems with his feet, he was frustrated that black veterans had fought and died overseas for freedoms they didn't enjoy at home. He was an astute businessman who had married into the family that owned the largest funeral home in Montgomery, Ross-Clayton Funeral Home. He was also the owner of the Citizens' Club, a night spot for members only, and you had to be a registered voter to become a member. My Aunt Mae, who adored my father, was a member. At all times Lewis kept in the trunk of his car copies of the so-called literacy tests, the prerequisite barrier that potential voters had to pass before they became registered by the state government.

As football coach, businessman, and night club owner, Lewis was by nature and necessity a methodical person. He brought all his experience into the planning and operation of the MIA transportation committee. He also meticulously applied his organizing skills to the voter registration clinic. He had a form for everything: intake and assessment forms for people who attended voter clinics; canvass forms for "block captains" on every block in Negro voting precincts to determine who was registered or not, who had attempted to register and was denied; affidavit blanks for people to fill out if they were denied; and so on. For those already registered, he had candidate forms to assess campaign positions that would impact on the Negro community; candidate-screening forms for Negro voters to tally their endorsements; sample ballots with large Xs next to the names of endorsed candidates; transportation forms for volunteers who drove voters to and from the polls on election days; and follow-up-forms that compiled data from the other forms.

Most of the formal leadership positions in the MIA were held by ministers. Not so with the Voter Registration Committee. Coach Lewis was the chair and he was surrounded by women who were sharp, smart, militant, and the best organizers ever. Coach Lewis recognized and publicly acknowledged the importance of women leadership. In addition to my education in the "citizenship schools" held in my paternal grandparents' home, I traveled with these incredible women, especially Mrs. Idessa Williams-Redden and Mrs. Bertha Smith, precinct captains who had a host of men and women as block captains working with them. Often we drove out to rural, outlying Negro communities to set up voters' clinics and to encourage local leadership. Many times my specific assignment was to talk to youth to encourage them to keep telling their parents and relatives to go down to the registrar's office to register to vote.

WITH ALL OF this activity, I still found time to enjoy a social life. I hosted elaborate tea parties in Mommy's home, and of course there were Sunday afternoon teas at our churches. Also, Montgomery girls had "petticoat parties," where we would gather at our friends' homes, petticoats in hand. The petticoat of all petticoats was the half slip of five layers of crinoline or white crocheted net with ribbed ribbons of green, yellow, white, pink, and blue at the hems. We dipped our petticoats in very thick starch and then hung them out to dry in the summer sun. When we put them on beneath our full gathered skirts, they would balloon from our tiny waists to almost a foot at our knees. Nothing was more elegant than for us to sit down with our legs crossed at our ankles and our skirts bouncing up, displaying the rainbow hems of our petticoats. We knew we were princesses when we promenaded to our friends' lawn parties or to dance socials at the bricklayers' hall or the community house, which also was our Negro library. I am convinced that the beauty of our petticoats was what invited boys to come over to ask us to dance.

I had two "beaus" that summer—Bernard Bailey who was my age and gave me a friendship ring, and Boonie Greene who was a year older. Most times, we walked to the movies, holding hands, or went to church functions and social dances. I had fun with them, but I was also interested in their thoughts about our people's freedom. Sometimes Bernard and Boonie came to mass meetings with their parents, but when they would not meet me at the MIA office, I knew that our friendships were just that—friendships.

My PARENTS AND brother drove to Montgomery at the end of summer to spend two weeks with family. My father worked with his father and his construction crew to replace the roof on First Baptist Church where Reverend Ralph D. Abernathy—Dr. King's right-hand man in the movement, preached. It was a proud moment when we, as a family taking up two pews, sat together at a Monday night mass meeting.

When time came to head back to Michigan, my father and grandfather hoisted and carried my footlocker to the trunk of the car while my brother grabbed the boxes of road food from the kitchen table. My mother, MaDear, and I followed. We hugged each other and said our lingering goodbyes as my brother eagerly climbed into the back seat of the car—two weeks in Montgomery had been more than enough for him, though I was sad that my three-month summer vacation had come to an end all too soon. If I had been in charge of my life, I would have stayed in Montgomery.

Across town, we stopped by Aunt Chick's home. My mother's relatives, with more travel goodies for us, were waiting to say their goodbyes and to pray for our safe return home.

Soon we were headed north on U.S. Highway 31. My father drove non-stop through Alabama, Tennessee, and Kentucky, stopping only for gas or on the side of the road when we needed to relieve ourselves or if he needed to catch a cat-nap. Young people today can't understand the significance of that; they can't fathom a world in which black motorists could not find a restaurant they could dine in or a hotel they could sleep in or even a gas station bathroom they could use without fear of refusal or humiliation or confrontation. And to a proud black man, confrontation could become deadly. So you just kept driving. That was the point of all those carefully packed boxes of road food and goodies.

When we reached Cincinnati, Ohio, we breathed a collective sigh that we had made it across the Mason-Dixon Line without incident.

After driving through the Deep South for sixteen hours, we broke our "car fever" by stopping at a Howard Johnson restaurant. Its bright orange and green roof tiles symbolized freedom. We went to the restrooms to freshen up and then sat down together for a hot meal.

Though Ohio represented the historical land of freedom for Negroes, you could quickly deduce that the Ohio state troopers had not gotten that memo. Negro motorists without Ohio car tags were constantly stopped by the troopers for so-called moving violations or speeding. You would see dozens of passenger cars along the roadsides with Ohio trooper cars, red lights flashing, behind each one.

My father had encountered this ordeal too many times. For this trip from Montgomery back to Inkster, he made certain that our car was in tip-top shape and he carefully drove just a bit below the speed limit; road-weary by that point, we felt that it was taking us longer to drive through Ohio than it had to drive across Alabama, Tennessee and Kentucky.

THE PRESIDENTIAL ELECTION cycle was again before us in 1956. Our civics class decided to hold mock campaigns and elections. I chose to represent incumbent President Dwight D. Eisenhower although I personally liked the contender, Adlai Stevenson. I campaigned vigorously, stressing that Americans "like Ike." I lost the mock election and conceded with these words: "I, portraying Eisenhower, lost at Fellrath Junior High, but Eisenhower, the president, will win the real election." So he did, with a landslide victory.

My special project for my civics class was an essay on the Montgomery Bus Boycott. My paper was laced with primary-source interviews of my relatives I had gathered over the summer in Montgomery and from our Montgomery family in our weekly phone calls.

The Montgomery Bus Boycott is not a story about one person or even a few people. It is a compilation of personal stories of the tens of thousands of black people who collectively made the movement successful.

The boycott actually came to an end not because of the year-long protest triggered by Rosa Parks's principled defiance, but because of a federal civil lawsuit filed by black attorney Fred Gray on behalf of four or five other women who had been arrested prior to Mrs. Parks under similar circumstances. Originally, the goals of the bus protest—the boycott run by the Montgomery Improvement Association—had been modest: courtesy toward black bus patrons, black drivers on routes in the black community (there were zero black bus drivers), first-come, first-served seating in the middle section of the bus. The original boycott demand did not even include an end to segregated seating. The black community just wanted a policy that allowed blacks to fill seats from the back, and whites to fill seats from the front, until the bus was full. This change in policy at least would have avoided the ridiculous humiliation of blacks standing in the back of the bus while there were empty seats in the white section in the front.

But Montgomery city officials would not give an inch. So attorney Gray and the MIA filed a lawsuit in the local United States District Court challenging the segregation ordinance itself. This was only eighteen months after the U.S. Supreme Court had ruled in the historic *Brown v. Board of Education* case that so-called separate-but-equal public education violated the United States Constitution. Fred Gray's *Browder v. Gayle* (Amelia Browder was a local woman; W. A. Gayle was the Montgomery mayor) lawsuit sought to extend the *Brown* doctrine to public transportation.

A three-judge federal court panel in Montgomery heard the evidence submitted by attorney Gray and shortly ruled that segregated bus seating was unconstitutional. The City of Montgomery naturally appealed, but because the ruling had been made by a three-judge panel, the appeal bypassed the U.S. appellate courts and went directly to the U.S. Supreme Court, which then, on November 13, 1956, affirmed the lower court ruling. It took another month for the Supreme Court ruling to be certified and the paperwork to arrive in Montgomery and for sullen city officials to announce that Jim Crow had lost.

But by the end of 1956 segregated seating on Montgomery buses was history, and black riders could both pay and board through the front door and then sit wherever they wanted. And then, in January 1957, all hell broke loose. Rabid racists wreaked vengeance on the black community. On January 10, four black churches and two parsonages in Montgomery were ripped by dynamite bombs. All the explosions took place about 2 a.m. It was an obvious, orchestrated conspiracy and it was later proven by law enforcement that the bombings were the work of local Ku Klux Klansmen and their sympathizers. The parsonages were those of First Baptist Church, occupied by the Reverend Ralph D. Abernathy and his family, and Trinity Lutheran Church, occupied by the Reverend Robert Graetz and his family (Graetz was white, but he pastored a black congregation in the black community; he was the only white Montgomery minister who supported the boycott and was a part of the Montgomery Improvement Association). The four bombed churches were First Baptist, Mount Olive Baptist, Bell Street Baptist, and Hutchinson Street Baptist (our family church; the Patton family home sat next door).

My grandparents called my parents to report the bombings. Though they heard the blast and felt an earthquake-like tremor, my grandparents relayed that little damage had been done to the church and no damage to their own house. My father accepted the report, but he wanted to see for himself. After he arranged for someone to handle his business, he drove to Montgomery.

While in Montgomery, he joined his family's construction crew and helped replace the roof on First Baptist Church. My grandfather's Patton Construction Company was also contracted by the Reverend Uriah J. Fields and the congregation of Bell Street Baptist Church to rebuild it. Bell Street Baptist had been completely destroyed by the bombing.

MY FATHER HAD carried with him to Montgomery a copy of my junior high school essay on the boycott and he told me that he shared it with people everywhere he went, from crap games to church. As my junior high school days came to a fun end in May 1957, I was eager to return to Montgomery for the summer and to see for myself the successful results of the boycott.

You can imagine my surprise when I rode the desegregated buses for the first time with Mommy, my grandmother, and she walked to the back of the bus and took a seat.

"Mommy, why do you sit in the back of the bus when our people protested the law that forced us to sit in the back of the bus?" I asked her. "Gwendolyn," she said, "the boycott was not about sitting next to white people. It was about sitting wherever you pleased." Mommy's matter-of-fact response broadened my perspective on the movement and deeply informed and shaped my race to freedom.

Still, at every opportunity when I rode the bus, I always plopped in a front seat next to a white person.

Monday night mass meetings still drew hundreds of people. The main concern had shifted to getting black men—and eventually black women— hired as bus drivers. There was a quiet discussion on purchasing and running a public bus company, but the concept did not take hold. This was my first instance of seeing how black people placed limitations on themselves. I had always wondered why black people traveling in the South wanted to stay in white hotels and motels instead of promoting, for instance, the establishment of a chain of A. G. Gaston Motels. Gaston was a black businessman who became a millionaire in Birmingham with an insurance company that served the black community. He also owned a hotel and restaurant. Why couldn't he have had a chain of motels serving black travelers in the South, I wondered.

The weekly mass meetings of the Montgomery Improvement Association continued to be full of the Spirit. A new feature was to have the music provided by youth singing groups. The Bradford Sisters—Verdell, Josephine, and Viola—were members of Holt Street Baptist Church (where the first boycott mass meeting was held on December 5, 1955), and the Howard Sisters—Rubye, Princilla, Barbara Ann, and Wilhemina—of Mt. Zion AMEZ (where the MIA was organized) were two of the outstanding groups. With the Montgomery Gospel Trio— an ensemble of the sensational a capella voices of Mary Ethel Dozier, Minnie Lee Hendricks, and Gladys "Cookie" Carter—these groups took Montgomery's movement by storm with their original compositions. When the legendary folk singers Guy and Candie Carawan heard the Trio sing their original "Why Don't White Folks Know,

We Ain't Gonna Ride the Bus No More," the Carawans promoted them for a fundraising concert in New York City's Carnegie Hall.

These youthful, innocent voices, yearning for freedom, delighted the old souls with their voices, often *a capella* and in perfect harmony. It was clear that the old souls' passion to fight for freedom was to create in their lifetimes a better world for the children.

THE SOUTHERN CHRISTIAN Leadership Conference (SCLC) formed in 1957 as a way to extend the Montgomery movement to the larger issues of all black Americans. Led by black ministers such as Martin Luther King Jr., Ralph Abernathy, Fred Shuttlesworth, Joseph Lowery, and C. T. Vivian, the SCLC made it clear that we had to advance our movement with direct action (boycotts) and demonstrations. The National Association for the Advancement of Colored People (NAACP) frowned on demonstrations and fiercely argued that the legal route was the only realistic challenge to Jim Crow. At a young age, I was able to discern class conflicts and the attendant problems of who would be the leaders in our movement. The ministers—some formally trained and some simply called—directly represented the masses, who filled their churches every Sunday morning. The lawyers, all formally trained and an elite class, were concerned with "civil behavior" and not with "civil disobedience," which they considered unruly and undignified.

My loyalty rested with the ministers. I recognized that we needed both tactics—mass demonstrations *and* the legal component—to mount a strategic movement for social and structural change. The "street heat" of marching and demonstrating could not effect fundamental social change without a legal component. But the legal component could not get anywhere without public demonstrations that pushed the envelope of public opinion to examine the laws and customs of structural discrimination and institutional racism.

From my youth to this day, I have struggled with lawyers who have a problem of seeing themselves as surrogates and not as advocates, supplanting the rightful leadership of the masses, whom they called "clients."

A debate in 1957 in Montgomery was whether the Montgomery Improvement Association (MIA) would become the Southern Christian Leadership Conference (SCLC). In tow with my paternal grandfather at the

MIA's Thursday night business meetings, I was firmly on the side of keeping the name of the MIA. The organization under that name had spearheaded and maintained the success of the bus boycott. Why should the MIA give up an identity that resonated with the masses of the people? I understood the need to coordinate regional movements, but was it necessary for a local grassroots organization to be subsumed into a regional organization?

The MIA won that debate, and thus became the local parent to the regional SCLC, which then went on, under the leadership of Dr. King and Reverend Abernathy, to lead the civil rights movement on a broader basis. But for decades that followed, the MIA continued to have a presence in Montgomery with its programs of direct action for social change.

This debate took hold with me in my future organizing efforts. While serving as 1965–66 student body president at Tuskegee Institute (now Tuskegee University), I stood firm that the students' Tuskegee Institute Advancement League (TIAL), the grassroots organization in Black Belt Macon County, should not become a chapter of the Student Non-Violent Coordinating Committee (SNCC).

SNCC stationery would be more impressive and would connote a breadth of support by listing the names of local organizations on the left side. Grassroots, local organizations' recognition guaranteed ownership and self-interest in continuing the movement.

Thus the concept of coalitions began to germinate in my mind as an organizing principle. That seed had been planted during my summers in Montgomery when I was a petticoat-wearing junior high school student who already was taking notes on the movement in my race to freedom.

6

Leaving Childhood

For the first seven years of my formal schooling. I thought "recess" was a waste of time. But in the eighth grade, physical education became my new favorite class. I loved playing softball and learning to pitch the ball underhanded instead of overhanded as in baseball. I learned that the rules of girls' basketball were different than the rules for boys' basketball. Each position had specific rules of play. Though short, I played "forward," which gave me the opportunity to jump for rebounds and to shoot at the basket. No doubt I had a head start from the years of playing "round robin" with my brother and his pack on our garage-mounted hoop.

Meanwhile, I continued to excel in English, math and in the new subjects of civics and biology. Biology was especially fun as we watched tadpoles grow into frogs, with the culminating hands-on activity of dissecting one. Biology was also a course on studying the human body and the distinction between female and male organs that was somehow analogous to "bees and flowers" and cross-fertilization. The analogy did not, and still does not, make sense to me.

I was not "developed" like many of the girls. My mother bought me training bras though I barely had "nubs" on my chest. Occasionally, the developed girls suggested I stuff my bra with toilet paper when I wore sweater-cardigan sets. I cared less one way or the other, but I obliged the girls to keep them from hounding me.

I remembered special "Very Personally Yours" meetings in the sixth grade for girls only. Here, we were informed that our bodies would transform with the growing of breasts and hair on our legs and in unseen places. The overload of information was accompanied by pamphlets on the menstrual cycle. It puzzled me that hygiene and cleanliness were emphasized, yet we were admonished not to take baths nor shampoo our heads during our monthly periods. Now, in the eighth grade, studying bees and flowers was to solidify the connection.

One day my gym teacher, Sandra Dennard, called to me as PE class was ending: "Gwen, I need to speak to you after you dress."

I dutifully went in to see her. "Gwen, you don't seem embarrassed when you suit up and take showers," she said, looking at me as though she could read my mind. "I want you to talk with the girls. Some are sad because they do not have breasts nor have monthly periods."

I wondered how Mrs. Dennard knew I did not yet have periods, but then I never complained of stomach cramps nor had the accidents some girls did when spots of blood seeped through their skirts or dresses—sometimes they paraded about with these "spots" as signs that they were grown-up. I was in no hurry to grow up. I wanted to stay young as long as possible.

Mrs. Dennard gave me a list of girls who were at the same stage of puberty as I was. I talked with them one-on-one, but most lamented that they were still "little girls" and not teenagers. I could not understand why they wanted to lose blood every month. Being anemic, I had learned at an early age to like spinach, broccoli, Brussels spouts, beets, and smothered liver and onions so I could build up iron in my blood. I concluded that losing blood would make me weak. I wanted to keep my blood in my body as long as possible.

In gym class I also learned square-dancing, with its graceful "now, promenade" and "do-si-dos," and the polka, bouncing all over the gym floor. These dance classes were held jointly with boys as our partners. The hat-dance was a lot of fun as we danced to the song, "La Cucaracha," around a gigantic Mexican hat on the floor. My mother bought me a paisley-print skirt and halter set that I always wore when we performed the hat-dance for assemblies. The halter had a collar that you slipped over your neck and the bodice buttoned down the front. Your arms and back were exposed. I could not wear my training bra because the straps would show on my back. This halter symbolized for me that I was a teenager. I did not need a bra—let alone to stuff it with toilet paper—to remind me that I was thirteen.

I WAS BEGINNING to develop an adult awareness of life, both at home and in the world.

I enjoyed watching beauty pageants on television, not so much to look at the women as at the gowns. For a brief moment I thought I would be a dress designer.

"*Ladies and gentlemen,*" the Miss World Pageant television host announced, "*Miss South Africa!*" I could not believe my eyes. Promenading down the runway was a light-haired white woman, probably blue-eyed. I had thought there was only one white woman in Africa: dark-haired Jane, the mate to Tarzan. Now I *had* to get an understanding as to how this blonde white woman came out of Africa.

My father explained the colonization of South Africa and the development of its apartheid system, which was akin to Jim Crow laws in the South. I knew all about those from my summers in Montgomery and was startled to realize that racial history in the U.S. had parallels in other parts of the world.

I became a student of world events, scouring the *Detroit Free Press* for articles on Africa. The Congolese, under the leadership of Patrice Lumumba, were striking blows of freedom to throw off the yoke of Belgian imperialism. Native peoples in Ghana in West Africa, under the leadership of Kwame Nkrumah, and in Kenya in East Africa, under the leadership of Jomo Kenyatta, were waging similar struggles against imperialistic colonialism.

Over the next few years, I kept abreast of African developments for independence. U.S. Secretary of State John Foster Dulles, an influential Cold War figure, died in 1959. I had become convinced that the U.S. was thwarting African liberation struggles, and for my tenth grade world history class I wrote a research paper entitled: "John Foster Dulles—the Balance of Terror Is Dead." My teacher, Mrs. Irene Cobb, did not submit my paper in the regional history contest because it might have been considered "anti-American" by white judges. I did, however, earn an "A" in her class. In 1960 the Congo won its independence from Belgium. It was breathtaking to watch on the television news as an African in his splendid native dress took his seat in the United Nations. Still later, after I had become a student at Tuskegee Institute, Congo President Lumumba was assassinated by Mobutu/Belgian/U.S. interests in 1961. That same year, UN Secretary General Dag Hammarskjold died in a plane crash. I had no doubt that these deaths and events were intertwined and they heightened my growing interest in the liberation struggles at home and abroad.

BUT I AM getting ahead of myself. It is still 1957 and I'm a Detroit teenager and at the beginning of a series of life lessons and experiences that made me grow up fast.

I began to wrap a pink plastic tea set in Christmas paper.

"No, Gwen, don't wrap that set. Wrap the tea set with the silver creamer and sugar bowl," my mother instructed.

"Why should Sandy get the pretty tea set?" I pursed my lips into a pout.

"Sandy is your sister. Your daddy is not home with her every night as he is with you and your brother."

Sandy was my father's proven "outside" child, five years younger than me. She looked exactly like a Patton.

My mother knew that Lois, Sandy's mother, was my father's "other woman." At first my mother and father argued and fought over this affair. Mother soon resignedly accepted the reality that my handsome, smart, urbane, and suave father was "a lady's man." Lois was not the only recipient of his charms. But as long as he provided for our family, bought Mother fur coats and diamonds, and she was on his arm as Mrs. Patton for events that mattered, she found it within herself to keep marital peace. She simply did not want her children to grow up fatherless as she had.

My mother claimed Sandy as our half-sister. She made it clear that Sandy had nothing to do with the circumstances of her coming into the world. Besides, my mother said with loving words, there is no such thing as in-laws, ex-laws, out-laws, half-children and step-children: we are all family. Most Sunday afternoons Mother, with my brother and me in tow, would drive to Sandy's home, where she lived with her mother and her grandparents. Sandy would run out and jump in the backseat with my brother. The three of us would spend Sunday afternoons playing in our home.

Whatever new back-to-school, Easter, or Christmas clothes I received, my mother bought the same for Sandy. Mother had Sandy's measurements, and when the family tailor made special dresses for me, winter coats, muttons, and muffs, Sandy got the same.

In August 1958, I had just returned from my annual summer vacation in the South. Mother took me to People's Drugstore for a soda fountain treat. I thought she wanted to have a special outing with me so I could tell her about the great time I enjoyed while in Montgomery.

As we entered the drugstore, I headed to the counter with the round stools. Mother gently steered me to one of the booths. After settling in, I ordered my banana split and my mother ordered a chocolate-fudge sundae.

Between bites, I enthusiastically told her about my summer adventures. She always listened to me, conveying tangible love, nodding her head and laughing at my fantastic life-learning exploits. But this time her gaze at me was too intent.

"Gwen, I have breast cancer. The doctors have given me three months to live."

I stopped breathing. Air returned to my lungs as tears cascaded down my cheeks.

"There is hope," Mother said. She reached across the table to hold my cold hands in her warm ones. I felt her love reviving my body. "The doctors said if they remove my pituitary gland, the cancer will stop growing. Let's pray this will work. I don't want to leave you. But, if I must go, I know you'll be okay. You are a smart girl and you will make your mark on this world."

My mother was thirty-six years old.

I later learned that she took my brother with her to Dr. Watson Young, her primary physician who had delivered my brother into this world, to discuss her condition and her impending death. My brother dearly loved our mother. Only he knew how to make her brewed-coffee and cheese toast just right. She knew her death would have a devastating effect on him, mentally and emotionally.

Mother was in the hospital at the University of Michigan, recuperating from surgery, when I had my first period. She already had had her left breast removed. When I visited her after the removal of her pituitary gland, she appeared wider than before. I knew she was in pain so I did not tell her that I had started menstruating; my monthly inconvenience paled in the light of her suffering.

Life somehow went on. I entered high school and, along with my girl-friends, the "Flip Jips," cheered the Inkster High School Vikings to victory at the opening of the football season.

Soon after, my mother was home from the hospital. Our dachshund, Duchess, followed her every step and had transferred from sleeping with me to sleeping at the foot of my parents' bed. Duchess brought much comfort to my mother and sat next to her at our kitchen table.

ONE DAY MY father cooked our favorite family dinner of calves' liver smothered with onions and gravy; steamed lemon-pepper broccoli, which my bother and I called "tree-tops"; his famous three-step, tender, every grain-to-itself steamed rice; and rolls. Throughout the day my parents had engaged in quiet, serious discussions. I knew we were going to have a family meeting at dinner.

"Kids, I have been called to testify before the grand jury," my father said. "A grand jury is like a private, secret courtroom. The jury listens to testimony and decides if the situation warrants a public trial."

My father had been notified that he owed the Internal Revenue Service $56,000 in back taxes over the past ten years. The prosecutor offered my father a deal if he would provide evidence of the numbers business.

"I don't know what the outcome will be," he said. "But, if I have to go to prison, I am prepared to rob a bank to get enough money to take care of you and your mother."

A few days later, his photograph graced the front page of the *Detroit Free Press* with the caption: "Bob Patton to Testify on the Numbers Racket."

People in the Inkster community were supportive and very warm towards my family. Many visited our home, did chores, provided comfort, and assured my parents that they would take care of us whatever the outcome.

With the astute legal counsel of our family attorney, Harry Fowler, and his partner, Kenny Cockerel (later a judge), my father and his crew avoided prison. He gave up the numbers business, which I thought was the real objective of the prosecution, instigated by the "old Negro mafia" in collusion with the district attorney's office.

MOTHER WAS IN and out of the doctors' offices. Her pain had returned. Every night, my brother and I slept with her until our father came home. Some nights we would prop her up on the left side; the elevation alleviated the pain caused by fluid build-up as a result of the radical mastectomy.

"Kids, Daddy's home!" my father would call out as he entered the side door. He always had Chinese food, shrimp, or barbeque. Nothing was more loving than to see him feed Mother, who found it too painful to lift her arm (she was left-handed). My parents' bedroom became our primary living quarters.

When Mother had to be readmitted to the hospital, my mother's mother, Mommy, and my father's mother, MaDear, came up from Montgomery to be with her. After a week, MaDear returned to Montgomery. Mommy stayed.

Not much later, Mother was admitted to a convalescing home. Mommy stayed with her. After a visit with my mother when she had cracks in her skin and fluids oozing from every crevice, I leaned over, kissed her, and told her that I was not going to bring Little Bob back to see her. She nodded understanding and approval. My brother could not have endured seeing her suffer so.

About 4 A.M. on October 31, 1958, the phone rang. My father was not at home. After a few pleasantries, the caller said, "Your mother has passed."

I lay in my bed and decided I would not tell my brother until he came downstairs to fix our breakfast at 7:30. He made pancakes. While we ate, I said, "Mama is dead." I knew I had to be strong for him.

Tears streamed down his cheeks but all he said was, "Oh, no!" He went back upstairs and did not come down until the day of our mother's funeral five days later. We placed his meals on the steps. Many times the tray was not touched.

My mother's funeral must have been one of the biggest ever in Inkster. More than two hundred cars were in the funeral procession. My father and brother took my mother's funeral hard, especially when the choir sang "Soon I'll Be Done with the Troubles of the World, Going Home to Live with God," one of my mother's favorite spirituals and the signature song in the movie, *An Imitation of Life*. Mommy and I did not cry at Mama's funeral; we knew she was in a better place.

As we rode to the gravesite, I told my father that Little Bob and I would not get out. I did not want my brother to see our mother lowered into the ground. I feared he would fall over into the crypt and beg to be buried with her.

THE REST OF 1958 was a blur. I was in deep conversation with God, constantly asking why he took our mother. My concern was not about me, but for Little Bob, who began to show signs of coldness and detachment. I reconciled my relationship with God by reading *Death, Be Not Proud* by

John Gunther. My renewed faith strengthened my resolve to press on with life and reassured me that God makes no mistakes. I accepted that I would come to understand in the by-and-by; I just had to keep on living.

Weeks at a time I stayed with my girlfriends and their families, especially Marilyn Russell, the "Flip Jips" pantomime saxophonist. Her family had moved from Jacksonville, Florida, to Inkster and bought a home in the middle-class subdivision Annapolis Park. Marilyn exhibited Southern charm and manners, reminding me of my friends in Montgomery.

At the kitchen table one night, Daddy gave my brother Bob and me $300 each to buy our own and others' Christmas presents.

Bob and I had been taught that our father had supernatural powers as Santa Claus, the Easter Bunny, and the Tooth Fairy. I never had the desire to sit on Santa's lap when I went Christmas shopping. I made my list of what I wanted and what I wanted to buy as gifts for others. As I read my list to my father, he would assess my behavior for the year, recalling the times I had been placed on punishment for "talking back" (I earned excellent grades in my subjects, but only satisfactory in deportment), when I had gone to Sunday School with or without complaint, or when I had helped other kids who were not as fortunate as I in our community. My "niceness" always out-weighed my "naughtiness." At the end of these sessions, my father handed over a stack of $50 bills. Our hugging embrace epitomized that special relationship between a father and his daughter.

But this Christmas season was different. Not only was my father's money short, but, more importantly, my mother was not there to advise while I did my Christmas shopping nor to help me wrap the presents.

EASTER 1959 CAME quickly. I was spending the holiday with my father's girlfriend, Edith Mae, in River Rouge. My mother knew about this affair, too, yet she was friendly to Edith Mae and her sister, Lucretia Simmons, who owned the record shop in Inkster. Lucretia's daughters, Larretease and Bernadette were my best friends. It was not unusual for our family to visit with the Simmons family, including Edith Mae, who lived with her sister.

Edith Mae had a philosophy similar to my mother's. She truly loved my father. I was my father's daughter. Therefore, she loved me as his daughter. She took me Easter shopping and bought me the most exquisite and expensive mohair blue suit, accessories, shoes and purse at Lord & Taylor, one of the most exclusive shops in Detroit.

Again, my brother and I were at the kitchen dinner table with our father. He had prepared his famous, crisp-fried pork chops, mashed potatoes without a lump, lemon-pepper steamed Brussels sprouts, and rolls.

"Kids, I have to marry Lois. She is pregnant. What do you think I should do?"

My brother said nothing, staring off in space.

"I love Edith Mae, but marrying Lois will make our family whole," I offered my father for consideration. Lois was Sandy's mother. We had known and loved Sandy as our sister all of her life. Now, Lois was pregnant with our future sister or brother.

Of course, I was baffled as to how a woman in her thirties could allow herself to get pregnant. This fact alone cautioned me to be wary of Lois. Moreover, she had not been friendly towards me as a child on the few occasions I entered her home to get Sandy when my mother was waiting outside in our car to take us shopping or to bring Sandy to our home to play with my brother and me.

I attended, along with my father's sister, Carrie, and Lois's relatives, my father's wedding to Lois. I knew not where my brother was.

HOME ECONOMICS BECAME one of my favorite classes in high school. During my summer vacations in Montgomery, Mommy taught me the quality differences of cloth—Indian head, linen, cotton, and muslin, and the thread counts that made the distinctions; tissue paper (raw) silk and synthetic fabrics of nylon and rayon. I knew how to unravel material to make fringe and to secure the fringe evenly with hand-sewn blind stitches. Mommy and I spent hours embroidering pillow slips, hand towels, and handkerchiefs with tightly placed hoops over the desired place on the fabric and stitched with tiny back-and-forth strokes of various-colored threads into elaborate flower designs and monograms. I knew the distinctions between stemware, from a water goblet to a sherry glass; from a demitasse to specially designed cup and plate tableware for sit-down luncheon teas; from short-pronged salad forks to long-handled teaspoons. My home economics teacher, aptly named Mrs. House, marveled as I methodically taught my classmates how to set a formal dining room table, to include the choice of the table centerpiece to complement the occasion.

I was uninterested in learning how to cook full dinners though I enjoyed making finger and pinwheel sandwiches, garnishing deviled eggs, carving fruit and raw vegetables to resemble flowers, and arranging trays for tea parties.

What I wanted Mrs. House to teach me was sewing. Sandy, who now shared my princess room in our home, was my living model. I made several outfits for Sandy and entered her in our high school fashion show.

Inkster High School was a predominantly Negro school with about 20 per cent white enrollment. The white boys, mainly Italian and Irish, mimicked the Negro boys in attire and hair styles. Or was it vice versa? The Italian boys Brylcreemed their hair into high pompadours while the Negro boys did likewise with their processed hair, held stiffly in place with Duke hair grease. Both sets wore pointed-toe shoes, taking every opportunity to stand in front of a wall with the shoe-toes pressing against the wall to get the turn-up effect. Both sets wore the pants high, secured with belts, and could cuff their shirts while wearing sport jackets.

The only assimilation between the girls was that Negro girls began processing their hair into permanents to get the straight, "fly-hair" effect. The girls wore mainly plaid pleated or straight skirts, blouses with yokes in the back, sweater sets with removable decorative collars or kerchiefs around their necks, hush puppies or saddle-oxford shoes, and white or cream wool socks not folded nor rolled down to their ankles.

Only one white girl, Charlotte Hanson, was on the cheerleading squad. The quarterback of the football team was white.

The district school superintendent was a Negro man. The administrative staff of the school was all-Negro. The teaching faculty was 90 per cent Negro. Two white male teachers taught me chemistry and American history, and my father probably got the history teacher fired.

This came about because one day in class while we were covering the Civil War—which the teacher insisted was the "War Between the States"—my friend Judy and I were working on a new cheer for the upcoming basketball game instead of paying attention. When we completed the cheer on paper, we excitedly jumped into the air, interrupting the class.

"Will the Gold Dust twins please sit down," our teacher said sarcastically.

I thought it was a term of endearment. That evening, telling my father about the school day, I mentioned what had happened.

"The Gold Dust twins were the wrapper drawings of two coal-black children, 'pickaninnies,' on soap products," my father said without expression.

The next morning he drove my neighborhood girlfriends and me to school. He accompanied us into the building and stopped by the principal's office. For the rest of my eleventh-grade school term, my American history teacher treated me with deference. I earned an "A" in the course. His teaching contract was not renewed for the following school year.

ON A BRUTALLY cold winter morning. I decided I would wear my virgin wool bunny-pink pants suit to school since my father was not home to drive me to school and Lois had already left to take Sandy to her elementary school. I was not about to wear a skirt and walk to school with the cold wind whipping my legs.

As I settled in my first class, my teacher said, "Gwen you forgot to take off your pants and to put on your skirt." Miss Primrose Zennia Robinson was my English teacher and one of my favorite teachers. In addition to English, she taught Latin and Spanish. She was extremely formal, always straight-backed and erect, with a neatly coiffed hairstyle of a tiny upward roll gracing her nape from ear to ear.

"I didn't bring a skirt, Miss Robinson. It's very cold outside."

"Well, I have no choice but to send you to the principal's office."

While sitting in the principal's office, he called my father. Fortunately, he was home. In fifteen minutes my father was in the principal's office. The principal explained the policy that girls could not wear pants in classes except for gym classes.

"That makes no sense," I chimed in. "Pants are not thick muttons, leggings, that need to be removed when entering a warm building. Besides, children wear leggings. I am a teenager. I had to wear pants to ward off the cold and to keep my legs from being chilled to the bone. My locker is already filled with books, my gym suit, and other stuff."

My father sided with my explanation, and I was sent home for the day.

An emergency school board meeting was held to discuss "girls wearing pants to school policy." My father and I attended the meeting. After discussion and deliberations, the policy was changed: girls could wear pants to school when the temperature dipped below 32 degrees. Not to flaunt this victory, I did not wear pants to school during the rest of the winter season. When the temperature dipped below freezing, my father drove me to school.

LOIS WAS MY stepmother during my challenges with the school system. She remained aloof and did not interfere. She was enjoying her marital bliss and was abiding her time to secure her authority in our family.

"Gwen, you are spoiled. You are going to have to learn that you cannot always have your way in the world," Lois said one day out of the blue. I was ironing clothes, including hers, in the den. I said nothing.

"You think you have your daddy wrapped around your finger," she continued. "I'm determined to change that."

I said nothing, unplugged the iron, and began sorting her clothes into a separate basket of clothes that I intended not to iron.

"I am the lady of this house, not you!" She shouted and abruptly left the den.

I was only sixteen, and here was a grown woman challenging me to a battle over the affection my father had for me as his child. I matured ten years in that moment and knew I had to match Lois's jealousy woman-to-woman.

Lois was tall, could pass for white, and thought she was a gift to men, especially my father, who was tall, dark, and handsome. He still maintained his affair with Edith Mae. Lois could not tolerate this arrangement nor assume my mother's posture of being my father's wife and the mother of his children while he had affairs with other women. Lois had loved the glamour of being "the other woman" and taunting my mother with phone calls, demanding to know where my father was and declaring that my sister, Sandy, needed this or that. When my mother would ask what were Sandy's needs and she would make certain that my father would respond, Lois would slam down the phone.

Lois simply did not have the emotional makeup to be my father's wife nor to extend the love for his children by my mother as my mother had for her child, Sandy.

When Lois and I school-shopped together, she took me to Federal's Department Store. I only went to department stores to buy dolls, bikes, toys and school supplies, never to buy clothes. But here I now was in such a store to buy school clothes, which ended up being only a rain/snow-resistant parka with a lining and a hood that Lois selected. I had never been in Federal's before, and its dozens of dresses, all alike and made of synthetic materials, had no appeal to me.

My mother had shopped with me at children's, teens and tweens, and ladies boutique shops, especially Winkleman's in the lily-white community of Dearborn, Michigan. She bought my shoes at stores which stocked Buster Brown or I. Miller brands.

Lois had no clue to quality. I knew my father had given Lois loads of money for shopping when she was his "other woman." It was clear that she spent the money on low-quality apparel and goods.

Lois brought this lifestyle to me when she married my father. I knew I could never abide it. The contradiction was not that my father did not have the money he once did—the numbers racket was over—but, rather about a choice of lifestyle. Chalk it up to class contradictions. After all, Lois was a cab driver and my mother was a college-trained bookkeeper/accountant.

When I asked Daddy one day for money to buy a pair of beautiful straw mules and he responded that I already had enough shoes, I was astounded and recognized that he had capitulated to Lois's pleadings to distance himself from me and to establish a lifestyle of what I considered a poverty mentality. If he had responded that he did not have the money, I would have understood. But, to say that I didn't need a new pair of shoes belied his teachings. He had always proclaimed that if workers assembled Cadillacs in the factory, they ought to have the right and the wherewithal to own and drive them. So I stole a pair of straw-mule sandals in J. L. Hudson Department Store in downtown Detroit and was caught. The manager sent me to juvenile detention center and tried to locate my father, who unbeknownst to me, was at the wedding of Lois's brother.

After the intake counselor talked with me and I told her my situation of my mother's passing, of my father and his second wife, and whatever else a sixteen-year-old tells a counselor in this circumstance, she, a Negro, seemed sympathetic. She gave me books to read. After about two hours, my father came. He talked to the counselor and then came over to talk with me. He was crying. I explained my actions and told him that he had changed since mother passed. His crying became audible gasps. I hugged him, crying as well, and promised him that I would never shoplift again.

When we arrived home, Lois was standing in the kitchen, scowling and shaking with fury. "I know, Bob, you are going to give her a whipping of her life," she said as a greeting.

I went to my room. Sandy was not home. Lois had taken her to her grandparents for the night. She did not want her daughter to be around a juvenile delinquent. I was relieved that I could sleep in my own bed alone. I needed solitude to sort out how I was to find security and happiness in my young age.

Lois insisted that my father should put me in reform school. She did not succeed with this demand, nor did my father whip me or even place me on punishment. He bought the straw mules that I had wanted in the first place. He, too, was trying to find a balance in his life that would not put him between Lois and his first-born children.

LOIS BECAME MORE combative towards me. "Did you see your mother last night?" Lois sneered with hatred darting from her eyes. "She was slamming doors and cabinets all night long!"

My father did not come home that night. No doubt Lois thought he was with Edith Mae, when I knew from the bottom of my heart he was at a craps game trying to make money.

When I came home from school that day, Daddy gave Little Bob, Sandy, and me $100 each to go shopping. He gave $3,000 to Lois.

Through Robert Simone's influence, my father regained his job at Ford Motor Company. His union members immediately elected him as their committeeman to handle their grievances. This meant that he did not have to work on an assembly line, but rather he visited assembly lines for inquiries with shop stewards about fair worker treatment. His salary, coupled with his gambling genius, put him almost back to the income level he had enjoyed with my mother.

But Lois was not satisfied. My father's affairs, especially with Edith Mae, were a thorn in her side. They argued and fought incessantly.

Lois's second child by my father, my half-brother Frank, was born in 1959, five months after she married my father. Frank was an adorable baby and I did not mind taking care of him. Frank absolutely fascinated me when sitting in his high chair and throwing his toast, peas, or whatever foods he could grasp with his tiny hands to the floor. He would look down at the food on the floor, then a puzzled expression would come on his face as if he wondered why the food did not bounce back to his high-chair tray. I figured he was trying to understand gravity.

In fact, tending to him and playing with Sandy were a respite from Lois and her mean attitude towards me. Her meanness had no bottom. For Easter 1960, she bought Sandy and Frank new outfits. She bought me a red umbrella to go with a gray suit I already had and told me I had enough clothes. She bought Little Bob nothing.

When she boldly announced to me in 1960 that she was pregnant again, I began to plan an escape to Montgomery to live with relatives who loved me unconditionally.

"DADDY, LAWRENCE SIMMONS has asked to take me to the amusement park tomorrow. A whole bunch of us are going. Can I go?"

We were sitting around the kitchen table, eating dinner. Before my father could reply, Lois snapped, "No. I need you to take care of the kids tomorrow night."

I could not believe my ears. Fridays are sacred to teenagers who at the end of the school week looked forward to being together and having fun. I did not say anything and waited on my father to respond. About ten minutes into our meal, Daddy said, "Let me think about it." Later that evening he said it was "okay" for me to go to the amusement park. I assumed that he and Lois had talked and worked out the many other options they had for a babysitter.

I was sixteen; Lawrence was eighteen. At 6 the next evening, he arrived in his father's car to collect me. When he came in, my father said, "I want you to bring Gwen home by 10 tonight."

"Yes sir, Mr. Patton," Lawrence replied.

I had looked forward to going to Edgewater Amusement Park. It was a thrill to be on the daring rides with neon lights blazing in the night. However, Lawrence did not drive to Edgewater. Instead, he drove to Belle Isle Park's "lovers' lane." After he parked, he began to grope me. I resisted. He became aggressive.

"If you rape me, you better kill me," I said in a no-nonsense tone. "If you don't and I live to tell my father, he will kill you."

He abruptly stopped his manhandling of me and took me straight home. I told him that there was no need to walk me to the door. I was not about negotiating a "good-night kiss" from him.

Surprisingly, my father was home. He had opted to babysit Sandy and Frank while Lois was the honoree at a baby shower hosted by her girlfriends. I told my father that Lawrence tried to rape me.

"Gwen, take care of the kids," my father said as he hurriedly left.

I later learned that he cornered Lawrence on the forbidden "Harrison Road," where old and wannabe gangsters congregated. He whipped Lawrence with a belt like a father would whip a child. Lawrence had been a protégé of my father in the numbers business. My father was outraged that Lawrence had not internalized the respectful culture of the Negro Mafia.

I CAME HOME from school. Lois had glued artificial flowers to two oval paper Chinet plates, spray-painted them gold, and nailed them above our living-room sofa. That was it. She was not only mean to me, but we had different tastes in all things. I foresaw myself devolving into Cinderella with a wicked stepmother. I had to escape.

The impending birth of another brother or sister heightened my apprehension of what my future would be in my father's new and consolidated family. When my father married Lois, she prohibited my summer 1959 vacation to Montgomery, the first time I was unable to visit with my relatives. Sandy and Frank had never visited with their paternal grandparents and relatives. It was if my father's bloodline had no significance to the emotional, physical, and mental makeup of his children by Lois.

Separation from my extended family, my roots, was impossible to contemplate. I was determined to change that. Plus, I needed to find peace and happiness, which I knew resided with my family on both sides in Montgomery. Montgomery, Alabama, was truly my home.

My dear friend Marilyn Russell and her family were motoring to visit their family in Jacksonville, Florida, the summer of 1960. I asked them to take me and drop me off in Montgomery.

The Russells knew my plight with Lois. Mr. Russell and my father talked about my situation, and my father agreed that I could move to Montgomery. Lois eagerly approved; she could not wait for me to be gone.

While packing my footlockers for the move, with tears welling in my eyes, I begged Lois not to create a wedge between me, my father, Little Bob, Sandy, Frank, and the unborn sibling.

Lois only said, "I think it is best for you to leave, Gwen."

I saw that Lois viewed me as a woman—her peer—not as her stepchild. Her relationship with my father while my mother was alive had tainted Lois's subsequent marriage to my father. I had become "Dot," my mother, in her eyes. It was deep.

The last image I had of Inkster was that of my father's forlorn face as we pulled away. I do not remember the drive South. Though the car was crowded with Mr. and Mrs. Russell, their five daughters, and me, I felt no discomfort.

I was happy that I was free of a family situation destined to be unhappy. Yet, I was sad that my sister and brothers were still in the snare. My prayer every day was for my siblings to chart their own independent races to freedom. I had faith that they would succeed.

7

Coming Home

In Montgomery, I could live with several different relatives during my senior year of high school. I chose my Great Aunt Chick, my mother's favorite aunt, and her daughter, Flora. Both were schoolteachers. Since childhood, I had wanted to be a teacher. Living with Aunt Chick and Cousin Flora would give me the inside on the day-to-day life of a schoolteacher.

Flora offered me several options to finish high school. Laboratory High, a private school affiliated with Alabama State College, was out; it had no cheerleading squad. Attending boarding school was completely out of the question. I opted for George Washington Carver High School, known as the "academy." It had a cheerleading squad. And Aunt Chick taught at the adjacent elementary school, which meant I could ride with her to school on rainy days.

My senior year at Carver was a dream come true. I was captain of the cheerleaders, editor of the student newspaper, *The Wolverine*, and ofttimes I was the lead singer in the choir. I joined and was baptized at Holt Street Baptist Church, which was attended by Aunt Chick and other relatives and was the site of the first Mass Meeting that launched the Montgomery Bus Boycott. Many churches throughout the community invited me to be their youth day speaker.

When the time came to apply to colleges, the Carver High guidance counselor, Mr. William Martin, talked to me about attending the University of Alabama. He said he thought I could do the work and was strong enough to handle the responsibility and weight of integrating Alabama's all-white flagship university. This was six years after *Brown v. Board of Education*, and Autherine Lucy had already integrated the school in 1956, but only briefly; no blacks had enrolled since Lucy.

I thought back to Mommy's words about riding the buses after the Montgomery Bus Boycott and replied, "The struggle is not about sitting next to white people, but, rather to sit wherever you please." That's the real meaning of freedom. I don't choose to sit next to white people in a classroom as my aim in life. My idea of freedom is to sit next to whomever I choose. And I choose to sit in a classroom at Tuskegee Institute, an institution that has distinguished itself with the genius of Booker T. Washington and George Washington Carver.

Besides, I had wedded my ambition to be a teacher with the ambition to be a cheerleader coach and advisor, and I wanted to continue cheerleading in college. I thought I could do that at Tuskegee.

Mr. Martin was astonished that I would reject this opportunity "to advance our cause," but years later he told me he was proud of my decision. When the community was in a raging debate about me and my peers in our militant "Black Power!" race to freedom, Mr. Martin was one of our staunchest advocates. Movement activity in 1960–61 Montgomery had a steady pace, especially in the area of voting rights. Aunt Chick and Cousin Flora were quiet supporters of the Movement. Schoolteachers were vulnerable to the powers and could be fired for any cause, particularly if they were visible and vocal in the Movement. On the other hand, my grandparents on both sides were activists. My paternal grandparents owned the Patton Construction Company and business was flourishing. My maternal grandmother, Mommy, was a nanny. White women could care less what their "help" did in their off hours as long as they showed up on time to take care of their children and to clean their houses.

I LEARNED FROM my elders in the MIA office that the "freedom riders" were coming to Montgomery. One group of freedom riders already had their bus set afire by Ku Klux Klan terrorists in Anniston, Alabama. Another group had been beaten by Klan thugs acting in collusion with the police in Birmingham, and a third group had been escorted by the same police to the Tennessee state line and abandoned in the night at a remote location.

These Negro and white freedom riders were members of the Student Non-violent Coordinating Committee (SNCC); the youth affiliate group to the Southern Christian Leadership Conference (SCLC); and the Congress for Racial Equality (CORE). I vaguely knew about the founding of SNCC after the spontaneous sit-ins in February 1960 at the Woolworth's lunch counter in Greensboro, North Carolina. By late spring of 1960, students at the all-black Alabama State College in Montgomery were sitting-in at the lunch counter in the Montgomery County courthouse and holding protests at the state capitol. As a result, the city police raided Alabama State College, routed the students, and held them hostage. The president of the college was forced by the state board of education to expel some and suspend others of the students who organized the sit-ins.

High school students had yet to become actively involved in the sit-in movement though I "worried" my elders into putting together a youth plan of action. After all, I had staged a personal "sit-in" at a lunch counter in 1952, when I was eight years old. I thought kids had a responsibility, too, to fight for freedom.

Many in the black community anticipated that white mobs would be at the Greyhound Bus Station, as they had been in Birmingham, to viciously attack the freedom riders. In Birmingham, the KKK beatings of the freedom riders, as was later proven, were carried out in collusion with the local police who deliberately stayed away from the Trailways bus terminal for fifteen minutes. The state and federal governments wanted to avoid a similar re-sult in Montgomery, and state troopers escorted the Greyhound bus from Birmingham to the Montgomery city limits. And then, despite promises by Montgomery police officials, the same thing happened: there were no police present to keep order at the Montgomery Greyhound terminal. What erupted at the hands of the white mobs with chains, brass knuckles, and baseball bats hurled upon the freedom riders was an attempted massacre on May 20, 1961.

Some of the black freedom riders escaped in Negro-owned taxicabs. But the black cab companies, because of city segregation laws, could not transport white passengers, and no white cabs would take the white freedom riders to safety or for medical treatment. Herbert Young, a hearse driver for Ross and Clayton Funeral Home (co-owned by the family of Coach Rufus Lewis's wife) rushed to the bus station to pick up some of the severely injured freedom riders. One of the most brutally beaten white riders was transported by a state trooper. The injured were taken to St. Jude Hospital, a Catholic facility that served the black community.

Later that day, the freedom riders were hidden in the homes of second-generation pharmacist and drugstore owner Richard Harris and the Reverend Solomon S. Seay Sr. The latter, later to become the third president of the MIA, lived in the outlying community of Madison Park, an all-Negro com-munity established by a group of ex-slaves led by the patriarch Eli Madison. There was one way in and out of Madison Park. Most of the men living there were armed to protect the community from white terror. Few white men, including police officers, would dare enter Madison Park without first consulting community leaders.

THE SUNDAY EVENING after the violence at the bus station, a mass meeting was called in support of the freedom riders. The freedom riders were supposed to be there, and Dr. King was coming over from Atlanta. I wanted to attend.

First Baptist Church, where the Reverend Ralph D. Abernathy pastored during the Montgomery Bus Boycott, was the site for the gathering. First Baptist was a beautiful church with a history of race pride. According to church historian Robert Beasley and his nephew, Benjamin Beasley (his mother, Mrs. Mildred Lewis Beasley, was the church organist), during the antebellum period blacks worshipped from the balcony of the white Baptist Church on Perry Street. By 1870, the black congregants outnumbered the whites. The blacks voted to establish their own church in a vacant wood-frame structure on Columbus Avenue.

When that church burned down around 1912, the congregation voted to build a new church on the same property but with the entrance on Ripley Street. Pastor Andrew Jackson Stokes, a funeral home owner, envisioned a grand brick church with imported pews and pulpit furniture, a pipe organ, a vaulted ceiling, and exquisite stained-glass windows, all of which came to pass in collaboration with a Tuskegee Institute architect. The grand First Baptist Church opened on Ripley Street in 1916. The church had 5,000 members, the largest black congregation in the nation.

Reverend Stokes's portrait was in one of the stained-glass windows above the panel of John the Baptist baptizing Jesus Christ. This juxtaposition of images spoke volumes of Reverend Stokes's personal conviction to strike a blow for freedom.

This was the church where so-called bourgeois Negroes left and founded Dexter Avenue Baptist Church in downtown Montgomery, and in so doing split family and friends into separate congregations based on delusional class distinctions in a racist society. This was the church that through the friend-ships of Ralph Abernathy and Martin Luther King Jr. and the Montgomery Bus Boycott reunited family and friends.

The rebuilt edifice is known today as the "brick-a-day" church.

People were filling up the church by 4 p.m. for the 6 p.m. mass meeting. I was with Mommy and my paternal grandparents. Initially the meeting opened up and proceeded like our regular mass meetings during the Montgomery Bus Boycott. However, there were white media correspondents from everywhere in the sanctuary. Suddenly, the meeting became deadly intense. A white mob had assembled outside the church. They threw rocks at the church windows, overturned a car and set it afire, and threatened to break down the doors of the church.

I was not aware that Dr. King was in the basement office, on the phone with U.S. Attorney General Bobby Kennedy requesting protection to secure our safety. As a teenager with invincible naiveté, and looking upon the faces of my family and elders, I sensed we were ready to lay down our lives with joy in our stand for freedom. Music by the church organist, Mrs. Mildred Beasley, helped calm our fears, and our resounding singing of old spirituals and freedom songs renewed our spirits despite the raging mob outside.

Meanwhile, we later learned, 400 U.S. marshals had been rushed to the scene and were holding off the mob while Dr. King was calling Kennedy and Kennedy was calling Alabama Governor John Patterson—at the time, a staunch segregationist—exhorting Patterson to mobilize the Alabama National Guard to assist the marshals, which he eventually did. There was even a rumor that an armed group of black cabdrivers, some of whom were Korea and World War II veterans, had sent word to Dr. King that they would take on the mob if he wanted them to.

After sixteen hours of being held hostage by the white rioters, we were able to leave First Baptist Church under protection. Patterson had arranged for coffee, juice, and sandwiches to be given to us as we exited the church to ride home in awaiting military jeeps and local transportation owned by Negro businesses, but by that point we didn't trust anything coming from local whites so we threw the food into the heaps of burned and smothering trash that the mob had piled up during our hours of captivity. We wondered if the so-called breakfast peace-offering might be poisoned.

I do not remember the Monday after the life-and-death all-night ordeal inside the First Baptist Church. I probably slept all day.

ON TUESDAY, NEGRO and white freedom fighters and their supporters visited Carver High School. They talked with students about joining the civil rights movement. These discussions were mainly on the campus because the freedom riders were not permitted to enter the school building, I connected with the freedom riders. I vowed that I would be a permanent freedom fighter, and without thought I invited some of them home.

We were all sitting in our living room discussing the importance of fighting for freedom and human rights when Aunt Chick got home from school. She looked at the Negro and white freedom riders and said, "Gwen, come with me." She briskly walked with me behind her to the kitchen. It dawned on me that I had put Aunt Chick and Cousin Flora at risk by inviting the freedom fighters to our home. I thought she was going to chastise me for putting their teaching jobs in danger.

Instead, I was stunned when Aunt Chick said, "Gwen, I don't want any white people in my home." She quickly made a pitcher of Kool-aid and placed cookies on a tray as she continued, "I can't go through the front doors of white people's homes and they are not to come through my front door. Do you understand?" Nonetheless, she walked in her always elegant manner to the living room, with me trailing behind, and was gracious to the freedom fighters as we laid the trays on the coffee table.

I cordially ended our visit and the freedom fighters left. Aunt Chick and I never discussed this incident further, but I took to heart her admonition not to accommodate white people if they were not doing anything in their own communities to dismantle Jim Crow USA Southern-style apartheid.

IN THE FOLLOWING days and weeks, school life went along as if nothing had happened. Though perplexed, I took the routine in stride. Negro teachers always had been schizophrenic as they on the one hand imparted race pride while on the other hand teaching and modifying the behavior of their pupils and students to stifle their potentials and to undermine their God-given talents that could not soar in a state-sanctioned racist society.

I made all A's at Carver, and with my transfer grades, when grade-point averages were calculated, I was designated salutatorian of the senior class. Everybody congratulated me but Rose. She was a book-worm and very smart. She never engaged in social activities. We were academic friends and had spent much time together in the library. Now, she was very distant and even hostile towards me.

One day I asked her, "Rose, what is it? Have I hurt you in any way?"

"I would have been salutatorian if you had not come down here!" Rose said with anguish, tears streaming down her cheeks. I nodded and went straight to the counselor's office.

"Mr. Martin, we have to have co-salutatorians, Rose and me. She would have been the salutatorian if I had not transferred from Inkster High School," I said with authority.

Mr. Martin smiled and let out a short, funny laugh. "Okay, Gwen."

At our graduation, Rose and I shared the podium as we each gave addresses to our cheering classmates, families, and friends.

AFTER A WHIRLWIND of graduation parties, I decided I would stay with Mommy the summer of 1961 before going off to Tuskegee Institute. All of my life I had access to televisions and telephones. Mommy had neither.

If I lived a charmed life in Inkster when my mother was alive, I lived a life of a princess when I stayed with Mommy. I slept in the main bedroom with her in one of the beautifully carved maple twin beds that my mother had slept in when she was a girl. There was a lovely vanity beneath a hanging mirror. One day I was sitting on Mommy's twin bed and looked over at the mirror. I smiled as I saw the reflection of the sofa in the adjacent living room. That sofa was the "courting settee" when young gentlemen came calling. Mommy could lie in her bed and see all that was happening in the courtship.

"Mommy, I found out your secret," I said.

"Well," she replied.

"How long has the mirror been in that place?"

"Since your mother took an interest in boys in the 1930s."

"Well, don't move it." I hugged her with every fiber of love in my body.

I had several beaus, Bernard, John, Elbert, and Ocie, and I felt secure that they could not get out of hand because Mommy was watching in our "secret" mirror and would come immediately to my rescue.

Mommy and I spent many hours perfecting my crochet, embroidery, and knitting stitches. I gained more speed in manipulating the tatting shuttles to make lace. We spent long hours in her garden, tending to mint, oregano, and basil and miniature tomatoes, hot peppers and eggplants. We attended mass meetings. We traveled on bus to Birmingham and Mobile to help with the founding of the Alabama Democratic Conference (ADC), the Negro state-wide political organization that united the county civic and voting leagues into one organization. I was instrumental in making certain that there would be a youth component to the ADC. I continued teaching in the citizenship schools to help my elders learn how to pass the literacy test, the prerequisite barrier to their obtaining their right to vote. I continued running the "go get me, go fetch me, go bring me" errands in the MIA office. I did not miss television nor the telephone. I came to realize that these creature comforts were deflectors and pacifiers to detract the human spirit from the real issues in life.

Mommy was in courtship with Mr. Benjamin Washington, considered one of the most handsome seniors in Montgomery. As he courted her, I would lie in her bed and glance at our "secret" mirror to make certain that he made no ungentlemanly moves. Mommy and I got a kick out of our reversed roles.

Saturday evening was always a special time to prepare for the following day's Sunday school and church. Mommy belonged to several churches in walking distance of her home. As a church was razed to make way for construction of interstate highways 85 and 65 that were tearing up her community, she simply joined another church in walking distance, regardless of denominations.

After studying our Sunday school lessons together, I laid out my church attire: dress or suit, matching purse and shoes, handkerchief, gloves, and hat. Mommy was a simple dresser, seldom with hat and gloves but always with a laced and embroidered handkerchief. I felt so worthy as God's child when I walked with Mommy to church.

Grand-aunt Mary, Mommy and Aunt Chick's baby sister, was a retired home economics teacher and a first-class seamstress. She made me several outfits for college. Cousin Flora bought me coordinating blouses, skirts, and jackets from fashionable women's shops. MaDear gave me money. Throughout the summer Mommy and I labeled my clothes and linens that I would need to take to Tuskegee.

At one of our sittings on the front-porch swing, I asked, "Mommy, if I could give you anything in the world, what would it be?"

"A round-trip bus ticket to Mound Bayou," she replied.

"What and where is Mound Bayou?"

"It's an all-Negro town in Mississippi, run by Negroes. They just got their first fire truck."

The love my grandmother had for our people, with no malice towards whites, became the bedrock of my personal philosophy. Other important lessons Mommy taught me this summer were that of being positive and firm, of standing on principle, of following through on commitments, and, above all, of being a lady in demeanor and decorum in all matters. There was no contradiction in being a freedom fighter and a lady.

On a special Saturday, I woke from a fitful sleep. As I gathered my night jacket about my shoulders, I looked over to the other twin bed. Mommy had made her bed and was out and about doing chores.

After washing up and brushing my teeth, I went to the kitchen to start breakfast. No need. Mommy had set the dining room table. The small waffle iron was waiting on its pad. Mommy had sectioned portions of a fresh pineapple and cantaloupe and diced the skinless fruit into large chunks and placed it in a covered bowl. Alaga syrup had been poured from its colorful bottle, with its label of a clenched handshake around sugar cane stalks, into a special syrup pourer with a sliding lever atop for easy pouring. Earlier in the week, Mommy had removed the cream that curdled at the top of a bottle of whole milk and scooped it into a Mason jar. All week, I shook the cream that eventually churned into butter. Mommy then scooped the churned cream into a narrow butter mold with a cover and placed it in her new Frigidaire to form a butter stick. Now, it was on the dining room table warming to room temperature for easy splattering over our hot waffles.

The table was set with plates, fruit bowls, water and juice glasses, fruit spoons, silverware, and cloth napkins. There were matching coffee cups and saucers. A creamer of milk and a sugar bowl that matched the butter dish were in the center of the table. This was to be a special Saturday breakfast. In fact, this was going to be the last Saturday that Mommy and I would spend together for some time.

I looked out the window above the kitchen sink. I saw Mommy in the fruit orchard on the south side of her home. She was plucking fruit and placing it delicately in the basket draped over her arm. The orchard had a small arbor for muscadine grapes that she picked to make wine for her Christmas teas. She would can as preserves and marmalade the fruit from the laden fig, peach, pear, and plum trees.

The backyard on the west was the home of the vegetable garden of tomatoes, onions, cucumbers (some to be made into dill and sweet, or as Mommy called them, "butter plate" pickles), green, yellow, and red bell peppers, and hot red and green peppers. Mommy would blanch a mix of these vegetables with vinegar and sugar and seal them in Mason jars for "cha-cha" sauce to be added to boiled greens such as collards, turnips, mustard, and cabbage. The adjacent herb garden contained oregano, sage, basil, and mint.

A hundred-year-old giant pecan tree was in the north side of the yard. A sturdy tire swing hung from one limb. My brother Bob, first cousin Al, and I had unlimited fun swinging in that tire as we pushed each other as high as the rope would permit.

The living and dining rooms were on the east side of Mommy's home. The early morning sun cascaded its brilliant warmth into this part of the home. On the front porch outside the living room a porch swing was suspended with strong chains from the ceiling rafters. I had much fun with my brother and cousin on the porch swing, naming cars that passed by the busy intersection of Holt and Early streets where her lot was located.

Mommy's front yard boasted green hedges aligned to the porch that led to white- and pink-blossomed azaleas and impatiens. One of Bob's and Al's greatest pleasures was to leap over the hedges onto the grass of the front lawn. Many times they missed and landed in the midst of Mommy's flower beds. And then we found extra joy, me included, in replanting the smashed flowers. I later realized that Mommy not only found joy in watching her "leaping" grandsons but she knew we were propagating new flowers that would bloom well beyond Thanksgiving. No matter how much damage they did to her impatiens, Mommy was never impatient with her grandchildren.

"Gwendolyn, where are you?" Mommy called as she came through the back door into her deceased son's bedroom, now converted into a den where her grandchildren spent countless hours playing games, reading books and magazines, drawing and coloring our self-made images on butcher paper that Mommy obtained from the meat department in her neighborhood grocery store. One of my favorite pastimes was cutting out paper outfits and folding the tabs of the outfits over my stand-up paper dolls.

The den's major feature was a black-pot-bellied coal stove with a chimney pipe that extended through the ceiling and the roof. During our Christmas vacations with Mommy, she stuffed the belly of the stove with hickory wood and small nuggets of coal. The fire in the stove accompanied with the blaze in the living room fireplace and the flame of the gas heater in the bedroom caressed Mommy's home with loving warmth. I felt so grown-up when I had the responsibility to mix white corn meal and hot water or to form leftover grits into patties and place them in a greased iron skillet on the hot stove to make water bread. Nothing was more exciting than lifting the eye-plate of the stove and stoking with a poker the fire in the belly to keep it burning.

Mommy's foot-pedal sewing machine sat in one corner. It took more than a notion to feed the thread from its spool through a series of loops atop the sewing machine, through the needle, the bobbin beneath, and pull a thread to the top of the sewing plate. I had to learn to find a patting rhythm with my feet on the wide bottom pedal and then to stitch fabrics together while pushing the material through the sewing plate feeder in sync with the up-and-down movement of the threaded needle and bobbin, all generated by my feet on the foot pedal. Mommy was a whiz; I sewed in slow motion, but my dolls never noticed a missing stitch in the clothes I made for them.

"I'm in the living room, Mommy," I called back.

Mommy had moved my two footlockers and the graduation gifts of white Samsonite luggage to the living room, where they were open and packed to the brims. The inventory list rested in the inset tray of the cosmetic suitcase.

Later, we would check the packed items against the list.

Mommy did not come to the living room. Soon I smelled and heard the sizzling of frying streak o' lean, my favorite breakfast meat I had come to love during past vacations in Montgomery. This cut of pork was never considered fit breakfast meat in Inkster. Perhaps, my parents considered it "slave food," and their race to freedom shunned what they considered "Jim Crow victuals." Or, I wondered now, was it really vital food that sustained our people's survival to this day?

I joined Mommy at the dining room table as she set the streak o' lean in a dish lined with paper napkins to absorb the grease.

"Gwendolyn, say the blessing."

I repeated the Fifth Commandment to honor our mothers—especially my mother—and fathers, and thanked God for blessing me and Mommy and for giving me another opportunity to enjoy my life with purpose and joy.

"Amen," we said in unison. Tears streamed from Mommy's eyes as she poured the pancake batter in the miniature waffle iron.

Tags had been sewn with my initials, "GMP," scripted in indelible ink, in all of my clothes, including my underwear. My sheets, pillowcases, towels and facecloths had been embroidered with my initials. Mommy and I spent all summer crocheting a bed coverlet of rope-like threads of red and white into connecting hearts.

Mommy had also packed a family quilt, a "Path and Stiles" pattern made by her mother, "Big Mama," for cool nights in the dormitory. This hand-pieced, block fabric quilt with cotton batting was a special heirloom. It would be my security blanket and a covering reminder of my responsibility to uplift the family and to continue the legacy of our people in our quest for true freedom.

"Gwendolyn, let's check the boxes."

Mommy called off the items as I checked the inventory list. Hangers. Iron. Table-top ironing board. Radio. Alarm clock. Fan. Hot plate. Jiffy Pop corn. Two throw-rugs.

We were to leave for Tuskegee Institute the following day after church. Cousin Carnell, my father's first cousin, was the designated driver.

I felt so truly blessed. Family on both sides cared about my well-being.

They loved me unconditionally. They placed their hopes in my doing well at Tuskegee Institute. I was indeed an offspring of the extended family. I was at home.

8

Off to College

Arriving and seeing Tuskegee Institute's campus was breathtaking. I noticed that all of the buildings facing inward, away from the major corridor, Old Montgomery Road, that the students called "Campus Avenue." I surmised that the architect designed the buildings thusly as a measure of safety for students. My deeper thoughts concluded that Tuskegee Institute as a private black college did not want the gawking eyes of whites who also traveled the Old Montgomery Road.

On the campus proper, I saw that the entry doors to buildings faced each other. Tuskegee Institute was a cocoon, a haven to develop and sharpen the minds of "the talented tenth" while instilling an appreciation for self-reliance and economic independence.

Cousin Carnell drove through the campus to James Hall, my assigned dormitory. As we unloaded my suitcases and boxes, Mommy noticed with a keen eye that there were shades, but no curtains. She eyeballed the window widths and heights and said, "I'll send you curtains next week. Tell the college people you'll need curtain rods." (That would be my first demand on Institute officials; more were forthcoming.)

College life was all that it purported to be: exciting, fun, and contemplative. Staying up all night chatting and studying with dorm mates was the dominant activity. During this first year at Tuskegee, I learned to play chess and bridge and even joined the bridge club, which won first place in several tournaments among collegians in the Southeast.

My greatest fun was playing "dirty hearts" in the "Rec," the student center. The student king of dirty hearts was a senior, Scotland, a Gullah brother from South Carolina. No one could verbalize college life like Scotland. As he slapped the penalty card, the queen of spades, on a play, he would lament his school woes. He called our math teacher "the dick"—she was tough and hard. He shared with us at the card table that math exams gave him "locked bowels" and he simply could not figure out the answers. When someone got on his nerves, he suggested that they "dig a hole, descend, and cover the hole with dirt." We cheered madly when Scotland crossed the graduation stage with his baccalaureate degree clutched tightly in his hands.

I was chosen as a Golden Tiger cheerleader in the first round of tryouts, along with Elizabeth Davis and Doris Comer, who became my best friends. We added pyramids and tumbles to the repertoire of spread-eagle splits on the floor and in the air. We executed our cheers with clean, precise movements. Our classmates roared when Doris and I ended a cheer with a jack-knife leap in the air, pom-poms uplifted, as Elizabeth completed the cheer with a perfect cartwheel that finished with a split on the hardwood. During halftime, the athletes would come out of the locker room early to watch us.

I ALSO FOUND my way to the "intellectual underground." Most of our discussions were philosophical with abiding interests in the "freedom rides" and "sit-ins" that were sweeping the South. We knew that a direct-action movement for freedom was afoot. We met with Tuskegee's community activists, especially Mr. Detroit Lee (who would be the lead plaintiff in *Lee v. Macon*, the precedent-setting 1963 lawsuit that desegregated the public schools in Tuskegee and ultimately throughout Alabama). We were determined that the local working class Negroes who made up the majority of the people in the 87 percent black county, would be a part of the school struggle, not just the children of the middle class and the educated elite. We spent much time creating scenarios that might electrify the student body to become conscious and consistent foot-soldiers as freedom fighters. I was particularly interested in establishing "citizenship schools" in the outlying rural community.

Many student discussions centered on the fundamental differences between desegregation and integration. I favored desegregation, which meant to me that black culture should remain intact and flourish, and opposed integration which meant to me that black culture would self-destruct. I was an adamant proponent of the "salad bowl" conceptualization that would respect all cultures in a pluralistic society and a fervent opponent of the "melting pot" theory that would neuter the rich black culture that was the soul of the USA.

I contemplated troubling second and third thoughts about integration, particularly in the educational setting. It made absolutely no sense to me to hand over our children to white teachers and administrators whom we knew were racists to the core.

EVEN SO, THESE discussions simmered on the back burner; social activities on the campus dominated our chatter.

One day while I was walking between classes in Huntingdon Hall, Mr. "Bucky" Buchannan stopped me and asked me to join the Little Theatre.

"You look like Diana Sands," he said. "I want you to play the part of Benitta in Lorraine Hansberry's play, *A Raisin in the Sun*. I was flattered. For several days I looked at myself in the mirror. My profile did resemble that of Sands, the 1950s star of stage and screen. I daydreamed about becoming an actress. After all, I had been in several plays since elementary school, including *The Mikado* and *Wuthering Heights*. I never paid attention to the plots nor the messages of the plays. I simply memorized my lines within the context of the scenes. I guess I was a method actress. My friends teased me and called me Olivia de Havilland. No doubt I was a ham.

Now that I was in college I thought it was important to read *A Raisin in the Sun* first to decipher the nuances of its deepest meanings. After two weeks, I showed up for rehearsal. I was chosen to play Benitta, to the consternation of a seasoned Little Theatre actress who was chosen to be the understudy; she was a senior, I was a freshman.

A Raisin in the Sun had achieved national acclaim and rave reviews. The play highlighted the "dream" of a black family that wanted to move out of the ghetto into a "lily-white" suburb where white homeowners went to extreme lengths to thwart them. A subtle sub-theme portrayed the black man, Walter Lee—a son, husband, father who made a living for his family as a chauffeur for white executives—as reckless. Knowing that his family had decided to use his late father's insurance settlement to purchase the home in the suburb, Lee instead pooled the money with a friend in a scheme to buy a liquor store. The friend absconded with the money.

Raisin deepened my understanding of the black man's frustrated effort to find his niche, his manhood as a provider, in a white-male-dominated racist society. In this search for meaning and purpose in a hostile environment, many black men became detached and lost, the "walking wounded." This predicament was the essence of Hansberry's play. The "raisin" was really the black man, whose hopes and dreams could either fester like a running sore, dry up in the sun, or explode.

My next role was as Inez in Sartre's *No Exit*. This existentialist play broadened my perspective as to how deadly collaboration with Nazis, fascists, and racists can be. In my actual world, collaborators were called "Uncle Toms." The play offered solace that collaborators would eventually confront their consciences (God?), and as a result, they will be confined in hell with "no exit."

My last play during my freshman year was as one of the leading characters in *Marriage-Go-Round*. I do not remember the details of the play. But the plot to procreate children from parents of good looks and brains resonates with me to this day, especially in the current preoccupation with genetic engineering. Of course, in the play the "good looks" were attributed to the woman and the "smart brains" to the man. This play planted in my subconscious the seed of feminism that would later blossom in my fight against sexism.

Between studying, attending classes, cheering, and rehearsing and performing with the Little Theatre, Elizabeth, Doris, and I planned our mini-movement. I simply could not wait for the student body to rise up and to strike a blow for freedom. I had to do something *now*. Elizabeth from Ohio and Doris from Oklahoma had not experienced raw racism as I had in Alabama, but they willingly joined my crusade to challenge "Jim Crow."

The community was boycotting the town stores in Tuskegee. Elizabeth,

Doris and I would walk to town and enter the stores. White merchants and clerks fawningly leap to their feet to wait on us, glad to see customers. We would examine the merchandise and set aside items that the clerks assumed we would purchase.

"Gosh, I'm thirsty. Is there a water fountain?"

"Oh, yes!" The clerk responded, giving us directions to where the water fountains were located.

When we arrived at the designated area, there were, of course, two water fountains, labeled with large signs that read "Colored" and "White." We returned to the main area of the department store.

"Is the 'Colored' water crimson or gold, Tuskegee Institute's colors?"

The clerk turned blood red.

"We would prefer clear, white water," we continued.

Getting no response but a baffled look, we walked boldly out of the store. By the time we got to the third store, the merchants had telephoned each other and locked their doors. We had a good laugh and walked back to campus.

ELIZABETH AND DORIS decided to spend their summer vacations in their hometowns. I was attending summer school as part of my plan to finish college in three years.

Summer school was filled with reading and writing papers. Campus activities came to a standstill.

The summer's most exciting event was the marriage of my grandmother, Mommy, fifty-six, to Mr. Benjamin Washington, seventy-one. Mr. Washington was a tall and strikingly handsome man. His thick salt-and-pepper hair was like a horse's mane in length and in silky texture. For years he had been targeted as "the catch" by single women in their twenties and older.

Mommy and Mr. Washington had been courting for years. Now, that I had arrived and was considered their child, Mommy finally accepted Mr. Washington's proposal, his solitaire diamond engagement ring, and his payment for her divorce from the husband she had been separated from for more than thirty-five years.

The wedding and reception were held in the Foster family home. Friends from far and near and families on both sides, including Mr. Washington's children and grandchildren from New York City, attended. Mommy's baby sister, my Aunt Mary Thomas, was the maid of honor. Aunt Mary's husband, Tom, was the best man. I was the ring bearer, a memory I will forever cherish.

Mommy continued to call her new husband "Mr. Washington." I called my new grandfather "Poppa" Washington. I felt so secure when Poppa, in his tuxedo tails and pinstriped pants escorted me and danced the first waltz with me before handing me over to my date, John Sparks, a senior engineering student at Tuskegee, at the fall debutante-cotillion ball hosted by Montgomery's Negro elite women.

On the weekends I rode the Greyhound bus back and forth from Tuskegee to Montgomery to help Mommy move special items from her home to Poppa Washington's home. His dogtrot home had a large living room with a piano, dining room, and kitchen on one side of the hallway, and two large bedrooms and a bathroom on the other side; it became a weekend haven for my friends who wanted a respite from Tuskegee Institute.

ON ONE OF my visits to Montgomery, we were sitting down for lunch when we heard a gentle yet persistent knock on the front porch screened door. Poppa Washington was home from lunch. He was a retired union butcher who still worked part-time to select special cuts of meats for elite whites who hosted endless sit-down dinner parties. In essence, he was a consultant, though this term was not applied to Negroes. Mommy helped Poppa Washington with the herbs and spices used to marinate the select cuts of beef, pork, and lamb. (Mommy also knew how to make goat, possum, coon, and rabbit meat into tasty fare, but elite white people did not partake of these meats, or so they claimed.)

"Come on in," Poppa Washington called out. "Make your way to the dining room."

We saw standing in the archway between the living and dining rooms a man with a skull cap on his shaved head and a slender, attractive women in a smart navy-blue pleated skirt with a boxed jacket.

"We are Reverend James Bevel and Elizabeth Hayes," the voice announced in the doorway. "We are full-time community organizers for freedom. We were told to contact Gwen Patton when we arrived in Montgomery." Looking straight at me, Reverend Bevel asked, "Are you Gwen Patton . . . the fearless freedom fighter?"

Before I could nod "yes," Mommy was on her feet and had set two additional places at the empty chairs around our dining room table.

"Please join us for lunch," she said. Reverend Bevel, without shame, heaped piles of food on his plate. It was obvious that he was hungry.

The Reverend James Bevel, a lieutenant in Dr. King's Southern Christian Leadership Conference (SCLC), was the first full-time civil rights organizer I met. He was dispatched, along with Elizabeth Hayes of the Birmingham movement, to rebuild the Montgomery movement back to the level of the Bus Boycott days.

Bevel, as we called him, was a small-framed man whose physical signature was a skull cap, overalls, and a denim jacket, whether he was organizing block parties for teenagers or preaching in church pulpits. He was a powerful orator who drew many of his sermons from the Bible stories of the prophets Isaiah and Ezekiel.

Bevel often told the story about Mr. Jones, who couldn't join the movement until he paid off his car notes. After paying for the car, he still could not join the movement until he sent his children to college. After they graduated, he still could not join the movement until he paid off his house notes. The day after the mortgage was paid off, Bevel went by Mr. Jones's home to ask him, again, to join the movement. Bevel was met at the door by Mr. Jones's daughter who told him that Mr. Jones had died that morning. Bevel would end the story with a powerful punch.

"Are you going to die before you strike a blow for freedom!" he exhorted.

Bevel lived in a cramped, damp basement apartment in Montgomery. We held strategy sessions there. For entertainment we listened to comic albums on his only possession, his hi-fi record player. He especially liked the comedian Buckley, who told hilarious homespun stories about country life. We also listened to Lenny Bruce. Though his parodies reeked of profanity, I intellectually resonated with Bruce's social and political criticism and commentary.

At one of our strategy sessions, Bevel said he needed a larger place. The

SCLC was sending another full-time organizer, Reverend James Orange of Birmingham, to Montgomery. One Sunday after church, while we were having our family dinner that included Reverend Bevel at Mommy and Poppa Washington's home, I related Bevel's plight. Mommy looked straight into Bevel's eyes:

"Young man, you can rent my furnished rental house for a nominal price, pay the utilities, and maintain the upkeep," she offered. I beamed with joy. We finally had our first "freedom house" for Montgomery. My grandmother made it possible.

FALL SEMESTER 1962 at Tuskegee Institute started off with a bang, and again, in the social realm. Our small intellectual, politically conscious group was respected by the larger student body, but we had yet to put our ideas of fighting for freedom into the collegiate social consciousness, and more importantly, to prick the minds and souls of our classmates to offer their own ideas of freedom and their own strategies to attain freedom.

I settled for raising social consciousness in my philosophy, sociology and literature classes by asking pertinent questions that related to the Negro existence and experience in white America. Gunnar Myrdal's *The American Dilemma* became my secular Bible. My companion readings included Kenneth Stamp's *The Peculiar Institution of Slavery* and W. J. Cash's *The Mind of the South*. Running against the grain of who I thought I was as a human being, yet finding resonance, were my reading of the rave author Ayn Rand's *The Virtue of Selfishness* and William Golding's *Lord of the Flies*.

Of course, I read W. E. B. Dubois, Frederick Douglass, E. Franklin Frazier, Paul Lawrence Dunbar, Ralph Ellison, Langston Hughes, Erskine Caldwell, Booker T. Washington, and other scholars and authors on the "Negro Question." I wondered why there were no Negro women authors, or, if there were, why they were not on my course lists of required readings. I knew about the heroic exploits of Harriet Tubman and Ida B. Wells, the compassionate entreaties of Dr. Mary McLeod Bethune and the poetry of Sojourner Truth and Phyllis Wheatley. But they were not considered writers of serious analysis.

I did find assurance in my philosophy class taught by Dr. John Eubanks.

The only thing permanent in the world is change. I knew, eventually, that a change was going to come for the better in the lives of Negro people, now lost and locked in white USA. I buried these thoughts of freedom in my subconscious while, literally, social activities governed my conscious behavior. I concentrated on being the best cheerleader ever, getting invited as a date to all of the fraternity Greek balls, and being "rushed" to join sororities. Delta Sigma Theta, as a legatee, was my choice.

It was a rain-drenched-filled night as Elizabeth, Doris, I and the other four cheerleaders cheered the Golden Tigers football team to victory over the Morehouse College Maroon Tigers. The game was played in Columbus, Georgia. The contest was a yawn as Tuskegee stomped Morehouse 63–6. At half-time the score was 42–6. We wished Morehouse would concede the game and the referees would accept so the fans, the bands, and we cheer-leaders could take refuge from the pelting rain. Nope. The second half of the game went forward.

By game's end, I knew I had caught a death of a cold. My immune system had never been strong as evinced during my childhood as an anemic and a sufferer of whooping cough.

But I had already and creatively secured special permission for Elizabeth, Doris, and myself not to travel back to Tuskegee on the college bus. We had an extended curfew to be back in our dorm by 12 midnight. I had arranged for Columbus friends to take us after the game to a Columbus nightclub where Bobby Moore and the Rhythm Aces of Montgomery were playing. Bobby was to take us back to Tuskegee, about forty miles from Columbus.

Despite feeling poorly, I had a fun time at the club. It was still pouring rain when we left and on the drive to Tuskegee. As Bobby approached the campus, he switched off the headlights and quietly coasted. It was 3 A.M. and we had a midnight curfew. Elizabeth and Doris were roommates and stayed on the first floor of Thrasher Hall. The back of their dorm room faced Campus Avenue. We had left the window imperceptibly cracked so we could climb through if we returned to campus after curfew. We took to heart Dean of Women Mrs. Kelly West's admonition that it was not about being off campus, but rather about being caught returning to campus past curfew.

As we ran from Bobby's car to the window, we were again drenched. I usually was the first one to leap to the window ledge and to raise the window. But this time I was too weak. Doris went first, and then Elizabeth hoisted me on her shoulders while Doris pulled me through the opened window. Elizabeth followed.

I was chilled to the bone and could not stop my teeth from chattering. Elizabeth and Doris quickly removed my wet clothes, dried me off, especially my hair and head, put me in flannel pajamas, and wrapped me snugly in a blanket. Elizabeth went to my room and told my roommate, Janet Peebles, a veterinary science major, that I would be staying downstairs. Elizabeth grabbed my great-grandmother's quilt off the foot of my bed, brought it downstairs, and wrapped it securely around me as an extra layer of warmth.

I simply could not catch my breath. For the remainder of the early morning, I sat on the windowsill and deeply inhaled the cool air into my lungs. Knowing that my great-grandmother's quilt was wrapped about me gave me the emotional strength and security that I would soon be okay. I began to breathe evenly and without labor. I stayed in Elizabeth and Doris' room, not going to my dorm room on the second floor. I slept for two days.

My dorm mates, with Elizabeth and Doris in charge, became my nurses. At regular intervals they brought chicken and tomato soup and a plethora of over-the-counter cold remedies. I steadily coughed up mucus and slowly regained my strength. After a week, I felt normal.

WHEN I RETURNED to my classes, I realized that "studying" had advanced to "booking." My first-year friend, Scotland, came to mind. I spent long hours in Hollis Burke Hall, the library, gathering research to write a slew of papers for my liberal arts classes. I made a conscious decision to cut back on my social life and to concentrate on my studies.

On the other hand, I wanted to celebrate my nineteenth birthday in style. This was the last year I would be a teenager. I did not dread becoming an adult, but I knew I had to put away my childish, innocent and adventurous behavior. I had to be more responsible and accountable for my actions. One promise I made to myself was never to go outside when there was a downpour of rain. Or even the threat of rain. I contacted my cheerleader coaches, Mrs. Letitia Williams and Mrs. Margaret Chenier, and asked them to replace me with a junior-squad cheerleader for the weekend's football game.

It was a bright, warm Indian summer day and evening on my birthday, October 14, 1962. I was ecstatic that the weather was cooperating. It was the best birthday present ever. Elizabeth, Doris, and I were spending my birthday weekend at Mommy and Poppa Washington's home in Montgomery. They always enjoyed our silly antics of practicing cheers in the living room or acting out spontaneous operettas while I played the piano.

"Okay, girls," Mommy said at our luncheon meal of fancy sandwiches, decoratively cut raw vegetables, and fresh-squeezed lemonade. "You have a 2 a.m. curfew. Remember, you will be getting up in the morning to go to church." My usual curfew was between 10 p.m. to midnight.

Of course, I had to have a date who was approved by my grandparents. They made it very clear to him their expectations of his being nothing less than a gentleman, or there would be serious trouble for him, including the possibility of being shot by Poppa Washington with his trusty shotgun.

Alan Woods, who called himself "Jerry," was my beau. He was a soldier stationed at Maxwell Air Force Base in Montgomery. Mommy at first was leery of Jerry. She thought soldiers were irresponsible "runabouts" with pregnant girlfriends at every base.

Jerry was six years older than I. He had light hazel-brown eyes with a glint of green, depending upon how the sun caught his stance. His almond-shaped eyes widened to complement an easy open-mouthed smile that revealed his beautiful, strong, even teeth. He was not just cute; he was downright sexy.

He was from Belize, the only English-speaking country in north Central America. Belize is a small coastal country between the Spanish-speaking countries of Guatemala and Mexico.

"The small town, Gorda, where I grew up is seven miles long and seven miles wide," Jerry reminisced. "The fine sand is white, white and the water of the Caribbean Sea is blue, blue." I was enthralled as Jerry described his homeland, the culture, and the foods. His soft, sing-song accent added mystique to his storytelling. Often he would speak in Spanish, and then translate for me. I had Spanish in high school. Now, I knew that Spanish would be my second language and made a mental note to take Spanish while at Tuskegee.

"Belize's greatest resource was mahogany trees. When we finally won our independence, the British had cut down all the trees and shipped the wood to England to make furniture. The colonialists did not replant the trees. So now we have self-government, but no economic base. We planted new trees. My father, a logger and wood sculptor, is head of one of the brigades. It takes at least fifty years for a tree to mature for industrial-commercial purposes." Jerry was no longer talking to me. He was talking to his hurt soul and spirit. This was my first direct understanding and contact with a victim of international racism, which I later learned is called imperialism.

"The British cut down the trees in a fell swoop while my countrymen were in the mountains of Guatemala and Mexico planning means to take control of our homeland. I probably will not ever live in Belize again. Besides, I don't want to live beyond fifty years. That's half of a century and that's long enough for anybody to be on this earth." I was stunned by his nihilism.

"I was forced to leave Belize. There was no work. My mother and brothers are in Los Angeles. My father is still in Belize. He will die there as a broken destitute and heart-broken man."

He abruptly ended the narrative. "Pshaw! You don't want to hear this sad story!" And with that conclusion, he lifted me out of my seat to dance as Bobby Moore and the Rhythm Aces played their popular arrangements of current R&B hits, especially the "slow-dance" songs.

Soon after my nineteenth birthday, Jerry and I began a serious courtship. Mommy was still skeptical. In her eyes I was still a teenager and Jerry was an "old man" at age twenty-five. She was concerned about my finishing college and not being sidetracked with what she called the "purple passion." But when Jerry showed up at the front door with cut flowers in his hand and his idea of a date was for him and me to swing on the front porch when I was home for weekends, Mommy's heart melted too. I was falling in love with Jerry.

THE CHRISTMAS HOLIDAY came quickly. I had planned to go to Michigan to visit with my brother and family. As Mommy and I were packing my suitcases for the trip, I came down with a spasm of coughing. I smelled blood in my nostrils. I became weak.

Poppa Washington carried me to my bedroom. Mommy placed Vicks salve in my nostrils and an ice-pack on my forehead and rubbed my chest with beef grease, called "tallow." She placed a pot of boiling water mixed with Vicks salve on the gas heater and closed the door to my bedroom. After a night and day of this home remedy, which included regular intervals of eating homemade chicken soup and taking aspirins every four hours, my breathing returned to normal. I spent the entire holiday in bed with this regimen.

When Jerry phoned and he learned about my "terrible cold," he was by my bedside every day. He became even more endeared to Mommy. Poppa Washington put away his shotgun.

At the end of the holiday and feeling much stronger, I returned to Tuskegee and registered, among others, for that Spanish course I had promised myself. But my stamina soon dissipated. Though I had consciously scheduled my spring-semester classes every other hour so I could go to my dorm to rest and nap, what with the rigors of walking to classes, cheerleading practices, and performing at basketball games, I grew steadily weaker.

I returned to staying with Elizabeth and Doris on the first floor; walking up the stairs to the second floor hall to my room took too much energy. Again, my breathing became extremely labored. The smell of blood in my nostrils was so pronounced that I was puzzled why Elizabeth and Doris didn't smell it, too. Finally, I was overtaken with fever with profuse sweating and constant chills. I began to cough up mucus mixed with blood.

Elizabeth and Doris reported my alarming condition to the dorm mother. In the middle of the night I was admitted to John Andrews Hospital. After three days in a regular room, I was transferred to the isolation unit. When I woke and looked up at the doctor and nurses, they were naturally in all-white uniforms, but they also had on white head gear, masks, and gloves. I was under an oxygen tent.

"You have been diagnosed with a far-advanced case of tuberculosis," I was told.

TB.

The words struck me as a death knell.

I was transferred by ambulance from the John Andrews Hospital isolation ward to Batson Memorial Sanitarium in Lafayette, Alabama, on January 23, 1963. I do not remember the fifty-mile ambulance ride.

Meanwhile, Elizabeth and Doris suffered not only isolation, but ostracism from our dorm mates in Thrasher Hall. My own roommate was terrified that she might have caught TB from me. When I learned later that she, along with Elizabeth and Doris, had tested negative, I was so relieved.

Elizabeth and Doris packed my clothes and belongings and sent them to my grandparents. No one else would dare enter my contaminated room. Thrasher Hall was fumigated and campus life resumed to normalcy.

Except, that is, for Elizabeth and Doris. My illness and the reaction of our classmates had deeply affected Elizabeth and Doris. Neither returned to Tuskegee for the fall 1963 semester.

9

A Movement Where You Are

Tuberculosis, like cancer, was a dreaded disease. Eventual debilitation or sudden death was the presumed outcome for both.

Cancer in the popular culture had the peculiar stigma of being a woman's disease, somehow associated with reproductive functions. Breast cancer, the grapevine said, was because a mother did not breastfeed her infant. It was whispered that a woman who had her fallopian tubes tied to prevent pregnancies, or had a hysterectomy for medical reasons, made herself vulnerable for cancer. In other words, a woman brought cancer onto herself. Of course, these misrepresentations were perpetuated by men who frowned upon women who underwent these operations. These women were undesirable as wives. After all, a woman's main purpose was to have babies. Though cancer was not contagious, the cancer-ravaged woman was shunned by many. The scarlet letter "A" had been replaced with the "big C."

Growing up in the 1950–60s, I never knew a man who had cancer. On the other hand, I never knew a woman who had tuberculosis, which was considered a man's disease. Men had to be out in the elements to provide for their families. Though TB was contagious, men rallied around its victims; their virile sense of themselves was their shield. My father hired Tommy Dokes, who had had tuberculosis and had the infected lung removed. Tommy was a welcomed friend in our home. No one went behind him, sanitizing everything he touched.

After I contracted the disease, I wondered if I would be treated differently? Would friends rally around me? And, if I didn't die but was cured of the disease, would people still go behind me, sanitizing everything I touched?

While I was in the sanitarium, my English professors Dr. Saunders and Emma Walker—she had taken special interest in me after I raised my hand in my freshman English class to volunteer that I had read *Studs Lonigan* while in high school, and I placed the two dots over the "i' when I wrote "naïve" on the blackboard—came to visit and brought Elizabeth and Doris with them.

At my insistence, they reluctantly told me the truth about how my illness was being perceived on campus; the reaction, mainly by coeds, was that I should be "quarantined for life."

I knew that if I overcame this illness, I had a challenge before me. I resolved that I would fight the sexist stigma, believed by both men and women, that could devastate the soul and spirit of women almost more than the dreaded diseases themselves.

The front of the sanitarium was impressive, but the ambulance went to the back. Negro orderlies helped me out of the vehicle and up four rickety wooden steps into a large, dimly lit vestibule. Metal folding chairs lined the walls. A white nurse beckoned the orderlies with her forefinger to bring me to a chair beside her small desk. After they exchanged medical papers, the orderlies took me to my room. I don't remember talking to the nurse. I was so weak.

I was led down a hallway to the left of the intake room. Beds with female patients—all Negroes—lined the hallway. I saw the backs of patients sitting in metal folding chairs watching a black-and-white television screen at the end of the hall.

My room was the first on the left. The room— smaller than my brother's upstairs bedroom in Inkster—was sized for two beds, but four were crowded in. Three older ladies greeted me as the orderlies put me in the empty bed. A white doctor and nurse were soon at my bedside. After taking and recording my vital signs, the doctor asked me to cough up sputum into a specimen cup, and then they left the room.

After a liquid meal, I fell into a deep sleep. The last thing I saw upon my admission to Batson Memorial Sanitarium was the one window in the room, opened to its fullest extent. I remember thinking, "Oh, this is why they call the TB sanitarium the 'fresh-air camp.'"

The following day the same doctor and nurse came to my bedside.

The doctor said, "You have a far-advanced case of tuberculosis. You have a fair chance of getting well. I am prescribing a daily injection of 1 gram of streptomycin for a month. If there is improvement, that is if your lungs clear up and the cavity in your left lung begins to heal, then you'll be on pills that you'll have to take three times a day. Turn over."

The doctor injected the medicine into my left buttock. For the next twenty-nine days I received daily injections, the doctor rotating the shots from my left to my right buttocks.

DURING THE FIRST month, I rarely got out of bed except to go to the bathroom that had three stalls, three face bowls, one shower and one bathtub. My diet progressed from liquids to solid foods. I ate heartily because I knew food would help me regain strength.

Cousin Carnell drove Mommy and Poppa Washington to the sanitarium, eighty miles from Montgomery, for monthly visits. On their first visit, Mommy brought a suitcase full of pretty pajamas, nighties, and robes, all embroidered with my initials. There were my comb, brush and toiletries. The sanitarium provided generic items, but having my own lifted my morale and determination to get well. My three elder roommates never had visitors. I quietly asked Mommy to bring presents to them on the next visit.

As my relatives were leaving on their second visit, I said to my room-mates, "Oh, by the way, we have presents for you."

They were very happy to receive the gift-wrapped presents of crochet threads and various sizes of crochet hooks, fabrics, and cotton for stuffing our hand crafts. My senior roommate—I didn't know her age but her hair was totally gray—said, "Gwen, never say 'by the way.' When you say 'by the way,' it's off-handed, not important. These gifts are important, and you gave them to us after serious thought and with love."

I knew there was wisdom in this chastisement. "Yes, ma'am," I said.

Mommy smiled and nodded her head in assent to my senior room-mate, thus assured that I was in good hands in furthering my upbringing in good manners.

My elder hospital mates and I spent many hours crocheting. My favorite craft was heart-shaped pillow coverings. I perfected my stitches of crocheting flowers and petals and then hooking the appliqués to loose chain stitches. I cut heart-shaped patterns of satin fabric, sewed the patterns together, stuffed them with cotton, and then slid the satin pillows into the crochet coverings. I made very large pillows and sent them as presents to family members, Elizabeth, Doris, and the Saunderses. My other favorite craft was stuffed ducks, the pledging mascot of Delta Sigma Theta Sorority.

As I became stronger, I visited with the patients in the hallway and the other two rooms. One room had eight patients; the other, larger room had fifteen. The rooms were crowded and there were no chairs. I sat on the foot of beds. I learned that one of the patients had been moved to make space for me in my four-bed room. I realized that the bed arrangements were a crude class structure within a disgusting, racist caste system—at the time I was the youngest and most-educated patient.

I offered to swap beds with the "removed" patient. She was surprised at my willingness to give up a bed in what was considered the "elite" room. She shrugged and said, "No, that's okay." I think my offer to exchange satisfied her and boosted her sense of worthiness.

I began to read my Bible that Mommy and Poppa Washington had brought on their first visit. Finally, I was able to attend church services, at first in the back vestibule, and then, when spring came, in the backyard in a circle of folding chairs under an oak tree. I learned how to "line out a hymn," especially the Methodist standard, "A Charge to Keep I Have," written by Charles Wesley and arranged for our Baptist hymnal by Lowell Mason.

Male patients were permitted to worship with us and I could easily determine who was courting whom. Early on I had shared my weekly letters from Jerry with my hospital mates; no male patients attempted to "make a move" on me.

Most of the patients identified with Job. My own favorite books were Kings I and II, Psalms, and Proverbs. I recalled my father's teachings about King Solomon, the son of David and Bathsheba, a black man, a direct progenitor of Jesus Christ.

By THE TIME I regained a considerable amount of strength and was breathing more strongly, a mother and her nine-year-old daughter, Nancy, were admitted. I asked to be moved to the large ward so I could be near the child. The request was granted, and I became even closer to the other patients.

The child's mother was very ill. She was thin as a reed and her breathing was extremely labored. She did not have enough strength to inhale oxygen through the tubes and her oxygen tank and tubes were replaced with an oxygen tent. Death was approaching.

The mother began to make painful gurgling sounds that words cannot describe. She then would go through a period of gasping for air, then a moment of silence as if she were not breathing. Then the cycle of gurgling, gasping, and silence would reoccur. For the first and only time in my life, I heard and witnessed the "death rattle."

I took Nancy from her bed, placed her in my bed, and cradled her in my arms. I softly sang hymns and children's songs to her as her mother struggled between life and death. The other patients lay awake and quiet in their beds, no doubt wondering if they were destined for the same fate.

The "death rattle" became louder. I began to talk to Nancy about death, heaven, and that Jesus would provide an everlasting life for her mother. Nancy, crying silently except for sniffles in the attempt to stifle tears, fell asleep as I rocked her in my arms.

After ten hours, the sounds of struggle were no more. Death had offered its relief. Orderlies came to take the mother out of the ward. My hospital mates began to chant, the 23rd Psalm and the Lord's Prayer. I was grateful that Nancy was still asleep.

From that day, Nancy became my "charge to keep." I taught her crocheting and other crafts. Mommy and Poppa Washington brought her "paint by numbers" gifts. I read and interpreted Bible passages for our daily school.

In September while watching TV news, we learned that four Negro girls had been killed in a church bombing in Birmingham. The screen flashed an image of the bombed church, and then the TV went on the "blink." We knew that the Klan with the tacit support of the police and Governor George Wallace were responsible for the bombing. We looked at each other, said nothing, went to our beds, and cried silently. I became even more protective of Nancy.

Then in November we were watching on TV President Kennedy's motorcade in Dallas, Texas. Before our eyes, we saw the assassination of a U.S. president who had reluctantly befriended Dr. Martin Luther King Jr. and was moving to champion our cause for dignity, freedom, and equality.

In our Jim Crow sanitarium of pitiful accommodations, inadequate diet of fried and boiled foods, one bathtub for thirty-three patients, no recreational room and no library, open weeping was our only form of protest.

THE NEXT DAY, I went to the kitchen. For more than nine months, I had never crossed the forbidden threshold that led to the main hallway. I could look down that hallway, our end of which led into our vestibule, our all-purpose room. But it had never occurred to me to walk past the vestibule into the "forbidden hallway" that led to the part of the sanitarium reserved for white patients.

On my way to find the kitchen, I passed a large recreational room with well-appointed card tables and matching chairs, lounge furniture, board games stacked on shelves, and a piano. I started to enter the room, but my objective was to find the kitchen. I was tired of the tasteless, yet salty food. As I made my trek, I became extremely cognizant that I was not only strong, but I felt fit, physically and mentally. My new concern was whether I could constrain my emotions in this despicable place or tear it apart. Were

Negroes to forever exist in this inhumane dilemma? Lying on our backs with a debilitating disease, praying to get well, and when we did get well finding ourselves in humiliating surroundings, designed to scream at us, "Yes, you are well, but in white eyes, you are still inferior, you're still *Nigras!*" "Nigra," of course, was the word used by whites too polite to say "Nigger" but not able to bring themselves to say "Negro."

I pushed open the swinging doors labeled "kitchen." The dietician and cooks—all white—were startled. "What are you doing here?" the dietician inquired officiously.

"I want to know what you're cooking," I responded in my polite manner.

The dietician rattled off a litany of foods, including oyster stew.

I said, "I've never had oyster stew served here."

"We thought Nigras didn't like such stews."

"Well, I do, and I would like some," I replied. "Is it possible for you to let us know your menus beforehand, so we could have the opportunity to choose?" From that day forward, while I was a patient, the menu options were posted on our new vestibule bulletin board.

The following day, with Nancy in hand, I ventured further down the "forbidden hall." We marveled at the shining floors, sparkling like glittering glass. The floors in our section were always dull. I don't recall if housekeeping came in our area to mop, let alone, wax our floors. I knew that those of us who were getting stronger swept our rooms. I assumed it was a part of our regimen to gain stamina. We did have Negro nurses' aides who changed our beds when we were weak. But when we gained strength, we made our own beds. Again, I thought it was part of the regimen. Now, I had second thoughts. No doubt the hospital administrator bragged on running an economically efficient sanitarium.

As Nancy and I continued our "march" to the front of the sanitarium, white bodies, clad in sleepwear and robes, suits and medical whites, darkened the doorways. No one attempted to stop us.

When Nancy and I reached the front of the sanitarium, there was a resplendent visitors' sitting area with another piano. This commodious area onto another hallway and on its right there was an open-stacked library. We went into the library and I began selecting books.

"You're not supposed to be up here," a hospital staffer said reprovingly.

"May I see the hospital administrator?" I said straightforwardly. Led to the office and upon entering, I wasted no time with my verbal petition.

"I'm a college student. Nancy needs to continue her schooling. We should have the right to visit the library and to check out books. My people, too, pay taxes which makes it possible for this sanitarium to be and for you to have a job," I said in one breath, proving my lungs were strong.

After what seemed an eternity of hesitation, the administrator offered, "We will bring a variety of books to your section for your choosing."

"Will you bring the entire collection?"

"That's impossible."

"Well, I would recommend that one day a week, Nancy and I and other patients in our section be permitted to visit the library to check out books and magazines."

The request was granted. Though no other Negro patients dared to trek up the hall to the "White" section, I was admired for my boldness.

THESE SMALL VICTORIES buoyed my spirit. However, I was weary of the daily Jim Crow accommodations. I was physically strong, but I found myself morose and not wanting to leave my bed.

My mind was saturated with thoughts of how many more of my people would be killed by the police, by bombs, by the Klan with state-power approval. The "death-mask" of murdered Emmett Till's swollen and battered face was a permanent image in my mind and heart . . . not as a nightmare, but as a call to fight for our freedom in this racist society.

When Mommy and Poppa Washington came to visit me, I told them about my desperate need to be home. After a series of communications with strong support letters from the sanitarium administrators to the vocational rehabilitation administration, I was finally released from Batson Memorial Sanitarium on January 1, 1964.

This was the happiest New Year's Day ever. My New Year's resolution was to fight injustice wherever I was. The movement was not an extra-curricula activity outside of my day-to-day existence. This I had learned while lying on my sickbed, the ideal repose for racism to ravage the souls of its victims.

It has always fascinated me that traveling home always seems faster than the journey away from home, going to an unknown destination. No doubt the anticipation of returning to a secure haven rapidly whiled away the time. I was coming home. I had conquered tuberculosis.

So it was that in what seemed like lickety-split time I was standing on my own front porch. The porch swing moved slightly in the January wind. I answered its beckoning call by going to it, sat down, and began a slow rock. Soon the swing and I were comfortably synchronized.

I had no luggage. I had left all of my belongings, except my Bible, in the sanitarium for Nancy. Mommy and Poppa Washington opened the front door to go on into the house.

"Gwendolyn, I'll make lunch for us," Mommy said.

I lingered for a long moment on the porch swing. Finally, I got up and went inside. My thought was to play the piano. Though there were two pianos in the sanitarium, I had never told the administrators that I could play, especially classical music. I didn't want to risk being put on display for the white patients as some kind of "Negress" oddity.

Now I went straight to the piano in the living room. My music books and sheet music were still in the seat of the piano bench. I placed the hymnal on the piano's music stand and played "My Faith Looks up to Thee" and "Have Thine Own Way." Then without thought, I moved into a soft and slow rendition of "Canadian Sunset." I knew the notes by heart.

"Gwendolyn, lunch is ready," Mommy called from the dining room. The dining room was still elegant with its antique furniture on rollers. Of course, the table was formally set—Mommy had probably set it before she and Poppa Washington came to the sanitarium to "collect" me, as we say in the South.

Poppa Washington offered prayer and thanksgiving to our Lord for bringing me safely through my ordeal back to my home of love, comfort and security.

Mommy's spread was a seafood extravaganza, starting with a piping hot oyster stew in a beautifully painted tureen with ladle. Oyster crackers were in a matching bowl. We ate that, then Mommy disappeared from back into the kitchen, soon to return with a platter of steamed shrimp and rice with a garlic-lemon-butter sauce and steamed broccoli ("tree tops," I had called them since childhood). Quiet tears of happiness cascaded down my cheeks.

After lunch, I slowly made my way to my bedroom. I don't know why I made this the last step in my home-coming journey. I knew it would be perfect. Perhaps the reality that I would be in my own private room and bed after a year was overwhelming.

I stood frozen in the doorway of my bedroom, Mommy and Poppa Washington behind me. It was exactly as I had left it, with the addition of a new Singer electric sewing machine next to my study desk. The gas heater in the fireplace glowed with loving warmth. My framed photographs on the mantle were still in their original arrangement. The novels on my nightstand were precisely where I had left them.

"Gwendolyn, you are to take two naps a day. You missed your morning nap," Mommy said as she placed a medicine cup of pills and a glass of water on the nightstand. She helped me change into my nightie. I took my pills and fell into a deep sleep of pleasant dreams.

I INDULGED COMPLETE mental and emotional relaxation during my first month of convalescence. Family and senior friends—my movement mentors Mrs. Idessa Williams, Mrs. Hazel Gregory, and Mrs. Bertha Smith—visited between my nap times. They told me about the murder of Medgar Evers, shot down by the KKK in his Jackson, Mississippi, driveway while his wife and children were inside. A busload of Alabamians had joined the 250,000 people for the "March on Washington." Mrs. Williams, a member of that Alabama delegation, now carried a copy of Dr. King's "I have a dream" speech with her at all times. She removed the copy tucked in her *Gideon International Bible* from her handbag and read the speech to me, nodding her emphasis when she got to the part that referenced the unfulfilled Reconstruction promise of forty acres and a mule: the promissory note had bounced, stamped "insufficient funds." Mrs. Gregory gave me a copy of L. D. Reddick's *Crusader Without Violence: A Biography of Martin Luther King, Jr.* Mrs. Bertha gave me an update on the voting registration drives and the several lawsuits filed by Coach Rufus Lewis challenging discrimination and racism of boards of registrars in central Alabama. As my movement mentors briefed me, I realized I had not read a daily newspaper the entire year I was in the sanitarium. I vowed to make up for lost time.

I had just one friend my own age to visit with me, Gladys Carter, nicknamed "Cookie." I was neither surprised nor disappointed that my peer group did not visit. As far as I knew, I was the only Negro person in Montgomery who had survived tuberculosis. The disease was still considered a contagious, deadly plague. Young people by nature wanted to live forever.

Cookie was smartly attractive and had a beautiful singing voice. She was enrolled in Alabama State College. I say "enrolled" as opposed to "attended." Cookie did not want to go to college. Her goal was to be a wife with a husband who would take care of her. Her model was not the wives of the 1950 television sitcoms of *Ozzie and Harriet* or *I Love Lucy*, but more like the perky, romantic wife of Detective Jimmy Halligan in the 1948 Hollywood movie, *Naked City*.

Instead of going to classes, Cookie visited with me. No matter how much Mommy and I tried to impress upon the Cookie the importance of a college education, she resisted. Mommy talked with Cookie's mother—we called her "Mommy," too—about our concern. Both Mommies agreed that it might be more productive and educational for Cookie to visit with me than to continually flunk out of college.

Cookie came every morning after breakfast. She loved to design smart outfits and could cut patterns, using old newspapers. I was a better seamstress. We spent hours in my bedroom, she cutting material and I at the sewing machine, stitching sharp outfits for us to wear to church. When it was time for my nap, Cookie would doze in the bedroom rocking chair that Mommy had bought when I was an infant. We would wake at noon and eat lunch together. Then Cookie was off until the next morning. I spent several Saturday nights with Cookie and we alternated going to each other's church the following Sunday morning. When I was around Cookie, I completely forgot that I ever had tuberculosis.

I BECAME CONCERNED that I had not heard from Jerry. Was he just patronizing me when he wrote me weekly letters with the closings of "Yo Amo Tu" and "Siempre" while I was in the sanitarium? Now that I was released, was he afraid to be around me? I mustered up enough nerve to call his best friend, Cherry, at Maxwell Air Force Base and learned that Jerry had received orders to go to Vietnam.

My heart sank. What little I read about Vietnam raised questions. I had no doubt that the "American advisors" would soon become soldiers in combat in a full-scale war.

However, Cherry then told me that the day before Jerry was to report for shipping out, he had gone AWOL. Cherry went on to say that when Jerry was caught he would be put into the stockade then court-martialed and eventually given a BCD, a bad-conduct discharge.

I did not fully understand the negative consequences of a BCD. I simply was relieved that Jerry was not in Vietnam. I knew he would eventually get in touch with me. I stopped worrying.

After a while, I began to visit after my midday naps with family members in their homes. After eating dinner with them, I always offered to wash the dishes, asking where was the bleach. At first they balked, but I assured them that I needed to sanitize the dishes. "Hey, I don't want to catch *your cold* and have a relapse!"

We lovingly laughed together as the Clorox was handed to me and I poured an ample amount in the dishwater. Resilience requires levity.

My indulgent relaxation turned into boredom after three months. Though I was still on my pills, I no longer had to take naps. I volunteered to work in the Negro library and read all about British Honduras and Belize. I had yet to hear from Jerry.

My movement mentor, Mrs. Bertha Smith, and her husband, Charlie, owned a dry-cleaners within walking distance of my home. They offered me a job from 8 a.m. to noon. I had never had a job and accepted the offer as a new adventure.

Clothes were cleaned with a gasoline-like fluid in a special tumbler. Then the clothes were placed in another tumbler to dry. It was decided that I would not work in the cleaning process because of the harsh chemicals in the fluid and the harm inhaling the fumes might cause to my lungs. So I became a presser. The ironing board, permanently attached to the floor, was thickly padded and wide. Overhead was an equally thickly padded steam presser that you pulled down onto the clothing spread out on ironing board. For pleated skirts, I pinned the pleats at the waist with another pin inside the pleat at the hem and pulled the steam presser down onto the fabric, making the pleats permanent. The pins were removed when the garment was hung.

Mrs. Smith's sister "Sweetie Girl" also worked in the cleaners. She was a milliner. Hats were the rage for church-going women and a necessity for men. Sweetie Girl taught me how to shape brims and to block hats over standard head-sized forms. My greatest thrill was when on occasions I returned to the cleaners after lunch and accompanied Sweetie Girl on her shopping jobs. She pointed out the differences and purchased various millinery materials, from basic hat shapes, ribbons, fabric flowers, bric-a-brac, scarves, and meshed nettings.

Five months had come and gone since I left the sanitarium. I felt stronger than ever. I was ready to return to Tuskegee Institute and the challenges of reentering the community of my peers.

10

Returning to Tuskegee Institute

Tuskegee Institute was even more beautiful in the early summer of 1964 than when I had left the campus in an ambulance in January 1963. New women's and men's dorms had been constructed, though not enough—some male students still resided in barracks, a leftover from when Tuskegee Airmen lived on campus in the 1940s.

I registered for a full load of sixteen hours with breaks between every other class in case I needed to go to my dorm to rest. I was assigned to the renovated honors' dorm, Thrasher Hall, the same one where I had lain on my sickbed eighteen months earlier when tuberculosis was devastating my body.

My new roommate tried her best to be friendly, but she was deathly afraid of me. I requested a room to myself and offered to pay for the unused bed. Tuskegee granted my wish and only charged me as a single boarder. My roommate felt guilty, but she was relieved when she moved down the hall. I later learned that she took all of her clothes to the Institute's infirmary, John Andrews Hospital, to have them fumigated. I understood.

Just two weeks into the 1964 summer semester, a thousand volunteer students, mainly white, heeded the call of the Student Nonviolent Coordinating Committee (SNCC) and arrived in Mississippi for Freedom Summer. Mississippi was known for its vicious reputation; SNCC would make it a battleground in the new push for civil and voting rights.

The very next day, two white volunteers from New York, Andrew Goodman and Michael Schwerner, and one black Mississippi voting rights activist, James Chaney, went missing. Their disappearances shocked the world. Everyone knew that the KKK had murdered them. It was just a question of whether and when their bodies would be found.

Despite the real threats of violence and murder at the hands of racists who seemed to have full protection and sanction from the State of Mississippi, Freedom Summer went ahead. Freedom Schools were established in black churches throughout the state. Black Mississippians opened up their homes to house and feed white volunteers. The Mississippi Freedom Democratic Party (MFDP) organized congressional district by congressional district to challenge the dominant all-white Democratic Party.

It was a dangerous situation. Meanwhile, Tuskegee students traveled to Mississippi to assess the MFDP as a possible model for our ongoing struggle in Alabama for the right to vote and for political power.

Tuskegee Institute also became a refuge for Mississippi SNCC organizers who came by the dozens to find respite and to renew their strength, resolve and spirit. TI was dubbed a "liberated zone" by SNCC and later by Congress of Racial Equality (CORE) freedom fighters.

Students provided the activists housing and food on and off campus. Some SNCC sisters stayed with me in my dorm room. The fact that I had had tuberculosis was of no concern to them. This more than anything boosted my self-esteem.

TUSKEGEE INSTITUTE HAD a rich, militant history of standing up to the

KKK. In the 1920s, when the U.S. Veterans Administration authorized construction of a VA hospital in Tuskegee for Negro soldiers and veterans, the white powers assumed that the professional staff of doctors, nurses, and medical technicians would be white while the janitorial and housekeeping staff, nurses' aides, and orderlies would be Negro.

"Not so," said Dr. Robert Russa Moton, second president of Tuskegee Institute, who had negotiated the sale of Tuskegee Institute's property as the site for the hospital.

The local white authority in charge of personnel then warned, "If Negroes show up at the hospital to apply for positions, the Macon County KKK will be there to greet them and to run them back to your school."

President Moton, it is reported, did not respond. But when he returned to campus, he alerted the local Negro Veterans of Foreign Wars. The ignorant arrogance of some white people never ceases to amaze. Macon County was 87 percent Negro. The number of white males in the county was a thimble-full by comparison.

On the day in question, armed Negro veterans and soldiers intermittently lined all routes leading to the new VA hospital. The KKK obviously got the word. They were nowhere in sight. The hospital was staffed with Negro professionals and paraprofessionals; the white staff worked mainly under Negro supervision.

During the 1940s, Alabama Negro workers helped establish the Congress of Industrial Organizations (CIO) in Birmingham and fought to be included in the United Steel Workers and United Mine Workers in north Alabama. In the port city of Mobile, Negroes stood shoulder to shoulder with the International Longshoremen Union to prevent the transformation of a natural industrial site into a man-made resort of white sandy beaches for the leisure class of whites to frolic on the Gulf of Mexico. Tuskegee Institute students stood ready in the cause to support union efforts.

Under the fearless leadership of the 1941 student body president James Woodson, his fellow student Chappie James, and others, students prohibited a nonunion bakery company from delivering bread on campus.

"Students blocked the truck as it approached the dining hall, Thomkins Hall. When the nonunion workers climbed out of the truck to see what was the holdup, male students stormed the truck, opened up the tail doors and threw loaves of bread every whichaway," Woodson recalled with a knowing smile when I interviewed him for my sociology class. "Yep, we ambushed that scab truck!" Woodson later became the Institute's alumni director; Chappie James became the U.S. Air Force's first African American four-star general.

Now, IN THE 1960s, Tuskegee Institute students were making their mark in our people's ongoing fight for freedom. We knew we were standing on mighty broad shoulders.

SNCC meetings at Tuskegee Institute collapsed the model of the Montgomery Improvement Association's Monday night mass meeting and Thursday night planning meeting into one weekly session. There would be singing of freedom songs, a report from a SNCC organizer about the development of Freedom Summer in Mississippi, and then a full-fledged discussion of what to do next.

"We need Tuskegee students to join us in the Mississippi Movement!" exhorted a SNCC organizer.

After intently listening to the rationale as to why students should drop out of summer school to go to Mississippi, I raised my hand and was recognized: "I disagree. We need to continue our movement in Alabama and particularly in Tuskegee where we are now living. We should not abandon our own movement by becoming interlopers in another movement."

I remember that the room fell silent. Then James Forman, the brilliant "old man" at age thirty-two, executive secretary of SNCC, walked to the podium. "I agree with Gwen. I suggest we form a Friends of SNCC chapter on campus and wherever possible assist the students with their local struggles."

We already had a fledging student movement in Tuskegee to test the enforcement of the just-enacted 1964 Civil Rights Act with sit-ins at "white only" establishments and by applying for jobs at the establishments. Moreover, our struggle was not only against Jim Crow but also against class division within the black community. We wanted to develop harmony and respect between Tuskegee's middle-class, educated elite and the poor and working class. Tuskegee Institute had fostered a disgusting class structure within a racist caste system. Poor and working-class youth swam in the Negro pool on certain days while middle-class youth swam in the same pool on other days. Even the president of Tuskegee Institute hosted several Christmas parties that differentiated between the support and professional faculty and staff. We Tuskegee students knew there had to be a strategy to bring together—as JoAnn Robinson, one of the key architects of the successful Montgomery Bus Boycott, put it— "the Ph.Ds and the No Ds."

With that background in my mind as Forman spoke, I stood and started walking towards the podium, saying, "I disagree." By the time I reached the podium and stood beside Forman, the crowd was groaning.

Undaunted, I said, "We as students should have our own organization with our own identity and leadership. Of course, we would work with SNCC based on mutual terms of agreement."

Again, mostly silence.

I remembered the discussions in 1960 between the Southern Christian Leadership Conference (SCLC) and the Montgomery Improvement Association (MIA) held in Montgomery at my church, Hutchinson Street Missionary Baptist. The MIA persuasively argued to preserve its local identity as the organization founded and owned by the local people who spearheaded the bus boycott.

"Let's put together a subcommittee of Tuskegee students and SNCC organizers to discuss these two issues, come to a consensus and then report back to this larger body," I said. The crowd applauded that.

Tuskegee students George Ware, a smart if eccentric and enigmatic graduate student in chemistry; Wendell Paris, a community activist who came from a strong movement family; Sammy Younge Jr., a native Tuskegeean who had attended Cornwall Academy in Massachusetts and was a Navy veteran; and myself were selected for the Tuskegee team. James Forman, Willie Ricks, and later Bill "Winky" Hall headed up the SNCC team.

It was subsequently decided that Tuskegee students would form their own movement organization, eventually called Tuskegee Institute Advancement League (TIAL), that would be affiliated with SNCC. Officers were elected and I was appointed to serve as chair of the Direct Action Committee. Movement activity in Macon County intensified with citizenship schools, sit-ins, wade-ins, voter registration drives and related activity. A TIAL office with two phone lines and a "freedom house" were opened in the community.

MEANWHILE, ENTHUSIASM WAS high that the MFDP would be seated as the bonafide delegates and would thus unseat the so-called lily-white regulars at the Democratic National Convention in August 1964 in Atlantic City, New Jersey. SNCC organizers were confident that their white allies would deliver this political victory. I was skeptical and stated so, to the consternation of my SNCC friends.

Thirty-three democratically elected delegates under the banner of the MFDP boarded the bus to Atlantic City. Mrs. Fannie Lou Hamer, with whom Tuskegee students had the closest ties, was part of the Mississippi leadership.

On televisions in our dorms, we watched with great anticipation for Mrs. Hamer's presentation at the DNC. We were saddened though not surprised to learn from her televised remarks that a compromise, orchestrated by the MFDP's so-called liberal allies, had arranged for five of the MFDP delegates to be seated. The lily-white delegates would retain their seating and voting privileges.

"We did not travel all the way from Mississippi just for five peoples to be seated," said Mrs. Hamer before the credential committee on television. "We's all tired and we all want to sit down."

This debacle would have serious implications as to how SNCC, particularly its white and Northern members, could or could not organize in Alabama.

11

Returning to My Childhood Source

As the summer semester drew to a close, my emotions were on both civil rights and personal issues, particularly my family. In Montgomery, Mommy and Poppa Washington were very pleased with my progress, physically, emotionally and academically. I made the Dean's List. My summer grades lifted my grade point average to a B-plus. As a gift, my grandparents bought me a round-trip train ticket to visit with my family in Michigan.

Since I was last in Inkster in 1960, Daddy had lost our home house. Lois was very happy about that; she had sworn that my mother was haunting the house. Lois then bought a home in her name, but with the help of my father's money, in Annapolis Park, which had been a new middle-class subdivision in Inkster when I left four years earlier.

As I eventually learned, the new house was not as commodious as our family home had been. The layout was awkward. There were two entrances, not three, and you had to walk through the living room to get to the three bedrooms and the bathroom. There was no hallway. Thus, there was a footpath across the living room to the bedrooms. There was no space a family member could claim as a cocoon for privacy. You were in each other's faces at every turn. One bedroom was for my father and Lois, one for Sandy, and the last was for Frank and Jeff. There was no bedroom for my brother Bob, who was then a senior in high school.

In fact, Lois gave my brother's exquisite maple twin beds and accessories to my father's sister, Edith Mae. She bought new twin beds for her sons but did not buy a bed for my brother. During his senior year, Bob stayed with an array of friends and family in Inkster and downtown Detroit. His girl friend, JoAnn, became pregnant. Bob got an after-school job as a busboy in a Howard Johnson's restaurant, the chain where our mother worked before cancer wracked her body and God took her out of her pain. Upon his eighteenth birthday and still a senior in high school, Bob married JoAnn. My father, by then regretting his marriage to Lois, was tormented by his allowing her to drive his two older children practically into homelessness. Fortunately, Bob and I had a loving extended family and friends to stand in the gap for us during our tender teenage years of crisis. Daddy was now somewhat on his feet financially, though Lois was still a hindering thorn in his side. He did much monetarily to support his son and his family.

I HAD NOT seen Bob in three years. While I was in the sanitorium, he wrote me twice. His last letter informed me that he had a daughter, Tamanee, who looked like her Auntie Gwen. When I called him to tell him I was coming for a visit, he told me had he another daughter, Teresa, then two months old. I was very excited and could not wait to see my nieces.

Bob was basically a quiet person, yet you knew he was a deep thinker. He rarely talked about himself, especially his feelings. However, if you sought his advice, he would listen to you, sometimes willingly and often times impatiently. He offered sage advice as if he were three times his age. Elders would say, "He's been here before."

I never knew my brother as child-like even when he was a child. He played childish games with me in pretending to eat my glass-covered dirt cakes and my mixed salads of weeds and flowers. But I knew he just tolerated my fantasies. He saw his role as my great protector. Though I was older, he considered himself as my big brother. He recognized that I was academically smart, but in his eyes I was immature and a hopeless dreamer. He often said, "You have book sense, but no common sense."

On the other hand, my brother had a keen understanding and appreciation for "street sense." He abhorred talking about the past and would rudely cut you off if there was an inkling of reminiscing about the "good old days." Though he planned for the future, more as a provider for his children, he thought it a waste of time to talk about dreams. He quickly would say, "You don't know what tomorrow may bring. The past is over. Just concentrate on today!"

My father was to pick me up at the Detroit train station and drive me to the apartment Bob and his growing family shared above the Poseys' home. The Poseys were longtime family friends and like godparents to my parents when they were young and had Bob and me.

Bob was at work at Ford Motor Company when Daddy and I arrived at lunchtime at the apartment. The apartment had a better layout than Lois's house. There was a large living room that led to spotless French doors that opened into the dining room. The kitchen was off from the dining room. A zigzag hallway led from the back door to the two bedrooms and bathroom. JoAnn was in the kitchen feeding the babies, Tamanee in the high chair and Teresa in her arms. I took Tamanee out of the high chair, cradled her in my arms, and began to feed her. Daddy gave JoAnn a hundred-dollar bill, me a fifty, and told us he would see us later.

Bob came home from work, greeted me as warmly as he knew how, and said, "I'm glad you're well." After changing out of his work clothes, he went to the bathroom to wash the daily diapers. His meal, reminiscent of the heavy mid-day dinners at MaDear's when granddaddy came home between construction jobs, was piping hot. We ate together as a family, Bob saying very little. After our meal, Bob began washing windows.

Our families on both sides were cleanliness and neat freaks. Bob and I inherited the trait, probably to a flaw. JoAnn was not as tidy and really detested house work. I sensed that this marriage would have problems.

Bob worked the time and a half shift from 3–7 A.M., and then from 7 A.M. to 3 P.M., which was his regular shift. With the new baby, he wanted to earn more money and the time and a half pay was 150 percent of the regular hourly wage as a bonus for coming in so early to work those extra hours. I was up at 1 A.M. to have breakfast with him. My brother never started his day, regardless of the time, without first having a hearty breakfast. I wanted to give him a special gift. After he cooked our breakfast, as he always had since our youth, I placed a shoebox on the table.

"Bob, these are Mama's shoes. The last pair I bought her before she passed. I want to give them to you to save for the girls as a remembrance of their grandmother." The high-heeled, white-strapped, quality leather mules were exquisitely dainty. Mama wore a size four shoe.

Bob stared at the shoes then looked at me angrily. Or was it in pain? "Why would you think I want these shoes?" he growled.

Startled, I said, "They are not for you, but for the girls. It's called legacy."

"Gwen, that's in the past! I'm not interested in the past!" Then a slew of insults and profanity tumbled from his mouth.

Hurt, I put the shoes back in the box and left the kitchen. My brother was truly unhappy. My silent prayer was my hope, my dream, that he would find happiness and that I would be present when this blessing occurred.

AROUND NOON, I called my teenage sweetheart, Toots. By 2 P.M. he was at the apartment. Bob arrived shortly thereafter. He greeted me warmly as if nothing disconcerting had happened at our breakfast. He and Toots talked and laughed about the things men laugh about. My brother liked Toots.

After a while Toots and I were finally alone in the living room. We had not seen each other in three years but I kept thinking about Jerry; the flame for Toots had extinguished.

That afternoon, I called Marilyn Russell, my best friend in Inkster. "I've been waiting on your call," Marilyn said. "Sharon has a new convertible Catalina and the Flip-Jips are going to New York City to see the Beatles. Hope you can join us!"

My dear friends Marilyn, Sharon, Judy, Lenora, and Audrey were still "the group." We were all cheerleaders except Marilyn. In our youth, we were the Flip-Jips, pantomiming Bill Doggett's band to cheering audiences. Marilyn was the leader of our band. She stole the show when she blew in sync with the saxophone solo featured on "Tequila."

I was practically packed already and quickly said yes. A road trip to New York would be a godsend reprieve from my brother's unhappy home.

The mop-head Brits had crossed over into the black culture with "I Want to Hold Your Hand." I heard the transitional link in the Beatles' incorporation of Little Richard's voice filler of "oooh!"

The 600-mile drive over to New York City was exhilarating. With the top back but the windows rolled up, our hair was slightly blowing in the wind, and passing cars were honking at us, acknowledging six brown beauties.

It was reaffirming to chatter with my friends about our youthful fun-filled days of yore and what we were presently doing with our lives. Lenora was happily married to her high school sweetheart; Audrey was having second thoughts about her marriage to hers. Sharon was contemplating marriage and becoming a model and wondering if she could manage both simultaneously. Judy was still sorting out her dreams for the future. Marilyn had partied out of Howard University and was leaning strongly to joining the Army to find herself. My Northern friends were mesmerized with my stories of the Southern movement and our people's struggle to be free of Jim Crow. I pressed upon them the need to get a college education and my determination to attain the highest degree offered.

New York City was all that the postcards depicted: skyscrapers, glittering marquees sparkling even in the sun-lit daytime, preoccupied people filling the sidewalks, and bumper-to-bumper traffic with yellow cabs daringly darting in and out of lanes to get away from the slow-driving private cars.

We had been delayed getting through the Lincoln Tunnel and into the city—were the police barricades due to Beatlemania; they were playing in town—so we decided to go to the Commodore Hotel to check-in. Thank goodness, Marilyn had made reservations. When we arrived, it was absolutely busy and so full of other people who had also come to see the Beatles, that we realized we probably could not get tickets. So we were already rethinking our plans when suddenly I heard a voice calling across the crowded lobby.

"Gwen, Gwen Patton is that you?!"

It was my Montgomery neighbor, Douglas McCants, who lived up the street from me with his aunt, Miss Helen, who owned the neighborhood grocery. Douglas became our escort in New York. The following day he took us to a hip party on Central Park West. We left there and had a blast at Small's Paradise Club in Harlem. Douglas introduced us to the famed basketball player, Wilt Chamberlain. Then we had an early morning breakfast of waffles and chicken at Well's Restaurant. Later that morning we went sightseeing in midtown Manhattan. Finally, we caught a Broadway matinee of *In White America*, a play about the abuse heaped by white citizens of Little Rock, Arkansas, upon the nine Negro students who were pioneering in school desegregation.

The following day, we drove back to Inkster.

There was no need to share my New York City adventures with my brother. He had made it clear that he did not value the experiences, let alone the thoughts of single college women. And for married women to take a weekend trip with single women was beyond his comprehension. He dismissed their husbands as wimps who had no control over their wives.

SOON AFTER RETURNING to Inkster, I telephoned my father's home and got Lois. Her curt response when she answered made it clear that she was not interested in conversation. Neither Daddy nor Sandy were at home, so it was a short phone call.

Still, I concentrated my thoughts on my half-siblings. Children should not be separated from each other because of the sins of their parents. As my baby sister, Sandy was special to me. I had seen such talent in her when she was a little girl. I learned she was working in a dentist's office and reflected that my father never would have permitted me to have a job as a teenager. I had not seen my brother Frank since he was a little over one year old. Now, he was four. I never laid eyes on my baby brother Jeff.

Daddy came by Bob's that afternoon after work. He had a 9 to 5 shift with his union office and secretary as the elected committeeman for grievances at Ford's River Rouge plant. His sense of worth came from workers in his shop and union officials who held him in high esteem. He had no value in his own home where Lois ruled. He had no say-so in rearing his children.

I told him I had decided to leave the next day instead of on the coming weekend, that it was best that I get back to Montgomery. He nodded with understanding and agreement and told me he would pick me up at 6 p.m. so we could have dinner in the station before I boarded the 9 p.m. train.

And so he did. After checking my luggage, we went to the station restaurant and dived into our food—smothered liver and onions—and serious discussion.

He said he would leave Lois if not for his sons, but he dodged my question about how much real influence he could have on them given how Lois ran the household. As for Sandy, he said he had no influence on her. "She's just sixteen and is going with a guy older than you. He hangs out on Harrison Road with me. It's clear that he respects me. I don't know what he does for a living, but he keeps plenty of money and drives a 'Deuce and a Quarter'"—that was slang for the must-have Buick 225 in the black community in that era—"and when he is out of town, Sandy keeps his car. Lois has no problem letting Sandy drive her around to go shopping and to do other errands in the car."

I shook my head in disbelief.

"I want you to continue to love your sister," Daddy implored. "She is a stone Patton, and that gives me hope that she will eventually land on her feet. My prayer is that she will come to Montgomery to be with you and the family. She wants to go to college. Maybe she'll choose Tuskegee."

I replied, "She doesn't have to wait to go to college. What about her visiting her grandparents? By the time I was her age, I had been to Montgomery more than sixteen times."

"Lois will never permit it. She is bent on poisoning the kids' mind that the Pattons are of no substance. Of course, she knows better. She's a jealous-hearted woman. And she is especially jealous of you."

There seemed little more to say about my Detroit family's home life. Our talk turned to my stay in the sanitarium, the fun I was having in college, the possibility of falling in love with Jerry, and the progress of the civil/voting rights movement. We talked about family and Montgomery. He wanted to know every detail about his favorite haunts; he had not been in Montgomery since Mama died in 1958.

"Gordon's Patio will stand forever. Uralee is always asking about you." Uralee Gordon was my father's best friend in Montgomery. He built, practically with his own hands, Gordon's Patio Club with beautiful ceramic tiles. The high walls surrounding the patio, some of the umbrella-covered tables, the floor and the dance floor with a large "G" in the center were covered with colorful tiles. His work of folk art was a cultural icon in the city. Adjacent to the Patio was the best shoeshine parlor with six high chairs and stirrups on a tiered platform. Uralee and his staff of spit-shine polishers were known on both sides of the Mississippi River. White and Negro tourists made it part of their Montgomery itinerary to see the radiant ceramic tiles and to have their shoes shined.

I told him that Squirrel, Hiawatha 's middle son, was continuing the business at the shoe store. He had expanded its merchandise to include the best of men's suits and hats. Squirrel was a genius with numbers. By day he was a popular math teacher. By night, he ran a successful business and a gambling operation.

My father smiled at that news. I was certain that visions of his youthful, foolhardy days came to his mind. Slipping out at night and going across the street, my father cut his gambling teeth in the back of Hiawatha's Shoe Store, shooting craps with the big boys in the late 1930s.

(Sadly, I was wrong about the permanence of Gordon's Patio. In the 1990s, the expansion of adjacent Alabama State University swallowed up the property; Uralee's carefully laid ceramic tiles, the colorful neon lights, and the silver-painted tree trunks in the open-air patio—it was all demolished to make way for new academic buildings.)

We still had some time before my train boarded.

"Now, let's talk about Bob. I find him very disturbing," I said.

My father looked out in the distance. "Bob has seen me at my lowest. Thank God, you had left and gone to Montgomery." He turned, looked sincerely in my eyes, his left hand on his forehead.

"Daddy, he is just nineteen years old! He acts like an old, old man!"

"I know. He's always been peculiar. He's more like your Mama and your Mommy and their side of the family."

I thought about that for a moment. Several relatives came to mind who, when they spoke, were short and to the point.

"You must love your brother as he is. I know he and I will have a tough time. I have done much to let him down after your mama died. And, then I had to marry Lois. I was in total turmoil. I plumb forgot Bob's high school graduation. I was on Harrison Road, gambling, trying to make some money. He will never forgive me for that. I promised God that I will do everything I can to make it up to your brother and to you."

Tears welled in my father's eyes. I leaned over, kissed him on his cheek, and wiped away his tears with my napkin.

"Daddy, I forgave you when Mr. Russell's car pulled out of the driveway on Henry Street. You were in an abyss and trying to do the best you could. I love you and will always love you. You are a good father."

My father sighed, composed himself and leaned back in his chair.

I told him I was still worried about Bob and didn't think I could stay with him on my future visits because of his intolerable disdain for college women. "He called me an 'educated fool' and said I didn't know how to boil water."

"I know your brother can be insulting. It's his way of fighting back. What he is fighting, I don't know. I know his words can be hurtful, but try to throw them off. Your brother loves you."

Soon the loudspeaker announced that my train was boarding. My father paid the restaurant bill, and we walked hand-in-hand to the train. He gave me money for the trip—it was 1964; thanks to the mighty struggle of our people we no longer had to pack shoebox meals but could eat in any dining car we desired and sit in any car we chose—and reminded me to keep my purse close to my body.

As the train slowly began to move out of the station, Daddy stood on the platform adjacent to my window. We blew kisses and waved at each other. We were crying tears of joy for our reunion.

The reverse of my spending three summer months in Inkster as I did in Montgomery could never be. Montgomery transplants, especially their first-generation children born in Detroit, transformed into cold beings like the harsh Michigan winters. Their air of northern coldness communicated a disdain of southern warmth that was generated by family and friends embracing each other. To use a southern expression: "Every tub has to stand on its own bottom." My brother epitomized this mandate. However, in Montgomery if your tub had a leak, family and friends would come to your aid to help you plug the leak, or take up a collection to buy you a new tub. There seem to be a disconnect in connecting independence with dependence with inter-dependence. I wrestled with these thoughts

This hope motivated me to visit with my brother and his family at least once a year. I could withstand the insults because I knew, regardless of the number of years it would take, that my brother would eventually pour out his love for family and friends. He would surely replace somebody's "leaking tub."

I WAS GLAD that I shortened my vacation in Inkster. It was clear that Montgomery was my true home in mind, heart, soul and spirit. As always, my cousin Carnell picked me up at the train station and drove me home. Poppa Washington and Mommy were glad to see me. Mommy sensed, yet she said nothing, that my visit with my brother and his family had been disturbing and disruptive.

I was soon settled and happy to be back in the family groove. As Mommy puttered around the kitchen making fruit preserves, I saw that my brother had inherited some of her quick-motion mannerisms and other traits.

Mommy was a lady of few words, and when she spoke, the words were always wise. I remembered what she said after the success of the Montgomery

Bus Boycott when I challenged her continuing to sit in the back of the bus: "The Montgomery Bus Boycott was not about sitting next to white people. It was about sitting anywhere you please."

In conversation with my brother about materialism, conspicuous consumption, and false status symbols, he said impatiently, "If we as workers make Cadillacs, why can't we own and drive them!"

Yes, Daddy was right. Bob and Mommy were much alike in their outlook on life. Bob at this juncture had not inculcated pleasantness and grace in his demeanor as Mommy had. But I had faith that, in due time, these "Mommy" traits would manifest in my brother.

Preserving figs as a topping for toast or as a side dessert dish was a Southern Negro tradition. Fig leaves covered the bodies of Adam and Eve when they disobeyed God in the Garden of Eden. Figs were food staples for Jesus and throughout the generations, all the way down to Mommy. Coming home early from my Inkster vacation had given me the respite to be with her and for her to show me how to continue the tradition.

I carefully poured green figs from my apron into the sink. I set the washed figs on paper towels to dry. After about an hour, Mommy laid the figs in a large pot. She sprinkled sugar on the first layer. Then she laid another layer of figs, sprinkled sugar, and so on until the pot was half-filled. After the juice from the figs absorbed the sugar and had sunk to the bottom of the pot to make syrup, she cooked the green figs under a low flame on the kerosene stove until they turned a deep-brown color. We then scooped the figs and syrup into Mason jars and tightly sealed the tops with red-rubber rings and caps to preserve the freshness. Placed then on the pantry shelves, the preserved figs would be a Thanksgiving delicacy for our Northern family members who motored down for the festive holiday.

JERRY HAD WRITTEN me while I was in Inkster. He was in the Maxwell Air Force Base stockade for going AWOL (absent without leave), a serious infraction in the military. His letter asked me to visit him.

The ride from my grandparents' home to the base in a taxi was unexpectedly short. I had never been on an air force base, let alone in its prison complex. I followed Jerry's instructions not to bring a purse and to bring in my pockets money I needed for taxi fares and a piece of identification.

I was escorted with a military guard to a cell door. The guard unlocked the door, and I was let into a large room with rectangular tables and chairs. Vending machines lined a wall. Women and children were sitting at the tables, visiting their imprisoned loved ones.

Jerry, dressed in pocket-less khakis and a white button-down shirt, was standing at the far entrance that led back to what I learned was the "lock-up." He smiled when I entered. Though I was bewildered, I caught his smile and suddenly relaxed. He started walking to an empty table and I met his steps. As we came face-to-face across the table, I leaned over to kiss him. Immediately, a guard touched me on the shoulder, and said in a pleasant tone, "Signs of affection are prohibited."

I asked Jerry how long would he be in prison.

"Probably three months. I first have to be court-martialed. Then I'll receive a BCD, a bad-conduct-discharge."

"What does that mean?"

"I'll lose all military benefits. I will never be able to make a living anywhere in the South. This region loves soldiers and wars. Doesn't matter who's right or wrong. Southerners just love to fight."

"Well, what are you going to do after your discharge?"

"I'm going to New York City. I have countrymen there."

I told him how proud I was of him in his refusal to go to Vietnam. I was adamantly opposed to the U.S. presence in that country, which I knew would lead to a full-scale war. Civil wars ought to be fought by indigenous people, just as the American Civil War was fought by soldiers from the North and the South. No foreign troops were on U.S. soil to settle the dispute between slave and free labor. Now, almost one hundred years later, capitalists were bent on sacrificing American citizen-soldiers to fight and die on foreign soil for hegemony, greed, and to exploit the foreign labor force with near-slavery wages to maximize profits by any means necessary.

"Don't worry about coming back out here," Jerry said. Looking me directly in the eyes, I felt his warm hand on my thigh. I slipped my hand under the table and covered his hand with mine. He gently embraced my hand. The tenderness was more powerful than a kiss.

"I'll write you once a week. We've been separated before and our love for each other grew stronger. It will grow even more stronger. Okay?"

I nodded my head in agreement.

"While we weather this separation, I want you to stay out of bad weather. Stay strong. Make all A's in your classes. We'll be together soon. *Yo amo tu.*"

He squeezed my hand again under the table. I left the prison, feeling secure in Jerry's love.

12

Movement on the Rise

SNCC organizers flooded the campus in the fall of 1964. They were still trying to overcome the disheartening betrayal—believed to have been orchestrated by Allard K. Lowenstein, later a U.S. congressman out of New York City—of the Mississippi Freedom Democratic Party at the Democratic National Convention in Atlantic City.

Lowenstein, incidentally, is an interesting footnote in SNCC history. James Forman had been suspicious of him since 1956, when he blamed Lowenstein for defeating certain platform planks at that year's National Student Association convention. In 1963, Lowenstein appointed himself a recruiter of white students from Yale and Stanford to SNCC's forthcoming Mississippi Summer project. Lowenstein did not go to Mississippi himself, but his white recruits there often opposed Forman's and Bob Moses's strategy and tactics. Then, at the 1964 DNC convention, Lowenstein sided with the "compromise" contingent in offering Mississippi Freedom Democratic Party members only two "delegate-at-large" seats rather than substituting the MFDP for the entire fraudulently elected Mississippi regular-party delegation. At a subsequent NYC conference to evaluate the Mississippi Challenge, Lowenstein argued that SNCC should be contained or removed from the Mississippi movement, validating Forman's suspicion of him as a destructive force and a SNCC nemesis. Yet Lowenstein continued to pop up like a bad penny wherever SNCC had a presence, including in 1967 when a SNCC delegation was invited to Dar es Salaam as guests of the newly formed independent government of Tanzania.

In 1964, however, Tuskegee Institute offered SNCC activists a refuge for reflection as students boldly argued with administrators to allow organizers to live on- and off-campus and to have meals in Thompkins Hall. The fact that Tuskegee students in the 1920s had made the bricks and built the dining hall conveyed a poignant righteousness to our demands.

SNCC Mississippians Willie Peacock and C. J. Jones registered for courses as full-time students. Bernard and Colia Lafayette departed to return to work as full-time SNCC organizers in Selma and Dallas County. SNCC phenomenon Stokely Carmichael made his debut on campus and wowed the students into action. His thrust was always for the vote to gain power so we as a people could make political decisions about our lives and our future. Courtland Cox, in his flowing cape, penetrated our minds with the undergirding philosophy as to why we felt compelled to fight for our freedom. William "Winky" Hall was our movement counselor with whom we could confide and discuss our differences with SNCC. Jean Wiley, a new instructor and a Woodrow Wilson Fellow, was our big sister who conveyed to the administration and faculty councils our student aspirations of having the freedom movement included as a core curriculum across the disciplines. Such inclusion, we asserted, would make our education more relevant. After all, we were not in college to land a job but to hone our skills, deepen our insights, and broaden our perspective for lifelong service to our community. Jean met hostile reaction from administrators. They assumed that a Wilson Fellow would be an advocate of the gradualism approach to attaining constitutional rights for Negro citizens. The administrators gave her pure hell and did all they could to derail her professional career.

I WAS AGAIN assigned to the honors' dorm without a roommate. This arrangement pleased me. I discovered that despite my extroverted demeanor I was really a loner. I valued solitude to read, study, reflect, and write. A roommate would have been an annoyance.

Two underclassmen stand out in my mind: Michael Wright and Ruby Nell Sales. Both were sixteen when they enrolled. Both were precocious and budding scholars. Michael was the son of Sarah Wright, author of the novel, *This Child's Gonna Live*, and the nephew of author Richard Wright. Michael immediately shed his collegiate sports jacket and soft leather loafers for the SNCC uniform of overalls, denim jacket, and brogans. He had every movement button pinned to the bib of his overalls. We called him "Super SNICK." Ruby was the daughter of loving and protective parents who sent her to prestigious church schools during her formative years. Ruby soon exchanged her pleated skirts, matching cardigan sweater sets, and high heels for SNCC overalls and marching shoes.

Tuskegee's enrollment increased from 1,900 to 2,300. Some of the increase was due to the student-exchange program of white students from the University of Michigan and St. Olaf College in Northfield, Minnesota.

An influx of professors, also mainly white, was added to accommodate the increased enrollment. Dr. Richard Wasserstrom from the University of Michigan became dean of Arts and Sciences. This school of liberal arts became the incubator for thoughtful classroom discussions on what freedom is and who should have the right to it. Dr. Eric Krystal, a white South African exiled because of his anti-apartheid activism, shared with us in his classroom and home his experiences, using documentary films about the terror and horrors of state-controlled international racism. Jim Crow in the American South was the first cousin to apartheid in South Africa. Maggie Magee was a close friend to Jean Wiley. One day when I went to visit with Maggie, I was surprised to see her straightening her hair with a heated straightening-comb just like the one that black women used. Gone was the myth that all white women were born with straight, fly-away hair. Rounding out the progressive circle of white faculty was Leslie Sherover; with her dark hair usually pulled in a long ponytail, she reminded me of the 1950s' Detroit beatniks who always wore black, played bongos, and talked in rhyme and poetry about social issues.

I liked the white instructors, but I was determined to gather my formal learning at the feet of black professors. I was still smarting from the white high school teacher who had called me a "gold dust twin." Racism, like a phantom, eludes white people, even the best-intentioned white people who consciously struggle with their racism, especially when they are in the presence of conscious, movement-driven black people.

I had several favorite black professors. Dr. Jimmy Henderson, our lead biology lecturer, was a "race man" on and off campus. Mrs. Norma Gaillard, my physical science teacher, saw her spunkiness in me. On several occasions she asked me to come to the high-rise teaching podium to explain principles and concepts before my two hundred fellow students in this huge class. Dr. Stanley Smith, a magnificent lecturer, often deviated from the core concepts in his "Marriage and the Family" course to debunk de Gobineau's theory of the inherent inferiority of the Negro. Dr. John Eubanks, my philosophy teacher, taught Hegel and encouraged us to read Marx, Plekanov, Kiergergaard, Neibur, Thurman, Parento and other philosophers who were on and off his required reading list. Professor Frank Toland mesmerized his history class by lecturing from notes that he would pull from his pockets while standing with one foot in a chair. There was no required text. Thus, we had to take enough notes to fill a textbook to pass his tests. Dr. Joseph Fuller was a legend. Legend had it that students once stole his final mathematics exam and everyone aced his test. From that day forward, Dr. Fuller had a mimeograph machine and portable typewriter in his classroom. On the day for an exam, he typed the questions, which he had sequestered in his mind, onto stencils and mimeographed the day's exam on the spot.

My favorite professors were Dr. Saunders Walker and his wife, Emma. They taught English and English and American literature. Both were brilliant lecturers. Dr. Walker always stood with an opened book in his hand. Mrs. Walker always sat and asked probative questions in our American and English novel and poetry classes. Dr. Walker was a natty dresser. He was not satisfied with our mastery of Chaucer and Shakespeare—he was bent on our becoming "cultured students." I do not think his desire was from a class-structure analysis. He was more about cultivating "refined" demeanor in his students, both in mannerisms and expressions.

THE EXPANSION OF enrollment and the bringing in of new faculty had not come without struggle. To expand the already diverse faculty of blacks, whites,

Western and Eastern Europeans, Asians, and black and white Africans in nine degree-granting schools, President Foster had embarked on a faculty exchange program, also with the University of Michigan. Several professors and instructors, most of them white, joined the Tuskegee faculty in September 1964. Huntingdon Hall, the education building, was renovated to accommodate offices for the new faculty, half of whom were teaching freshmen courses and the other half were teaching political science courses, laying the foundation for a pre-law curriculum. There were ruffled feathers when Dr. Richard Wasserstrom, white, was appointed dean of Arts and Sciences. The chair of Literature and Languages, Dr. Saunders Walker, had to vacate his commodious office to make room for the new dean.

Meanwhile, movement activity was escalating on campus, with more and more students joining consciousness-raising sessions and volunteering to teach in citizenship schools in the outlying, rural Macon County communities. The tension was palpable between the old-guard black professors, who had nurtured thousands of students to make their mark on the world, and the new guard of mainly white professors, who demonstrably supported the movement-driven students.

TIAL had adapted the MIA model of holding motivational mass meetings/rallies on one night and then movement assessment/planning meetings on another night. At one of the planning meetings, the black-white faculty issue dominated discussion. Movement strength and unity demanded a resolution, so it was decided that TIAL would call a gathering of faculty and students to air the issue. As TIAL's direct action chair, I was assigned "to make it happen."

The direct action committee got permission to hold the gathering in the neutral domain of the Student Center Ballroom in lieu of any faculty office or home. Professors sat in a central circle, one black, the next one white, and so on. Students sat in outer concentric circles. That seating arrangement broke the hierarchal rank of deans, chairs, professors, and instructors—everybody was equal.

Facilitating the meeting, I put forth the challenge: How do black and white professors work together in mutual respect to engage students to continue the mission to realize human dignity and freedom for all peoples, i.e, the movement? The discussion was lively, frank, and honest. I wish we had recorded it.

As THE FALL went along, I wanted to return to cheerleading, if I had the time and the stamina. At our first exhibition basketball game of the year, I made my return to cheer the Golden Tigers. My classmates rose to their feet and chanted, "Go, Gwen, Go!" Tears of joy met the broad smile on my lips at this assurance that I was welcomed back into my collegiate family after having overcome tuberculosis.

I settled into a routine of classes and movement work. The two had not yet melded at Tuskegee. We still had a distance to go to make education relevant to serve our people and not simply to prepare us to do the bidding of racist America as white-approved tokens to advance a society that was hostile to the masses. The risk was in training a potential black elite to be the new overseers and neo-colonialists. This cycle of personal success, at the expense of destroying our people, our family and friends, had to be stopped. I had come to fear that higher education closed as many doors as it opened. This disturbing contradiction preoccupied my mind and emotions.

Twice a week I traveled ten miles from Tuskegee Institute to the Macon County community of Little Texas to conduct citizenship classes. The country people there wanted desperately to become registered voters. Passing the literacy test, which a political science major would find difficult, was the prerequisite racist barrier. These humble, God-fearing people could barely read and write, but they knew within their hearts that they had a claim to be a part of a government that proclaimed to be "of, by and for the people." I spent a lot of our time tutoring classes on learning and reciting portions of the state and U.S. constitutions. The people's memorization skills were remarkable. The highlight of the sessions, after teaching the alphabet, using phonics, and the spelling of one-syllable words, was for my people to write their own names, replacing the "X" that had signified their invisible and discounted humanity.

Sammy Younge Jr. drove me to and from Little Texas in his souped-up, powder-blue Volkswagen. I always wore Sunday outfits with heels. Sammy always wore his badge-of-courage outfit of overalls with white shirt and wide tie under the bib of his overalls. Sammy, who had attended prep school in the Northeast and then been in the Navy, was a solid member of Tuskegee Institute's middle-class, educated elite. He was lighter than many white people with his blue veins prominently exposed through his ivory skin. His hair was a ringlet of curls. He looked like a Greek god.

MEANWHILE, THERE WAS also campus social life. I was elated when Delta Sigma Theta Sorority rushed me. Since my childhood this sorority had been my choice of sisterhood. The fact that black women in 1913 founded a sorority based on service and social action and then joined the picket lines for women's suffrage resonated with my spirit. I had learned much about Dr. Mary McLeod Bethune, a revered Delta, in my sixth-grade class from my teacher, Mrs. Frances Webb, also a Delta. I wanted to continue the legacy of Soror Bethune, who charged us to lift as we climb.

I enjoyed the rush parties and the get-acquainted gatherings of "Big Sisters" and pledgees. Too soon I became disappointed at my one-on-one interviews with my Big Sister. I wondered if the Tuskegee coed sisters understood the same Delta principles of respect and integrity that I had learned from Mrs. Webb. After the interviews, I was still a pledgee, but I had yet to make the next stage to be a "duck."

Odetta, the renowned folk singer who upheld the legacy of Paul Robeson in lifting up the plight of black people in racist America, was to be in concert on campus. I knew that "Bucky" Buchannan, the Little Theatre director, had made her performance possible. Some months earlier Buchannan had sponsored Pete Seeger, the acclaimed union and folk singer. Seeger was a rave with white college students, but he was not a hit on black campuses. Bucky had talked to me about the dismal turnout of students for Seeger. I suggested that he invite Odetta whose Birmingham roots and black rhythms would resonate with our students.

As I entered Logan Hall for the Odetta concert, I noticed that the Deltas and Pyramids had on black dresses, heels, pearl necklaces, and earrings. I did not remember getting a memo on the dress requirement, and if I did, I probably ignored it. I was going to a folk concert. I dressed appropriately with loose-fitting plaid skirt, fringed at the hem, coordinating cardigan sweater set, stylish black knee socks, and hush puppies.

Odetta rocked the standing-room-only audience. When she started singing "Take this hammer and take it to the captain" and called students to come onstage, I was one of the first to leap out of my seat.

The following day, Big Sister summoned me.

"Gwen, you did not follow the dress code for the concert last evening," she said with disgust. "This is your second meeting to discuss, first, your attitude, and now, your behavior."

I searched her face for a sign of reasonableness. "Big Sister, I am obliged to say that I was the only one dressed appropriately. You, the other Big Sisters and pledges were out of place. When I looked about me on the stage, I did not see any of you. You don't wear corsets, girdles, and garter belts to folk concerts."

I aced my community service project. Big Sister accepted my already committed work as a reader for Solomon Greene, a blind and super-smart political science major. My work with Solomon prompted a prominent Tuskegee family to ask me to work with their blind son. I took great joy in gluing toothpicks on paper in shapes of triangles, squares, pentagons, octagons and the like for him to feel so he could visualize in his mind the shapes based on the number of sides.

For awhile my pledging continued without incident. But I continued to chafe at the pledgee requirements. Jewel, a pledgee, always had swollen lips. I asked if she was suffering with a medical complaint. She responded, "Wait until you advance to the 'laughing brush.'" I was dumbfounded by her reply.

When Big Sister asked to borrow my portable typewriter, I gladly obliged. Then Christmas season was quickly approaching, the time for final exams and papers due before the holiday break. I told her, "Big Sister, I need my typewriter." She said, "Oh, I loaned it to Kay. She lives in White Hall. You can go to her dorm and get it."

That did not sit well with me. I had not loaned my typewriter to Kay. Nevertheless, I went to White Hall. Kay, a member of another sorority, was out singing Christmas carols, in French, in an 87 percent black community. I was outraged. I went to the oval balcony of the top floor that overlooked the ground floor lobby and shouted to all who might hear to tell Kay to return my typewriter to my dorm.

Of course my righteous request was viewed as a belligerent demand by Big Sister. Eventually, probably inevitably, Big Sister said, "Gwen, we are taking you off the line." I nodded my head to register mutual agreement. That was okay with me. I was done with the childish antics.

The experience did not dampen my spirit to become a Delta. I simply had to be patient in finding the right chapter, one which upheld the mission of the sisterhood above the need of sisters who suffered with the "I've got the power syndrome."

The news that I was "de-lined" from Delta prompted a contingent of coeds to join the effort to establish a campus chapter of Gamma Sigma Sigma. After being convinced that this sorority was exclusively dedicated to community service and that there were no hazing activities, I readily agreed. At the founding initiation meeting, I was elected parliamentarian.

I SPENT THE Christmas holiday with my grandparents. Jerry wrote and called from New York City. He had landed a factory job in Brooklyn and was on probationary status. It was not wise at this time for him to take leave. He did not want me to come to New York City. The weather was brutally cold. He reminded me that we had weathered absences before and that he would send for me to visit with him during spring break.

I hosted two parties and served Mommy's famous homemade plum sherry. Lama Alford, a Morehouse student, was always the life of the party. He played a mean gospel piano and had a strong voice we just knew was heard in Third Heaven. Lamar was destined to find his way to Broadway. He was the son of the Reverend W. F. Alford, pastor of Beulah Baptist Church, one of our prominent movement centers during the Montgomery Bus Boycott. I was close to the Alford family and had been a bridesmaid in the wedding of Lamar's sister, Stella, also a student at Tuskegee Institute.

My friends, home from college, gathered at my parties. We talked about movement activities on our respective campuses. Black colleges from Howard University southward were on fire in the fight for freedom. Some friends had even been jailed for movement activity. As we shared our reports and analyses, we concluded that 1965 was fated to be a banner year in our "struggle," the new term that replaced the word "movement."

The civil rights anthem for college students became "Freedom is a Constant Struggle." Its key words meant that the fight for freedom will be a human condition forever; thus, you had to pledge a lifelong commitment to attain, maintain, and sustain freedom. The fundamental question—to borrow from Courtland Cox—was in which venue you choose to wage the freedom struggle. One camp ardently argued that we had to have a permanent cadre of "freedom high freedom fighters." If you did not unconditionally join this camp, you were somehow a "back-slider, a sell-out" and were off the freedom train track.

I wrestled with this position. What is the nature of a cadre? How will this cadre sustain itself? Will it give rise to vanguardism? What is the difference between vanguardism and elitism?

13

Marching and Demonstrating

Back on campus after the holidays, registration lines choked Logan Hall; the bookstore was no different. I congratulated myself for having had the foresight to preregister for spring classes and buy my books before leaving for Christmas.

After a hectic first week of 1965, our small Tuskegee Institute Advancement League issued a campus-wide invitation. About a hundred students heeded TIAL's call. Most notable in the contingent were Jimmy Rogers, Gene Chenault, Joseph Pequease, Warren Hamilton, "Pinky" LeBlanc, Eldridge Burns, "Duke" Barnett, Simuel Schutz, Lenard Huntley, Demetris "Red" Robinson, Lee (a white brother from nearby Auburn), Jennifer Lawson, Laura Payton, Ann Pratt, Ann Anthony, Ruby Taylor, Aufait Williams, Elizabeth Hayes, Betty Gamble, and drop-dead gorgeous George Davis who had transferred from Brown University to be where the action was hot. In his thick Boston brogue he said, "I know Alabama whites are in the main murderous rabid racists, but I feel safe and secure knowing that Alabama blacks are more dangerous."

George Ware assumed the chair of TIAL; I was again chosen as direct action chair.

George lived off campus with two veterinary majors, Ernest "Trap" Stevens and George "Sneaky" Copper. The inner circle of TIAL had hilarious fun in their apartment. The ceiling was covered with black footprints—George had wet his feet in black paint and Trap and Sneaky held him upside down as he walked across the ceiling. They made a very good collegiate version of white lightning. Jazz was the only permitted music; Miles Davis's "Sketches of Spain," Coltrane's "These are Some of My Favorite Things," and Donald Byrd's "New Perspective" were favorites. George and I proselytized about jazz being the only true U.S.-born classical music, a gift from black Americans to racist America. My mother's insistence that I learn and appreciate music had not been for naught. Later, George Davis added Bob Dylan to our play list.

Our freedom activities continued with sit-ins, wade-ins at public pools, filling out job applications, teach-ins, citizenship schools, and taking county people to the registrar's office on the designated days—only to find that the registrar was "out to lunch" for the remainder of the day.

HERMAN JAMES FROM New York City was president of the Institute Council (student body). He had invited Malcolm X to speak in early February at one of our mandatory mid-week vespers. Students often grumbled about being required to attend ballet performances, classical piano recitals, and chamber music concerts. But there were no grumbles with Malcolm X coming to town. Logan Hall could not hold the crowd. Many community people were outside with the hope of just getting a glance of this magnificent warrior who championed our cause with simple and unflinching words. Malcolm X had recently returned from Mecca, where he had witnessed black Muslims and blue-eyed white Muslims worshipping together. As he reassessed his views on race, he also revisited his nonsupport of the civil rights movement.

"It's the ballot or the bullet!" he exhorted to thunderous applause. "If the racists touch one nappy hair on the head of Dr. Martin Luther King Jr., then they will have to deal with me!"

The audience was electrified. Malcolm's presentation was the long-awaited olive branch for his organization to join forces with the civil rights movement. Because of him, I broadened my awareness of our struggle to embrace an international perspective. The following day Malcolm X journeyed to Selma, where Dr. King was then jailed, to meet with the Selma movement, especially with the children. Less than three weeks later, Malcolm was dead. We had feared he would be murdered by racist whites if he stayed in the South, only then to be shocked and saddened when he was assassinated by blacks in the North.

Malcolm X's visit and the students' heartfelt response motivated Doris Mitchell, a veterinarian and daughter of physician Joseph Mitchell, to offer her family home in rural Macon County as a TIAL retreat for reflective-thinking and a refuge for rest and relaxation as our struggle for freedom escalated.

Meanwhile, Institute Council President Herman James was content with having invited Malcolm X to campus, but radicals demanded more from our student government association. To us, hearing Malcolm X was not an ending, but a beginning to advance the struggle.

ON FEBRUARY 18, 1965, Jimmy Lee Jackson was shot by a state trooper in Marion, county seat of Perry County, west of Selma in Alabama's Black Belt. The unarmed Jackson was attempting to protect his mother and grandfather at a nighttime demonstration for black voting rights after police, deputies, and state troopers attacked the marchers. Jackson was shot by trooper James Bonard Fowler and died of his wounds eight days later.

In Birmingham, at the motel owned by black millionaire A. G. Gaston, SCLC and SNCC held meetings to plan a joint demonstration that would protest Jackson's murder and petition for black voting rights. The tactic they settled on was a march from Selma to the State Capitol in Montgomery to deliver the petition to Governor George Wallace. Thanks to the invitation of Jim Forman of SNCC, George Ware, myself, and other TIAL members were able to participate in the strategy meetings.

The march from Selma was to start on March 7 and culminate in Montgomery on March 10. There the marchers from the western Black

Belt would be met by a similar group that would march from Tuskegee in the eastern Black Belt.

The Black Belt was and is important. It comprised a dozen or more counties across central Alabama and took its name from its rich, dark soil that was excellent for growing cotton. That is why the wealthy white planters moved there in the early 1800s. Thus, that is why there were so many black people in these counties, because they had been brought there as slaves to produce the white planters' wealth. And, really, to *be* the white planters' wealth. After emancipation, the majority of the ex-slaves had no place else to go and no resources to go anywhere with. So they stayed as sharecroppers, tenant farmers, and wage hands.

The populations of most of the Black Belt counties were more than 75 percent black. Yet, two of these counties had not a single registered black voter as late as 1961. Selma, Montgomery, and Tuskegee were all in the Black Belt, as was Marion where Jimmy Lee Jackson was murdered.

Marion, moreover, was interesting for a couple of other reasons. Even though it is a small town, it had been an early seat of education in Alabama and even today has two historically white colleges. And it was in Marion that what is today Alabama State University, the HBCU in Montgomery, was founded in 1867; it moved to Montgomery in 1887.

Lastly, Marion has a special if odd role in civil rights history in that Coretta Scott, Juanita Jones, and Jean Childs grew up in or around Marion. These three young black women would become, respectively, the wives of Martin Luther King Jr., Ralph D. Abernathy, and Andrew Young, marriages which all took place before the husbands became forever linked through the civil rights movement.

So Marion and the entire Black Belt had the weight of history, large black populations, great wealth juxtaposed against crushing poverty, and significant native citizens. What it did not have was black voters and equal rights under the law. Is it any wonder that the Alabama Black Belt played such a large role in the freedom struggle?

A CALL WAS issued for hundreds of people from Tuskegee to march. When we returned to campus, George Ware immediately went to Herman James to elicit his support and the resources of the student government association. But James was a frat man, not a movement man, and he balked. As Herman had abdicated his responsibility, not only to the student body, but to our people as a whole, George without hesitation took over the Institute Council's office. It became the staging area to raise money to rent buses and to encourage people with cars to join our movement pilgrimage to Montgomery. The Council office had a telephone with long-distance privileges. Sammy Younge Jr. was one of our chief fundraisers. He telephoned many of his rich former classmates from Cornwall Academy and asked them for donations and for them to come down to the march to witness how their money was being used and to see freedom fighting in action. Sammy organized a brigade of fundraisers with buckets to collect money from motorists when they stopped at the traffic light on Campus Avenue, the main street from campus to the black middle-class enclaves.

By early March, TIAL was poised to lead at least 1,500 people to honor the commitment to have an eastern Black Belt contingent at the State Capitol on March 10, 1965.

But then Bloody Sunday happened in Selma on March 7. Whether in the dorms, the student center, or at our instructors' or friends' homes and apartments, our eyes were glued to the early evening news on television. Some SNCC organizers who had been in Selma that morning to be a part of the kick-off of the Selma-to-Montgomery Voting Rights March returned to campus and told us about the state troopers' onslaught. Their verbal reports were amplified as we watched the malicious attacks on our people—many in their Sunday clothes—as they walked to the foot of Selma's Edmund Pettus Bridge. State, county, and local police on foot and a sheriff's posse on horseback hurled teargas canisters, wielded cattle prods, billy clubs and guns, and generally ran amuck, demonstrating their racist depravity by brutally beating our people back across the bridge into downtown Selma. It was a horrific sight, evoking the images of the 1963 Birmingham police riot and their hateful use of fire hoses and dogs in a futile effort to stem the tide of our freedom movement.

The next day, Tuskegee Institute's administration issued an edict that students could not participate in our March 10 caravan-march to Montgomery. President Luther Foster invoked the doctrine of *in loco parentis*. We countered with arguments that eighteen-year-olds were drafted into the military without parental consent, let alone consent from surrogate parents. Some students called their parents, who wired telegrams that their children could participate. Other students feared that their parents, who were schoolteachers and held state jobs, might face reprisals. A great many students were twenty-one, like me, and did not need permission.

On the evening of Tuesday, March 9, the day before we were to go to the State Capitol, the administration circulated at least two thousand copies of U.S. District Judge Frank M. Johnson Jr.'s injunction that prohibited any marches to Montgomery pending a hearing. Now we understood, to our dismay, why a second attempt to march in Selma on the morning of March 9 had "turned around" and returned to its church headquarters; Dr. King was reluctant at that point to violate an injunction from a federal court that had up to this point largely supported civil rights issues.

However, after our TIAL meeting, we were determined to proceed with a march that wouldn't turn around. It was important to us that we dictate our own terms in our fight for freedom. It was an insult to our dignity to seek sanctions outside of ourselves.

Later that evening, we learned from Tippy Jackson, a Macon County grassroots community leader and ham radio operator, that the Reverends James Reeb, Orloff Miller, and Clark Olsen had been brutally beaten by whites in Selma. The three Unitarian Universalist ministers had answered the call from Dr. Martin Luther Jr. to join the demonstrations in Selma and had barely gotten there before being assaulted on leaving a cafe. We were saddened by this news and realized anew how dangerous the struggle for freedom could be when white folks began to beat up other white folks. Reeb would die from his injuries two days later.

Wednesday, March 10, was a "great getting-up morning!" Unbeknownst to us student activists, the greater Macon County community was prepared to join in our caravan-march. More than fifteen hundred students, faculty, and community people assembled at Thompkins Hall. An encouraging number of private cars was there to join our caravan of several buses. The administration, having been unable to daunt our freedom fervor, relented and provided sack lunches of bologna sandwiches, apples, and juices for our pilgrimage.

During our slow ride to Montgomery, some students got out of cars to walk a distance and then were picked up by cars further down the line. A relay-marching contingent became a steady presence. We were determined that the eastern Black Belt march to the Capitol be a true complement to the western Black Belt march to the Capitol. I will be forever indebted to my cousin, Lenard Huntley, who organized the community "marching contingent."

We arrived at Montgomery's First Baptist Church about 9 A.M. As described earlier, this was the famed church pastored by the Reverend Ralph D. Abernathy during the 1955–56 Montgomery Bus Boycott. First Baptist was the appropriate site from which to start our march to the State Capitol to petition for our voting rights and to register our demand for first-class citizenship.

Someone who assumed a position of authority said we did not have a march permit, as if that mattered to us. But by the time we assembled in formation, two-by-two, man and woman, a march permit that had a starting time but no ending time was in hand. We had to make adjustments to disperse the local ministers, who had commandeered the front line, by telling them to mingle with students in their ministerial responsibility to provide a protective covering. Those of us who were in "the Word" knew as we looked the ministers directly in the eyes that we had bared their naked egotism.

Governor Wallace's refusal to accept the students' petition transformed what had been planned as a one-day march into a protracted freedom struggle odyssey. After Wallace refused to meet with student representatives George Ware and George Davis, students vowed to sit in front of the Capitol until he did so or at least sent a representative.

The night descended and it became cold as the three hundred students began a vigil before the Capitol. The police had surrounded us and we began to realize that anyone who left to find a bathroom was not being allowed to rejoin our ranks. The creative solution was for the students to form two circles, one of men, and one of women, with their backs to the insides of the circles. Anyone who needed to urinate could retreat within their respective circles and do what had to be done. Thus did the great "pee-in at the Alabama Capitol" join the civil rights lore.

When it began to rain, I knew I had to find dry quarters. The thought of recontracting tuberculosis crowded my mind as I began to cough. Even though I knew that I would not be permitted to reenter the ranks of my dedicated peers, I left the circle of now-shivering students and found a SNCC car with organizers who had not been allowed past the police line.

I climbed into the car, exhausted to the bone. I learned that there were several cars filled with SNCC organizers who had come to Montgomery in full force. I told them that we could go to my grandmother's home—it had been the SCLC Freedom House for Jim Bevel and James Orange.

Three of the SNCC cars did go to my grandmother's home, now occupied by my aunt, first cousin, and my U.S. soldier uncle who had just returned from Japan. After my aunt rustled up some food, about sixteen SNCC organizers slept wherever they could lay their tired heads and fatigued bodies. I slept like a log in my own bed.

The Tuskegee insurgents finally left the Capitol and slept on the concrete basement floor of First Baptist Missionary Baptist Church. Forman and other SNCC organizers brought food and blankets to the church.

THE NEXT DAY, March 11, six hundred Alabama State College students, organized by Willie Ricks (Mukasa) and students Donna Smith and Timothy Mays, joined the Tuskegee students. This time, the marchers were about 1,000 strong as they paraded to the Capitol to present the petition. Governor Wallace again refused to accept the petition. That evening we sought refuge in the Dexter Avenue Baptist Church, Dr. King's pulpit during the Montgomery Bus Boycott. The church was one block from the Capitol, the ideal "staging location." During the middle of the night, the trustee board had the lights, water, and heat cut off. I was not surprised. This was the same church that broke from First Baptist based on pretentious class distinctions. This was the same church that gave the Reverend Dr. Vernon Johns a hard time and later extended the same treatment to Dr. King. This was the same church that never hosted a mass meeting during the Montgomery Bus Boycott.

The following day, March 12, George Washington Carver High School students (led by Viola Bradford, the Howard Sisters, and Leon Hall) and St. Jude Catholic High School students (led by the Smith and Bethune girls) joined the Alabama State College students. As they attempted to march from Jackson Street to Dexter Avenue Baptist Church to join the Tuskegee student contingent on the last leg to the Capitol, the students were beaten back by club-wielding sheriff's possemen on horseback. Galloping horses forced students to find safety on the front porches of homes. Neighbors who were home opened their doors to let the students in to avert their being trampled. Jackson Street Baptist Church opened its doors as students retreated into the sanctuary. It was in this church that Jim Forman uttered the words, "If we can't sit at the table of democracy, we will knock its fucking legs off."

A small contingent including SNCC's Annie Pearl Avery finally made it to Dexter Avenue Baptist Church, now surrounded by police while Tuskegee students were inside, including me. We feared that if we walked outside, the police would beat us to a bloody pulp. The small contingent stood between the police and us in the vestibule with the door opened. When we saw Annie Pearl snatch a billy club out of a cop's hand, we were fortified and boldly walked down the front stairs. We reentered the church through the basement door. A debate between SCLC's Jim Bevel and SNCC's Jim Forman ensued. I was not interested. My contribution to the discussion was simply that the Tuskegee march that didn't turn around had guaranteed that the Selma march would go forward because, as we had shown, people will march for their rights.

My colleagues and I got back on the waiting buses to return to Tuskegee. Bevel was left to debate with himself.

However, when we were back on campus, another debate, called by George Ware, took place with Jim Forman. Forman and SNCC organizers were blamed for manipulating students into our extended protest stay in Montgomery. I was insulted. No one had manipulated me. Tuskegee students had every opportunity to return to campus. Those who stayed had done so of their own free will. I concluded that as we withstood the police blows, we struck a blow for freedom. Students cut their freedom teeth with this harrowing experience. I grew a wisdom tooth.

TUSKEGEE INSTITUTE COUNCIL elections were held annually in March, and I had decided in January that I would run for president. I had told only Clarence Jones of this personal ambition, and he had agreed to be my campaign manager. Clarence and I had graduated together from George Washington Carver High School in Montgomery. He was an honor student and a bookworm who studied the dictionary like a textbook, and as a result had the most extensive vocabulary of anyone I knew. Clarence was not a student activist, but he supported our cause for freedom. He was active in the YMCA/YWCA. I had been pleasantly surprised when I saw the Y delegation, probably encouraged by Clarence, with adviser Lois Reeves in the lead, join our caravan-march to the Capitol. Mrs. Reeves was a bubbly lady; her strong singing voice could lift any downtrodden spirit. When we sat down in front of the Capitol on the first day, she led the students in a singing round of her favorite, hilarious song, "Zoom, Golly, Golly!"

Clarence and I discussed a budget, campaign literature, and signs. He recommended that my campaign signs be made of wood with waterproof paint. My theme was, "Elect Gwen Patton. Student Body President. Total Representation for All!" I asked Clarence to pull together a crew to paint the wooden signs and at the appropriate time to hang them where students congregated and at the married students apartment complex.

SNCC's "Winky" Hall introduced me to Ann Anthony from Mississippi. She was tall, stunning, and sporting an afro that rivaled Angela Davis's. I asked Ann to run for "Miss Tuskegee." I sought out Ruby Taylor who did not join our march because she was afraid her mother, a science teacher in Pickens County, would be fired. A large number of Tuskegee students' parents worked for public school systems, the largest employer of Alabama's black college graduates. As such, they were middle-class, yet vulnerable because they were always subject to being fired by white segregationist school system administrators. I wanted to create a space for students like Ruby to feel included. I asked her to run for corresponding secretary, a key position. Howard Foster, already looking like a business executive in his daily attire of three-piece suits, was my choice for treasurer.

Immediately after our freedom-struggle odyssey with Tuskegee and ASU students attempting daily marchers to the Capitol for six consecutive days, I launched my campaign. George Carter Jr., whose family owned the sweet shop, the campus grocery, and three small enclaves of attractive trailer houses near the campus, offered the use of his Cadillac convertible to open up my campaign. I sat on the trunk and tossed candy and trinkets as he drove me through the Tuskegee campus. George provided the candy and trinkets. I made special appeals to the African Student Union and the Married Students Association with promises that they would be integral components in my "Total Representation" pledge.

I was summoned to President Foster's office. He said he had already asked my four male opponents to take down their campaign signs because they had become weatherbeaten in a recent downpour. He said all four had complied and he asked the same of me. I replied that surely my signs—wood and waterproof—were not a problem. Exasperated, he said he wanted them down anyway because the board of trustees was coming. I responded that my signs should stay up and the others should go back up because the trustees, of all people, should see student activity.

When I left the president's office, I pulled together a petition that received over 1,000 signatures from students, faculty, and staff supporting my stand to keep all campaign signs up.

MEANWHILE, A FIERCE legal battle had been underway in the federal courthouse in Montgomery. Hosea Williams of SCLC, John Lewis of SNCC, Peter Hall of the Birmingham movement, and Mrs. Amelia Boynton of the Selma voting rights movement had filed a lawsuit against Governor George Wallace, Public Safety Director Al Lingo, and Dallas County Sheriff Jim Clark asking the U.S. District Judge Frank M. Johnson Jr. to order the government to provide equal protection under the law to allow the march from Selma to Montgomery, to petition for voting rights for Negro citizens, to proceed. Lingo and Clark had led the brutal assault against the initial marchers on "Bloody Sunday."

Our local black legal team of Fred Gray, Solomon Seay Jr., Charles Langford, and Charles Conley coordinated with ACLU attorneys Bill Kuntsler and Donald Jelinek and Arthur Kinoy of the National Lawyers Guild. There was a flurry of motions and restraining orders surrounding whether the march could proceed. At one of these legal meetings in Charles Conley's office in the Brick Layers' Hall on Union Street, I met with Hosea Williams. James Forman of SNCC had asked me to report on the student strength to support the march. Forman often insisted that I join SNCC folks at planning and logistical meetings (in Selma at the black-owned Torch Motel, at Birmingham's black-owned Gaston Motel, and at Montgomery's black-owned Ben Moore Hotel, which my Grandfather Patton designed and his construction crew built). SNCC had opened an office in the Ben Moore after the continual "march(es) that wouldn't turn around" Tuskegee and Alabama State College students. These meetings discussed the ongoing court battles and such logistics as housing/tents at the designated sites, portable toilets, and meals for the marchers.

Judge Johnson Jr. ruled on March 17, 1965, that the march could go forward. In part, he ordered the defendants Wallace, Lingo, and Clark, and anybody under their authority, be restrained and enjoined from "arresting, harassing, threatening, or in any way interfering with efforts to march or walk . . . by plaintiffs, members of their class, and other who may join them, along Highway 80 from Selma . . . to Montgomery; and otherwise obstructing, impeding, or interfering with the peaceful, nonviolent efforts." President Lyndon Baines Johnson soon afterward federalized the Alabama National Guard and ordered them to provide safety and protection for the marchers.

Finally, on March 21, 1965, two weeks after Bloody Sunday, the march from Selma got under way, with the protection of the U.S. government.

CONCURRENT WITH CAMPAIGN activities I had been traveling back and forth to Montgomery to work with my elder mentors and relatives to set up housing in their homes for marchers who would find it difficult to sleep on the grounds of St. Jude, the final campsite for the marchers. I reunited with the ladies who served as voting rights block and precinct workers with Rufus Lewis. These ladies lived in the adjacent communities surrounding the City of St. Jude. The closest community was Washington Park with Wescott Street as the main corridor. On this street resided Mr. and Mrs. Charlie and Bertha Smith, Mrs. Blanche Watson, and Mr. and Mrs. Frank and Hazel Gregory whose home was located at the end of Wescott Street on

Early Street. Mrs. Emma Madison Bell, a militant voting rights activist and niece of Attorney Arthur Madison who brought the first class-action voting rights lawsuit on behalf of Negroes in 1943, lived on Early Street. Mrs. Bell, affectionately called "Shine," was a plaintiff in the 1943 lawsuit. These ladies and their families opened up their homes for housing the marchers. Across the street on Fairview Avenue from the City of St. Jude were the communities of Mobile Heights where the Bethune family organized housing and Carver park where my Aunt Chick and her daughter, Flora, housed Lutheran ministers Edwin Peterman and John Reynolds from St. Louis.

Mrs. Zecozy Williams's family on Hill Street, across from St. Jude Catholic School, promised to prepare tons of fried chicken, greens, corn on the cob, cornbread, and desserts. The Montgomery Improvement Association (MIA), especially Georgia Gilmore, the famed movement cook, would assist with the food brigade. Water stations along the route from St. Jude to the State Capitol had to be designated and manned. Mrs. Mary Bibb, who owned the sunshine yellow clapboard community grocery store at the corner of Oak and Early streets, agreed to provide water and soft drinks. Community activist Peter Shine agreed to set up a lemonade and water table on the corner of Oak Street and Jeff Davis Avenue. Mt. Zion AMEZ Church on the corner of Holt and Stone streets, would provide a water station and a restroom stop.

Local physicians had to organize and to coordinate with the Medical Committee for Human Rights physicians, mainly from New York and Chicago. Local physician John Winston Sr. miraculously made arrangements with administrators at St. Margaret's Hospital, which had yet to integrate, for use of the emergency room to complement the services which would be available at the black hospital in the City of St. Jude.

ON THE SAME Wednesday that Judge Johnson ruled the march from Selma to Montgomery could proceed, I was elected Tuskegee Institute student body president, with 75 percent of the vote. The other candidates on my slate were elected as well: Howard Foster, treasurer; Jacqualine Banks, secretary; Ruby Taylor, corresponding secretary; junior Benny James, vice president—when he acknowledged me as "Madame President" at our victory celebration,

I knew he was a team player and would make an excellent student body president the following year—and Ann Anthony, Miss Tuskegee (sadly, she became ill and had to leave school; first runner-up Majorie Love did a beautiful job representing us as Miss Tuskegee, and was escorted by Benny).

I asked Benny to draft a new constitution to change the name "Institute Council" to "Student Government Association" and to change titles to SGA president and officers. The newly elected officers agreed on the need for a student senate with two representatives from each dorm and from campus-wide organizations. That feature had to be added to the draft for student ratification.

I met with TIAL Chair George Ware and insisted that there would be no TIAL takeover of the SGA—nor any need for one—as he had done when Herman James failed to step up. Instead, I saw two distinct entities with different priorities, duties and responsibilities. Of course, we would work together on mutual causes and programs. I had the general support of the student body and strong support from TIAL members Wendy Paris, C. J. Jones, Jimmy Rogers, Eldridge Burns, and Sammy Younge Jr.; Sammy served as liaison between SGA and TIAL.

Warren Hamilton, an astute underclassman, served as my assistant. The SGA office was always swamped with students wanting to get involved in student governance and programs. They constantly congratulated themselves, especially the guys, for duly electing the first coed president, which I appreciated but didn't dwell on. My aim for running for SGA president was to help motivate and to encourage my peers to become consciously engaged in our struggle for freedom. My 1965 message to my colleagues read:

> Our society is dynamic. It agitates, churns and spurts forth new ideas and events. The stagnant society is crushed, causing its members to mumble and shout complaints. Let us not at Tuskegee become stagnant but (rather) get in the mainstream of dynamism and move forward in all directions.
>
> Tuskegee Institute has just commenced (in) moving forward and the students have been instrumental in this progress. However, this progress cannot continue unless every student occupies his (her) position on the ideological spectrum. I challenge the student body of 1965–66 to take

their places respectively and look to the prospective [sic] of human dignity.

Tuskegee Institute is *OUR* school. We can make it the best institution or the worst institution in the world. Let us make it the best institution by believing in consideration, deliberation, action, and above all, commitment. Let us exhaust every potential and exalt ourselves to the highest in dedication and determination to motivate changes for the betterment and progress of our campus and campus life.

ON MARCH 21, 1965, a motorcade of Tuskegee students, along with our young and progressive dean of students, Dr. P. B. Phillips, arrived in Selma. We were directed to a prominent position within reach of the Reverends Martin Luther King Jr. and Ralph D. Abernathy, in the line of 1,000 marchers, headed to Montgomery to petition for our voting rights. I was certain that our "Tuskegee March That Didn't Turn Around" gave us such recognition. Moreover, the students' three-day protest before the Capitol and ensuing protest marchers thereafter moved Tuskegee's administration to be one of the key sources to provide meals for the hundreds of marchers on the four-day trek from Selma through Lowndes County and on to Montgomery.

Each day a contingent of Tuskegee Institute students joined the marchers. At the campsites each night, we shared in the folk and freedom songs of Len Chandler, Joan Baez, and the SNCC Freedom Singers. Walking the last few miles into Montgomery to the final campsite at the City of St. Jude was a complete joy and an occasion for celebration. Montgomery's movement infrastructure was working with the precision of an army, as it had during the 1955–56 Bus Boycott and in rescuing the Freedom Riders in 1961. People marveled at the support organized by the Montgomery community.

That night during the "Stars for Freedom" rally, residents of the adjacent Washington Park community sat on their rooftops with their children to watch and hear the singers and movie stars. The children were thrilled when the "Bonanza" theme song blared and "Adam Cartwright" (Pernell Roberts) stepped up to the microphone. The old-timers swooned as the deep, melodious voice of Billy Eckstein filled the cool, crisp night. All joined in when Harry Belafonte swayed into his calypso beat of "Day-O (The Banana Boat

Song)." And, of course, Odetta and Nina Simone's protest songs energized the freedom fighters in the crowd.

Other stars who appeared at the rally were singers Tony Bennett, Leon Bibb, Ina Ralls, Pete Seeger, Joan Baez, Peter, Paul and Mary, and the Chad Mitchell Trio; actors Sammy Davis Jr., Ossie Davis, and Shelley Winters; comedians Nipsey Russell, Alan King, Mike Nichols, and Elaine May; conductor Leonard Bernstein; writer James Baldwin; and heavyweight boxing champion Floyd Patterson.

We were jubilant and well prepared to march the next day, and through our chosen collective voice of Dr. Martin Luther King Jr., we were ready to tell Governor Wallace that it wouldn't be long before all of God's Alabama children would have their right to vote, to be first-class citizens.

DURING THE RALLY, a light but steady rain fell. Always conscious of my weak immune system, I asked Cousin Flora to drive me and her Missouri Lutheran minister guest to her home before the evening ended. I knew the minister was tired after the 54-mile trek from Selma and would appreciate a good night's rest in a warm, comfortable bed. I knew I needed the same thing.

After a hearty breakfast the following morning, Flora drove us to the Carver High School parking lot. I was surprised and delighted when she, with her trusty Brownie camera in hand ,stepped out of her car to walk with us across the street to the staging area on the St. Jude campus. Flora had informed her principal, Robert Pierce, at Lowndes County Training School in Hayneville the night before that she was not reporting to her classes on this day. Flora and her mother, my Aunt Chick, were already registered voters, but on this day she would risk her teaching job to join in our fight for the right for all of Alabama's black citizens to vote. I beamed with joy as we walked across to St. Jude.

The drizzle of the previous evening had lightened into a mist from an overcast sky. The air was cool and damp. I was glad I had worn my fur-lined boots and three layers of clothes.

No sooner than we melded with the crowd, we were instructed via a bullhorn to assemble at the campus west gate, facing Hill Street, for the line-up. The National Guardsmen from their various posts joined the assemblage.

We marched out of the gate onto Hill Street. Neighborhood people were on the sidewalks and they soon joined the marchers. The marchers, about 20 across, men on the ends of each line with women concentrated in the middle, filled the street. Some men wore orange vests to denote that they were parade marshals. I was somewhere in the middle of the huge gathering. The array of strong, purposely erect backs before me fortified my conviction that we would make democracy work for all Americans. There would be no backsliding.

Our multitude turned left onto Fairview Avenue. St. Jude High School students, with my cousin Ella Bell in the midst, filed out, led by math teacher K. T. Brown, to join the march. On the right side of the avenue, elementary school principal Herman Harris, defying the Board of Education mandate, had lined his pupils near the street curb. They waved and cheered as the marchers passed by. A few yards onward, Carver High School students streamed out. Timothy Mays, with his gigantic American flag waving, left the ranks momentarily to lead the Carver students in chanting "Freedom Now!"

The crowd swelled as we marched down Oak Street. People left their homes, churches, and businesses to join our ranks. They also opened up their homes, churches, and businesses if any needed to use their bathrooms. As I looked back over my shoulder, the crowd was still making the turn onto Oak Street. There were thousands of us by the time we crossed Early Street.

Mrs. Mary Bibb, owner of the community grocery store on that corner, unlocked her outdoor vending machine for marchers to take free Nehi and RC colas. Further down Oak Street near the intersection of Jeff Davis Avenue, Peter Shine had set a table with cups of lemonade and water.

Flora had left our line to take photographs (now displayed in Lowndes County Voting Rights Interpretative Center) of Stokely Carmichael, Dr. and Mrs. King, and others who were at the front of the march. Riley Lewis, a black professional photographer, darted everywhere, snapping pictures of the marchers.

We turned right at the corner of Jeff Davis Avenue, the crown jewel district on the west side. More people streamed out of businesses. Principal Raul Dobbins at Loveless School obeyed the school board edict that students were not to join the march. The eager children's faces pressed against the windows as we passed by made us only more determined.

We made a left onto Holt Street. It was apparent that every black church on this corridor had organized their congregations. As the march reached Mt. Zion AMEZ Church, tables laden with sandwiches and beverages were at the ready.

The marchers moved forward to Day Street then to Mobile Street. I had been on Mobile Highway and Mobile Road, but never on Mobile Street. I did not know it even existed. The magnificent homes with climbing steps up to the homes' entrances made the street appear to be in a valley. I knew Montgomery was a hilly city, and the high-top homes on this two-block street were confirmations. Moreover, Mobile Street seemed to be a demarcation that separated the black west-side community from the white enclave that led to the downtown white business and government districts.

The march proceeded to Five Points hill where Mobile, Clayton, Montgomery, and Goldthwaite streets converged. At the apex of the hill that dropped down into the heart of Montgomery, the marchers became quiet and solemn. Someone murmured, "We're going to meet the man." "The man," everyone knew, was Governor George C. Wallace.

A prayer was offered. The marchers came to a standstill to gather collective strength, then moved forward down Montgomery Street, not knowing what awaited around the bend at the fountain at Court Square, the foot of Dexter Avenue, leading the last quarter-mile up to the State Capitol. We were on our way to meet Pharoah; Dr. King was our Moses collectively chosen to deliver the message: "Let our people go."

At the bend onto the last leg of our 54-mile journey, we saw the Capitol majestically sitting atop Goat Hill. We saw federalized National Guardsmen, standing in sentry formation, on rooftops along Dexter and lined on both sides of the avenue as we approached the Capitol. We felt safe.

By the time the march reached Dexter Avenue Baptist Church, the crowd was still turning the bend at the fountain. News media estimates were that 25,000 to 50,000 people were marching up the street.

BEFORE US WAS a stage fashioned from a flat-bed trailer parked in the street just in front of the Capitol—the marchers were not permitted to stand on the

Capitol steps nor its marble platforms, especially not on the upper landing to the massive doors of the Capitol before which a bronze star embedded in the marble marked where Jefferson Davis had stood for his inaugural 1861 swearing-in as President of the Confederate States of America.

Dr. King and other dignitaries were by now standing on the makeshift stage, an array of microphones before them. The Guardsmen lined the breadth of the Capitol grounds behind the stage on Bainbridge Street. Cameramen were busily recording the event for the historical record.

Dr. King stepped to the microphones. He opened his message with a primer on racial discrimination in the historical context of forced African importation coupled with U.S.-born Negroes as enslaved laborers for economic exploitation. His teaching-sermon picked up a cadence in the traditional Baptist delivery of "call and response." Dr. King concluded with the now-famous refrain, "How Long!" The crowd roared back, "Not Long!"

The clock atop the Capitol dome began to chime. The Confederate flag was flapping in the wind. Within what seemed a blink of an eye, the rally was over. The National Guardsmen removed their helmets and placed them beneath their right arms on their right hips. Their helmets that had displayed American flag decals during the march and rally were now turned around to display the Alabama flag, signifying that the Guard was no longer under federal auspices, but now and henceforth under the authority of the avowed segregationist, Alabama Governor George C. Wallace. Was this an omen?

That night Viola Liuzzo, the wife of a Teamsters Union member, mother of four little children, who drove from Detroit, Michigan, to be a part of the Selma-to-Montgomery March for Voting Rights, was shot and killed by the KKK on the highway between Selma and Montgomery.

The movement did not end at the Alabama State Capitol on that cool March day. It just moved to a higher, yet deeper, plane. The movement would and must continue. Our race to freedom is a constant struggle.

14

Student Affairs

After the Selma-to-Montgomery March, I recharged at my grandparents' welcoming home. Jerry phoned from New York City. I gave him a detailed account about the march and all the developments that led to that critical event. He was proud that I had been elected student body president in a landslide. He asked, "Do you want me to send for you?" His question was a way out for me to place my visit with him on the back burner.

I was grateful and replied, "Jerry, I think I should stay home and rest. I'll have a two-week break between spring and summer semesters. That will give us more time together."

"Okay. It's still chilly up here anyway. I'm going to send you the money for the train fare so you'll have it in readiness," he said. I was beginning to feel guilty. "Don't feel bad. Absence makes the heart grow fonder," he said.

Or it makes the heart grow farther, I thought after we hung up.

I spent the next five days in hibernation, trying not to think about Jerry or anything else. I was tired. Mommy was happy that I was getting much-needed rest. She waited on me hand and foot, bringing my meals to my bed on the rolling butler tray.

Soon I was back at school and plunging into my studies and into my new responsibilities as SGA president. One of the privileges of the office was to sit on the President's Council. I know I was supposed to be impressed to sit at the table with all the president's men. But, I have never been impressionable. At first during the weekly meetings, which I thought was too often, I did not know what my role was to be. Was I to report on student activities and their concerns or was I to "tattle-tale" on students and divulge what they were "up to"? Most of the seven male administrators on the council were polite, though from time to time they would ask me to stem the daily pickets at the Big Bear Supermarket and at the bank, whose CEO was Allan Parker, president of the Tuskegee City Council. Sammy Younge Jr. and Wendy Paris led the bank picketing, which was in response to Parker stonewalling the federal appropriations to build another low-rent housing project. The city fathers apparently thought the one existing project was enough.

"Gwen, aren't you concerned that students are missing classes with their pickets?" asked Dr. Herbert Wilson, director of development.

"No, Herbert. We have arranged with students who have cars to carry students to and from campus to downtown between classes."

My replying to Wilson by his first name—as he had addressed me—jolted the council members in their cushioned chairs.

"*Miss* Patton, that's good planning," responded Dr. P. B. Phillips, dean of students. (Later, I advised SGA Vice President Benny James, heading off to sit in for me at a different meeting, "If they address you by your first name, you respond in kind. I promise there will be only one round of the first-name salutations.")

Dean Phillips was closest to me in age and an excellent advocate for students. However, I knew it would be only a matter of time before he would find himself between a rock and a hard place as students pressed for changes and the administrators insisted on the status quo. I had confidence that Dean Phillips would side with the students, but just in case he wouldn't, we would call for his resignation. Likewise, we would call for student action in the event he was fired for supporting us.

I bided my time with the weekly President's Council meetings until the students at our monthly SGA meeting overwhelming endorsed the new constitution at the April meeting, with at least 1,000 students present.

At one of the May President's Council meetings, I requested a change of SGA advisors and to purchase a mimeograph machine that the current advisor had blocked. The SGA's recommendation for a new advisor was Danny Williams, a young assistant librarian and archivist. Through the years we had cultivated a wonderful intellectual relationship as he assisted me in locating excellent resources for my research papers.

Williams, thanks to Dean Phillips, became the SGA advisor, but President Foster denied our request for a mimeograph machine in the SGA office. We took up a collection and purchased one anyway; students had to have ready means for mass communications.

At the May SGA meeting I appointed my six-person cabinet, and the student body ratified the appointments. The cabinet accompanied me at all subsequent President's Council meetings. Of course, the council balked. When I explained to President Foster that I needed accountability and that the SGA cabinet would provide that, he understood.

I asked William "Bill" Clark to work with Dean Phillips to establish a student judiciary council. Gone were the days when a dean of one of the schools could expel a student from the Institute as a whole. The Frankie Chambliss situation was the case in point. She had been expelled from the renowned School of Nursing by Dean Lillian Harvey. Chambliss, without question, had breached the curfew policy while on internship in Baltimore, Maryland. Her removal from the School of Nursing, was one thing, but fellow students took exception to her summary expulsion from the Institute. I asked Montgomery lawyer Charles Conley, who also practiced in Tuskegee and was one of SNCC's favorite counselors, to take up the issue. Our argument was that Frankie had not breached any policies of the other seven schools in the Institute. We won. Frankie transferred to the School of Education. But for the sake of the Institute and to avoid needless lawsuits, we needed a student judiciary council to mediate these types of issues.

I asked SGA Treasurer Harold Foster to serve on the college union board that determined appropriations for student organizations. I reserved the right to sit on the entertainment committee. When I learned that the Harkness Ballet, the 604th Air Force Band, the Four Freshmen, and the Paul Winters orchestra had been contracted, I pushed to include Nana Dinizulu and the African Ballet, and Bill Doggett. Dean Phillips accepted the responsibility to contract these additional acts and his staff made it all happen.

I also sat on the Lyceum committee because I sensed my obligation as student body president to provide a broad political perspective at this pivotal junction in our people's race to freedom. I cannot remember all the monthly scholars and lecturers in the SGA's "Ideology Spectrum Series," but I remember vividly the presentations of Dr. Herbert Aptheker, the noted historian on slavery; Gus Hall of the Communist Party USA; and Dr. Lonnie Shabazz, head of the Muslim Mosque in Washington, D.C. All were SGA recommendations.

Dr. Herbert Aptheker's appearance on campus was especially memorable for a personal lesson it taught me. I was to collect Dr. Aptheker at the Greyhound Bus Station in downtown Tuskegee at a specific time. The driver of the Institute's transport was on time and drove me to the station. When I entered the station, I saw only a distinguished-looking, middle-aged white man. I returned to campus, assuming I had mixed up the arrival time. I was surprised when the dorm mother told me to call Dean P. B. Phillips immediately. Dean Phillips informed me that Professor Aptheker was waiting at the station. The transport driver quickly drove me back over there, and when I reentered the station, a baritone voice asked, "Are you Gwen Patton?" I replied, "Yes, are you Dr. Aptheker?" He nodded. He was the same white man I saw previously in the station. I had read Professor Aptheker's analytical, insightful books on slavery, racism, exploitation, and their links to the accumulation of wealth for the few and the powerful. I presumed the author to be a black writer. Our first meeting thus turned into a teaching lesson about the pitfalls of presumptuous thinking that can be dangerously prejudiced and judgmental. Whenever we saw each other in subsequent years, Professor Aptheker and I greeted each other with a hearty laugh.

STUDENT BODY PRESIDENTS were always invited to a myriad of national and regional meetings. The 1965 meeting of the U.S. National Student Association (NSA) was the premiere conference, and it was to be held at the University of Wisconsin in Madison.

To get to the NSA confab, I took my first plane flight. I sat securely buckled up and practically motionless in my seat. The stewardess in a monotone demonstrated the safety features and told passengers what they should do in an emergency. Her safety tips did not allay my fears. The plane slowly taxied to the runway. Okay. Soon the plane raced down the runway, and as the giant iron bird lifted into the air, I heard a "clunk," the wheels folding underneath the belly of the plane. Mommy's words echoed in my mind: "If the Lord wanted us to fly, he would have given us wings." But when the plane was aloft, I felt peace. The cumulus clouds that I had read about in my sixth-grade science class were indescribably beautiful. The sun was radiant and brilliant. Yes, the Lord wanted us to fly so we could see his omnipresent handiwork. I began singing "Somewhere Over the Rainbow" as the plane gracefully glided through what I considered was First Heaven.

The NSA conference was fascinating. Among the groups present was the Student Nonviolent Coordinating Committee (SNCC), Students for a Democratic Society (SDS), Young Americans for Freedom (YAF), Youth Against War and Fascism (YAWF), Young Republicans, and Young Democrats, and other student groups known by their acronyms. I observed that male delegates outnumbered females by four to one.

I spent most of my time listening. Two discussions caught my attention. "Fast for Freedom" was a nationwide project of college students who forfeited lunch and donated their lunch money to the NSA Civil Rights Desk to help underwrite projects in the South. I signed up Tuskegee Institute to participate.

The other discussion was on the Vietnam War and the draft. Most of the discussion, led by white students, opposed the war in Vietnam, calling it an imperialist venture. I was taken aback when the student body president from historically black Talladega College in Alabama passionately argued in support of the Vietnam War. He wore his ROTC uniform and saluted the flag before and after his fervent plea. After listening to his patriotic rant, I knew we needed a draft counseling center at Tuskegee to offer an option for male students if they lost their deferment status. Black students should have the choice to fight for freedom at home on their own behalf or to fight for freedom on behalf of capitalists bent on exploiting and destroying the world for their personal greed.

The draft counseling center became a reality the coming fall. I mentioned that historian Dr. Herbert Aptheker had been a Lyceum speaker for us. In the fall of 1965, I was happy to welcome to Tuskegee his daughter, Bettina Aptheker. She was as insightful and as sensitive as her famous father. I invited Bettina to Tuskegee Institute to help establish an anti-war, anti-draft counseling center. Though Tuskegee's strong anti-racist military tradition included the famed Tuskegee Airmen, I felt strongly that current Tuskegee students should have options if they did not want to go to war against other people of color in Vietnam, a country 10,000 miles away that was in the midst of a civil war.

Bettina arrived on campus the day of an "Appreciation Parade" for

Tuskegee Airmen hero General Benjamin O. Davis Jr. General Chappie James was leading the military parade with its display of weaponry. Bettina's eyes were big as flapjacks as she watched. However, after I explained the difficulty black students faced in financing their college educations, she shook her head with understanding of the number who might choose the ROTC for the financial support it provided.

The campus counseling center was established. Outreach community programs were put in place to encourage brothers to come on campus for draft counseling and to exercise their right as "conscientious objectors." Five "safe houses" were arranged in Montgomery, including my grandmother's rental home, as way stations for conscientious objectors to make their way to Canada for political asylum.

Over the Christmas 1965 holiday, I traveled with Bettina to the University of California at Berkeley to become one of the founding members of the Student Mobilization Committee Against the War in Vietnam.

HOWEVER, BEFORE THAT, my second meeting of consequence was the gathering of Southern Christian student leaders at a religious retreat in Ocala, Florida. By coincidence, President Foster and I arrived separately at the Montgomery airport for the same flight to Atlanta (with connections to different destinations). Dr. Foster arranged for us to sit together. No doubt we both hoped to exchange views on how students and administrators could work harmoniously.

After settling on the plane, I suggested to Dr. Foster that the Institute could save money if we both rode the same transport to the airport when our travels coincided.

"I agree," he said with a smile. "You know, you are a young lady beyond your years."

"My grandmother always tells me that I've been here before." We both laughed.

What I didn't tell him was that while I was resting for a few days in Montgomery after the Selma March, I learned from Poppa Washington that Dr. Foster, before reversing course and deciding to support Tuskegee students in the "march that wouldn't turn around," had called Mommy and pleaded with her to talk with me in an effort to curtail what he called "my extra-curricula activities" that could negatively impact my studies and grades and even my health.

Mommy understood coercion and took exception to Dr. Foster using my health as a tactic. She knew full well that if anyone attempted to intimidate me, I would stubbornly dig in my heels.

Dr. Foster and I eventually developed a close relationship. We both knew that when necessary we could take off our gloves and fight on a question of diverging principles, yet the fight would not be personal.

After that first warm encounter at the airport, Dr. Foster and I traveled often together. Our plane conversations were learning experiences for me. Dr. Foster was a marvelous speaker with great command of English—my major—and its vocabulary. Many times he would share his presentations with me and give me pointers to make my own presentations more effective. We had an abiding, mutual respect for each other, although forty years later I learned at my Inkster High School class reunion from Thelma Belcher, school librarian and Tuskegee alumna, that Dr. Foster had called her and suggested, jokingly, I hope, that the area alumni association make sure not to send another "Gwen Patton" to the Institute.

I was fully aware during my time at the Institute that Dr. Foster was being pressured by the powers, all the way up to Governor George Wallace, to smash the militant Tuskegee student movement. Tuskegee Institute, though a private university, had received public funds dating back to when its founder, Lewis Adams, a politically savvy Negro farmer and tinsmith in Tuskegee during Reconstruction, had negotiated the black bloc vote for state legislative candidates Arthur Brooks and Civil War Colonel Wilbur Foster in exchange for state appropriations to open a school for Negroes. Tuskegee Institute opened in July 1881. The intent of the white legislators was to keep Negroes in the county as part of the labor force and for economic development. Both Negroes and whites agreed that this would be necessary if Tuskegee was to remain a viable agricultural community.

Eighty years later, the loss of state funds would not break Tuskegee Institute. The first president of the Institute, Dr. Booker T. Washington, had seen to that by cultivating external sources of funding that subsequent presidents had built upon. Nevertheless, a university needed all of the funds it could garner. Dr. Luther Foster was the fourth president of the Institute. I fully understood his predicament. He was not the enemy.

I first came to this discernment when students from Alabama State College (ASC), which did receive the bulk of its funding through state appropriations, wanted to hang their president in effigy. A crowd of ASC students gathered at President Levi Watkins's home. They were angry because he had issued an ultimatum that students would be expelled if they joined Tuskegee students in the demonstrations at the Capitol. Someone in the gathering, it was rumored, had a gun.

The student leaders of the group, Timothy Mays, Douglas McCants and Dorothy Frazier, learned that I was present. I was called to the front. I climbed the steps and stood on the front porch. I looked down at the front row of the rally and saw the effigy, made of bed sheets, lying on the ground. Across its chest was "Levi Watkins."

I stood frozen for a moment, collecting my thoughts, then said, "We need your support. We need each others' support. We need Dr. Watkins's support!"

The crowd cheered approvingly.

"And, we need to support Dr. Watkins!" I cried.

The crowd became suddenly quiet.

I went on, "Dr. Watkins is not our enemy! He has been appointed to stifle our race for freedom! But we have to look into his heart! What we do in the streets gives Dr. Watkins the leverage to do what he needs to do in the suites. It's a one-two punch strategy. And we of all people should never talk about hanging anybody or anything!"

The crowd erupted into thunderous applause as if waiting for me to utter those precise words.

"Those kind of inhumane KKK tactics don't belong in our struggle! Let's go back to the student center to reorganize and regroup!"

I left the porch and began walking across the street to the campus and was gratified that the crowd joined me.

15

Harlem Interlude

I chose a back car, next to the dining car. In an earlier "Jim Crow" era, blacks rode in the front cars, those closest to the train's coal-driven engine, where they would catch the brunt of the soot and sparks. Racism is a pathetic pathology.

This was the first time I had boarded a desegregated train from the South, and it was thanks to the youth of Birmingham who had braved the undulating power of water hoses and police dogs simply because black people wanted to exercise their fundamental rights to public accommodations. Thanks to the Birmingham movement, the 1964 Civil Rights Act was passed.

The train ride was twenty-four hours. Before I placed both feet on the Penn Station platform in New York City, Jerry was there with a beaming smile and extended hand to help me down the train steps. We embraced and greeted each other with an enduring kiss. We had not seen each other for over a year.

I assumed Jerry would have a car or a taxi waiting to take me to his home. Nope. After getting my luggage, we went to another platform, this one underground, for my first subway ride. The gleaming white ceramic tiles, though not as beautiful as the multi-colored mosaics of American workers in the Cincinnati train station, had their own elegance.

The doors of this underground train automatically opened. A rush of people emptied from the car and then an inrush of people, including Jerry and me, filled it. Jerry laid claim to a bright orange plastic seat and pushed me into it. All the other seats were taken. The people, many reading expertly folded newspapers, were oblivious to one another. The train jerked into motion.

After two stops, Jerry said we were switching trains. "We're going to take the A-train to Harlem," he said, looking at my bewildered face. Was this the train that motivated Billy Strayhorn to compose his famous jazz tribute that was recorded by the fabulous Duke Ellington Orchestra? "Yep," Jerry responded.

We ascended one set of stairs only to descend another set of stairs on another platform. A speeding train displaying a gigantic "A" screeched to a halt. Again, Jerry commandeered a seat for me. I noticed that all the people in this train car were black. Was this a "Jim Crow" car? A voice over the intercom said, "Next stop, 125th Street!" The train hurtled ahead, traveling 66 blocks nonstop.

When we emerged from underground, we were in Harlem. It still had its splendor though there were signs of decay. I was puzzled as to why black men were stooping on the sidewalks and in the medians as if in a stupor, trance, or deep sleep. After a few minutes, they would alertly stand and walk briskly away. I later learned that these men were drugged out on heroin, which caused them to stoop down in a deep sleep for a few minutes and then to arise fully alert. If I had only known what lay ahead.

As Jerry and I walked from the station at 125th and Lenox, my mind lifted up the glorious days of the Harlem Renaissance, an inspiring module in my American Literature classes. Later, I tried to locate the haunts of Langston Hughes, Richard Wright, Claude McKay, and others, but none of the locals knew.

Jerry registered us in the Braddock Hotel. Though the hotel had maid and room services, it was quite obvious that the hotel was on the decline. I was disappointed that Jerry had not made accommodations at the famed Theresa Hotel, where Fidel Castro stayed with his chickens after the successful 1961 people's revolution in his country.

I never said anything to Jerry about my disappointment. Maybe his money was not enough to cover my week's visit in New York City. Besides, dining at the sidewalk café of Frank's Steak Restaurant, taking in a revue at the Apollo, and capping off the early morning with cocktails at the Baby Grand, where jazz greats like Houston Person, Etta Jones, and Dakota Staton performed, made up for the disappointment.

Jerry knew I loved intellectual outings. He escorted me on a whirlwind tour, riding the city buses so I could see New York City from uptown to downtown, from east side to west side. We visited the Guggenheim and the Museum of Modern Art. Viewing the artworks and the modern architecture of the museums, I conjured up thoughts of Ayn Rand and her novel,

Fountainhead. We took a horse and buggy ride through Central Park and had a late lunch at Tavern on the Green. We strolled through Central Park and crossed 110th Street back into Harlem.

Soon my vacation was over.

As I rode the train back to Montgomery, I wondered why I didn't ask Jerry direct questions about his life in New York City. He introduced me to only one of his friends, a school teacher who lived on 110th Street and taught in Paterson, New Jersey. He appeared to be gay. When we were at Jerry's favorite neighborhood bar, "The Honduras Headquarters," I made acquaintances with his Belize homeboys. The major attraction in the bar was when a regular patron would push a handkerchief up one nostril and pull it from the other nostril. I thought it was a magic trick. Later I learned that his nose cartilage had been eaten away from snorting heroin. I was more dismayed than disgusted.

I put thoughts of Jerry away while spending my last week's vacation at home in Montgomery. Out of sight, out of mind.

16

SNCC and Black/White Issues

Summer school resumed its regular routine of classes and picket lines in downtown Tuskegee. White exchange students from St. Olaf College of Minnesota and the University of Michigan were a visible critical mass within the student body. Charlene Kranz, a white coed from Washington, D.C., enrolled outright as a Tuskegee student; her father worked in the government and had ties with the Community Relations Program that mediated race relations in Tuskegee. Charlene had learned firsthand from her father about the Tuskegee student movement. She wanted to be part of it. Charlene and I became fast friends.

Tuskegee continued to be a staging area from which SNCC organizers—mainly brothers and two extraordinary sisters, Martha Presod and Gloria Larry—operated in the Alabama Black Belt counties of Lowndes, Wilcox, Dallas, and Greene. In Macon County itself, leadership was mostly provided by Institute students—especially Wendy and George Paris, Simuel Schultz, Eldridge Burns, Demetrius "Red" Robinson, and others who grew up in Tuskegee.

Soon we saw an influx of northern white women who had remained in Mississippi after the 1964 Freedom Summer. Many said these white women were chasing SNCC black men. I couldn't have cared less. I recognized that some sisters will find some brothers absolutely incompatible for personal companionship, and vice versa. People should have the right and the freedom to choose their own companions. However, the problem with many white women, after they coupled with their black companions, was their "White African Queen Syndrome" and their arrogance to tell black people what we should do in *our* struggle for freedom. I knew it would be a matter of time before we would send these white women packing. If they insisted on staying in Tuskegee, then their contribution must be one of listening and learning from the grassroots people, not one of talking and directing.

James Forman asked me to serve as a guide for some of these white women. We were driving on Highway 80 through Lowndes County where there was not one black registered voter although the county was 90 percent black. Many residents had been evicted from the land they worked on and tenant houses. They were living in tents because they dared to try to register to vote after the Selma March.

"Slow down the car," one of the white women said. "The cotton is so beautiful. It looks like clouds on earth."

I said nothing but I was incensed. It was clear that these women did not comprehend the relationship of black people and cotton that was the economic foundation for slavery and then for sharecropping and tenantry. While white plantation owners' children played and frolicked during the summers, black children were forced into the blistering heat to chop and hoe cotton. In October, black children were dismissed from the shabby county schools to pick cotton with sacks on their backs. In March, the children were dismissed from school to plant cotton.

When we returned to campus, I immediately sought out James Forman. "These white heifers have to go," I said.

"Gwen, you have a latent hostility for white women!"

"Latent?" I retorted in a huff. I explained to Forman how a fact-finding mission degenerated into a romantic "cotton as clouds" excursion, absent any understanding of the life and struggle of our people in the Black Belt. "We are not in this struggle to raise white people," I said. "We are in this struggle to fight for our freedom."

I don't know what happened to the white SNCC women, but they were no longer visible on campus.

Tuskegee students took to heart SNCC's organizing technique of listening to and letting the people talk. Movement work in Alabama was not all about action. Many times we spent days and weeks talking about a freedom strategy. One such lengthy discussion was the selection of the symbol for the independent political organization, the Lowndes County Freedom Organization. It didn't matter if Stokely Carmichael—and he would agree—suggested the black panther as the symbol: the people had to decide what symbol would best represent their aspirations.

During some of these discussions, some local people wanted the "buzzard" which would "eat up the rooster" symbol of the white supremacist Democratic Party of Alabama. No one became impatient nor angry in these prolonged discussions. We asked each other probing questions. Are we scavengers, like the buzzard? Do we want to fill our political souls with racist white meat? SNCC also had to do research as to the nature of a black panther. We learned that the black panther was not an aggressive but rather a defensive animal that had no reservations in protecting its family and habitat. Others pointed out that the black panther was an indigenous part of our culture. Ceramic, sleek panthers graced our fireplace mantels and served as doorstops. Black squadrons in World War II often called themselves black panthers. Thus, the Black Panther Party symbol was a product of the people, not of an individual.

Likewise, Tuskegee student organizers took exception to anyone outside of the community telling local people what to do. The greatest infraction was to tell local people to go to the registrar's office to register to vote. Tuskegee students were concerned about encouraging local leadership. It was crucial that the neighbor up the road insured confidence and trust in his neighbor down the road. We considered the outside agitator, the interloper, as dangerous and if not disciplined as a potential provocateur. It didn't matter if this person was black or white, male or female, Southern or Northern; such behavior in community organizing simply could not be tolerated.

The students' Tuskegee Institute Advancement League (TIAL) drafted a code of conduct for SNCC organizers: 1) only freedom fighters who intended to live in Alabama could organize in Alabama; 2) SNCC organizers, black and white, who came in and out of Alabama would be directed by the local people and were not to design leaflets and movement paraphernalia without consultation from the local people nor to control the mimeograph machine (they were to teach local people these skills); and 3) they were not to usurp the natural leadership of the local people by becoming surrogates, but were to respect grassroots people as their own leaders and advocates. Needless to say, several SNCC people, mostly white, left Alabama.

On another front, Tuskegee students strongly supported the *Southern Courier*, a weekly newspaper founded by Northern whites Jim Peppler from Yale University, Mary Ellen Gayle, and Ellen Lake, who accepted the mission to report, not to interpret, the movement in Alabama's Black Belt. The *Courier* hired as writers and stringers Viola Bradford and Rubye Howard, and her sister, Barbara Howard. They were black Montgomery high school students who had talent and potential as journalists.

Another argument between SNCC and Tuskegee students arose. Tuskegee students were content that five to ten students could command picket lines every hour on the hour so students would not miss classes. SNCC was accustomed to building mass picket lines and demonstrations. Tuskegee students were more concerned with the quality of the messages of freedom, not with the number of students.

SNCC constantly attempted to recruit students to drop out of school to become full-time SNCC organizers. TIAL vigorously fought that. We reasoned that freedom fighters needed all the education they could obtain to become present and future leaders in our community. After all, Kwame

Nkrumah, our revered president in Ghana, was a Lincoln University graduate. James Forman was a former certified school teacher. Even Stokely Carmichael took a hiatus from the movement to earn his philosophy degree from Howard University. Students stressed that our parents and relatives were spending more money than they had for us to earn our college degrees. We were not about to thumb our noses at their sacrifices. The movement needed smart leaders and our people had faith that we would become smart. Quitting school and/or cutting classes mitigated against this objective. Tuskegee students won the debate.

MEANWHILE, THE ADMINISTRATION again began to apply pressure on my student presidency. I was told that white and black city fathers were coming to terms for Tuskegee to be a "model city." The notion was ridiculous on its face. There were no black elected officials in this Black Belt county of 87 percent black population.

Sammy Younge Jr. was serving as liaison between SGA and TIAL. He spent most of his time in the SGA office as SGA officers tutored him with his studies and research papers. However, when TIAL decided to test the "model city" myth, Sammy dropped his studies and became a full-time strategist. The plan was for students to visit white churches in downtown Tuskegee. The National Presbyterian Synod had passed a resolution urging black and white parishioners to visit each other's churches. TIAL convinced a black Presbyterian, armed with the resolution, to visit the white Presbyterian church the following Sunday. Concurrent with this action would be a delegation of students, dressed in their Sunday best, to visit the white Methodist church. We thought white Methodists would be more civil than white Baptists. As the Presbyterian congregation slammed the door in the face of one of Tuskegee's upright black citizens, the Methodists physically pushed us out of their church and locked the doors. We decided to hold a church rally on the steps.

The following week, plans were made to revisit the Methodist church. The student delegation swelled to well over 500 students with a large contingent of white exchange students. When we marched from campus and made the turn to downtown, we were met by a seething white mob, armed with chains, baseball bats, and stink bombs. The mob attacked the students, singling out a white St. Olaf student who wore a leg brace due to a childhood bout with polio. Wendy Paris and other brothers battled the vicious vigilantes and pulled the student out of the melee to safety. The following week plans were made to again march to the Methodist church.

Dr. Foster summoned me to his office and pleaded with me not to lead students to the church on Sunday. I replied that he was overestimating my influence and that the students would march with or without me. He stressed that he was concerned about the students' safety.

"Perhaps if you lead the march, the racists will not attack us," I said. I told him I was certain the white city fathers would not like the national headlines to read: "Tuskegee Institute President Attacked by White Mob!"

Dr. Foster almost fell out of his chair. He called Washington, D.C., and requested that Justice Department community relations representatives come immediately to Tuskegee.

Meanwhile, community men, led by Wendy and George's father, Mr. George Paris Sr., organized themselves into an armed brigade to protect us if necessary. The Deacons for Defense and Justice out of Bogalusa, Louisiana, came up and led our march with pick-up trucks, driving in legal shotgun style. The whites remained on the sidewalks, chains and bats going limp in their hands, as they gawked at our obvious determination to defend ourselves. The Methodist church still locked its doors. We held our last church rally on the steps. We had proven the point that Tuskegee was far from being a "model city."

TUSKEGEE STUDENTS CONTINUED their movement activities in other Black Belt counties. Tuskegee student Ruby Nell Sales, SNCC's Gloria House, seminarian Jonathan Daniels and Father Richard Morrisroe, Stokely Carmichael, and sixteen other organizers were in jail in Hayneville, Lowndes County, Alabama. After Stokely was bailed out of jail, the jailers suddenly decided to release the freedom fighters. Something sinister was afoot. As several freedom fighters approached a local store to buy cold sodas, Tom Coleman, a self-appointed deputy sheriff with close ties with State Trooper Chief Al Lingo, commander of the savage attack known as "Bloody Sunday" on the Edmund Pettus Bridge in Selma, aimed his shotgun. Daniels pushed Tuskegee student Ruby Sales out of Coleman's line of fire and took the point-blank blast. For years Ruby was traumatized by this harrowing experience.

Upon Coleman's subsequent acquittal by an all-white jury in Hayneville, Tuskegee students spearheaded by Sammy Younge Jr. carried a coffin with the prominent inscription, "Justice is Dead in Alabama" to the state Capitol. As SGA president, I sent a telegram to Governor George C. Wallace about this miscarriage of justice. His lame response was,

> Under our Constitution and laws, both state and Federal, every person charged with a crime is presumed innocent until proven guilty before a jury of his peers. A jury has acquitted the accused (Tom Coleman) after hearing all of the evidence. The accused was accorded every right to which he was entitled under the Constitution, insofar as I know, and was acquitted.

THE LONG HOT summer finally came to an end. We all needed and welcomed the reprieve. Less than two weeks into the 1965 fall semester, SGA officers met with President Foster and his cabinet.

The items on the agenda included: male students had burned down World War II barracks that were still being used as dormitories but were unfit for the purpose; students had been picketing the financial aid officer because of his surly and rude behavior; and athletes had threatened to boycott the opening of football season until issues of insurance and scholarships were cleared up.

The SGA offered several proposals:

1) The burning of the barracks should be considered a minor infraction, really a favor to the Institute, for there had been dire fire violation codes.

2) The financial aid officer should borrow professional personnel from the dean of students office to assist him with the paperwork and he should work on his behavior to function as a facilitator, not as a dictator.

3) Attorney Charles Conley, legal counsel for the athletes, should draft a contract that included injury insurance and scholarship provisions in case an athlete was hurt on the playing field.

All the SGA recommendations were accepted. The students in the barracks-burning were assigned to help paint and landscape new dormitories built to replace the old barracks; no one was expelled. Conditions improved in the financial aid office. The athletes got the protections they deserved.

That fall, I was able to be a cheerleader for the Golden Tigers—and appreciated an ovation from my fellow students for my efforts—at one of the early season football games and at an exhibition basketball game; thereafter, I did not cheer until the Thanksgiving game with Tuskegee.

SGA Vice President Benny James escorted Miss Tuskegee Majorie Love, and the ROTC escorted her court of Maria Thomas and Patricia Williams at all athletic events. Homecoming in Tuskegee, for the first time, did not parade downtown for blacks and whites to view from separate sidewalks. The SGA had decided that to continue this "Jim Crow" buffoonery was offensive. The 1965 Homecoming parade ended at the edge of campus before the Dance Theatre House on Fonville Street. Peter Scott, student editor of the *Campus Digest*, wrote a supportive editorial, "Pomp Without Circumstances," explaining our position.

The parade thus did not go downtown to the Confederate statue on the courthouse square that memorialized whites for their participation in the Civil War. Since the 1930s, Macon County's rural black folks from the outlying communities—Little Texas, Fort Green, Society Hill—had to see Tuskegee students in this hostile downtown environment. Rural blacks seldom visited the campus except as patients at the campuses' John Andrews Hospital. This year they were personally invited to visit on campus to view the parade. They beamed with joy as they lined Campus Avenue, some on horses and in buggies, to watch the Crimson Pipers (under the extraordinary baton of Lucius Wyatt), the most limber drum majors and majorettes, cheerleaders, freshmen pep squad and mascot, and student organizations. The greatest shout came when the ROTC organizations performed their theatrical drills. No doubt the black war veterans found comfort that the students understood their sacrifices in fighting for democracy abroad so that their sons and daughters could fight for democracy at home. The homecoming theme was "Profiles of Future." Indeed, Tuskegee students were giving a new meaning to "profiles of courage" by dismantling local "Jim Crow" tradition.

A new pride was instilled in Tuskegee as students saluted rural black folks.

Lewis Adams, the blacksmith and farmer who founded Tuskegee Institute, was finally lifted up and placed in proper perspective with Dr. Booker T. Washington, the first president, whose brilliance had led to economic development and the founding of the National Black Labor League.

At that night's homecoming dance, "movement" students wore the freedom fighter uniform of denim overalls, sport coats, and wide 1950s ties. The underclass coeds were fascinated with, if a little frightened by, the new contemporary "after 5 attire." My cousin Ella Bell was thrilled by the "new black man," but she kept her distance. When Wendy Paris in his movement attire and hard hat with *freedom fighter* stenciled on the brim asked Ella to dance, she almost fainted. Needless to say, Ella, who eventually served on the Alabama State Board of Education, cut her movement teeth as a student at Tuskegee Institute. Today, Ella is one of the most outspoken advocates for excellence and fairness, calling out names who work adversely toward these goals to the detriment of our children.

For my last exhibition game, I cheered at the 1965 Thanksgiving Alabama State College Homecoming at Cramton Bowl in Montgomery. Tuskegee was the traditional rival to Alabama State College in this much-awaited annual event. I did not march in the parade from downtown Montgomery to the bowl, and I only cheered during the first quarter. My lungs were not what they used to be.

As CHEERLEADER, FREEDOM fighter, and student body president, I had a gratifying and almost unbelievable amount of trust from my fellow students. Several coeds confided in me about their pregnancies. I comforted them and convinced them to tell their parents—and prayed that the parents would take care of the babies. I instilled in my coeds that it was now more important than ever to get a college degree so they could take care of their babies. In one sad instance, a coed could not tell her family. She was raped by her stepfather, and she didn't think her mother would believe her.

My former residence, Thrasher Hall, was now an office building housing the Community Education Program. Dean P. B. Phillips had taken to heart the progressive students' demand that our education should be relevant to the uplift of our collective community and that the doors to post-secondary

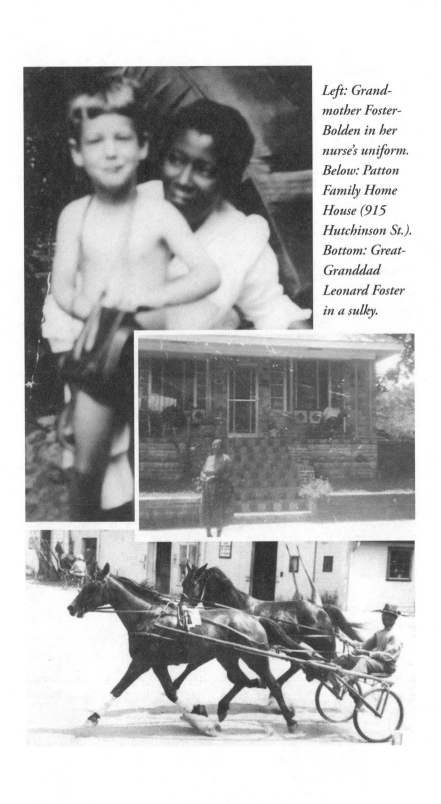

Left: Grand-mother Foster-Bolden in her nurse's uniform. Below: Patton Family Home House (915 Hutchinson St.). Bottom: Great-Granddad Leonard Foster in a sulky.

Right: Mama and Daddy when they were young. Below: Granddaddy Patton at the dedication of the repaired Bell St. Baptist Church #2 that was bombed by the KKK during the Montgomery Bus Boycott. Granddaddy was the contractor for the restoration.

Above: The Patton family home that Gwen grew up in, located at 3125 Henry Street in Inkster, Michigan.

Center: A children's birthday party that Gwen attended in the Inkster neighborhood.

Left: Gwen (kneeling, far right) as an Inkster High School cheerleader. She was also a cheerleader after she transferred to Carver High School in Montgomery, and later at Tuskegee Institute.

Right: Gwen at age seventeen. Below: Gwen and her escort attending her senior-year prom at Carver High School.

Above: Gwen as Benita in A Raisin in the Sun *in a Tuskegee Institute Little Theatre production.*
Below: Gwen (center, seated) served as the president of Tuskegee University's Student Government Association.

Above: Gwen, circled, on the Edmund Pettus Bridge in Selma, Alabama, March 21, 1965, for the start of the final Selma-to-Montgomery March. Martin Luther King Jr. is nearby at the left center of the photo.

Right: Robed and hooded members of the KKK made an appearance at one of Gwen's National Student Association meetings.

Top: In happier times, Gwen with her former husband, Jerry.

Bottom: Gwen with sax player Houston Person and jazz singer Etta Jones.

News clipping of Gwen as an organizer with hospital workers' local 1199. She and another official are in the office of U.S. Representative Frank Thompson (D-NJ), the sponsor of a bill protecting the workers.

At seventy-four, Gwen was a woman of influence and respect.

education should be an open door. He had received a multi-million grant from LBJ's Great Society programs of Opportunity for Economic Development and Equal Education Opportunity—both programs were spearheaded by black Southern youth who bravely withstood the brutal blows white supremacist police and state governments in the turbulent 1960s.

Now I was living in Emery I Dormitory, the first time coeds lived in the three nice Emery dorms that were initially built for males. Betty Gamble and Elizabeth Hayes, both from Birmingham, were my roommates. I had met Elizabeth when she and Reverend Jim Bevel visited with me in Montgomery to join the Southern Christian Leadership Conference in 1964.

The pregnant coed in question had a botched abortion by a midwife in a makeshift clinic in Montgomery. In the aftermath, she wanted me to sit with her. She was aware that Elizabeth and Betty were activists, but she did not know them well enough for trust. I asked if another friend, Linda Way, could sit with us. Linda was popular in another kind of way on campus. Her musician boyfriend, Joe Lovelace, was an accomplished bass guitar player. I told the distraught coed that there had to be at least two sitters. In the wee hours of the morning, Linda and I went to the coed's room in White Hall. She was sitting in the bathtub filled with hot water up to her chest. Blood was oozing from her vagina. It was obvious that she was in cramping pain as she pushed her feet hard against the front of the tub. Soon the head appeared and the mother pulled the stillborn baby from her womb. She cut the umbilical cord with the scissors she had placed on the tub's ledge. She washed the stillborn baby, wrapped it in a blanket, and handed it to Linda. She sponged herself off and dressed in blue jeans and a plaid shirt. She grabbed in one hand a small shovel that Linda and I had not seen leaning against the bathroom wall, and she took the baby from Linda in her other hand. We went out to the "valley" behind White Hall, where she dug a small hole under a tree, placed the dead baby in the makeshift grave and covered it with dirt. None of us said a word. I insisted that she go to John Andrews Hospital where I told the intern-residents (probably from Meharry and Howard medical schools) and nurses (from Tuskegee) that the student was experiencing severe menstrual cramps and needed immediate attention. I do not know what the interns wrote in their reports. But I was extremely happy to see the coed march at our 1966 graduation.

Another weird yet touching experience was when a male student came by my dorm to tell me that he had just left his girlfriend in a coed's apartment. He said he could not retrieve his semen-filled condom from his girlfriend's vagina. He asked me to go to the apartment to see what I could do. I went. The coed was crying and terrified that she might become pregnant. I had to go to the store to buy a pair of cooking tongs with rounded scissor edges. I boiled the tongs in hot water and then poured alcohol over them. I carefully gripped the lip of the condom and slowly pulled out the prophylactic. The semen was still in the condom.

In another situation that truly frightened me, a coed had twisted a Coke bottle up her vagina in an attempted self-abortion. The bottle became lodged in her vagina and she could not remove it. I begged an intern to come to the dorm, and after removing the bottle, he admitted her to John Andrews Hospital for follow-up.

OTHER INTERVENTIONS ON behalf of students were less dramatic, but still meaningful. While in the Hollis Burke Library one day, I overheard students squabbling over a copy of the *New York Times*. They were economic majors and one of their assignments was to track the returns of the New York Stock Exchange.

Eldridge Burns was a TIAL activist. His family was part of Tuskegee's black elite class. His mother, Mrs. Freddie Burns, was one of our librarians and she supported our student movement. I learned from her that the library only received one copy of the *Times*. When SGA treasurer and economics major Harold Foster looked into this, we found that about fifty economics students needed the paper and that the shipping costs for fifty copies would not be much more than for the one copy.

So we soon had fifty students signed up as subscribers to the *Times*. John England, a work-study student in the SGA office, picked up the papers at the bus station and delivered them to student subscribers' dorm rooms every morning. (John England would go on to law school, serve as as a city councilman in Tuscaloosa, Alabama, and eventually as a justice on the Alabama Supreme Court.)

THUS 1965 PASSED. It was no ordinary year. It was a watershed year in which ordinary black people achieved their fundamental constitutional right to vote as a result of unrelenting struggle since Reconstruction was dismantled in 1877, and it was a transcendental year during which we realized that further relentless struggle, with divine inspiration, would be required to make the black vote permanent this time.

I had incredible experiences as student body president. I had to come to grips with the contradictions within the black community. I had to rethink incest as a reality within the black family. And then there were coeds who would risk their lives not to let unintended pregnancies abort their college educations. Surely these deadly decisions demanded priority discussion in our freedom movement. I reflected on the lectures, framed as "the Epistemological Question," by philosophy professor Dr. John Eubanks. The lay interpretation of the question asked: What is value of my decisions? In the broader scope, the question begged: What is the value of my education? The response raised further questions: Will my decisions/education uplift me, my family, my community, my race?

Jubilant yet weary from nonstop activism, I looked forward to my Christmas holiday with Mommy and Poppa Washington. The two weeks were festive with friends home from various HBCUs in Louisiana, Georgia, Tennessee, Virginia, and the Carolinas. We gathered at each other's homes to talk about what was happening on our respective campuses. At my annual Christmas tea parties, one of the highlights was caroling while I played the melodies on the piano. The centerpiece of our impromptu cantata was Lamar Alford's solo rendition of "O Holy Night." (A Morehouse music and theater major, Lamar's musical talents landed him a starring Broadway role in *Godspell*.)

Buoyed with the Christmas spirit, we retired to Mommy's large dining table, elaborately set, including exquisite sherry glasses for Mommy's homemade plum and cherry wines. The centerpiece was a miniature ceramic nativity scene. We took our seats with Poppa Washington at the head of the table. He offered blessing and thanks, being mindful to thank Mommy for preparing the spread. We said Bible verses and thanked God for bringing us through an eventful year. Then Mommy served finger sandwiches and festive cookies.

After Mommy and Poppa Washington retired, our movement discussions began in earnest. Were we the "talented tenth" with options to escape the horrific slavery history of our people? If so, was it the purpose of our education to swell the ranks of the "black bourgeoisie," oblivious to our history? Or did we presume a role in the "vanguard" to liberate our wretched people? We did not yet have the constitutional right to equal opportunity in this racist society. Did democracy in its present administration work for us? Our consensus was a resounding "NO!" We would continue our activism to strike a blow against Jim Crow. With this collective resolve, my guests cheerfully said "Merry Christmas" and departed.

The remainder of the Christmas holiday was a restful respite. Nevertheless, I expected the upcoming year would be tumultuous.

17

Sammy Younge Jr.

Someone shouted from the kitchen: "We need a bottle of mayonnaise!"

Our habit was that SGA officers, TIAL organizers, and student leaders would meet at the TIAL "freedom house" after students returned from extended breaks. January 2, 1966, was such an occasion after the Christmas holiday. As soon as we unloaded our suitcases, we beat the familiar path to the freedom house.

Sammy Younge Jr. was a large presence in these gatherings. Sometimes "Sammy and his Lemon Drops," also called the "Shades," an informal doo-wop chorus consisting of Sammy, Wendy Paris, Henry Holtzclaw, Eldridge Burns, and William Winston, would give us a private concert—in terms of our enjoyment, they could rival Smokey Robinson and the Miracles. Cornelius Jones had the meanest "shing-a-ling" dance steps this side of the Mississippi.

Refreshments always consisted of an array of Mogen David, Boone's

Farm, and Cold Duck wines. George Ware often brought fancy chianti in exotic basket-covered bottles—the empties served as candleholders and gave a decorative touch to the table. Of course, Sammy's Catawba Pink wine was in abundance. And the centerpiece was a plate of bologna sandwiches on white bread, slathered with mayonnaise, which apparently had run out.

"I'll get the mayonnaise!" Sammy shouted.

I caught him as he was leaving and asked to be dropped off at the campus on his way to the store. "I need to rest and be ready for registration on tomorrow," I said. I had preregistered for my own spring semester classes, but as SGA president I felt a responsibility to be present as our 2,000-plus students jammed into Logan Hall for the sometimes stressful registration process.

We jumped in Sammy's souped-up, powder-blue Volkswagen and dashed off. It was about 10:30 p.m. when he dropped me off.

And then, just like that, he was gone.

Around 12:30 a.m., a firm knock on my dorm door startled me from a deep sleep. "Dean Phillips wants you on the telephone in the office," a voice on the other side of the door shouted in alarm. "Please hurry!"

Dr. P. B. Phillips had never called me in my dorm, let alone at this time in the early morning. I groggily got to the phone and asked him what was the matter.

"Sammy has been shot," he said.

He went on to explain that Sammy had apparently argued with a white gas station attendant about using the inside restroom. Notwithstanding the 1964 Civil Rights Act that had barred segregation of public accommodations, many white store owners in the South, including at the Standard gas station near the Tuskegee bus depot, still tried to restrict the use of their toilets to whites only. Navy veteran and SNCC organizer Sammy Younge Jr. was not one who would have accepted that kind of discrimination. It was natural that he would have resisted. In any case, the white gas station attendant, Marvin Segrest, had shot Sammy.

Dean Phillips confirmed that Sammy was dead.

I struggled to process this shocking news. Finally, I asked Dean Phillips if he would have dorm parents and resident counselors post announcements for a student body meeting at 7:30 a.m. in Logan Hall. He said he would.

Then, inexplicably, I went back to my room and fell back to sleep.

I AWOKE WITHOUT an alarm clock at 5:45 a.m. It was January 3, 1966, the day of Sammy Younge Jr.'s murder. Almost in a daze, I dressed, walked to Thompkins Hall, and was the only student in the dining hall for breakfast at 6:25 a.m. Twenty minutes later, I slowly walked down the stairs to the student center where the SGA office was located. Mrs. Beulah Johnson, a community leader, was sitting in a metal folding chair in front of my locked office.

More often than not, Mrs. Johnson was furious with student activism. A native Tuskegeean of the elite class, she viewed student activists as "outside agitators" heaping dispersions on her idyllic and culturally enriched community haven. She was convinced that the local elite Tuskegee students like Sammy Younge Jr., George Knox, Eldridge Burns, Demetrius Robinson, Wendy Paris, Patti Jones, Shirley Irving, George Poole, and other born, bred, and protected Tuskegee "kids" were unduly influenced by unruly militants. She constantly called us a "bunch of communists."

We did not dislike Mrs. Johnson. She meant well. She truly loved her beloved community. But we could not resist playing a joke on her. We called the FBI in Montgomery and told them that we knew a woman who knew a lot of communists and no doubt was a communist herself. She was livid when FBI agents visited her home and interrogated her. We had a good laugh over it. Humor could be like high-octane gas to help the Movement get over some humps.

But this morning, there sat Mrs. Johnson, stoic and firm. She stood, grabbed me by the hand, and led me out to her car. "Please, get in," she said. "I want to talk with you before you meet with the students in the gym."

We drove around for awhile in the neighborhood and then toward the edge of town as she urged me to stay calm. Soon it dawned on me that Mrs. Johnson was kidnapping me and driving me out into rural Macon County. At the next stop sign, I opened the passenger-side door, leaped out, and ran as fast as I could until a passing motorist picked me up and drove me hurriedly back to campus.

By the time I arrived, the bleachers in Logan Hall were packed with murmuring students. Dean Phillips, SGA adviser Danny Williams, and President Foster were already on stage. I joined them and stepped to the microphone. I asked all SGA officers, cabinet members, and dorm reps to join me on stage. SNCC and TIAL organizers were in the audience, but I did not call them forth. This was a student assembly as to how we would deal with the murder of our colleague.

Our immediate message was to remain calm, go to class, let the police investigate, be courteous and forthcoming if you saw anything connected to the shooting, and feel free to come to the SGA office if you want to talk.

As classmates slowly and sorrowfully left the gym, I asked Wendy and Eldridge to join me in paying respects to the Younge family. My nervousness dissipated when Mrs. Rennie Younge, Sammy's mother, greeted me with a hug and asked me to help with the funeral program. She had always been there with the "movement kids," sometimes joining Mr. George Paris Sr. at our planning meetings. Little Stevie, Sammy's baby brother, who truly admired his big brother, was distraught. The tears would not stop as he kept repeating his brother's mantra, "What are we gonna do?"

Mr. Younge Sr., though forlorn and quiet, was visibly angry. I could not tell in that moment if he was angry with me and the other students or with the shooter. Twenty-three years later, I came face-to-face with Mr. Younge at the dedication in Montgomery of the Southern Poverty Law Center's Civil Rights Memorial for those who were martyred during the movement days. Sammy's name is one of the forty inscribed on the memorial. Mr. Younge leaped out of his chair to hug me and said, "Gwen, I understand now what you kids were doing. My son was a revolutionary. I am so proud of him." As we embraced each other with tears of reconciliation, I replied, "Sammy was a good man. You raised him to be giving and caring. He will always be remembered and cherished. His memory will live forever."

THE STUDENT BODY reassembled at noon in the dining hall. I stood in the intercom music booth in the center of the hall with nothing to report except that Segrest had been taken into custody and released on bail. I learned that some students, mostly Northerners, had withdrawn from Tuskegee

Institute at the behest of their parents. Many of these parents knew first-hand the horrors of Jim Crow and had left the South with the hopes that their children could be spared the type of mean racism sanctioned by the state of Alabama. The Tuskegee Institute of Booker T. Washington, George Washington Carver, the Tuskegee Airmen, and so many others, had seemed a safe oasis, but now even a Tuskegee student could be murdered, and some parents could not abide their children being in harm's way.

I had already met with President Foster and urged him to write all Tuskegee parents to quell their fears and to assure them that Tuskegee Institute would be relentless in bringing the murderer Segrest to justice. I was convinced that Segrest was an emboldened racist who felt he could kill Sammy with impunity because the local black elite did not embrace the moral purity of the black students' movement for freedom and fundamental social change, right there in Tuskegee. I do not know if Dr. Foster dispatched such a letter. If he did, I never received a copy.

Nonetheless, I told my fellow students, "I understand that some of us want to withdraw from school. But more than ever this is the time for us to remain and to fight for our rights. Sammy was murdered because of our righteous struggle for freedom in racist America. Let's not abandon his life, our lives, by withdrawing and leaving."

I sensed that the students wanted, needed an action to channel their pain and anger and spontaneously called for students to assemble at 2 p.m. at Logan Hall to march downtown for a vigil "in honor of our slain revolutionary brother, Sammy."

With the murder of Sammy, we transformed from "freedom fighters" to "revolutionaries." We had lost a soldier in the heat of the battle.

At 2 o'clock, it felt as if all 2,300 students were gathered at Logan Hall, along with professors and community people in great numbers. SGA officers and cabinet members, TIAL and SNCC organizers, Dean Phillips, and SGA adviser Danny Williams were at the front of the line. We silently marched from campus to the bus station. We blanketed the area with our bodies in a collective message that we would continue our fight against USA/Southern-style Jim Crow apartheid.

Wendy, wearing his freedom fighter attire, had an amplified bullhorn.

Several TIAL leaders urged the students to hold strong, to "keep their hands on the freedom plow," and to cling to the blood-stained banner of freedom. SNCC organizers led us in freedom songs, including one of Sammy's favorites, "I Know That Freedom Is a Constant Struggle." We were sad but energized as we marched silently back to campus.

WHILE WE AWAITED the legal course for justice, a series of actions were planned and implemented. We called for a boycott of white businesses. We demanded that Tuskegee Institute withdraw its account from Alabama Exchange Bank, where Tuskegee City Council President Allen Parker was CEO. Students regularly attended city council meetings and raised poignant questions as to the progress of the murder case.

As SGA president, I wrote U.S. Assistant Attorney General John Doar in the Civil Rights Division, asking him to look into the violation of Sammy's civil rights. Doar's response infuriated me:

> An extensive investigation by the Federal Bureau of Investigation has failed to produce evidence of a violation of a federal criminal statute. In this case, possible federal crimes would have been willful deprivation of federal rights under the color of law or the deprivation of such rights pursuant to a conspiracy.
>
> The Department of Justice is continuing to follow developments bearing upon civil rights in Tuskegee. Where we found violations of federal law in Macon County (Tuskegee), we have acted to correct them. In this connection, the United States moved in court to eliminate racial discrimination in voting, schools, public accommodations, and jury selection in Macon County. Most recently, on January 20, 1966, the federal court ordered the Macon County Jury Commission to compile a new jury roll on a racially non-discriminatory basis. This along with prior court orders against racial discrimination in the voter registration process should help insure the fair administration of justice by local authorities in Macon County.

What in the hell was Doar talking about! The registrar's office was always closed when we escorted black potential voters to the courthouse. If you were not a voter, then how could you serve on a jury? Hell, the racists were in charge, and they were hell-bent not to share power with a people they still thought should be their personal property. Their attempt to put on a liberal face in working with black people as a whole, and not just with the black elite, was a farce. The ruling whites, in tacit agreement with elite blacks, demonstrated a class structure within a racist caste system. The students found that arrangement unacceptable. We cared about our people in the rural areas—most of whom were poor farmers—and were not going to be gulled by the town and gown class.

Attorney Doar's officious letter was "sound and fury, signifying nothing." To hell with U.S. Attorney John Doar.

Sammy's "Celebration of Life" was held at Mt. Olive Baptist Church, in the heart of Tuskegee's black working-class community, on the north side of town going towards Auburn, and across town from the black elite enclaves. Sammy was not a member of the church, but this was where his people were, with down-home services. He was a regular worshipper, often singing in the choir, rousing the spiritual wherewithal to carry out the freedom struggle for the next week. It was from this congregation that Sammy encouraged people to go to the voter registrar's office. He had helped at least 700 people to get registered.

There was a solemn motorcade from the Younges' home. Immediately after the family car came a fleet of SNCC cars, souped-up to outrun racist vigilantes, now driving in a slow dirge of grief. Packed student cars and campus buses were next in line. At the church, Mrs. Younge had asked that all the pews on the left side, behind the family seating, be set aside for SNCC freedom fighters, Sammy's comrades in struggle, SGA officers, and TIAL student leaders. The rest of the church was packed with community people and overflow mourners stood outside in the drizzling rain. Yes, God was crying.

There were wails of hurt as the church choir sang the fourth stanza of the "Battle Hymn of the Republic": "In the beauty of the lilies Christ was born across the sea / with a glory in his bosom that transfigured you and me / as he died to make men holy, let us die to make men free / while God is marching on. Glory, glory hallelujah!"

Then SNCC Freedom Singers rose to sing "We'll Never Turn Back": "We've been buked and we've been scorned / we've been turned back sure's you're born. But, we'll never turn back. / No, we'll never turn back, till all people be free. / We've hung our heads and cried for those like Sammy who have died. But we'll never turn back, / No, we'll never turn back, till all people be free. / Sammy died for you and he died for me. No, we'll never turn back till all people be free."

The sobs did not wash out our renewed commitment to "never turn back." Racist America would have to deal with us in the name of Sammy Younge Jr., the first U.S. black college student murdered in the line of duty for fighting for freedom, not on foreign land but on the home front.

A WEEK HAD passed since Sammy's "Celebration of Life." Students still were terribly emotionally distraught. I secured an appointment with Dr. Foster and went to his office. The guardian of his inner sanctum was his secretary, Mrs. Pauline Punch. She was a part of Tuskegee's black elite and vehemently resented the student movement. Her son, Ricky, wanted to be a part of our movement, but she adamantly vetoed his participation. On several occasions I asked her at least to allow Ricky to work with the SGA, strictly with campus-student activities. It puzzled me why people like Mrs. Punch had a dire need to establish a strict class culture in the black community of Tuskegee at the expense of the majority of black citizens. I was from the third generation of an education family, destined to be a college professor in accord with so-called class elevation. But all of us had working-class family members, and all of us rose on the strong backs of our people who were enslaved or, post-emancipation, became domestic servants and yardmen for white people. Mrs. Punch should have welcomed my intentions and efforts, but she always had a pithy response to my presence. Sometimes her verbal response and tone were extremely caustic. I was never ever to find common ground with Mrs. Punch. Sadly, her son, Ricky, became a drug addict.

On this day, she announced via the intercom on Dr. Foster's desk that I had arrived and he said to send me in. I got right to the point, asking him to suspend the regular order of classes so the campus family could come to grips with the traumatic thing that had happened to our Tuskegee family.

"We need our administrators to show grief with us," I told him. "We as students need to know what the mission of our school is. We need confirmation that it is part of the school's mission to train us to serve our people, not run away from them. Just as you exercised your *in loco parentis* status to try to prohibit our march for voting rights, I'm asking you to show 'in absentia parental' concern. I have lost a brother. You have lost a son."

Tears flowed from my eyes. They welled in his, too.

We came to an accord. Dr. Foster would call a two-day moratorium to discuss and share our grief of losing Sammy by the most foul means. Dr. Robert J. Havighurst from the University of Chicago School of Social Work would develop a convocation and facilitate the collective grief-counseling so much needed by the students. We needed to find purpose and direction in our ongoing quest for freedom in a society that despised us because of the color of our skin. We were clear that *e pluribus unum* was about Europeans melting in a cultural pot of whiteness. Black folks were never intended to be poured into the pot.

The second moratorium day would deal with the matters of the day: 1) school desegregation; 2) housing for people in the county; 3) scholarships for local rural people to attend Tuskegee; 4) apartheid in South Africa; and 5) the Vietnam War and the draft.

Bettina Aptheker helped put together a "teach-in" on the war and the draft, with attorneys Bill Kuntsler and Arthur Kinoy of the Center for Constitutional Rights out of New York City as moderators. Dr. Eric William Krystal, our white South African exiled professor, facilitated "teach-ins" on South Africa and what is now Namibia. African students from Rhodesia (now Zimbabwe), Kenya, Ghana, Nigeria, and other African nations were a part of the "teach-ins" to share their revolutionary struggles against colonialism. We were enlightened—and dismayed—that "neo-colonialism," with African puppets carrying out the bidding of white colonialists, was the new struggle on the continent. Yes, "freedom is a constant struggle," as Sammy had often reminded us.

The two-day moratorium was a tremendous success, bringing a sense of calm that the Tuskegee family was becoming whole and holistic. Administrators no longer sneered at our movement activity. Going to class *and* joining picket lines to fight for the right to vote, to get jobs, and to have decent housing were complements to our classes and became a routine way of life for Tuskegee students. If education is to have a real and positive consequence, it must be relevant to the uplift of the community.

MEANWHILE, SAMMY YOUNGE'S murderer was out on bail, walking the streets. Tuskegee's 1966 spring and summer semesters passed and the fall semester began and still no trial date had been set.

18

Student Teaching and Graduation

As SGA officers were preparing for the 1966–67 student body elections, a large delegation greeted me in the SGA office. "We want you to run for student body president again."

I knew they were sincere. I was moved by their request. But I was a senior and would graduate at the end of the semester; I had already been accepted in Tuskegee's graduate program for the summer of 1966. Further, the new constitution I helped enact did not permit a graduate student to serve as SGA president.

SGA Vice President Benny James was not an integral part of the student movement, but he was an excellent team member and was in line for the presidency. I wanted more than anything for him to succeed.

I listened intently to the delegation's rationale and was humbled by their support of my leadership. We agreed that I would run for the office of vice president, which would be a unique move but constitutional. I was elected overwhelmingly as the vice president for the 1966–67 school term, garnering more votes than any other candidate. I was elated that Benny was elected as president with a substantial margin.

One of my actions as SGA president was to secure the blessing of Dr. Foster to print our yearbook, the *Tuskeana*, in the campus print shop. Previously it had been published by a white firm in Montgomery. But I had taken an elective course in the School of Mechanical Industries and was amazed at the various industry-career development crafts taught, including printing. This was in keeping with the tradition of vocational education so important to the philosophy and success of Booker T. Washington. I wondered why we didn't have more community people enrolled in the School of Mechanical Industries.

Now I went back to see Dr. Foster to talk about our 1966 graduation and our signature yearbook that would chronicle our 1965–66 campus, community, and movement activities, and the murder of Sammy Younge Jr. Mrs. Punch was as terse as ever, but Dr. Foster received me warmly. We truly had developed a mutual respect. I explained that we wanted to dedicate the 1966 *Tuskeana* to Dr. P. B. Phillips, dean of students, who had never faltered in his support, especially during trying times. Dr. Foster was okay with that. He was also okay with my suggestion that our graduation speaker be Dr. Dorothy Height, president of the National Council of Negro Women (and a Delta, as I would become).

When I thought I could coast for at least a week, another ordeal cropped up. "You will not practice-teach here," the principal of the black Tuskegee high school said to me. In minutes, a campus transport delivered me back to campus. There was never an option for me to practice-teach at the downtown high school, which although technically desegregated was still predominantly white and had only white teachers.

Administrators arranged for me to meet with the Institute's legal counsel, attorney Fred Gray. He had successfully argued in the U.S. Supreme Court the landmark 1957 *Gomillion v. Lightfoot* case that struck down the gerrymandering by whites of the city limits of Tuskegee so as to exclude practically every black Tuskegee voter from the city limits. The gerrymandering was, of course, an effort by whites to retain local political control. They correctly saw the rise in black voter registration as the handwriting on the wall that spelled the end of local white domination of city and county elective offices. Gray had also been the attorney for Rosa Parks, Martin Luther King Jr., and the Montgomery Improvement Association during the Montgomery Bus Boycott. His lawsuit on behalf of Claudette Colvin, Aurelia Browder, Susie McDonald, and Mary Louise Smith had ultimately ended the 382-day boycott with a federal court decision that struck down Jim Crow laws requiring segregated seating on city buses.

Gray had also represented the Freedom Riders in 1961, sued numerous segregated school systems, and had successfully argued in federal court that the Selma March should be allowed to continue. He was a genuine civil rights legend.

But attorney Gray and I had strong differences. Though we eventually reconciled, I don't know if in the spring of 1966 he was still smarting from my successful challenge that stayed the expulsion of Frankie Chambliss from Tuskegee Institute. Attorney Gray did not like losing, especially to a militant student like me.

He suggested that I student-teach in Birmingham, but Birmingham was 148 miles northwest and I would have been away for the entire work week from campus and my responsibilities as SGA president and as a scholar-activist in the student movement.

"There is no alternative," he said. "Nobody in Macon County wants you at the schools."

I called attorney Bill Kunstler in New York City and asked him to call Dr. Deborah Cannon Wolfe, a master education professor at Hunter's Teacher College. She had sent letters of support for our student movement work, and she was from Shorter, a rural community in Macon County. A school was named in her honor in that community.

Dr. Wolfe called President Foster and insisted that I undergo my practice-teaching internship at the school named for her. Attorney Kunstler called attorney Gray, who backed off in light of a promised lawsuit as a breach of contract that Tuskegee Institute had promised, via tuition, to provide an unfettered opportunity for me to earn my baccalaureate degree to its completion.

SOON ENOUGH, I was sitting in the principal's office at Deborah Cannon Wolfe High School, sixteen miles west of Tuskegee Institute. The previous name for the school was Macon County Training School (for colored students) that served rural youth in west Macon County where Shorter was the central community amid with outlying smaller farming communities. A brick structure had replaced the wooden building of the Rosenwald School model.

"Miss Patton, you are by no means here to stir up our students. If it had not been for Dr. Wolfe, you would not be here." As he laid out *his* rules and *his* regulations, the phone kept ringing in a strange ring pattern.

"Yes, sir," I said to each rule. "Do you wish to answer the phone?"

"No, that's the party-line."

I suppressed my disgust that a public school would have to share a phone line with other parties in the area. What if there was an emergency? What if a party line subscriber picked up the phone while the principal was having a confidential conversation concerning a student or a teacher?

My orientation finished, the principal punched an intercom button on a miniature switchboard on his desk to ask the teacher who would be mentoring me to send a student "to fetch" me.

Miss Winifred Davis was known as one of the best English teachers in the school district. She was a spinster who lived in Tuskegee with her spinster sister. Both pulled their hair back into tight buns and wore glasses. They were part of Tuskegee's educated, black elite. I did not know their position on the movement or of Tuskegee students' involvement in it.

I found her warm, sincere, and dedicated. She taught the lesson for the day for five periods while I sat in the back of the classroom. At the end of each period, she enthusiastically introduced me as the student-teacher for the next six weeks.

During her home-room lunch period, I joined Miss Davis and the students to the multi-purpose room that served as a gym, convocation hall, and lunchroom with long tables. Male students were playing an impromptu basketball game on one end. I nodded to the fellow who had the ball and he impulsively tossed it to me. Maybe my three-inch heels gave me a luck advantage, but I launched the ball towards the net and it swooshed through, making me an instant hit with the students.

Most students brought sandwiches. There were milk, fruit, and snack machines. There was nothing hot to tide their tummies over before the long bus ride, sometimes ten miles, back to their homes in the rural community. Practically all of these students had chores, fetching water from the well, chopping and piling up wood to lay in store for the winter months, feeding chickens and collecting eggs, before coming to school. Many awoke by 5:30 a.m. to complete their chores. And for goodness sakes, don't let them miss the broken-down, rambling school bus. They would trudge the ten miles, hoping to get a ride in a passing pick-up truck, the first car in the rural community. School meant much to these rural children and youth.

When the Institute's driver picked me up at 3:30 p.m. that day, I asked to be dropped off at the Bell South Telephone Company office in Tuskegee. I asked to see the manager and told him I thought it was outrageous that a public school had to share a party line. He replied that private phone lines were more expensive and his company was in the business of making money.

At that time, we were boycotting downtown stores to protest the murder of Sammy Younge Jr., but on my walk home I broke the boycott to stop at a hardware store to purchase an electric hot-plate, a large soup pot, a can-opener, a water pitcher, fifteen plastic soup bowls, and spoons.

I had moved from the Emery I dormitory to a house trailer with a kitchen with a large, modern refrigerator. The trailer was owned by George Carter, whose family owned several businesses, including a small grocery store. I stopped by the store and purchased five pounds of beef tips and canned vegetables. Loaded down, I asked George if he would drive me home.

The following morning, I had to make several trips to the campus transport to load up before we made our trek to school. The driver helped me carry all the packages to my classroom. Before the students arrived, I placed the hot-plate on a desk and made several trips to the bathroom to fill the pitcher with water for the soup pot. Once the water was boiling, I spilled into it the beef-tips and some salt and pepper.

I did not teach the first day. Instead, I gave the students a survey of Elizabethan, Romantic, and Victorian literature. We then exchanged ideas as to how we could best learn together. But, of course, the students were fascinated with the soup pot before them. I explained the importance of a hot meal in the middle of the day. We talked about our culture as farmers, builders, and laborers with our heartiest meal at mid-day.

On the blackboard, we listed vegetables we could add to the soup pot: "Tomatoes, green peppers, onions, potatoes, okra—fresh. Home left-overs of cooked corn and pole beans." The students divided into groups and decided among themselves as to who would bring what and how much. Miss Davis beamed as she sat in the back of the classroom and I at the teacher's desk.

After I poured the canned vegetables into the soup, the aroma permeated the school building. The principal came stalking into the classroom.

"Miss Patton, what are you doing?!"

"Cooking soup and teaching."

He fumed that I was creating a fire hazard, and I replied that our students needed a hot meal and reminded him that the school had a kitchen where soup could be made for the entire student body. He threw up his hands and stomped out, mumbling to himself.

When the driver picked me up at the end of my second day, I asked to be taken to the home of Socrates and Connie Harper. What a powerful and historically insightful first name for a rural black farmer and businessman! The family owned an expanse of productive farm land in Tyson, Alabama. Mrs. Harper supported Tuskegee's student movement though she cautioned me that we were moving too fast for recalcitrant whites whom she thought would eventually come around. Her mantra to these whites was that we were human and should have an opportunity to sustain ourselves. She was an ardent believer in the philosophy of Dr. Booker T. Washington, the first president of Tuskegee Institute, who stressed that "black people must pull themselves up by their own bootstraps." Mrs. Harper's motto was "Be patient and love tough, both black and white."

I discussed the party-line phone issue with her and added that I had learned that the white and the black high schools in Tuskegee had private lines. "Why should our rural children be slighted?" Mrs. Harper took this cause personally, and almost overnight, the party line ceased at the school. (Mrs. Harper was later elected to the Macon County School Board.)

I cooked soup in my classroom for about two weeks. Thereafter, hot soup was provided for all students in the multi-purpose room. This became the antecedent to provide hot lunches at all public schools in Macon County.

I presented my six-week module to Miss Davis for her review, suggestions, and approval. She commented that it was a novel approach to English literature. I had been torn as to how I was to teach English literature to rural youth—how to maintain and transfer the beauty and rhythm of the words, yet with an appreciation that would have meaning, relevance, and application in the lives of my students today.

Shakespeare's *Macbeth* was not difficult. I employed the usual methodologies of students memorizing certain passages for recitation and elocution. Most of the girls chose Lady Macbeth's crazed soliloquy, "Out damn spot . . ." To be able to use "damn" in the school setting thrilled them. The boys reenacted the moving of Birnam Forest with their class-made props of trees, shields and swords. They enjoyed learning about military maneuvers. The students in teams reenacted scenes in homemade costumes. The three-witches scene was the favorite as we filled the black washpot with makeshift creatures while putting packs of dry ice into the water in the pot so that it hissed and gave off steam.

We did not only read the play in class. I played recordings of the play so students could hear intonations and expressions. Listening skills were high on my teaching agenda. I had been to too many rallies where speakers electrified the crowd to action, but when I asked people what the speakers had said, they would fervently reply, "I don't know, but they sure did sound good!"

Macbeth also provided a way to teach character skills and values, to teach about the flawed quest for power that can impel murder. The murder of Sammy Younge Jr. was all about power and the murderous determination of those in the "power class" not to share power. Sharing power, of course, was the cornerstone of participatory democracy, a safeguard for a civilized society.

Teaching the Romantic and Victorian poets was a different and more complex subject matter. We had fun as I taught rhyme and meter. Students composed their own poems, explained their poetic structures and recited their works before their classmates. I concentrated on the works of Shelley and Yeats because their brilliant poetry reflected the matters of their day—

the hardship of life in the transition from agrarian to industrial society, displacing farmers and the elderly.

We read and discussed the prolific young poet, Keats, who died at twenty-six. I stressed the importance for students to maximize their potential no matter how young they were. Sammy Younge Jr. was only twenty-two when he was killed, but he had left his heroic mark.

The Brownings were my favorite poets to lift up love for family and between a man and a woman. We talked about "girl and boy" relation-ships, courting and personal commitments. I displayed in the classroom an ornate calligraphy poster made by an artist in Tuskegee Institute's School of Mechanical Industries of the "How do I love thee?" sonnet. It was refresh-ing to see a boy and girl holding hands before the poster and reading the poem to each other.

I loathed Wordsworth and Coleridge but Alabama's school standards required that they be taught. Coleridge's cocaine-induced "Kubla Khan" at least was an outstanding piece for discussing poetic form, but I saw no redeeming grace in such poems as Wordsworth's "Daffodils." To balance this segment, I introduced the poetry of Robert Burns and Sojourner Truth and the poetic prose of Frederick Douglass, which enhanced my teaching that art must reflect the conditions of the people of the period.

At the end of the six weeks, Miss Davis handed me my evaluation. With apprehension, I slowly read her lengthy assessment, to find at the end that she had given me a grade of A++. She told me, "I've learned as much as the students, if not more, from your teaching. I definitely will have a new approach when I teach English literature next school term." I hugged her. It meant much to be validated by a master English teacher. I thanked her for understanding my commitment to our people, especially our youth.

Concurrent with my practice teaching, I had been writing my senior English thesis, for which I presented oral arguments before a panel of English professors. Professor Emma Walker, the wife of Dr. Saunders Walker, head of the English Department, was my thesis chair. Mrs. Walker was a stately, ultra-feminist in manner, yet handsome like the movie star Lauren Bacall.

My thesis title was "What Did the Romantic Poets (1752–1848) Do

During the Debacle of the Cato Street Conspiracy?" The title referred to a foiled 1820 plot to launch an uprising against British class structure and poverty and exploitation of the working people. I indicted the Romantics for not using their creative talents to inform on the inhumane conditions of their society.

My thesis committee, with a congratulatory note from Dr. Saunders Walker, awarded me the grade of A+.

ABOUT A WEEK before graduation, I was asked by a delegation of SNCC women warriors to join them as a full-time organizer. Jean Wiley, an English teacher at Tuskegee Institute, had resigned to work full-time for SNCC in its communications department and had recommended me to become a SNCC campus traveler. One of the strong sisters in the delegation was Rubye Doris Smith-Robinson, who had weathered the jails of Mississippi during "Freedom Summer." She was now SNCC executive secretary, succeeding the venerable James Forman. Another sister was Fay Bellamy, who was my mentor because of her militant, no-nonsense demeanor. Fay also co-authored the SNCC play, *Back to Black*, featuring Stokely "Star-michael" in one of the lead roles. I saw the play later with Fay in Atlanta and commented, "Back to black? Most of us never left nor desired to leave 'black.'" Miriam Tillinghast was also part of the delegation. We knew her well in Tuskegee when she denied SNCC cars for our organizing, and instead sent us money to buy mules to ride in rural Lowndes County. Gwen Robinson, a profound strategist for urban community empowerment, completed the delegation.

I listened intently as to why I should become a full-time cadre for SNCC. I was still struggling with "movement work" as separate from the ordinary life experiences of our people on a daily basis, regardless of where they were in the scheme of living. To me, the movement was an everyday responsibility in pushing back racism and pushing forward for freedom. The movement was not some extracurricular activity but was an inextricable part of my existence that shaped my very being, my purpose, and my outlook on the world and my role in it. People had to come to the movement with their own self-interest at heart to be free. Anything less than this consciousness to struggle for personal freedom from racism, or as an unconscious racist who did not see her/his perpetualization of racism, was paternalist and naïve at best, or was a sickening and disgusting ego-trip to assume the surrogate position of martyr/stardom to free other people and not him/herself.

My thoughts also concentrated on the sacrifice of my family who made it possible for me to earn my degree and who had pledged to underwrite my pursuit of the master's degree. They surely wanted me to enter the mainstream, wherever I could, to make a difference in that arena that would have a positive impact on the lives of black people in that sphere.

As I contemplated these heavy concerns, I said, "I will be in graduate school this summer. I was elected as vice president for the SGA. My community work is in Benton, Lowndes County and we must focus on electing our Black Panther Party candidates to important county-wide positions. We can never thank SNCC enough for the primer on the roles and responsibilities of county elected offices, especially that of sheriff, coroner, school board, tax assessor and collector. Moreover, here in Macon County, we are working hard to elect Lucius Amerson as the South's first black sheriff since Reconstruction. He asked specifically for Wendy Paris and me to work in his campaign."

"Okay," my sisters said, registering their true understanding. "We will come back after summer to ask you again."

We were all clad in our black robes; honor tassels to the sides of our mortarboard caps. Tuskegee Institute's traditional Mother's Day graduation was always blessed with splendid weather for our ceremony on the campus green. Dr. Dorothy Height, president of the National Council of Negro Women, delivered the commencement address. Her message was that no matter where we found ourselves in the professional world of work, it was not isolated nor insulated from our mission to continue our quest for freedom. Dr. Height, a woman of immense intellectual and purposeful stature, reinforced my rationale to my strong SNCC sisters that our race to freedom was the essence of our being.

As I crossed the stage to receive my degree, I marched directly to Mommy, my grandmother, and handed her my diploma. "This is yours. You surely earned it," I said with tremendous love.

She lovingly smiled at me and looked knowingly in my eyes and knew I was tired. Truthfully, I was not only exhausted, I was bone-tired. I couldn't wait for the between-semesters two weeks of pure rest during which I knew Mommy and Poppa Washington would wait on me hand and foot. I knew that after that respite, I would be ready for the challenges that surely lay ahead for me as a graduate student.

19

Macon, Lowndes, and Atlanta

Graduate school, however, quickly took a back seat to politics and organizing in Macon and Lowndes counties, and then on a broader scale.

Lucius Amerson, a husband and the father of two sons, left his job in the cafeteria at the Veterans' Hospital in Tuskegee to vie for sheriff in Macon County. He asked Wendy Paris and me to head up the student contingent in support of his campaign. We were not surprised by the backlash of the tiny white population that was still in political control of the county—the very thought of a black man in legal authority, with a gun, no less, was repugnant to them. But the internecine class struggle that developed around Amerson's candidacy within the black community was something else!

Amerson was a short and muscular Korean War veteran. And he was dark-skinned. Tuskegee did not *per se* have a color caste system; the entry into the elite class was to possess a college degree. Amerson had none, and the fact that he was dark invoked the invidious dictate: "If you're black, stay back!"

The incumbent sheriff was Harvey Sadler. He had been appointed by Governor George Wallace to replace the previous sheriff, Preston Hornsby, who resigned to run for probate judge. Sadler had been a member of the White Citizens Council, the suit-wearing counter-part to the Ku Klux Klan. He helped found Macon Academy, the white private school formed in response to school desegregation, and his children were students there.

However, Sadler had political savvy. He was cordial to blacks, which was truly welcomed. The memory of the earlier abusive Sheriff "Pat" Evans, a fanatic racist who called black people "niggers" quicker than he would call them by their first names, was still vivid in the minds of blacks, especially in the rural community. Despite his own racist background, Sadler did not want to be viewed as an Evans reincarnation. Before the 1966 primary election, Sadler appointed a black deputy to bolster his newly acquired "moderate-liberal" image. It has always floored me as to why white people think that their political-liberal shift, even if heartfelt, should replace the aspirations of black people in their quest to share power. And when black people press their right to sit at the table of democracy, these so-called liberals become "hurt." Our struggle has never been about finding white people to serve as our surrogates. We had already been there during four hundred years of slavery and segregation.

Students were not fooled by the white politicians' machinations. Wallace appointed Sadler to give him a leg-up on that office. Blacks, as a result of unrelenting efforts to register as voters, now outnumbered white voters in Macon County by three-to-one. Blacks were seeking political offices across the board, from the state legislature, county school board, county commission, to tax collector.

The reaction of Tuskegee's black elites to Amerson's candidacy was unbelievable! There actually was a public statement that the position of sheriff should be the *last* office that blacks should seek.

"Not so," said the rural folks. The sheriff's position was number one on their political agenda. The sheriff in most instances was the only elected official they encountered in their communities. Sadly, the leaders of the elite class supported Sadler.

Undeterred, students allied with the rural folks. We knew most of them because of our work in the county with voting education, citizenship schools, and voting registration. We publicly lambasted the black middle class and did not bite our tongues in calling them "uncle toms." In fact, we were ashamed of them. They should have been on our side in this historical campaign that added to the local legacy of the Tuskegee Airmen and the

hard-fought struggle to have the Veterans' Hospital under black professional leadership. The elite blacks were spitting on the grave of Tuskegee's
second president, Robert R. Moton, but then he, too, was dark-skinned.
President Moton had summoned black men to protect the VA Hospital and
Tuskegee Institute when the Ku Klux Klan threatened to harm any black
who applied for a professional position at the hospital in 1923. Moreover,
it was Sheriff "Pat" Evans, referring to the Institute and the VA Hospital,
who had snorted in a public forum, "I think there ought to be law about
putting two big nigger [institutions]] like that in one county."

After a hard-fought campaign, Lucius Amerson became the first African
American sheriff elected in the South since Reconstruction. But racism
dies hard. Following Amerson's election, the governor appointed several
white Macon County men as constables, with police powers. There was a
nineteenth-century law allowing the appointment of constables, but it had
seldom been exercised and never in Macon County.

IN BETWEEN CAMPAIGNING for Amerson in Macon County, I was working
in the Benton community in Lowndes County where a slate of black candidates were running under the independent political banner of the Lowndes
County Freedom Organization—with the Black Panther as its symbol
and party logo. We were indebted to SNCC's venerable Jack Minnis, who
researched and found the obscure law for establishing independent parties
in Alabama. SNCC 's popular primer on the duties and responsibilities of
elected offices was a godsend to the candidates. As in Macon County, the
election of a black sheriff was high on the people's agenda. Other offices of
great concern were county school board members who could set policy that
our children would receive quality education and would not be compelled
to forfeit school in October to pick cotton nor in March to plant it. Further
down the agenda were the offices of county commission, coroner, tax assessor,
and tax collector. The 90-percent black majority of Lowndes County was
not interested at this time in municipal elections, viewing themselves more
as a county-wide community (whereas the citizens in Tuskegee, the county
seat of Macon County, viewed themselves as separate from the citizens in
the rural community).

Eldridge Cleaver came to Lowndes County during this period to write his observations on the Lowndes County Black Panther Party for *Ramparts* magazine. He was in complete wonder when he saw that black people owned long guns, and some carried them on racks in the back windows of their pickup trucks. Long guns are traditional in Lowndes and other rural counties. Shooting small game and deer was one way, sometimes the only way, these black families put meat on their dinner tables. Lowndes County blacks also had a tradition of self-defense. If an overseer with a gun came riding up on his horse during the tenant farming/share-cropping era, they would surely meet black farmers with guns the next day. Some women carried pistols in their bosoms and purses.

When we learned that Eldridge Cleaver had been convicted of rape, and that he raped black women as practice to rape white women better, we made him *persona non grata* on Tuskegee's campus.

I did not travel for the SGA during this period. I wanted SGA President Benny James to experience all that I had when I was in his position.

Intermittently with my movement work, my graduate studies at Tuskegee went unhitched. I took several philosophy courses which gave me insight to my movement as a scholar-activist. I read Hegel and Pleckanov. But I had yet to read Marx, Engels, Lenin, Adam Smith, Trotsky, Rosa Luxemburg, and George Padmore.

MEANWHILE I WROTE a short essay on "Black Power!" The call made by Willie Ricks (aka Mukasa) and Stokely Carmichael (aka Kwame Ture) on the 1966 "March Against Fear" in Mississippi was reverberating throughout the country. The essay, "Pro Black, Not Anti White," was later published in the *Journal for American State Colleges and Universities*. I had no idea how my article landed in this publication.

As a result of the published article, I was asked by Leslie Dunbar of the Field Foundation to work with the Student Human Relations Project (SHARP) to explain the meaning of "Black Power!" to students across the country.

After negotiating a salary of $6,000 per year (a beginning teacher's salary), with fringe benefits, insurance, and an operating budget to underwrite traveling and conferences, I landed my first job without looking. My family was very proud of me. This windfall job reinforced my belief that movement work was legitimate work and that it should be within the mainstream to carry the message for fundamental social change if America was to live up to its creed of participatory democracy.

I called the Atlanta-based office of SNCC and announced that I was on my way to Atlanta, where SHARP was located. I expressed my desire to stay with the SNCC collective in the Mennonite House on Houston Street. I told my comrades that I was able to pay rent and that the money was to be earmarked for necessities and that the collective should never run out of toilet paper and toothpaste. We all laughed at my survival demands. I further asked them to write a budget-prospectus for a "Black Power!" conference for Southern black and white students to be held on the campus of Tuskegee Institute.

Through SHARP, I already had speaking invitations from Bryn Mawr, Berkeley, Harvard, Columbia, and other ivy league schools. I had no invitations from the black colleges and universities or from Southern schools.

BEFORE MOVING TO Atlanta, I visited with Jerry in New York City, my third visit to the city. This time I took a plane to LaGuardia Airport, and then ground transportation to the downtown bus station that New Yorkers called the Port Authority, where Jerry met me.

We rode the subway train uptown. Jerry was living in an efficiency apartment that Harlemites called a "kitchenette." It was not my cup of tea for a living quarters, but it was better than the Braddock Hotel.

Jerry as always was lovingly gracious. He took me on city excursions to see "the big city, the big lights." We went to the Village in lower Manhattan. The Village was saturated with art shops, cafés, boutiques, and other eccentric and exotic sights inside and outside of historic buildings. It was breathtaking. I tried to imagine myself as an art dealer.

Later that evening, we meandered to the Village Vanguard, where black jazz geniuses Miles Davis, John Coltrane, Bill Evans, Elvin Jones, J. J. Johnson and Paul Chambers had appeared. The smoke-filled club had a reverent atmosphere as patrons appreciatively listened to musical masterpieces. Later we went to the Village Gate where drummer Max Roach and his ensemble were beating out joyful rhythms of be-bop. Max was suspended in air in what looked like a tailored drum platform, eye-level to the audience. To cap off the morning hours, we went to see the extravaganza of female impersonators at the Jewel Box Revue. As Jerry and I rode the train back to Harlem, I felt like a hip New Yorker.

THE STUDENT NON-VIOLENT Coordinating Committee (SNCC) "freedom House," rent-free as a contribution from the Mennonites, was simple and imposing at the same time. The wood structure was large with large rooms converted into bedrooms, dormitory style. The covered back porch, which reminded me of my Patton grandparents' home, was our dining area with a long table that could seat twenty.

My roommates were Ethel Minor, an ace in public relations; Freddie Greene, whose brother, George, souped up all the SNCC cars that ran faster than Alabama police cars; and researchers Myrtle Glascow and Doris Derby. A somewhat mysterious young sister from New Iberia, Mississippi, sat on the floor all of the time, taking in the wisdom of her older sisters. In fact, she slept on the floor in her sleeping bag.

Before I got around to telling the SNCC collective I was dissatisfied with the living arrangements, we moved into apartments on Gordon Road (now named after the late SCLC stalwart, the Reverend Ralph D. Abernathy). Stokely Carmichael was chosen as my roommate, I assumed, since I was an avid reader and Stokely was traveling incessantly, that I was to verbally summarize books for him when he was in Atlanta. I did so with Kenyatta's *Facing Mount Kenya*, Fanon's *The Wretched of the Earth*, Harold Cruse's *The Crisis of the Negro Intellectual*; and Nkrumah's *Consciencism*, which had special meaning for me.

Because I had funding and an income, I bought the living room and kitchen furniture. SNCC provided the beds for the two-bedroom apartment. I bought the linens and bathroom and kitchen necessities. The apartment complex provided the refrigerator. I bought the food. We needed a stove, but when Stokely came to the apartment with a one-eye hot-plate, I was done.

When Stokely left the following morning for an organizing tour, I packed up everything! I left a set of linens with pillow, a towel and face cloth, one fork, spoon and knife, a plate and bowl, one pot and skillet, and the hot-plate. I left the food in the refrigerator. Stokely would later tell others, and to tease me, "She even took the shower curtains!"

I moved into an apartment with Margaret Mills (now Efia Nwangaza), SNCC's Dwight Williams, and Bill Mahoney (one of my SNCC beaus at the time, though Jerry was still my fiancé). Bill was still traumatized by his brutal experiences in Mississippi's Parchman Prison. He was placed in the "hole" as excrement and rats floated in filthy water up to his neck. Bill, who could pass for any race except black, was from a solid middle-class black family in Montclair, New Jersey. He was a good writer.

The apartment rent was underwritten by Margaret's minister father; she was a student at Spelman College and was married to Dwight Williams, a key organizer in Vine City, one of the poorest urban black communities in Atlanta, near the Atlanta University complex. Vine City was the epitome of "town" that was forbidden to mix with "gown" on the college campuses.

Since Margaret's family was paying rent for the apartment, I felt obligated to buy the food. Of course, I bought wholesome foods: meats, fresh vegetables, fruits, snacks, and the like.

One night when we were reading each other's writings for criticism and suggestions, Bill commented that I shouldn't buy fancy foods.

"What foods do you think we should buy?"

"Peas and beans. That's what poor people eat, and we work with them. We should live their lifestyle."

"Bill, I'm not in this movement to romanticize poor people. I'm in this movement so poor people don't have to be poor. I thought that's what our struggle is about."

The following day I left work early. I went grocery shopping and bought large bags of black-eyed peas, butter beans, cornbread mix, T-bone steaks, broccoli, and baking potatoes. When I arrived at the apartment, nobody was home. I washed the peas and spilled them into a pot of boiling water. I washed and oiled the potatoes and placed them in the oven to bake. I mixed the cornbread batter and seasoned the steaks and placed them in the refrigerator to marinate. I then labeled the packages of peas and beans with

"Bill Mahoney" and placed them in the food cupboard. Six o'clock came quickly as my roommates came tumbling in, exhausted from their work in the SNCC office, Vine City, and school. The SNCC discussion about Black Nationalism and class analysis was fierce, and my SNCC comrades brought the argument to our apartment. I expressed succinctly that class within the black community was real. I could not escape my experiences at Tuskegee Institute. It was impossible to ignore the class question and to tout unconditional love for all black people. An analysis had to be made before a strategy could be put in place to unite black people. I was always puzzled by black nationalists, who later became black cultural nationalists, and their obliviousness in the face of this reality. Sometimes, I would engage lengthy debate, but this day my concentration was elsewhere.

My roommates were sitting around the kitchen table discussing their day's work. I placed the steaks, onions and green peppers under the broiler and began to steam the broccoli in the colander. The peas, potatoes and cornbread were done.

As my roommates began to fill their plates, I told Bill, "Oh, you don't have to eat the bourgeois steak, potatoes, and broccoli. Your dinner of peas is in the pot." I placed a bowl with a slice of cornbread in it before him. He was flabbergasted as the rest of us piled our plates with steak, potatoes, and broccoli.

The office of the Southern Student Human Relations Project (SHARP) was in an odd-shaped building at 41 Exchange Place in Atlanta. Other movement offices were housed there. I called it a "one-stop movement building." Connie Curry, a white SNCC organizer who strongly supported the "Black Power!" movement, was working in the building with the American Friends Service Committee, a Quaker organization that was red-baited by Southern officials and their so-called "sovereignty commissions." Connie and I became fast friends. She often read my writings and offered positive suggestions to make my essays better.

I was doing quite a bit of traveling in the Southeast. Black students were heeding the call for "Black Power!" Naturals, or Afros, began to frame the faces of female students. Male students were sporting Afros, too, as a complement to their dashikis, replacing sport shirts.

I realized that there needed to be at least five Gwen Pattons to carry out the work of SHARP. I wrote a proposal to underwrite expenses for SNCC campus travelers and for a Southern conference to discuss Black Power. SNCC campus travelers could help build a Southern black student base. In concurrence with the SNCC executive committee, we set February 11–12, 1967, as the date for the nation's first Black Power conference, to be held on the Tuskegee Institute campus where there already existed a seasoned student movement.

CONCURRENT WITH THIS work, I was also traveling back to Lowndes County to work with the Black Panther party. SNCC was out in full force leading up to and on election day. We had more black voters on the rolls than whites. But we knew that the minority white folks were going to steal the election because they held the positions that counted the votes. The election results for the November 1966 election were:

	Black Panthers		White Democrats	
Sheriff	Sidney Logan	1,426	Frank Ryals	1,943
Coroner	Emory Ross	1,391	Jack Golson	1,901
Tax Assessor	Alice Moore	1,557	Charlie Sullivan	2,234
Tax Collector	Frank Miles	1,556	Iva Sulivan	2,227
School Board				
	John Hinson	1,620	David Lyons	1,894
	Robert Logan	1,620	Tommie Coleman	1,933
	Willie Strickland	1,552	C. B. Haigler	2,139

Soon after the election, plantation owners put black sharecroppers and tenant farmers and their families off the land. James Forman of SNCC procured tents to house the displaced families. Prominently visible along U.S. Highway 80, the same corridor where people marched for voting rights in 1965, the makeshift community was called "Tent City." It was a harsh winter of discontent for these rural families. But their spirit to fight for freedom kept them fired up.

However, within a few years and continuing to today, Lowndes County had a black majority government, including a black "high sheriff." The community is as feisty as it was in 1966. Through their experienced and no-nonsense grassroots organizing, the community—black and white—stopped an Alabama governor from placing a landfill on U.S. Highway 80, now designated as a National Historic Trail, an All-American Road, and a National Scenic By-way to commemorate the 1965 Selma-to-Montgomery Voting Rights March.

ON THE HEELS of the 1966 elections came the travesty that was called a criminal trial of the murderer of Sammy Younge Jr.

Nearly a year had already passed without a trial since Sammy was killed, and a white grand jury had already reduced the charge from first-degree to second-degree murder. Then Marvin Segrest, the killer, succeeded on November 12, 1966, in having the venue of his trial moved thirty miles north from Tuskegee to Opelika, a cotton mill town that bordered Auburn, home to what is now Auburn University. Opelika was a well-known "redneck city." Blacks motored through it at least five miles under the speed limit and still got traffic tickets from police who probably were in the KKK.

Segrest's lawyer argued that a change of venue was necessary because of the Tuskegee students' protests after Sammy's murder. But the real reason was that the jury list in Macon County was now two-thirds black, thanks to concentrated voter registration drives. So the white judicial officials simply moved the trial to a majority-white county.

The trial began on December 7, 1966. The evidence against Segrest was overwhelming. Eyewitnesses said Sammy was walking away from Segrest when the service station attendant fired the fatal shots. No witness saw Sammy with a golf club, however, when the police took "forensic" photographs of the crime scene, Sammy was sprawled on his back with a golf club beneath his body, blood oozing profusely from the back of his head. The golf club was evidently necessary to support Segrest's lie that he had shot Sammy in self-defense.

Sammy and Segrest had argued in the past about the "inside" and "outside" restrooms. Segrest always directed black people to the outside bathroom. On January 3, 1966, when Sammy was at the gas station, he refused to go to the "outside toilet." I am certain that Sammy felt safe in confronting Segrest; a large number of Tuskegee Institute students were next door from the gas station at the Greyhound bus depot, awaiting taxis and rides to carry them to the campus. But, racists are not rational.

Perhaps Segrest thought murdering Sammy would send the age-old message: "Niggers, stay in your place or we white people will teach you a deadly lesson." The gun had replaced the lynching rope.

There were some highlights during the trial. One was desegregating in Sammy's honor the "White Ladies" bathroom in the Opelika courthouse. Believe it or not, two years after the 1964 Civil Rights Act, Opelika still had signs stipulating "White Ladies" bathroom on the first floor and the "colored women's" bathroom in the basement. While in the "White Ladies" bathroom, we left our collective signature in large letters on the wall: "Black Power!"

Another high point was when a black character witness, one of sixteen called to testify for Segrest, was asked, "How long have you known Mr. Segrest?"

"Thirty-five years," the witness answered.

"Well, how long has Mr. Segrest been a good man?"

"Thirty-four years."

Students and other black spectators roared in laughter at the obvious implication and at the defense attorney's surprise with this unanticipated answer. The judge pounded his gavel, demanding order.

After two days of testimony before the lily-white jury of county farmers and small businessmen, the young prosecutor made his closing argument, "All I ask is a verdict that you can sleep with. A verdict that you can walk down any street in this county and never need to deny."

When the prosecutor sat down, I went to his table and poured a cup of water from his pitcher. He was startled. As he turned to look at me, I said, "Whose side are you on," more as a statement than question.

I was relieved that Mary Ellen Gayle with the *Southern Courier,* the weekly newspaper published by journalists from the northeast who covered the central Alabama civil rights movement, was present in the courtroom and rushed up to the prosecutor's table during this exchange. I knew that the *Southern Courier* would accurately report this trial for posterity.

The jury deliberated only an hour and ten minutes before coming back in, and the foreman, who had slept through much of the trial, announced, "Not Guilty."

It was more than I could stand. "Let's go!" I shouted as I headed for the door.

"Young lady, sit down until I adjourn court!"

I looked at the judge incredulously, hoping my eyes conveyed that I had no respect for him or his kangaroo court. Looking around the courtroom at my friends, I said, "I'm leaving." When I got to the door, two burly policemen blocked it. I said, "I got to go."

Wendy Paris and Eldridge Burns, their eyes fixated on me at the door, then jumped up and headed to the door, followed by about thirty other Tuskegee students and faculty members. The police gave way. We were prepared to host a rebellion right there in the courtroom. There surely was going to be hell to pay in Alabama.

It was about 7:30 p.m. when we arrived back on campus. Some of us went to the SGA office where President Benny James was waiting for me. He had not been at the trial, which was a disappointment. But the verdict had spread through the campus and the community like wildfire. "Gwen, what do you think we should do?" he asked.

I was determined for Benny to accept his leadership role. "What would you suggest?"

"Well, I think we need to have a student body meeting."

I was encouraged. Leaflets were drawn up for circulating on campus calling for a 10:30 p.m. meeting. I called my cousin, Lenard Huntley, and told him to round up at least fifty community people to come to the meeting.

I was shocked when only three hundred people, including my cousin, community people, and SNCC organizers showed up. What had happened to the student movement spirit?

The meeting became a large seminar discussion of strategy, and we all dispersed as mobilizers to go back to the dorms and each bring at least five peers to a "midnight meeting," symbolic of "midnight schools" our ancestors held in secret during slavery time. I personally went to the home of Dean of Students P. B. Phillips and insisted that he join us at our "midnight meeting." He knew well enough not to argue and joined me right then and there.

We returned to Logan Hall to see how many people would show up. In the end, some two thousand people turned out at midnight. Student leaders rose to talk about the plight of black people in racist America. Others talked about how Tuskegee black elite leaders were allowing white folks to take over our institutions, particularly at the VA Hospital, desecrating its founding.

I sensed that students were becoming antsy. Meeting in Logan Hall was not enough. There had to be some type of motion, a movement of people.

A SNCC organizer said he was going to the downtown square to sleep in front of the Confederate statue. Student Carl Fitts volunteered to go with him. They picked up their sleeping bags and left the gym.

SGA President Benny James made an immediate transformation. "We will join them! Brothers we need marshals for the march!"

Every man quickly moved to the center of the gym as coeds moved inside with brothers on both ends of the lines. I grabbed Dean Phillips and Benny James, and along with Wendy Paris, Eldridge Burns, and other Tuskegee Institute Advancement League leaders, we moved to the front of the march.

At first we tried to sing freedom songs, but nothing seem appropriate. We were too angry to sing, so we marched downtown in silence.

As in many Southern towns, Confederate statue stood in the square. Even if downtown was not well-lit, the spotlights trained on the statue gave perfect illumination for what the students had on their minds and in their hearts for action on the square in downtown Tuskegee this wintry December 9, 1966, at 2 a.m.

After a round of rousing speeches, lifting up the memory of Sammy, someone yelled out, "We need some black and yellow paint!" Out of nowhere came cans of black and yellow paint and paint brushes. The base of the Confederate statue was serving as the rally platform. "Splash!" went the black paint onto the face of the Confederate statue. The crowd roared with approval. Each "splash" of black paint, covering the face and the upper torso of the statue, released the built-up tension. The action was therapeutic. When a brother painted a yellow stripe down the back of the Confederate statue, the cheer was greater than scoring a winning touchdown! Dean Phillips, standing next to me, turned and looked at me. We both smiled.

Racist America would have to reckon with a new firebrand of black people, the "new profiles of courage."

Someone started singing, "Take this hammer, take it to the captain. Tell him I'm gone. Captain called me a nappy-headed nigger. It ain't my name. Take this hammer."

Then someone painted the words "Black Power!" at the base of the statue. The crowd, contented for the moment, began to chant "Black Power!" as they started walking back to campus.

Some student and community leaders stayed at the statue to discuss what else could be done to register our anger at the acquittal of Sammy's murderer. All of a sudden, the chant of "Black Power!" became louder and louder. To our joyful surprise, eight hundred students had returned to the square.

They began to chant Sammy's mantra, "What we gonna do? What we gonna do?" Wendy Paris and I said, "Do what the spirit say do," the title of one of our freedom songs.

The "spirit contingent" destroyed downtown Tuskegee. Thirteen businesses on the main square were wrecked. Policemen were on the scene, but they dared not to touch these angry black men, who were prepared to battle them to the death with their fists. The Tuskegee Rebellion, a rural rebellion, was before Detroit, Chicago, Plainfield, New Jersey, and other urban rebellions.

TUSKEGEE INSTITUTE PRESIDENT Dr. Luther Foster called a campus-wide meeting for 9 that morning in Logan Hall. Most students had not slept since our "midnight meeting" and subsequent march to the Confederate statue at the downtown square.

Dr. Foster lambasted our actions and complained that the damages were costing the Institute. He reiterated his stance that the college is an educational institution and should be void of civil rights activity. He still had yet to accept that since the 1960 sit-ins and the 1961 freedom rides and all the other actions since, black students, the paying clients, had mandated that their black educational institutions had to become citadels of civil rights, to teach African-American history, and to be think tanks to design strategies for first-class citizenship and human rights. Some of the students rallied behind Dr. Foster while most listened to him politely as well-bred, middle-class black students knew how to do. There was a smattering of applause after his chastisement speech.

Then came a disconnect from Dr. Foster. He announced that we would break into groups in various classrooms in Huntington Hall to discuss civil rights issues. Probably Dean Phillips recommended this phase of the all-campus conference. As a result of students' civil rights activity, the college received millions of federal dollars for community programs under the supervision of Dean Phillips.

Student leaders instinctively knew that we must have scholar-activists in each workshop. We were certain that Dr. Foster would have his respective administrators in each workshop to control the discussions. As we went to various workshop rooms and saw one of our activists present, we went to the next room until all the workshops had a least one scholar-activist in the midst. As it turned out, we had more than ten activists in each workshop.

I chose the "Equal Opportunity" workshop. Much of the federal funds came from this office (OEO) for the college's program, "Tuskegee Institute Community Education Program (TISEP)." Though I lauded this program, I thought it should go further.

"Our concern in the Deep South is not about painting out-houses lily-white," I had testified before the OEO in Washington, D.C., earlier: "Our need is to lay pipes, sewer lines and accompanying drainage systems. Blacks who have expertise in these fields, such as graduates from Tuskegee Institute, should have an equitable share in the contractual work." I wanted OEO to move beyond President Johnson's "anti-poverty programs to build the Great Society" into the economic development arena for the black community in the South. I knew if white people murdered individual black people over sharing political power, they would surely massacre black people wholesale over sharing economic power. These thoughts were my underlying assumptions in my discussions in the workshop.

Even though I was not surprised, I was nevertheless elated when scholar-activists were pushing for Tuskegee Institute to buy up the downtown area, including the bank. Tuskegee Institute in the 1940s had owned a bank right there on campus, but for whatever silly reason, probably at the insistence of white people, gave up the charter. Students were recommending that the college purchase the downtown movie house, restaurants, clothing stores and the like and develop new enterprises like a skating rink and a bowling alley. Students had envisioned that all of Tuskegee should be a college town, capitalizing on students as the major market base and providing proprietary entertainment for community people as surplus revenue. Unfortunately, Dr. Foster and his administration could not grasp this leap for economic power. They were still stewing, just like the white folks, over the students' movement to gain political power. Throughout Dr. Foster's tenure as president, downtown Tuskegee with its mostly white business owners remained a ghost town as a consequence of the student and community boycott to protest the murder of Sammy Younge Jr.

BEFORE RETURNING TO Atlanta after the trial and its aftermath, I made an appointment to meet with Dr. Foster. "I don't mean to be disrespectful," I said to him, "but I have to ask, and I hope you will be honest with me and yourself, are you afraid of white people?"

"No, Gwen, I am not," he said, as if counseling me. "We must move circumspectly. We must separate white people and form coalitions with moderate and liberal whites who want to see Tuskegee become a model city for similar towns to emulate."

I asked if that was why he and other Tuskegee organizations had not publicly stated that justice was not served in the acquittal of Sammy's murderer. Dr. Foster did not answer.

I went on, "Are we to conclude that the right to life of a black man taken by a white man is of no significance in the light of forging alliances with so-called liberal Southern whites, an oxymoron from my set of experiences."

Dr. Foster grimaced.

"Sir, it is a historical fact that whites coalesce with each other in the face of black people fighting for their human and constitutional rights. We can look at our recent history and see how whites in suits and hoods, from governor to the KKK, from the white elite to what they themselves call 'trailer-park trash,' work together to stem the tide of our people's movement for equality, dignity and justice."

Dr. Foster looked off in space, but it was clear from his body language that my words were taking root.

"White folks see our movement for freedom as an encroachment on their power, which they think was ordained by their God as the sole inheritors of this control over our people and this country, probably the world. Sir, I learned about 'manifest destiny' at this college, my beloved alma mater."

I knew I had said enough on this matter, but I concluded that students wanted the college to sponsor a "Freedom Christmas for Sammy" and to name one of the male dorms in his honor.

"I think we can do those things." Dr. Foster replied, obviously grateful that we ended our conversation on a positive note and that he had had the last word.

20

Jailed for Talking

The Tuskegee Institute Golden Tigers were scheduled in late 1966 to play their annual pre-Christmas exhibition basketball game against the Fisk University Bulldogs. I decided to travel to Nashville, Tennessee, where Fisk is located, for this classic, which would be attended not only by Fisk's students and community fans and busloads of Tuskegee Institute students but also by students from the black colleges of Meharry Medical School and Tennessee State University. My purpose was not only to cheer for my alma mater but to encourage students from the various campuses to attend the February 11–12, 1967, "Black Power!" conference at Tuskegee Institute.

After the game, hundreds of students congregated at the University Inn, across the street from Fisk. We settled in for an evening of socializing with deluxe hamburgers, French fries and "spirits." The black proprietor was making tons of money as the festive crowd fed quarters into the juke box and chattered about the matters of the day.

I moved from table to table, talking about the impending conference. Some students remembered me from days gone by when I was a cheerleader at the classic and offered me seats at their respective tables. They were intellectually thirsty and wanted to know the meaning of "Black Power!" and how it was to be manifested. Future doctors among the students were especially interested. Roosevelt McCorvey, a Tuskegee Institute graduate then studying at Meharry, asked me if Black Power included a push for black medical students to serve as interns and residents at predominantly white hospitals in the South. Heretofore, black medical students in the South could only do their student-practice at the few existing black hospitals, sharply limiting not only their training but also their opportunities for future practice. Honestly, I had not focused on this perspective of institutional racism, but I got it, and I was restructuring the substance of the conference in my head as I replied with assurance that "Yes, there will be a special workshop on this issue."

As I continued to move from table to table, the proprietor came up to me and quietly said, "I don't want you to talk about civil rights in my business."

I replied, "Sir, we're talking about the freedom of our people and the future of students who are patronizing your business." As he left and went back behind the bar, I thought my response had satisfied him. I continued to move from table to table with my message.

Shortly a phalanx of police burst through the front doors. I realized that the proprietor had called the police when he returned to the bar. "There she is!," the proprietor shouted, pointing a finger towards me.

The police rushed and circled me. "You're under arrest!"

"For what?" I said without raising my voice.

"The owner has signed an arrest warrant against you for disturbing the peace." Unbeknownst to me a black undercover police agent had been watching my movements in the bar for more than an hour.

The police handcuffed me. As they began to hustle me toward the doors, Tuskegee student McKinley Harris stood and said, "You can't arrest Gwen!"

As the police rushed and circled him, I shouted, "Don't anybody else get up! Stay in your seats and stay calm!"

The police pushed McKinley, now also handcuffed, and me out the doors and into a waiting paddy wagon. After being booked, fingerprinted, and photographed, I was allowed to call the SNCC office. I was then led to a jail cell with a white girl who looked no more than nineteen and a black woman in her late twenties. The cell had two bunk beds. It was Friday night, too late for arraignment. I wondered where I was to sleep. I knew I would be in jail over the weekend

I took a seat on the cell's uncovered toilet. The black woman was obviously angry as she paced up and down the tiny the cell. The white teenager made small talk with me. After about two hours, the jailer came to let the white girl out of the cell. The sister promptly took the top bunk mattress from the concrete slab and placed it atop the one already on the bottom bunk and designated that place as hers.

I had been to jail before for movement activities, but always with my comrades. Jail was a lark. We would talk about the movement and our future and fervently sing freedom songs, driving the jailers crazy. Now, I was in jail alone, with a cellmate who could not care less about the movement.

I had on my finest wool herringbone skirt-suit, with a wide collar that gave way to a cape that draped my shoulders, bodice, and back. But that was not my biggest worry. Beneath the suit I wore a silk slip, panties, and bra that Grandmother Patton had given me as my college graduation gift. I knew my cellmate, a "street woman," would see a class difference.

My objective was not to do as the Tuskegee elite did with the rural and working-class blacks and exacerbate our differences. I had to soulfully communicate with my cellmate that we were sisters.

"Why are you here?" I asked, still sitting on the toilet.

"I took a life," she said without emotion.

"Do you have a lawyer?" I followed up without asking for any details. I did not want her to think I was a jailhouse informer.

"Yeah. When I was convicted, I wanted to kill him, too."

After some silence, I began talking about our movement, our struggle to be free so we don't have to be in circumstances to "take a life." She began to warm up to me. She put the other mattress back on the top bunk and told me that was where I would sleep for the night. I sincerely thanked her.

As we stripped down to our underwear for our night's sleep, she made no comment about my underwear. Placing my foot on her bunk, I climbed to the top bunk. There was a blanket but no sheet. I pulled the blanket over me and had a fitful sleep. The following early morning, a jailer pushed a broom and dustpan through the central slit of the cell. I knew I was the one to clean up the cell as my cellmate did not budge from her bunk. This was Saturday, and on Sunday, I also swept out the cell. The meals were not bad, though the breakfasts had too much grease floating around the fried fatback that spilled over into the sorghum and biscuit section of the tray.

My cellmate and I spent Saturday and Sunday talking about the movement and the importance of fighting for freedom for ourselves and for our people. She shared her despair and pessimism that black people would never be free. She was full of self-hatred. I did all I could to make her feel worthy. When the jailer pushed the broom and dustpan through the cell-slit Monday morning, my cellmate jumped from her bunk to catch them. She cleaned the cell, including washing the toilet and facebowl with the jail-issued soap.

Soon another jailer arrived and told me to dress quickly. After about ten minutes, the jailer led me to a police car that carried me to court for arraignment. After the quick procedure, I was bound over for immediate trial before the same judge. The judge asked me how I pleaded. "Not guilty," I responded. The black proprietor, the agent, and the arresting policemen were all present to testify against me. The judge found me guilty and fined me $500 or a month in the county prison. I refused to pay the fine.

I was then hauled off in a van to prison. I was again booked, fingerprinted, mug-shot, stripped, bodily searched, showered, and given prison-issue garb with my number stamped on a green blouse, with matching skirt, socks, and tennis shoes. I was immediately taken to the sewing section of the prison, where a jailer explained my work as a cutter of fabric that already had patterns pinned to it.

After about four hours, a jailer came to take me to the release room. I was told that my fine had been paid. I took off the prison garb, donned my personal clothes, and verified that my personal effects were correct. I learned that SNCC's Charlie Cobb had wired $500 to the court system on my behalf.

Before leaving prison, I asked if I could use the telephone book. I found the address of my cellmate's lawyer and took a cab there. When we met, I did not discuss her case with him. I told him about my ordeal and that I wanted to file a complaint against the University Inn proprietor and the authorities for what I considered a false arrest. He asked for a retainer to take my case, and I wrote a $100 check. Then I took a Greyhound bus back to Atlanta.

SAMMY YOUNGE JR.'s first cousin Bill came from South Carolina to visit with his relatives in Tuskegee. Stevie, Sammy's baby brother, was still taking his big brother's murder very hard. Segrest's acquittal had added another layer of pain. Stevie was happy to see Bill, who looked uncannily like Sammy. This was Stevie's first Christmas without Sammy; Bill brought him comfort.

Stevie had inherited Sammy's powder-blue Volkswagen. He loved driving the car and sometimes he would drive to the gas station to watch Segrest pumping gas. Stevie never got out of the car. With Bill visiting, Stevie hatched a plan. They drove to the gas station and Bill got out and asked Segrest, "Where's the restroom?"

Segrest, turning seven shades of pale, ran into the station. Bill followed him, and again asked, "Where's the restroom?" Segrest, quivering as if he had seen a ghost, pointed a shaky finger to the door *inside* the station. Bill's report of what had happened inside the gas station gave Stevie some comfort, at least.

I MADE SPECIAL plans for my 1966 Christmas holiday with my maternal grandparents in Montgomery. Poppa Washington's seventieth birthday was December 22. I invited my grandparents' friends to the special birthday party I hosted at the popular Laicos ("social" spelled backwards) Club, my favorite nightspot. Roscoe Williams, owner of the club, gave me permission to host the birthday party at 6 p.m., the time he and the house band came in to set up; the club opened to the public at 7 p.m. For an hour we had our private birthday party to eat ice cream and cake and for Poppa Washington to open up his birthday presents.

The band played various arrangements of the birthday song. It was a thrill to see Mommy and Poppa Washington dance. By 8:30 p.m. the club was almost full, mainly with college students and professionals. The band again played "Happy Birthday," in the traditional arrangement, dedicated to Poppa Washington, while the patrons sang. Mommy's eyes sparkled like a teenager's.

I spent the remainder of the Christmas holiday sitting at our dining room table and committing to paper my thoughts on Black Power. Was it a slogan, a demand, a plan, or a culmination of our civil/voting rights movement?

"Black Power" was articulated by the author Richard Wright in the 1940s during a rent strike in Harlem. In the 1950s, the Reverend Adam Clayton Powell preached "Black Power" from his pulpit, Abyssian Baptist Church, in Harlem.

Though Powell was elected to the U. S. Congress, it was clear that his pronouncements were not so much political as they were economic in nature. White America paid no attention to the call for Black Power during this period.

When Kwame Ture (aka Stokely Carmichael) and Mukasa (aka Wille Ricks) shouted "Black Power!" on the June 1966 "March Against Fear" in Jackson, Mississippi, white America went berserk. SNCC's Kwame and Mukasa had joined Dr. Martin Luther King Jr. and the Southern Christian Leadership Conference to continue the march across Mississippi started by James Meredith, who had been shot by the KKK. No doubt the KKK murder of Ben Chester White, a quiet black man and sharecropper on a plantation in Natchez, Mississippi, who was not involved in any manner in the movement, gave urgency to the fervent call for "Black Power!"

Black Power had many dimensions. Foremost from the voting rights movement in Lowndes County, and its Black Panther Party, was the right to self-determination and self-defense. Guns did not excite those who lived in rural areas. They were necessary tools to put food on the table—rabbit, possum, coon, deer. Moreover, the symbol of Black Power, the Black Panther, was not sensational. Practically every home had a ceramic panther on the fireplace mantel or as a doorstop. It baffled me that white America reacted in such a violent manner, physically and verbally, to what I considered to be a simple part of our culture. Even during World War II, black soldiers named their squadrons "Black Panthers." And, surely, black people ought to have the constitutional right to protect and defend their families against deadly assault.

Of course, there was the obvious dimension of voting rights, and the need to elect black people to positions that had the greatest impact on the collective community. Again, my experiences in Lowndes County and Tuskegee taught me that black folks were less concerned with what were considered figurehead positions like mayor. They were serious about the sheriff, who held life and death in his hands, or the school board, so black children could attend school for the full academic term and not be forced to tend the fields in October to pick cotton and in March to plant it.

The call for Black Power in the 1960s added another dimension—culture and a sense of black nationalism. I saw the need for black consciousness and a critique of U.S. institutional forms in every arena that demonized "blackness": calling a chocolate cake "Devil Food's Cake" and a white cake "Angel Food's Cake" was nothing short of psychological genocide perpetrated on black people.

Negritude was gaining import with movement organizers. The Algerian writer Franz Fanon's treatises on this subject internationalized the fervor for cultural black nationalism. Though I saw the merit of Negritude as a foundation for thought and as a prism to analyze the black experience in white America, I also saw the limitations. I was afraid that too many of our people would settle for wearing Afros, dashikis, and African attire and identifying romantically with Africa without knowing or wanting to know, that Africa was a vast continent and that Africans on the east coast, such as Kenya, did not connect with Africans on the west coast, such as Senegal. European colonialism and now the phenomenon of puppet neo-colonialism, with USA monetary and military support, was a complex contradiction that still had to be worked through by Africans, country by country and then by the continent as a whole. Black Americans calling themselves Africans and assuming African affectations were no resolve for the masses of blacks languishing in racist USA.

The economic dimension of Black Power continued to be buried. The 1950s–60s civil rights movement was overshadowed with the quest to sleep in a white hotel in lieu of, for instance, expanding the black A. G. Gaston

Motel to be franchised beyond Birmingham, Alabama. For me, the analysis of the economic dimension was the critical need to lift our people out of despair and desolation.

I codified my thoughts into two themes that I would present at the February "Black Power!" conference: the three C's—Capitalism, (false) Christianity and the supremacy of the Caucasoids wherever they exist—and the three M's—Money, Military, and Might.

21

If You Can't Run for Freedom, Then Hobble

January 1967 went by like a whirlwind. James Harvey from Southside Chicago came to Atlanta to help with final conference preparations. I had met James some six months earlier at a Midwest anti-draft counseling workshop. We shared a deeper understanding of the draft as the central component that institutionalized the USA standing military that made wars in Vietnam and other USA aggressions around the world probable. The might of USA foreign policy was predicated on the fact that conscripted troops could be sent anywhere to further the ambitions of capitalists at the behest of the government. Former President Dwight D. Eisenhower had laid out clearly the threat from the military-industrial complex. Within that context, the draft had to be a centerpiece in the upcoming "Black Power!" conference.

SNCC also had a strong position against the draft and saw it as a deadly tactic when tens of thousands of black men, especially militants, were called to report to the combat lines in Vietnam against a people who were engaged in a civil war to reunite their country and to rid themselves of French colonialism, now with the USA assuming military surrogacy as the French cut their loses and ran. The draft, a key cornerstone for USA imperialism, had to be discussed in a more fundamental and deeper manner.

I rented a car and James and I drove to Tuskegee the day before the conference. There was a snag about using the campus facilities, but Dean P. B. Phillips arranged for the Tuskegee Boy Scout Camp to be the conference site.

Meanwhile, Leon Ellerbe, a Tuskegee native, had been drafted. The draft board had not accepted his declaration as a conscientious objector. In fact, black men who declared opposition to the war itself were hardly ever granted CO status. Heavyweight boxing champion Muhammad Ali was a prime example. He loudly proclaimed, "No Vietnamese ever called me a 'nigger' and I ain't gonna fight in a white man's army." When he then refused induction, he was stripped of his championship title and the U.S. government tried to put him in prison. The handwriting was on the wall: Draft them, send them to Vietnam, then kill them under the pretext of war in the name of fighting for democracy.

On Leon's behalf, I called my anti-war friends in New York City. They arranged to send him a plane ticket to Montreal, Canada, where he would seek political asylum. The ticket was to be sent to my grandmother's home in Montgomery.

EN ROUTE TO Montgomery to take Leon to lay over at Mommy Washington's until his flight, I had a strange car accident. "Gwen, the car sounds funny. Pull over," Leon said, sounding worried.

When I pulled over and stopped on the shoulder on U.S. Highway 80 in Shorter, Alabama, the car imploded. Somehow I managed to open the driver's car door and to throw myself on the ground. I remember seeing vivid stars. I knew I was on my way to Heaven. I felt no pain.

When I awoke, I was in Tuskegee's John Andrews Hospital. My left leg was in a cast and my left jaw was wired shut. John England and other Tuskegee students were at my bedside. They had donated blood for the operation that had been performed on my leg. I had suffered a compound fracture in my left ankle. The crushed bone had been scraped out and my leg, ankle, and heel were now connected with metal plates and pins. Leon's arm was broken, but he suffered no other injuries. I was happy that at least he couldn't be drafted with a broken arm.

During my month-long stay in the hospital, SNCC Executive Secretary James Forman visited me often. He was still interviewing for what became his book, *Sammy Younge, Jr.: The First Black College Student to Die in the Black Liberation Movement.* I asked James to bring me books to read. I read polemical works by Marx and Hegel. For cultural insights, I read Langston Hughes's vignettes about "Jess B. Semple." Lying in my hospital bed, I constantly thought about the meaning of Black Power; the concept had sobered and was no longer exclamatory. I wrote a short article, "Booker T. Washington in Retrospect: The Father of Black Power."

After a month in John Andrews Hospital, my orthopedic surgeon, Dr. John Hume, released me. He said the metal plates and pins in my lower leg would serve as a bridge to connect my ankle with the heel in my foot. I was happy to go home to Mommy as I hobbled out of the hospital on crutches. However, after two months of total bedrest in Mommy's care, my leg did not get better. An ulcer developed at the base of my leg, oozing pus through the cast, emitting a foul odor that indicated infection. Concurrent with this setback, a painful abscess developed in my left jaw and gums where teeth had been surgically removed after the strange car accident. I was in excruciating pain. Mommy called Dr. Hume, who directed her to get me back to John Andrews as soon as possible.

There a dentist drilled into and drained my jaw and gums; the relief was instant. While still groggy from the anesthetic, I was placed on a gurney and rolled to an operating room. I don't remember anything after that. A nurse was sitting at my bedside when I slowly opened my eyes.

Dr. Hume, my surgeon, was soon at my bedside. He explained that he wanted to amputate my left foot and lower leg lest the infection spread and kill me. He said they would have amputated in the first surgery, after my accident, but I was unconscious and they had no signed consent form. This time, he had brought one. He wanted to do the amputation the next morning.

Obviously, I was distraught at this news. I asked if he had consulted any other physicians. Heatedly he replied, "That's what's wrong with you, Gwen! You always want to challenge! I'm your doctor, and I know what's medically best for you!"

Dr. Hume had made it known during my days at Tuskegee that he took exception to our student movement and to my leadership in particular. I could only wonder now if his decision to amputate was some sort of retaliation for my disrupting his notion of Tuskegee as a "model city" of race relations.

I told him I needed time to read over the release form and to think. As soon as he left my hospital room, shaking his head in disgust, I climbed on my crutches and hobbled to the nurses' station to call my grandmother. "Mommy," I said, "ask Carnell to come get me." Carnell was my cousin on my father's side who first drove me to Tuskegee Institute when I enrolled as a freshman in 1961. In less than two hours, Carnell was at the hospital. I left the release form, unsigned, on the bedside stand.

There was more than distrust of Dr. Hume as to why I would not consent to amputation. The deep-seated motivation was sex, pure and simple. I could not imagine myself in a romantic situation and in the heat of passion saying in a sultry tone, "After you take off my blouse and pants, don't forget to take off my leg!"

I LAY IN bed for a week contemplating my predicament. As always, Mommy tended me, including placing the bedpan under my bottom to keep me from getting up and hobbling to the bathroom on crutches. She brought the washbasin to my bedside in the mornings for me to sponge off and to brush my teeth. She wheeled my breakfast in on the rolling butler tray. Her friends would visit and stand around my bed and pray.

Out of the blue, I decided to call my movement friend, Bettina Aptheker, in New York City and explained my medical plight. "Gwen, let me call you right back," she said. In less than an hour the phone rang. It was Bettina, saying she had arranged for me to fly the next morning to New York for an appointment with Dr. Melvin Belsky, an internist with the Medical Committee for Human Rights. He had been one of the volunteers in that capacity during the Selma to Montgomery Voting Rights March in 1965.

When Bettina hung up, I related all to Mommy. As I hugged her, I said, "God has answered yours and your friends' prayers."

The next night I was at the International Guest House in New York City. Quilts from Gees Bend in Wilcox County, Alabama, graced the walls in the lobby-lounge. In the gift shop there was a section for the Freedom Co-op that sold goods made by grassroots people from Mississippi, South Carolina, and Alabama. Though I met and knew Africans while at Tuskegee Institute, this was my first time meeting Asian and South American peoples. I slept soundly that night despite my pain, knowing that the world is really full of good people.

Dr. Belsky examined me thoroughly and then referred me to Dr. Herman Robbins, an orthopedic surgeon and chief of staff at the Hospital for Bone and Joint Diseases in East Harlem. Robbins's private office was at 970 Park Avenue. I was considered an emergency case and he saw me immediately. After he sawed off the cast, now soft and soaking with pus, X-rays were made of my leg, heel, and foot. When Robbins came back into the examination room, he slapped X-ray negatives on wall-mounted screens. With his long, white doctor's coat flapping as he turned to explain the X-rays to me, he said I had severe infection of the bone, and the metal plates and pins from my initial surgery were making things worse. He said the metal had to come out.

I asked, "Do you think my leg and foot will have to be amputated?"

He replied, "I hope not. You will need aggressive antibiotic treatment to clear up the infection. Amputation is always my last resort."

His words were comforting. I instantly gained trust in him.

He wanted to schedule surgery for the next day and said I would need an aggressive around-the-clock intravenous antibiotics regimen afterwards; he predicted that I might be hospitalized for up to three months.

He was not happy when I said—somewhat shocked myself that I was saying it—that I had to go home to Montgomery to talk with my grandmother and to pack my books. "Time is not on your side," he said. We compromised that I would return for surgery in no more than a week. He bandaged the ulcer on my lower leg securely and put on a soft cast that covered my foot, except for the toes, and leg up to the knee. He gave me a week's supply of antibiotics and pain pills.

Maxine Orris, who would become my little sister, roommate, and best friend, picked me up at the doctor's office and drove me to the airport. I was back in Montgomery before midnight.

I told Mommy Dr. Robbins's prognosis. She prayed and gave me her blessings to return to New York City for medical treatment. I exchanged my hat-box luggage that I had used for my two-day stay in New York City for my footlocker. I packed mainly underwear, nighties, and books; I was to be in the hospital for a long time.

I flew back to New York and went directly to the Hospital for Bone and Joint Diseases. When I reported in the emergency section, the doctors were puzzled by my footlocker. I insisted that it had to go wherever I went. I was assigned to a ward as an indigent patient; my footlocker was placed under my bed.

Who said God takes care of babies and fools? At twenty-three years old, I was no baby. God truly takes care of his people, babies and fools alike. I am a living witness.

My year in the tuberculosis sanitorium had honed me into a professional patient, I easily adjusted to the hospital as my new home. I got to know my ten ward-mates, white and black.

After the surgery to remove the metal, my leg was placed in a bubbled cast. An intravenous needle was inserted on the back of my left hand, leaving my right hand free to hold books and to write. Thousands of units of antibiotics and saline trickled from the overhanging bag into my body. I was completely bedridden.

Movement people, most of whom I was meeting for the first time, visited on a regular basis. Even when I fell asleep, they would sit quietly by my bedside. I had become a "cause celebre," a Southern freedom fighter injured in an odd accident. Some of my visitors included, of course, New York SNCC organizers, most notably Mae Jackson from Brooklyn and James Forman, who was now international affairs director. SNCC Executive Secretary Ruby Doris Smith-Robinson couldn't visit, because she was in a hospital downtown, suffering with what some said was leukemia. I always found it peculiar that this strong, vibrant woman fell ill after her horrendous imprisonment in Parchman Penitentiary in Mississippi. She was happily married to an attentive husband, Clifford Robinson, and they had an infant son.

My other visitors, among legions, were Yuri (Mary Kochiyama), who cradled Malcolm X's head after his assassination in the Uptown Audubon Ballroom; James Baldwin, whom I met in Montgomery during the 1965 Voting Rights March; and Julia Wright, the author Richard Wright's daughter, who was visiting in New York City from Paris, France.

Mae Jackson and Maxine Orris became my two best and dependable friends. I gave Jerry's telephone number to Mae and asked her to let him know I was in the hospital. I had been thinking about Jerry since I arrived for my first examination with Dr. Belsky. But I hadn't called him. Truthfully, I suspected he was a drug addict. However, when Jerry learned I was in the hospital, he visited every day. He washed my nighties and my hair. He gave me my bedpan and changed my sanitary pads. A woman could not have had a better lover-companion; he exemplified the vow, "in sickness and in health."

One of my hospital mates was in a special rotating bed that would prevent her from getting bedsores. One night her bed slipped into a vertical position and she was sliding down towards the floor. I incessantly pushed my call button but it seemed a lifetime before nurses came to right the bed.

When Dr. Robbins visited that morning, I asked if the intravenous contraption could be hooked up to a wheel chair so I could have mobility. He took care of it. With my new wheels I could go to the bathroom on my own. And when my hospital mates needed attention, I could roll up to the nurses' station to report the concern. I became known as "hell on wheels."

One of my wheelchair ventures was to visit the ward that was beyond my own, though we could hear patients' moans. There I saw patients in full-body casts from their necks to the bottom of their legs. They were suspended spreadeagle from metal rods—no more wondering why they moaned. I thoughtfully put my own condition in perspective.

After I visited all the women patients on my floor, I wheeled myself onto the elevator and went to the floor below. This was mainly a men's floor for indigent patients. They were playing poker. I made regular visits to this floor as if I were in college to master a new profession. They taught me how to tell if someone was dealing from the bottom of the deck, or if a player "dropped" a card to the floor and exchanged it for one that another player had previously placed on the floor, and to watch for small tiny folds at the corners of cards. I learned how the "house cuts over and under" that was more than ten per cent of the pot. I learned the sequence of winning hands. I learned betting rules of check, call, call and raise, and that you could not check and then raise. I learned that all money had to be placed on the table for other players to see and that you could bet "all in" and win a portion of the pot. I learned that facial expressions and emotions had as much import as the cards secreted in your hands in calling a bluff or when to hold or fold. Poker, if played honestly, was a mind game. I was fascinated.

My father was a gambler, but his game of chance was dice. He never taught me how to gamble. When he learned that I was an excellent poker player, preferring five-card stud and draw with jacks or better, and that I remained a lady throughout the game even when challenging some under-handedness, he beamed, "I guess it's in the blood!"

I made regular visits in my rolling chair to the administrative nurse's office. Patients slipping out of special beds should never happen. "Hospital liability should be a concern," I said in earnest. "Ethically, I would have no other choice but to be a witness to such a mishap." The nurse administrator and I became friends. She often visited me at my bedside to ask how the night had gone for the patients.

My best friends in the hospital were the housekeeping and food work-ers. Union Local 1199 had expanded beyond pharmaceutical, nurses, and ancillary caregivers to include these sections of workers. I wheeled myself all over the hospital, telling workers I was a Southern freedom fighter and encouraging them to sign up with 1199 as their union representative. The hospital administration was furious with me, but there was little they could do when Dr. Robbins, chief of staff, was my strongest ally for human dignity. The workers overwhelmingly voted for 1199 to represent them.

My anticipated three months in the hospital extended to five months, from June to October 14, 1967, my birthday. About two weeks before my release a young white social worker intern from Columbia University came to my bedside to ask about my plans to earn a living. "Can you secure me a position teaching high school English or history?" I asked. Stunned, she replied, "No, I don't think so. You'll still have a cast on your leg, will be on crutches, and will have to make regular visits to your doctor as an out-patient. Have you considered babysitting? We have a referral list of people who need babysitters."

When I replied that I didn't go to college to be a baby-sitter, she said I was being childish, and I told her to leave and send a children's social worker to talk to me. Soon Dorothy Burnham, a children's social worker, was at my bedside. After we talked about our life philosophies, I concluded that we were in the same camp. She knew my dear friend, Maxine Orris, very well. Mrs. Burnham arranged for me to receive welfare for rent and transporta-tion, food and commodities, and a clothing allowance as an out-patient.

My first visit to a welfare office was an eye-opening experience. Irate clients, mainly mothers, were grumbling aloud about the disrespect they were receiving from social workers. Most of the people, clients and professionals, were black. Every now and then a white professional would come out of nowhere and agree with the black social worker who was giving a client grief. Tensions were mounting. I scooted my bottom onto a table, pulled up my crutches and stood leaning on them and in a loud, modulated tone said, in effect, "This disrespect has got to end. We are here because we are desperate. I'm a college graduate and I'm in a desperate situation. Circumstances bring about desperation on all of us, no matter what your background. Let's be civil and humane to each other. Nobody wants to be on welfare unless she has to. Besides, we, our parents, grandparents, our forebears, our ancestors in slavery, have paid taxes and deadly dues to make possible this safety net. This money does not belong to social workers or the welfare office. In fact, if it weren't for us, they would have no jobs."

I think the clients would have paraded me around on their shoulders if I had not desisted. But, things became more civil as clients talked with their social workers and were given their subsistence checks. Soon I met George Wiley, who was organizing the National Welfare Rights Organization (NWRO). I became an organizer and did much writing on the rationale to remove the stigma of being a welfare recipient. I organized motivational sessions with women to lift their self-esteem and self-respect.

My next encounter with the welfare office was when I presented receipts for payment of my clothing allowance. In 1967, you could put $5 down on lay-away plan. I had laid away nice wool pants and sweaters that averaged $20 a piece. This was considered expensive for welfare recipients. I did not argue with my welfare caseworker. I quietly asked her, "Why would you want me to continuously come to you for a clothing allowance to quickly replace cheap clothes that couldn't stand up to washing and dry cleaning? How much did the suit you are wearing cost? Because I am a welfare client, am I mandated to wear cheap clothes?" She quickly made arrangements for a check to be cut, payable to the clothing store. Soon afterwards, a policy was incorporated to give welfare recipients semiannual clothing checks, payable in their own names.

Still on a roll of how black professionals mistreat and take advantage of other blacks they consider beneath their class, I wrote the Tennessee State Bar Association. For over a year I had not heard from the lawyer who had taken my case with a $100 retainer for what I considered a false arrest at the University Inn in Nashville, Tennessee. Within a month I received my $100 and was notified that the lawyer was on a six-month suspension from practicing law.

I then looked into why I had not received workmen's compensation from my car accident that occurred during my legitimate work responsibilities. White liberals, too, were not going to escape from their mistreatment of blacks, regardless of the class, because of their racism. Attorney David Rein took my case pro bono and filed a claim for me to receive my back workmen's compensation in a lump sum. We won the case without going to court. I was relieved to be off the welfare so-called relief roll.

22

Among the Leftists in NYC

It was now fall 1967. The civil rights movement was transitioning, and both the antiwar and the women's movements were escalating. I didn't move back to Atlanta or Tuskegee or Montgomery at that time. Graduate school had long since been pushed to the background. My work with SHARP in Atlanta had basically ended with my accident, and I had been in New York now for half a year. My doctors were there, and the social services safety net was markedly better than in Alabama or Georgia. I was also doing work I liked with the NWRO and SNCC.

And, for better or worse, Jerry was there. However, I decided that I would not stay with Jerry. I needed my independence and time to be alone. I have always known that I am basically a hermit and a recluse. I opted to rent a room in Paul Boutell's apartment on 7th Avenue at 116th Street.

Paul was a sincere movement friend who was a member of the Socialist Workers' Party (SWP). Up to now, I had no clue as to the many left organizations that supported the Southern movement. I knew that Malcolm X was given a forum in the SWP, and this was the deciding factor as to why I rented a room in Paul's apartment. Paul introduced me to writings of Leon Trotsky, the SWP's leading theoretician. Trotsky, of course, worked with Lenin during the Russian Revolution and was detested by Stalin, who came to power after Lenin's death. Trotsky exiled himself to Mexico when he learned that Stalin planned to assassinate him. As I read Trotsky's works and talked with Paul, I learned that the Communist Party, which also supported the Southern movement, and had been especially active on behalf of Alabama's "Scottsboro Boys" before World War II, was considered SWP's archenemy. The rivalries of the Russian Revolution and the Soviet Union carried over in the various USA leftist groups in the 1960s.

Paul's apartment was in a building that had a mirrored foyer and had been considered top-of-the-line in 1940s' Harlem. I was across the street from the famous gated apartment building, "Grey Columns." Around the corner were a mosque and a Muslim restaurant. I often ate in the restaurant. For the first time I tasted curried foods. One of my favorite dishes was "kima," curried beef, but instead of slices of beef, the Muslims used hamburger.

I was not impressed with our apartment's layout. When you entered, you walked down a hallway. The kitchen was on the immediate right and Paul's uncle's room was on the left. He had been a member of Marcus Garvey's movement in the 1920s. I marveled as he donned his Garveyite uniform with plumes and epaulets and marched before me. Farther down the hall were Paul's quarters, loaded with books, in what was probably the original dining room. At the end of the hall was the living room, layered with years of dust.

Before the living room, the hall made a left, and on the left of this hall was my large bedroom. A seldom-seen night-shift worker occupied another bedroom adjacent to mine. At the end of this hall was the bathroom, with a footed tub and a toilet flushed by pulling a string connected to a tank above. The apartment was not my cup of tea, but it definitely was another experience for me in terms of the lives of my Northeast movement friends.

I transformed my spacious room by laying wall-to-wall carpet, setting up a writing station with a typewriter, and creating a small living room with a cushioned wicker sofa and chair. I had a telephone installed with my number listed in the phone directory. My bed was the centerpiece. My weekly rent was $15.

Jerry spent many nights with me in my apartment and I spent many with him in his kitchenette apartment. But we also had an agreement that we would have time alone and that we could visit by phone. I realized that I was drifting away from Jerry. I could not see myself living in a rented room, a kitchenette, or even an apartment for the rest of my life. Jerry seemed contented with such an arrangement, but I grew up in a home—a house—and I intended to own my home one day. Many New Yorkers, especially left progressives, thought owning a home was "bourgeois." I had several discussions with them on the importance of owning a home in the South. In many instances the home was put up as collateral bond in the event that a family member may be arrested. During the height of Montgomery's bus boycott, the home was a critical part of the strategy when people were harassed by arrest on the whim of the police.

AFTER ABOUT A week of getting settled in my new quarters, I continued my organizing work with the National Welfare Rights Organization, which was in walking or, should I say, hobbling distance from my apartment building. I had a hard cast and was on crutches.

My first mistake was taking the subway to the New York SNCC office, located downtown at 100 Fifth Avenue, to resume volunteer work. Negotiating the steps with crutches and changing platforms in the stations proved to be too much. Instead, I became an expert on the bus system routes and schedules. I could ride free as a handicapped passenger.

H. Rap Brown (later Jamil Al-Amin) was now chairman of SNCC. Under his leadership the organization replaced *Nonviolent* in its name with *National*. This was a statement that black people had the right to self-defense in the face of violence upon their persons and property, especially by the police, who were now being called "pigs" in the popular black movement culture.

James Forman was doing an excellent job setting up SNCC's International Affairs Division, securing non-government organization (NGO) status with the United Nations, and receiving scores of invitations for organizers to appear before UN committees to further William Patterson's 1951 petition, "We Charge Genocide: The Crime of Government Against Negro People." Mae Jackson and I were assigned to assemble press packages to accompany presentations. SNCC also received VIP invitations to receptions hosted by African nations; I first met Betty Shabazz, Malcolm X's widow, at a reception hosted by the government of Guinea.

Though SNCC was recognized with respect from international circles, the organization was in shambles. Barely enough money was coming in to cover the rent for the five-room office in high-rent downtown. The argument between the two warring factions within SNCC, centered around the 1966 call for Black Power, continued to boil. The book, *Black Power: The Politics of Liberation*, by Stokely Carmichael and the scholar, Chuck Hamilton, did nothing to abate the internal hostilities. The NYC-SNCC office basically had been the fundraising arm and was pretty much run by white SNCC members. When Southern black SNCC organizers called for white members to focus on organizing in white communities against racism, many whites balked. There were a few exceptions like Elizabeth Sunderland, but the majority became sulky and angry.

I later learned that many of these whites were Jews. Southern blacks looked at all white-skinned folks as white people. Yet somehow there was a notion that Jews were not really white people and that there should be a natural alliance with them because of their history, from the pharaohs to the Holocaust. But after deep and heart-wrenching discussions, many black

SNCC organizers concluded that all white people, including Jews, enjoyed a white-skin privilege. We were looking at Israel, its support from the U.S. government, its relation to the Mideast, especially Palestine, and the rise of Zionism. We reasoned that if Jews could not organize in the mainstream white community because of anti-Semitism, they surely could organize in the Jewish community around Zionism and Israel's rapprochement to apartheid South Africa. There was enough organizing work for everyone if all were genuine in trying to create a fair and just world.

Unfortunately, SNCC's white liberal financial base completely dried up. A few of our white radical friends like Carl and Anne Braden and Lucy Montgomery stood by the new SNCC. They not only saw the validity in calling for "Black Power," they moved to organize other whites around the need to fight racism. These brave organizers saw such a fight as in the self-interest of whites to end exploitation by the ruling class in their communities, in the Appalachian coal mines, and in the Chicago meat packing industry, to name just a few examples.

Though I saw SNCC's international work as necessary and invaluable, I was still preoccupied with the draft, a type of forced labor that fell disproportionately on young black men because of institutional racism. SNCC had written a position paper against the war in Vietnam upon the murder of Navy veteran Sammy Younge Jr. Many SNCC organizers, like Donald P. Stone, opted for prison instead of military induction. But still there was no deep analysis of the draft itself.

The Student Mobilization Committee Against the Vietnam War—"the Mobe"—was gaining national momentum. I sat on the Mobe continuations committee along with A. J. Muste of the Fifth Avenue Peace Parade Committee and Dr. Benjamin Spock, the famed pediatrician. They asked me to be a full-time organizer for $75 a week, then a high-end salary for movement organizers. NYC-SNCC Central Committee agreed that I should take the position. SNCC's John Wilson, later a popular city councilman in Washington, D.C., and who inexplicably committed suicide, was assigned to work with me. I requested that Mae Jackson work with me as well. The Mobe was planning a series of massive national actions against the war in

Vietnam. They needed someone, ideology-free, to organize the black community to join the actions.

The Mobe was my first time working with white radicals on a daily basis. I had already met Socialist Workers' Party (SWP) and Communist Party (CPUSA) members while in the hospital. They visited me often. My apartment mate Paul was in the SWP, and I had learned from him some of the various left factions. In addition to SWP and CP being a part of the Mobe, I met members of the Progressive Labor Party (PLP), who played a low-key role in the strategy sessions. Bill Epton stood out as a PLP leader. On a one-on-one level, Bill reminded me of the firebrand "freedom-high" SNCC brothers. Whereas SWP members were Trotskyites, PLP members were Maoists, after China's Mao Tse-Tung. CP members, however, were Stalinists and gave uncritical support for the Soviet Union line. Thus the CPUSA hated both the SWP and the PLP.

Maoism resonated with the growing national, urban Black Panther Party (BPP). After Eldridge Cleaver visited Alabama in 1966, when he wrote about the first Black Panther Party and its parent Lowndes County Freedom Organization, he transported the BBP concept to the West Coast. Cleaver, Bobby Seale, and Huey Newton formed the second BBP in Oakland, California. From there, BPPs were established in urban areas across the country. Mao's little *Red Book* became the BPP guide for urban revolution.

I found Maoism's demystification of U. S. imperialism as a "paper tiger" refreshing. The Vietnamese, in their successful effort to reunite their country, concluded that the USA military, coupled with its money and might, was nothing but a "paper tiger."

PLP's Bill Epton and I parted philosophies later over the question of Mao's "cultural revolution." I made it clear to Bill that if anyone raided my grandmother's home and smashed one piece of her demitasse china, I would cut his hand off. Bill had no clue to Southern black culture and values, just as many New Yorkers had no clue as to why owning a home was critical to survival. Bill and I, however, remained personal friends despite our differing views. This, too, was strange to many New Yorkers: they could not understand how people could remain personal friends while disagreeing peaceably on political questions. I chalked it up to the Southern experience of black people not disliking individual white people, many who were their employers and paid them subsistence wages, yet hating the collective system of "Jim Crow" that demanded subsistence wages "to protect the social order."

Factionalism and sectarianism took their toll on the Mobe. After participating in the discussions for awhile, I withdrew. I found no merit in arguing with the SWP that the movement to end the war in Vietnam should have a single issue approach, i.e., to just end the war without a multi-issue analysis of USA racism and imperialism as the underlying causes of the war in the first place. The CPUSA embraced the multi-issue approach, but they would not connect USA racism and imperialism with that of Israel. The "hippies" thought you could end the war by placing flowers in the barrels of soldiers' guns. The "yippies" saw the "exorcising and levitating" of the Pentagon as the solution.

I HAD MY fill of listening to dubious, shallow, and ludicrous arguments of the white left. I knew my responsibility was to help form a national black anti-war, anti-draft organization. I felt the black community was ready for it, and I wrote a proposal soliciting support to establish the National Black Anti-War, Anti-Draft Union (NBAWDU).

Throughout the years I had been a successful fundraiser. First, I talked face-to-face or over the telephone with potential donors and foundations, which were predisposed to supporting the concept. I incorporated their suggestions in my written proposal. A major feature in my proposal was the "implementation strategy," which needed people power doing paid work. I did not view "movement work" as "free labor"; such work was just as vital, if not more so, as a job in corporate America. After all, the movement was up against powerful corporate interests and the government to win the hearts and minds of Americans. Besides, people give their all and more if their survival—food, clothing and shelter—is secured. Second, I asked several foundations to match each other in support while NBAWADU would raise 20 percent of the overall budget. Donors and foundations trusted my integrity as I provided quarterly reports of expenditures, accounting for every cent. Measurable outcomes were noted as a baseline for the next level of work. I had indirect support from Panamanian Carlos Russell in Brooklyn and Omar Ahmad in Harlem who pressed the peace movement to support anti-war activities in the black community. NBAWADU received funding for a two-year program.

I persuaded James Harvey to leave his strong movement base in Chicago to come to New York City to work full-time for NBAWADU. I hired John Wilson, Mae Jackson and Diane Jenkins. NBAWADU had three major programs:

1) to build a massive black contingent to join the Spring Mobilization March for Peace in the nation's capital;

2) to convene a national conference that would look beyond Vietnam to arrive at a deeper understanding of how the hidden hand of U.S. imperialism was being used against the liberation struggles in Algeria, Guinea Bissau, Angola, Zimbabwe, South Africa, Namibia and other struggles on the African continent; and

3) to continue anti-draft counseling in black communities, especially in the South.

NBAWADU rented space in the SNCC office, which provided a financial support for the organization at a time when SNCC was plumb out of funds. There was not a donor in sight after James Forman, Stokely Carmichael, and Rap Brown violated SNCC's Central Committee's instruction and signed a SNCC "merger" agreement with the Oakland-based Black Panther Party. Forman became its minister of international affairs; Carmichael (now Kwame Ture), its chairman; and Brown (now Jamil Abdullah Al-Amin), its minister of defense. SNCC's Southern base in Atlanta—including me, though I was in New York City—was flabbergasted upon seeing the signing of the "merger" on the national television news. The central committee quickly convened and voted to censor the brothers, but to no avail—SNCC was falling apart.

IN THE MIDST of this organizing work, I joined a "poker club." There were six of us, one of whom was a police officer. This gave me comfort and security that the club was not a thug group. I was the youngest and the only woman. You had to have at least $50 dollars to sit at the table. Usually we placed $200 on the table. Members rotated and hosted the poker party as "the house" every Saturday night. The party started about 8 p.m. and would continue until about noon on Sunday mornings. Food was free. Mixed alcoholic drinks were available for a cost, but serious poker players do not drink that much while playing.

The poker grapevine heard about our club; I was an oddity and thus a draw of sorts. Players from all over the city would show up. Sometimes there were more than ten men waiting for one of the six at the table to either go bust or get up for a rest. I hosted my poker parties at my senior-organizer friend's apartment in Brooklyn's Bedford-Stuyvesant community and in Mae Jackson's apartment in the coveted Clinton Avenue community. Mae's mother, Melissa, who also lived in the apartment, prepared the food. Melissa had lived in Brooklyn for more than twenty years, but she still had her "Nawlins" accent. She would prepare delicious gumbo and other dishes, using New Orleans-style spices. Melissa was responsible to hold and to secure my "over and under cut" from each winning pot. Melissa's Brooklyn smarts, reinforced with Louisiana human nature insights, made it clear to all the male poker players that no one was to mess with her. Her facial expression conveyed, "Don't even think about messing with me, Mae, or Gwen unless you want to meet your Maker this instant." I did not know if Melissa had a gun, but my .38 was always close at hand.

Mae, my dear friend, more innocent than she realized, always watched in awe as I played poker. When I won a pot, she would say nonchalantly, "I knew you would win." She had no clue to the mental pressure involved. The quicker I won a pot to accumulate winnings was the better. On the other hand, when I was not playing, I wanted players to sit forever and to keep calling and raising. My cut from the pot increased accordingly.

From one of my good poker nights, I was able to buy a $600 mimeograph machine for the SNCC office. The organization was completely broke. Only the rent from NBAWADU kept the office space available. Kwame, miffed by SNCC's censure of him, sent his fiancé, Miriam Makeba, to retrieve all of his copies of *Black Power*. The removal of the books meant that SNCC would no longer receive any proceeds from selling the books. Even that small source of revenue was now gone.

NBAWADU organizers were being paid while SNCC office staffers were not. Irvin Davis, who self-appointed himself as the office manager, and his assistant, Jimmy Lytle, approached NBAWADU while we were in a strategy meeting.

"Gwen, NBAWADU needs to put us on staff," Irvin said more as a demand than as a request.

Accustomed to Irvin's officious style, I simply replied that there was no funding for additional organizers. I was not cold in my response. I recognized their need to have an income. I suggested, sincerely, that Irvin and Jimmy become cab drivers. They could earn a living while passing out flyers and talking about the movement with passengers all over the city.

But they became angry and hurled insults at me, castigating me as a black woman who stymied black manhood. Both were married to white women. I said nothing. James Harvey was ready to go to blows, but I stopped him. The following day I called the business office and asked them to come get the mimeograph machine and to return the balance of my payment.

I moved the NBAWADU office from SNCC to Jim Haughton's unemployment office in uptown Harlem, the heart and soul of the black community. Haughton, a brilliant theoretician on racism and cybernetics in the capitalist work-world, was dedicated to finding employment for black people in the construction industry. He worked diligently with unions, which were still mainly racist but needed workers as more and more white workers moved into managerial slots in corporate America, thus removing them as dues-paying union members. Haughton insisted that black workers get apprenticeships that would lead to journeymen's cards in the building trades.

I recommended to Irvin and Jimmy that they consult with Haughton about employment. The potential workers who came to the unemployment office attended workshops, and I facilitated some of the workshops on racism, social consciousness, and their roles as freedom fighters in the workplace. Sadly, Irvin and Jimmy found employment in construction—and probably its discipline of showing up on time and producing work—to be beneath them.

I needed time to reflect on the psyche of black men, especially those who called themselves "freedom fighters." Were they pimping the movement to get out of working as black people in the main had to as a responsibility to provide for their families? Were these "freedom fighters" really "wimps" who could not stand up to the vicissitudes of black life in racist, white America? They vowed that we would eventually win freedom, but did they find our current station in life hopeless, and if so, were *they* hopeless?

The words of my brother, Bob, came to mind. My brother was a Ford factory worker who often worked overtime to provide a comfortable living for his wife and three children. His wife did not work outside of the home. Her job was to keep house and to raise the children. When my brother visited me, I took him to a movement family's apartment. The husband did not work. He was a full-time "freedom fighter" with no income. His wife worked. The apartment was dirty and in disarray with mattresses for sleeping on the floor. The four children ran barefoot about the apartment, eating dry cereal from the boxes. The "freedom fighter" waxed eloquent about the movement and the impending revolution. My brother listened intently. When we left the apartment, he said, "If where I've just been is freedom, then let me stay oppressed."

MORE THAN 5,000 blacks joined the 1968 Spring Offensive for Peace as a response to President Lyndon B. Johnson's continued U.S. military use of napalm and Agent Orange to defoliate Vietnam's forests, which the U.S. government dubbed as "jungles where the gook guerillas [North Vietnamese] were hiding."

It was so moving to see the busloads of my brothers and sisters from Beaufort, St. Helena, Parris Island, John's Island, and Daufuskie Islands, South Carolina. NBAWADU had set up an anti-draft counseling center in that pristine region of black culture. This was alongside white doctors who physically examined black draftees and found that many had hypertension, diabetes, and other physical ailments that should have precluded their going into war. The health of black men was worthy of examination as part of the movement's overall strategy to end the war in Vietnam; a disproportionate number of soldiers on the front lines in Vietnam were black.

Other buses from the South—including Louisville, Birmingham and Atlanta—came rolling into Lafayette Park in the nation's capital for the peace march. Black folks came from Chicago, Detroit, Cleveland, Boston, New York, and Philadelphia to join the largest contingent from Washington,

D.C., led by brother Abraham Lincoln. As people got off the buses, they were asked to join the Black Brigade for Freedom and Peace.

NBAWADU thought it was important for black people to march together. This tactic was not to show separatism though this may had been the motive of some black nationalists. NBAWADU saw it as a media tactic. It was important for people, especially black people, who watched the nightly television news coverage of the peace march to see a strong black contingent opposing the war in Vietnam. If blacks intermingled with their compatriots by locales, many of whom came together on the same buses, the black presence would not look as strong and would be white-washed as television and photograph images.

There was also another philosophical reason to form the Black Brigade for Freedom and Peace: There was no resolve among black and white activists to issue the call for "peace and freedom" advocated by white peaceniks and "freedom and peace" advocated by black militants. White activists saw peace in Vietnam as the priority, while NBAWADU concluded that peace in Vietnam and throughout the world, including the USA, could only come *after* nations had the freedom for self-determination.

The other tactical reason for the Black Brigade was that black folks were not going to conclude their march at the Pentagon. Black folks knew intuitively that the Pentagon was a sacred cow and that anyone who attempted to vilify this icon of might was surely going to get his head beat. Instead, the Black Brigade turned left and marched to Banneker Field on Howard University's campus, where hundreds of students were waiting in the bleachers. As we were settling in at Banneker Field, several white peaceniks who were on the tail end of the march to the Pentagon, joined us at the NBAWADU rally. They reported that the Capitol police were beating the marchers into a bloody pulp. Johnny Wilson, the chair of NBAWADU, opened up the rally and welcomed the white peaceniks with these remarks, "We knew that the cops would go brutally wild. We know their wrath and hatred. Welcome to the club—the billy club that is." The crowd whooped.

However, when it was my turn at the rally podium, I took the opportunity to raise the question of choice: To take or not to take the (birth control) pill. Black movement men had made it adamantly clear that black women should refrain from taking the "pill." My thoughts for sometime reflected on the argument between my father and mother, who had an hysterectomy after my brother's birth. It did not matter to my father if my mother needed the operation for health reasons. My father's response to my mother's independent stance to control her own body was "I don't know if she's a man or woman." Too many black men felt that the preeminent role of women was to produce their babies.

On the other hand, I had attended several meetings with white feminists as a part of the Jeanette Rankin Brigade. Their mantra was the pill as the liberating force. I found this stance as oppressive as that of black nationalists. I suggested that if we were truly talking about freedom, women should have the choice to take or not to take the pill. Sometime after this, I observed that white feminist organizations began arguing the same "choice" mantra.

During this period, I recommended that SNCC form a Black Women's Commission. Mae Jackson and I drew up incorporation papers and registered them with the New York Secretary of State. Fran Beal, an international SNCC supporter who spent a large portion of her life in Paris and was fluent in French, joined Mae and me on the commission. Fran had the best intelligence in analyzing the "triple jeopardy of black women: racism, classism, and sexism." I translated Fran's analysis as in the larger society, in the workplace, in the home.

After the march in the nation's Capitol, NBAWADU called for a national conference to be held at the Biltmore Hotel in New York City. Two thousand people from around the country registered. We read letters from black soldiers we had received from brothers on the front lines in Vietnam. One of the poignant letters read:

> "I'm from South Carolina. The first sign of racism that I experienced was when I was in the fifth grade and we had to walk ten miles to school. We had to walk past two white elementary schools to get to the black school. One day I met this lady with her little white son walking down the sidewalk and he asked, 'Mommy is that a nigger?'
>
> It kind of took something out of me. I have been a Marine in Vietnam for 13 months. I have fought in the jungles and stuff. The day that Dr.

Martin Luther King was killed, we had spent all night trying to keep the Viet Cong from taking this one hill. I remember that morning as the sun broke, this white boy scrambled into the hole with me and he said, 'Leon, they killed that troublemaker.' "I said, 'What troublemaker?' 'That King guy! That King guy!' That sent something through me. Here I am in a foreign country, fighting somebody who didn't do anything to me and this white boy sliding in a hole, and I had protected his ass many nights, talking about they had killed this troublemaker, Dr. King."

Films were shown. Fran translated the French film, *The Battle of Algiers*, which did not yet have English captions. The film on the liberation struggle in Angola gave us new words in Portuguese that described our black movement in the USA: *a luta continua*, the struggle continues.

I was amazed that black conferees from organized, predominantly white left organizations insisted on raising the question of liberation struggles in Hungary and Poland, but knew nothing about such struggles on the African continent. I was more convinced than ever that NBAWADU made the right decision to extract itself from a peace movement that was mainly a coalition of white, left organizations.

At first the fire popped and crackled and then eventually gave way to a bright orange-yellow flicker. Soon warmth enveloped the room. It was the largest fireplace I ever saw.

I was sitting across from Angela Davis in one of the meeting rooms in the student center at the University of California-Los Angeles (UCLA) where she was an instructor. I was snuggled in an oversized, comfy chair. I laid my crutches aside as I pulled the matching ottoman closer to rest my feet and legs. .

I had been invited to UCLA to share a panel on the role of black women with actress Cicely Tyson, Davis, and Roosevelt University professor St. Clair Drake. My remarks were concise and to the point: There is no ascribed, and definitely no prescribed, role for a woman. Her skills and talents should be afforded every opportunity to be used in a productive and positive manner. A man who needs a woman to be subordinate or in an inferior status must examine his own insecurity. I stressed the necessity for serious conversations between men and women, individually and collectively if we were to uplift our families, our communities, and our movement.

Earlier that day the Black Panthers wanted me to "review" their sister "Pantherettes." I was heartsickened to watch them drill in their black leather jackets, pants, and berets at the commands of a brother Black Panther. They looked like flag-girls on a football field. But instead of flags, they held makeshift rifles.

Angela, sitting across from me in a likewise comfortable chair, was stunning; her coiffured Afro was at least thirty-six inches around. Though she used much Marxist jargon, her tone was soft and beseeching. Angela was so unlike my New York City friends who framed their Marxist arguments with a harsh and dogmatic flair; she had retained her Southern upbringing and charm.

We talked about her classroom experiences and her interactions with her students, and about our need to be mindful of the impressionability of young people to the examples we set. I also thanked her for making popular our responsibility to communicate with incarcerated brothers. Her relationship with the imprisoned George Jackson, who had received a harsh, racist sentence for robbing a gas station of less than $70 when he was nineteen, had helped inspire the movement to look at the capitalist prison industrial complex for what it was and to redefine "criminal inmates" as political prisoners. However, I was very critical of the movement's romanticizing prisoners, which I believe contributed to prison guards murdering George Jackson on the pretense that he was planning an escape with outside support. The shoot-out by Jonathan Jackson, George's young brother, in a California courtroom had some of its basis in youthful impressionability and invincibility. My heart ached for the deep hurt that Mrs. Georgia Jackson felt. No mother should have to bury her children.

LATER, I WENT to Peekskill, New York, to help the Johnson family, whom I did not know, organize a city-wide youth conference. Racism in Peekskill was just as virulent as in 1949 when white residents stormed a Paul Robeson concert and rioted, hurling rocks and racial epithets. The white sponsors of the concert hurriedly put Robeson in a car and sped him back to New York City. The white mob had seemed bent on killing Robeson, an accomplished actor and singer, and a vocal advocate for civil rights for black people, and was branded as a communist.

The oldest Johnson son, Lumumba, a Muslim, met me at the Peekskill train station. The family had read my articles in *Muhammad Speaks*, the national newspaper of the Nation of Islam. All U.S. Muslims had seen the coverage of the press conference by Muhammad Ali when he faced prison for not complying with the draft. His splendid, bejeweled heavyweight boxing championship belt lay across the press conference table. I sat next to Ali and read the NBAWADU statement of support: "If Champion Ali had capitulated to go fight in Vietnam, NABAWDU is certain that no Vietnamese would kill him. Our concern is for Champion Ali's life. Any white soldier in the U.S. military has an implicit order to kill "uppity Cassius Clay" on sight. Champion Ali has lifted the legacy of Joe Louis to a higher level."

Lumumba Johnson was as gentlemanly and polite as other Muslims I had met. The Johnson family had six children, from ages ten to twenty. Their warmth and determination to build a Peekskill movement reminded me of the dedicated families during the Montgomery Bus Boycott. The parents were from North Carolina, roots made evident in Mama Johnson's country cooking.

We pulled together a city-wide planning committee of black youth and their parents. I was elated that the group wanted a conference-plenary discussion on the war in Vietnam, the draft, and the ramifications these forces had on the black community. I knew my mission at the youth-parents conference was to instill in young people the importance of commitment. In the South we changed the word "commitment" to "conviction." My elders constantly imparted to my generation: "If you don't stand for something, you'll fall for anything."

Now, it was my turn to continue the teaching of values, to build and strengthen character in this present generation.

FOR SEVERAL DAYS I took the subway back and forth between Harlem and Queens to visit my friend and elder, Vida Gaynor. She was a consistent mentor and financial supporter of NBAWADU. I was helping her pack crates and boxes of small household items and clothing for overseas shipping. She was expatriating to Tanzania, East Africa. Vida was an experienced public accountant and she had decided to place her talents in service for this country that had rid itself of British colonialism in the quest for self-determination and governance of its national resources.

While packing Vida's belongings on April 4, 1968, the WLIB radio announcer interrupted the "straight ahead" jazz program with a calm and sad voice: "Dr. Martin Luther King Jr., while standing on the balcony of the black-owned Lorraine Motel in Memphis, Tennessee, has been shot." Then the announcer said in a sad tone, "Dr. King is dead."

Shocked and distraught, I plopped on Vida's bed. She kept on packing and said, matter-of-factly, "This is why I'm leaving this country."

I wanted to get back to Harlem as soon as I could. Vida counseled me to spend the night in her home. I accepted her sage advice and we exchanged remembrances and thoughts about Dr. King until the early hours. Many Northern black activists had mixed feelings about Dr. King. Many placed him in a Southern box of accommodating degrees of racism though Dr. King had delivered a powerful speech against the war in Vietnam at the Riverside Church in New York City.

I recounted to Vida Dr. King's profound, historical analysis of the inextricable relationship between slave and subsequent Jim Crow black labor and exploitation of white labor to accumulate wealth for the capitalists in the South and North. Dr. King delivered this analysis in his famous speech, "How Long, Not Long," at the conclusion of the 1965 Selma-to-Montgomery March at the Alabama Capitol in Montgomery.

"What stands out most in my mind," I continued, "was when Dr. King met with us SNCC organizers and told us that he understood and appreciated the concept of 'Black Power!', but the slogan was an unfortunate choice of words." Some of the SNCC organizers bristled at his assessment. I intrinsically agreed with Dr. King. We had appropriated, redefined and elevated a derogatory slur the racists hurled at us to debase our dignity and humanity. We had turned the "epithet" upside down into a positive description as how we defined ourselves, physically, historically and culturally . . .

and now politically via our right to vote.

The next mid-day morning, I left Queens for Harlem. When I climbed the stairs from the IRT subway and entered Harlem, it was visibly clear that black rage had wreaked havoc in the community as a reaction to Dr. King's assassination. The world soon learned that the rage was not isolated in Harlem. Over 110 looting and fiery rebellions erupted across the country, from east to west, from north to south. Dr. King, a peaceful soldier of the cloth, was gunned down because he was supporting black garbage workers in their struggle for livable wages and benefits. The poet, Leroi Jones, dubbed this period: "The Fire This Time."

23

Soldiers to Soldiers

In May 1968, my organizing and teaching was interrupted again by another car accident, resulting in further injury to my left leg. I was sitting in the front passenger seat while my Tuskegee Institute colleague, Clarence, then living in Long Island, was driving us from New York City to New Rochelle, New York. In the back seat were the newly elected SNCC program chair, Phil Hutchins, and two NBAWADU sisters from Boston. We were on the way to the wedding reception of Kwame Ture (formerly Stokely Carmichael) and Miriam Makeba.

Kwame and I had had a complex relationship since our first disagreement at Tuskegee Institute and my later decision to no longer be his roommate in Atlanta. But we had a deep and abiding respect and love for each other. We could listen to one another and disagree and never raise our voices. Our disagreements usually ended in infectious laughter. Kwame called me a "modern-day Harriet Tubman." Kwame loved black people unconditionally; I loved them conditionally. I had strong reservations about a sector of our people—now called the *lumpenproletariat* by leftists; I called them "street people"—who could be dangerous if they were unprincipled. I maintained my long-standing criticism of the unconscious black so-called middle class who believed that the road to freedom was to become capitalists, or at the very least to become high-salaried bureaucrats with the unspoken mission to keep other blacks stuck to the bottom of the lifeboat.

I had received the coveted invitation to Kwame and Miriam's reception; I didn't know who else in SNCC had received an invite, and no one else in the car had acknowledged one. I gradually realized that my colleagues intended to attend the reception on my invite. While we were en route, my Southern manners kicked in and I said I thought it would be in poor taste for "us to crash the reception. I'm sure the hostess has planned for a set number of guests."

Meanwhile, Clarence was driving very fast and not only my manners but my fear was kicking in. I had no sooner finished pleading with him to slow down than he lost control; "boom!" and we crashed into a tree. Before I blacked out, I saw stars. I felt no pain. I was convinced that this time I was on my way to heaven. My body in my mind was actually floating in the air.

When I opened my eyes, the pain in my leg was becoming unbearable. A doctor was standing over me as I lay strapped on a gurney.

"Where am I?"

"Harlem Hospital," the doctor said. He held a syringe of morphine that he was about to inject into my body.

I do not know why I refused the morphine. Perhaps I thought about Jerry, who was now a full-blown heroin addict. Heroin is a derivative of morphine. Perhaps it was a resistance to the racist medical methodology administered to black patients. I did not know if morphine was injected when I was a patient at John Andrews Hospital in Tuskegee after the first accident. But I did know that Dr. Herman Robbins never prescribed morphine to ease my pain. One time Demerol was ordered. I felt like I was spinning around in my bed, rising and falling with a strange sensation in my head, I was through with Demerol. Extra-strength Tylenol was sufficient for me.

Now I told the doctor not to inject me but to call Dr. Herman Robbins, chief of staff at the Hospital for Bone and Joint Diseases. "I'm under his care. I'm certain you don't want to interfere with his treatment," I said.

THE PAIN WAS so severe that I willed myself back to sleep. When I awoke again, I was in the Hospital for Bone and Joint Diseases. Dr. Robbins had sent an ambulance to Harlem Hospital to transport me, and now he explained that the accident had broken my femur but it had also closed the gap in my bones between my shin, heel, and foot. He put me on an every-eight hours course of antibiotic shots to ward off reinfection.

My injured leg was on a raised splint with weights attached. I had to pull myself up from my bed to sit on a bed-pan with a pulley hand-grip that was overhead. Mae called Jerry. And as before, he was attentive and lovingly caring. I realized that Jerry felt his strongest with me when I was incapacitated and dependent.

As Dr. Robbins was studying the next intervention that would enable me to walk on my own two feet, he sent his interns to talk with me. They explained that bone could be removed from my hip and used to mesh the bone in my shin, heel and foot.

While they beamed at me with this "good news," I thought about it for the proverbial New York minute. Then I said, "If the Lord wanted the hip bone to be in the shin bone, he would have done that in the first place. Pretend I am Mrs. Nelson Rockefeller. What would you do for her? Please ask Dr. Robbins to come see me." It was obvious that the interns were miffed with me as they brusquely walked out of the ward.

Soon Dr. Robbins was at my bedside. "Gwen, I'm trying to do the best I can to get you walking without crutches, a brace, or an artificial limb."

"I know, doctor. And, I trust you with all of my heart. There is an eye bank and other organ banks. Is there a bone bank?"

He said yes, but it was under the authority of the Navy in Bethesda, Maryland, with all of the bone reserved for U.S. casualties from the war in Vietnam. I bristled internally. Wasn't I a casualty of the Freedom Movement, a soldier of no less importance? I told him that if he would put in a request for the bone, I guaranteed a public campaign that would put the Navy to shame.

Dr. Robbins smiled. He knew I meant business. As he was leaving he asked if there was anything else he could do for me, and he was surprised when I asked if he could pierce my ears—I had always wanted to wear hoop earrings. He smiled, said, "Gwen, you are a remarkable young lady!," and promised to pierce my ears on his rounds the next day. Then he kissed my forehead and left my bedside.

As promised, Dr. Robbins pierced my ears with a hypodermic needle. With a surgical needle, he tied small threaded loops of suture in my ears to insure that the holes would become permanent. Then he handed me a dainty, velvet-covered box that contained a pair of small, gold-hoop earrings. They were shaped like graceful dolphins. The subtle message was a lovely compliment.

He said he had written the Navy with a plea for bone. I, too, had written letters and had asked my friends and family to write. The Navy probably received at least 100 letters.

A week before my hospital release, Dr. Robbins and his brightest intern, who later took over his private medical practice, performed an operation on my knee. They gave me only local anesthesia, so I was able to watch as they drilled a rod through my knee and placed bolts on each protruding end. They were realigning my shin as well as making it possible for me to walk with the aid of a patella brace. Flo Kennedy, the out-spoken lawyer who wore trademark large floppy hats, provided $250 to purchase the brace. The brace was secured around my knee with a cup. Two rods extended down each side of my leg and were attached to an oxford-looking shoe. Dr. Robbins wanted to see if the smaller gap, caused by the second car accident, between the anatomical components would mesh and cement together.

On the day of my release I held a press conference in front of the hospital. I had on my patella brace which made me look like a polio victim. The invited mainstream media did not show, but the progressive media was present in great force. My story and request to the Navy for bone was heard on progressive radio stations from coast to coast and was covered in several print organs. I cautioned my supporters to use the language of "request" and not that of "demand"—I was not in competition with casualties who were wounded in the godforsaken war in Vietnam.

After a couple of days, I took a Penn Central train to Washington, D.C., and then a Greyhound bus to Bethesda, Maryland. I gave the cab driver at the bus station the address of the Naval Hospital. When I arrived at the facility, I went to admissions. The administrators were baffled at my presence, but they listened politely to my plea. I thought I saw a glimmer of empathy in their eyes. After my presentation, I returned to New York City.

I hated the patella brace. It made me walk awkwardly and slowly. I exchanged the brace for my trusty crutches. I could make longer swings, covering greater ground and could keep up with a fast walker.

I CONTINUED TO travel throughout the country as a speaker, especially on college campuses. When I received international invitations to speak and lecture, my foreign sponsors gladly accepted the movement friends I suggested in my stead.

I met Mickey McGuire when I was invited by the Black Student Union to speak at the University of Houston. Mickey was from Mobile, Alabama, and had done time in the state prison at Atmore in south Alabama. He begged me to go to the Texas black schools, Texas Southern University and Huston-Tillotson College. I was reluctant since I had not been invited, but Mickey convinced me to see my visits as fact-finding missions for organizing.

My first unannounced visits with the student body presidents and student leaders reminded me of my days as student body president at Tuskegee Institute. I was impressed with their support for the movement, but I was disappointed that they did not see their college education and environment as inextricable components of the overall movement. These student leaders reverted to the "gown and town" dichotomy, perpetuating the class schism within the racist caste system.

I then visited the student unions and talked with students at random. I won the friendship of some students by going into the card rooms and playing with them. Their assessment of their college experiences was different than their student leaders. I urged them to talk with their student leaders and to become active in their student government associations.

Mickey was pleased with my interaction with the students. We quickly developed love, respect, loyalty, and admiration for each other. I was puzzled once when he commented on my college degree and said he had a degree, too—a "bachelor's degree from CSU, College of the Streets University."

We both laughed. I knew Mickey would soon work with me in raising the social consciousness and responsibility of black students.

As I flew into LaGuardia Airport one time too many, I knew there was a need to form a national black student association, and within that context, to form a national black student speakers' bureau. Partly my reasoning was based on a desire to share the opportunities, but partly it was selfishness—I was tired to the bone.

AFTER A WEEK of rest, reading, writing, and relaxation, I had an unexpected call from Dr. Robbins: "The Navy sent three jars of bone. Report to admissions tomorrow morning by 9 a.m."

Before he put me under, I asked Dr. Robbins if I could see the precious bone. I was expecting it to look like bone. Instead, it was finely crushed and looked like white corn meal. The procedure was to pack the crushed bone in the cavities and overlay some of it on my own bone. Bone grafting was like any other organ transplant. The critical factor was for the donor bone to match and adhere to my own bone. The delicate procedure also required that veins from my shin connect with veins in my ankle, heel, and foot via the overlaid bone; without blood circulation the foot would atrophy and die. Amputation would be the only remedy if the procedure failed.

I do not know how long the operation took, but when I groggily awoke from the anesthesia, I saw my toes sticking out from a hard cast as if standing at military attention. I still had my foot. I thanked God for blessing Dr. Herman Robbins with his medical genius.

I spent six weeks in the hospital while the bone was welding together and my ankle and heel were getting stronger. Dr. Robbins put a new, well-lined plaster cast on my leg, ankle, and foot, my toes still sticking out. This time he put a hard-rubber piece on the sole of the cast. He wanted me to walk on my own as a form of physical therapy to strengthen the bone even more. Gone were the crutches and the cursed patella brace. Dr. Robbins instructed me to pull a thick sock over my cast if my toes felt cold; it was important for the blood to circulate and that meant my toes had to stay warm.

While I was still in the hospital, a social worker with a built-up shoe came to visit me. She was an attractive white woman with a wonderful disposition and demeanor. She answered all my questions about her shoes.

I did not like the design of the oxford-style shoes, but the fact that she had a hand in their design told me she chose the style.

Around this time, Senator Robert F. Kennedy was assassinated. The country was unraveling. Amidst it all, my movement friends still gave me a coming-home party. This was the first time in over two and a half years that I placed my own foot, albeit in a cast with a rubber heel, on the ground. I danced the night away.

JERRY AND I subsequently visited with my grandparents and family in Montgomery. Mommy Washington was very fond of Jerry. She thought he was a jewel who had stood by me when I had tuberculosis and again after my accident. When she saw me walking without crutches, she never stopped thanking God aloud for my miracle.

I did not ask Jerry to accompany me to visit with my father and my brother and his family in Inkster, Michigan. I knew that my street-wise brother would instantly discern that Jerry was a junkie. And my father detested drugs of any kind; he thought if you took two aspirins you were a dope fiend.

24

Students and Workers Unite!

I hardly had been back in NYC for a "New York City Minute" when I was thrust into a month-long series of endless "Continuations Committee (CC)" planning meetings. I had been serving on the "CC" to plan and coordinate protests against the Vietnam War since December 1966, when I accompanied Bettina Aptheker to the founding of the Student Mobilization Committee in Chicago. I had known Bettina since I was student body president at Tuskegee Institute in 1965 when I asked her to come to the campus and help set up a Draft Counseling Center for black students and teens.

The "CC" meetings went on and on. At last a plan of action was agreed upon to protest the Vietnam War at the 1968 Democratic National Convention in Chicago and to support Eugene McCarthy as the Democratic Party nominee for the presidency. The hippies and Yippies (Youth in Politics, led by Abbie Hoffman and Bobby Seale of the Black Panther Party) were vocal participants in planning for the week-long protest in Chicago. By this time, I had my fill of "new left" politics, arguments and sectarians. I sensed the Yippies' theatrical antics and outlandish tactics would be no match for Mayor Richard Daley's 1,000-member police force. Daley had made it clear that he would order the police "to shoot to kill." What worried me about the hippie movement was their nonchalant attitude about police-state power—putting flowers into gun barrels was no deterrence to state violence. Moreover, the hippies seemed always to be in an altered state of reality. They were Dr. Timothy Leary's "turn on, tune in, drop out" groupies, experimenting with psychedelic drugs to expand the mind, but with no practical sense of reality. They were dancing in the streets but "out to lunch." The Yippies were a bit more attuned to reality, but then they had nominated a pig for president. I understood the satire, that it made no difference who was nominated or elected, the script for the presidency had been written. As H. Rap Brown of SNCC said, "A fourth grader could serve in this vacuous position."

But what I could not understand is how hippies and Yippies thought that their movements of overt zany and outlandish actions would not provide an amorphous cover for provocateurs, police agents and infiltrators. On the other hand, the Black Panther Party (BBP) was more covert and clandestine, despite their members wearing berets and leather black jackets, which emitted an aura of intrigue and oft-times danger. The BBP's persona and actions demonstrated a pure love for our community with its free breakfast, health clinics, after-school programs for youth and its righteous criticism of hostile police actions in the black community. However, the overall BBP mystique provided a perfect storm-cover for internal infiltration of police agents, informers and saboteurs.

The Chicago NBAWADU Chapter decided to participate in protest marches in a low-key manner. Chapter members knew how brutal Chicago police could be. Thus, protecting their personal safety and lives was foremost in their decision. This decision coupled with consultations I received from my Inkster family and UAW members, and my Montgomery family and elder movement mentors, who had waged a fierce political battle within the racist Governor Wallace controlled State Democratic Party, its spin-off of the Alabama Independent Democratic Party (AIDP), and the National Democratic Party of Alabama (NDPA), a spin-off the Alabama Democratic Conference (the black caucus within the State Democratic Party that sided with the AIDP and defeated the NDPA) as to why they were supporting Humphrey led me to decline any public appearances at the Chicago protest gatherings. The new coalition of the AIDP elected three black Humphrey delegates/alternates: Civil Rights Attorney Arthur Shores of Birmingham, Alvin Holmes, whom I knew as a youth parishioner member of our Hutchinson Baptist Church Family, and Joe Reed. The "peacenik coalition" literally considered Humphrey as a puppet with hand-strings being manipulated by President Johnson, who had escalated the war with greater aerial napalm and chemical warfare exposure in Vietnam, and then announced that he would not seek re-election.

Both positions were flawed with the single-issue tactic: End the war in Vietnam and all will be well, or fight against racism and poverty and all will be well. The intersection of racism and the war had yet to take hold though the arguments for a multi-issue approach had been raging in the peace movement since 1965. Without this thoughtful analyses of the war-machine, government, corporatism, capitalism and imperialism, both groups will inevitably find themselves consciously or unconsciously complicit with the "isms" they now found evil. Such complicity will manifest itself in one of the isms as "rank opportunism" that may mitigate against real freedom and opportunity for all Americans, black and white.

I left New York City for Chicago that Sunday, August 25, 1968, and was a guest of Lucy Montgomery, a long-time financial supporter of SNCC, and a resident in the garden condos of ritzy Old Town, Chicago. It was unbelievable that the Chicago police forced protesters into this area and that an all-out riot/rebellion between the police and the protesters occurred as Lucy and I watched from her condo veranda. I was determined to join the protests the next day in Grant Park. After joining the Chicago Chapter of NBAWADU line of march, I was bewildered when we arrived and I saw protesters swarming over the Park's larger than life statutes of military monuments. It was complete chaos. I wanted out of the Grant Park melee.

My challenged leg in the cast provided the reprieve. I approached the policemen's perimeter who were not allowing protesters to leave the Park and were corralling them for ultimate arrests. I asked them to let me through the police lines. The police looked at my cast leg and permitted me to pass through. I hobbled across the street to the Lakeshore Hilton restaurant, known for its delectable stuffed mushrooms, sautéed calf livers and bread assortments frequented by black Southside residents. I found refuge. I contemplated what these past events meant for American politics, and more specifically for blacks within this unsettled system. I concluded that my movement work could not be within this context.

WHEN I RETURNED to New York City, I put Jerry on the back burner of my mind and heart. My thoughts were focused on the unconsciousness of black students and their disconnect with the black working class.

I was still smarting from my 1966 visit to the National Student Association headquarters in Washington when I was student body president at Tuskegee Institute. By at least 1961, NSA had set up a Civil Rights Desk, which was manned by two white male students; NSA received large foundation grants for such activity. In 1964, NSA shepherded the "Fast for Freedom" project, whereby college students all over the country forfeited lunch for one day and sent their lunch money to NSA to support civil rights activity and programs in the South. Tuskegee Institute students participated in the project for two years. When I visited NSA again in 1968, the Civil Rights Desk was manned by another set of white male students. In fact, all the NSA paid staffers, perhaps twenty, were white.

I had no qualms as to how monies were used for civil rights activity. I knew that NSA had financially supported the Mississippi Project. However, no money was sent to the Alabama Project, which not only embraced "Black Power" but was acting on the concept by putting forth black candidates via an independent political party in five Black Belt counties.

I raised the staff contradictions in terms of racial composition with NSA. They offered me a job on the Civil Rights Desk. After a brief time, I resigned. This was not the resolve. NSA had raised hundreds of thousands of dollars under the banner of "civil rights." A more principled resolve had to be found.

I went back to New York City and pulled together all the black student contacts I had made over the past two years. I sent a letter asking those at predominantly white schools to ask their Black Student Unions to pay their way to the upcoming 1969 NSA national conference at the University of Texas in El Paso. I then sent letters urging the student body presidents at the hundred-plus historically black colleges and universities to attend the conference. I knew they would be bona fide delegates while BSU representatives could only be observers. At my first and second NSA conferences in 1965 and 1966, only a handful of black colleges were among the thousand colleges represented.

I asked Muhammad Kenyatta from Chester, Pennsylvania, Mickey McGuire from Houston, and my dear friend Mae Jackson to a strategy meeting at the NYC-SNCC office. I learned that NSA had invited Dr. Nathan Hare, a black psychologist who once taught at Howard University, and Reverend Jesse Jackson to be keynote speakers. NSA also contracted Stax Records, featuring the Staple Singers, Isaac Hayes, and others, to provide the entertainment. Though this was laudable, it did not speak to the plight of black students struggling with racism on predominantly white campuses and black students struggling with recalcitrant and reactionary administrators on black campuses. Struggling black students needed a black, national infrastructure to serve their direct needs. NSA had not been and could not be that vehicle.

I SHARED MY thoughts with James Forman. He had somewhat withdrawn from the urban Black Panther Party which by then was riddled with saboteurs, provocateurs, and FBI infiltrators (we didn't yet know the half of COINTEL-PRO's murderous assault on the Panthers, including imprisoning honest brothers like Geronimo Pratt for twenty years and murdering Fred Hampton and Mark Clark in their sleep).

Forman, however, still had a fascination with the intrigue that was rife in the beleaguered BBP. Once I traveled with him to Atlanta to check on the national SNCC office at 360 Nelson Street. When we visited the freedom house, I saw black college-aged women—my cousin among them—wearing army fatigues and combat boots. They were scurrying about and carrying missives to secret destinations in the wee hours of the morning. I was one of his most trusted and respected movement colleagues, yet he never asked me to undergo these "missions." He knew how I felt because I told him these were silly antics with dangerous ramifications.

On a more rational course, Forman was working closely with Detroit black workers, who had rebelled against the exploitation of speed-up and other indignities in the auto industry. The workers had staged sit-downs in the factories and wildcat strikes to lift up their grievances. They formed Ford Revolutionary Union Workers (FRUM), Dodge Revolutionary Union Workers (DRUM) and Eldon Gear and Axle Revolutionary Union Workers (ELRUM). Forman was an absolute genius in pulling these radical workers' groups together as the League of Black Revolutionary Workers, known as the League. When a black worker named Thompson could no longer withstand the dictates of the foreman bellowing orders to speed-up the assembly line, Thompson shot the foreman. Kenny Cockerel and his partner, Harry Fowler (also my father's lawyer), defended Thompson.

I resonated with the Detroit factory workers. There were at least 2,000 active and silent workers in the League. They were serious about political education. They were clear on working-class analysis in a racist and capitalist society. They understood the fundamental importance of reaching out to build strong coalitions. Some of the key players were factory workers General Baker, Marian Cramer, Luke Tripp, Mike Hamlin, and Chuck Wooten; Jerome Scott, a Vietnam veteran and factory worker, and his wife, Theresa, a registered nurse and a strong healthcare union member; Rita Valenti, a registered nurse and a close union ally with Theresa Scott; John and Edna Watson, married Wayne State University students; John Williams, a public school teacher and a strong advocate in the teachers' union; attorneys John Taylor and Justin Ravitz, who later became an elected judge and was known for standing to honor the people in his courtroom rather than vice versa; and Dan Georgakas and Marvin Surkin, later the co-authors of *Detroit, I*

Do Mind Dying: A Study in Urban Revolution.

The coalition formed a book club, "Control, Conflict and Change," that met once a month. There were 500 dues-paying members. I was humbled when they asked me to give a review and analysis of Kate Millet's *Sexual Politics.*

On this occasion of being in Detroit, I took Forman to meet with my father, a UAW committeeman in the Ford-River Rouge Plant. My father supported the League, but he cautioned against withdrawal from UAW. Too much was at stake, especially contract negotiating power and pensions. My father recommended to Forman that the League remain independent but serve as a strong black caucus to demand that the union stand up for fairness, justice, and the ongoing fight against racism in the union and in the factories.

"Many racists in the union would like anything better than for black workers to withdraw," my father said. "If this happens, black workers would catch pure hell and would be fired left and right with the assistance of white, racist workers on the line. There is no contradiction between black workers organizing inside and outside of the union."

FLYING WITH FORMAN from Detroit back to New York City provided quality time to share with him my analysis of the black student predicament. I was sorting through my concept of how we could realize the transition from "student to student worker to worker consciousness."

I told Forman I thought his generation of students was programmed to be teachers, my generation was programmed to be teachers, social workers, and lawyers, and the current generation was programmed to be businessmen, business managers, and journalists. I said that if there was no intervention in terms of consciousness and responsibility to the masses of our people, our "talented tenth" would become neo-colonialists, USA-style, the new overseers in black face.

Forman nodded in understanding.

I unloaded my analyses of NSA and the proposed strategy to demand reparations from NSA for its unconscionable, if unconscious, raising funds to support black movements in the South while spending the bulk of the funds on salaries for white students as civil rights workers and overhead for the three-story NSA headquarters and field offices, also manned by white students. With reparations from NSA as an acknowledgment of their white privilege in exploiting our movement, we could establish an infrastructure, the National Association of Black Students (NABS).

My concept needed principled worker allies like those in the League to provide political education to help students' transition of thought. Black cafeteria workers on college campuses were fighting for protection of their jobs and unionization in the face of being replaced by outsourced, private food services. Students' college experiences should include more than going to Greek balls; they should be joining workers on the picket lines to show solidarity and to break down the "gown and town" syndrome.

Forman promised his support. He said that if I would draw up a resolution he would present it to the League's executive committee.

However, I did not share with Forman the tactics the small strategy group had developed. We had promised each other to keep the plan under wraps, partly to see if there was a saboteur or infiltrator in our ranks who would spill the beans.

THE 1969 NATIONAL Student Association conference was held in August on the campus of the University of Texas at El Paso. That weekend I was a coordinator of the Third World Commission, comprising of African American, Native American, and Mexican American students, and I sought a meeting with NSA President Bob Powell. He rebuffed me. Without his leadership, it was virtually impossible for me to have a hearing before the NSA executive committee or its national advisory board.

Black and Mexican American students had widely circulated their respective position papers to the 1,000 NSA delegates and observers. Black students were asking for an official accounting of monies NSA had received since 1961 for civil rights activities and programs. We were demanding that half of that amount be set aside to establish the National Association of Black Students. NABS would have a principled relationship with NSA in the future.

At a press conference, I laid it out: "NSA as it is presently constituted is not relevant to black students and their problems. NSA can not any longer use black problems for its own purposes to gain financial grants from foundations. We are issuing this call for reparations so NSA can right its past wrongs."

The time was ripe to request reparations. Forman had demanded in his 1969 *Black Manifesto* that the USA superstructure—in this case the Church, which confiscated much land in Africa and left the Bible as the exchange—make amends for the historical wrongs the government had perpetuated on its black citizens.

At Sunday evening's opening plenary, representatives from the Third World Commission mounted the platform, to the consternation of Powell, who was presiding. Our hope was that he had added our resolutions to the agenda to be presented to the body for ratification. But if he did not, then we would walk off the platform and the roughly one hundred TWC delegates and observers would also walk out to join us in a strategy session to plan our next actions. Powell did not include us on the agenda. His tactic was to avoid discussion until after the elections the following night.

As agreed, Muhammad Kenyatta led the TWC representatives off the platform. As we were leaving the auditorium, an altercation erupted between two female delegates, one black and the other white. Muhammad stood between them to cool the situation. The black female student joined us in the walk-out. A few white students also joined us.

We had declared that all our actions would be nonviolent. If anyone at the strategy session could not adhere to this tactic, we respectfully asked them to leave the meeting. No one left. We subsequently decided that if Powell persisted in going on with the elections on Monday evening, we had no choice but to nonviolently disrupt the meeting. Over the past weekend Mickey McGuire had studied the auditorium's layout. He knew where all the electrical outlets, including telephone outlets, were located. He and his action group were to station themselves at the various outlets, and upon a signal from Muhammad were to pull the plugs. Immediately after this "disconnect" action, some of our delegates, in fake KKK outfits, would march in, chanting "NSA, KKK." We assigned all of the white students who walked out in support of our cause to be in the "KKK" march, with

Scott Douglas, a black student from Memphis, Tennessee, as the leader. We spent hours making KKK outfits out of white sheets and hoods out of pillow cases with "dunce-shaped" water cups at the apex.

The black contingent made it clear to the rest of the TWC representatives that our bottom line was $50,000 reparations from the NSA for their opportunistic exploitation of the black plight in racist USA. The money would be used to establish NABS. Neither the Native American nor the Mexican American (headed by Caesar Chavez of the United Farmers Workers) factions had a monetary plan.

At the Monday night plenary session, Powell proceeded to conduct elections. Muhammad gave Mickey the signal to "cut the juice." At another signal, the main door opened and our "KKK" march paraded throughout the auditorium, chanting "NSA, KKK!" Visibly shaken and angry, Powell walked off the platform. Muhammad and I mounted the platform and I went to the podium. Mickey reconnected the microphone. I said in a modulated and serious tone to the delegates, "The election had to be stopped. The race question is the number one question in America today." As planned, Muhammad came to the podium and I handed him the microphone.

"Now, let us break up into groups to discuss this question," he said. As he pointed to various sections in the auditorium, he said, "Black students over there. White students who care enough to do something about bigotry over here, and the group who is against blacks in the center."

A white male student ran towards Muhammad and yelled, "What are we supposed to discuss?"

Muhammad replied, "You've been running the U.S. for 400 years, and you don't know how to run your group meeting?"

No white group "against blacks" formed in the center. However, about 500 students left the auditorium.

The two remaining group discussions went on through the night. Finally, the white group who wanted "to do something about bigotry" came to the black group. Among them were some of the current NSA elected officials and all of the candidates vying to become NSA president. Also in that group was Patrick Rooney, the CEO of Golden Rule Insurance Company. He was one of the vendors at the conference. He said in the integrated group, "What the black students are asking is reasonable, historically sound, and modest."

It was agreed that reparations should be paid for the express purpose of establishing NABS, which would have a principled relationship with NSA. I suggested that we get a good night's rest and meet in the morning, and I insisted that someone bring Bob Powell to the morning meeting.

THE MEETING RESUMED the following morning. Oddly, fifty-plus years later, I do not recall if Bob Powell was there or not. But all the NSA presidential hopefuls were there and each promised that if elected he or she would honor the reparations.

We delegated to a smaller working committee the issue of how the reparations would be paid. I asked Bernard Nicolas, a Haitian exile and an economics major at UCLA, to represent NABS's interests.

The elections went forward that evening. The newly elected NSA president, Charles Palmer, past student body president at UC-Berkeley, succeeded Powell and announced that NSA would honor the reparations for the establishment of NABS. The remaining 500 delegates and observers loudly applauded. This was the first time that a white establishment institution had honored a call for reparations.

Caesar Chavez was sitting next to me in the auditorium. He leaned over and said, matter of factly, "I think $20,000 of the $50,000 should go to the UFW." I looked keenly in his eyes and responded, "You did not put forth a struggle for your cause and you did not struggle for this victory. And, besides, my people did not oppress your people."

AFTER THE NSA conference, Muhammad Kenyatta returned to Chester, Pennsylvania, and Mae Jackson to Brooklyn. Bernard Nicholas and Mickey McGuire accompanied me to Washington, where businessman Patrick Rooney joined us in amicable discussions with new NSA President Charles Palmer at the NSA headquarters.

We decided that NSA would pay two installments of $25,000 and that the NSA House at 3418 17th Street Northwest could serve as the NABS House; NSA had secured other housing accommodations for its officers.

Ironically, the new NABS House was located on the periphery of Rock

Creek Park and adjacent to the fabled "Gold Coast" neighborhood that has been home to many accomplished African Americans in Washington. The elegant brick house sat on a hill. Twenty steps led up to a landing and lawn before the front entrance. The main floor consisted of a large living room, which served as a receiving and conference room, an adjacent dining room that was converted into an office, and a spacious kitchen. A bathroom was to one side of the kitchen and on the other side were stairs leading to a large basement. Part of the basement served as a workroom with office equipment and storage for office supplies. Another part of the basement served as guest quarters for overnight NABS visitors. (One of our guests was jazz bagpiper Rufus Harley. His 1966 debut album, *Bagpipe Blues*, stormed the jazz world. Rufus, in Scottish kilts and attire, was the world's only black jazz bagpipe player. Sadly, by 1970 he was a gas meter reader in Philadelphia. NABS was attempting to revive his jazz career by booking concerts on college campuses.) The NABS collective lived upstairs, where there were four large bedrooms and a bathroom.

Bernard opted to take a year out of college to help establish NABS. Vince Benson, from the University of Pennsylvania, who had attended the NSA conference and vigorously campaigned to serve as NABS's co-coordinator, also wanted to take a hiatus from college to work with NABS. But he was married and he and his wife, Myrtle, had two small children. I told Vince that I first had to talk with Myrtle's parents, who owned a lucrative funeral business, in Philadelphia. I invited them to visit the NABS House to see if it was suitable for their grandchildren, not yet of school age. After their visit, they sent a year's supply of canned goods and food staples.

Bernard's fiancée, Dawn, wanted to leave UCLA to work for NABS. I suggested to Bernard that she should not come until we had secured more living space. I had never cottoned to the "freedom house" concept with mattresses everywhere on floors. Working in the movement was a 24/7 job. People needed space with comfortable surroundings for privacy.

The Muslims bought a mini-mansion less than a block from the NABS House. Colonel Hassan, who had a residential methadone program for addicts, bought a mini-mansion diagonally across from the Muslims' house. The three-story house next door to the NABS House was up for sale. I placed a three-month option to purchase it. My dream was to buy all seven of the commodious houses on the block.

PATRICK ROONEY ASKED what his Golden Rule Insurance Company could do to help establish NABS. The NABS collective had designed a brochure that laid out its founding, vision, mission, and programs. Another pamphlet described the "NABS Speakers' Bureau" with photographs, brief biographies, and topics. Rooney agreed to print 1,000 brochures and pamphlets. I was relieved. The bureau's speakers and topics included:

- Myself, on black and white coalitions, rural and urban politics and education, student power, psychology of the ghetto and black women's liberation;
- Leroi Jones, the poet and playwright who had won the Obie Award for the Best Play of 1964, on nationalism and black art;
- Topper Carew, an architect, on revolutionary thinking in design, lectured on art, culture, African and African American lifestyles;
- Milton Henry, an attorney and co-founder of the New Republic of Africa, on black separatism, land sovereignty and power, and black self-determination;
- Paul Boutelle, a member of Socialist Workers Party, on politics, economics, revolution, socialism and nationalism;
- Chuck Stone, a political analyst, special assistant to U.S. Representative Adam Clayton Powell, and author of *Black Political Power in America,* on brinkmanship and black revolution;
- Muhannad Kenyatta, minister and field organizer for SNCC who organized black cooperatives in the Tennessee-Mississippi area, on black reparations, racism and religion, black liberation and the Third World;
- U.S. Representative Louis Stokes of Ohio, member of the House committee on education and labor, on general politics and education in black America;
- Valerie Tucker, NABS regional director for central U.S., on problems blacks face in the Catholic church;
- Jeanette Michael, NABS regional director for the Northeast,

on problems that black people face in small Catholic churches;
- Bernard Nicholas, NABS regional director for the west coast, on comparative analysis of U.S. and Haitian blacks;
- Ossie Davis, famed actor and writer;
- Reverend Charles Koen from Cairo, Illinois, minister and Prime Minister of the National Black Liberators, on ideology and "It's a long journey from Little Egypt to Soul Valley";
- Conrad Lynn, an expert draft resistance lawyer and author of *How to Stay Out of the Army*, on justice for black people, Third World issues, war and USA imperialism;
- and Rosie Douglas, a West Indian, on connecting liberation struggles in the diaspora.

MY DESIRE WAS to put matriculating students on the college circuit as speakers, as well as leading personalities in the black freedom struggle, regardless of their ideologies. I was determined not to be the "star" of NABS. I knew that when an organization is centered on one person and when that person moved on to new challenges, the organization died. I had seen this in SNCC with Kwame Ture (Stokely Carmichael), who was sought by and hounded by the media as *the* SNCC spokesman. SNCC organizers lovingly and derisively called him "Star-Michael." I had also seen this in the church when an auxiliary president would stay in the post of the presidency with no program to develop younger leadership. When the "life-time" president died, so did the church auxiliary. Besides, I was bone-tired from speaking on the college circuit.

When the brochures and pamphlets were printed, I turned to writing proposals and fundraising letters. The Cummins Engine philanthropy section, headed by former SNCC organizer Ivanhoe Donaldson, who adamantly opposed "Black Power" from a practical viewpoint, awarded NABS a $20,000 grant. Individual donors of $10 to $1,000 included U.S. Representative Shirley Chisholm and Lucy Montgomery with the Chicago Gray Panthers.

NABS gained enough resources to take on a mortgage to purchase the mini-mansion next door. With more space available, NABS sent for Bernard's fiancée, Dawn. Soon students from around the country wanted to come to work for NABS. I wrote several college financial aid directors to have NABS listed as a work-study site. Antioch College was one that honored the request. Coretta Scott King, the widow of Dr. King, sat on the board of trustees at Antioch. I was certain that she approved NABS as a work-study opportunity equal to students traveling abroad to enhance their educational studies. Diane Jenkins, who as a New York City high school student had worked with me during the National Black Anti-War, Anti-Draft Union (NBAWADU) organizing, was now a freshman at Antioch; she signed up to do her external studies with NABS. The Neighborhood Youth Corps registered NABS as a community work site. Several high school students, even from Chicago, worked with NABS during the 1970–1971 summers.

Each member of the NABS collective received a stipend of $75 per week; housing and food were provided as part of NABS's overhead. Several frugal staff members saved money to help with their future college expenses.

My sister, Sandy Patton, had been a music major at Howard University. She wanted to major in voice, but her counselor recommended that she should become a music librarian. Disappointed, she dropped out of college. NABS hired her as secretary and as my administrative assistant. Like the Kennedys, I believed in nepotism. (I realized that my sister was extremely talented. I underwrote her tuition at the Corcoran School of the Arts. Sandy went on with her dream to be a singer. Presently, she is an international jazz singer and a retired professor of voice with the Swiss School of Jazz.)

Every Wednesday evening, the NABS collective held readings and discussions. Dr. Robert Rhodes, professor of political economy, and Jack O'Dell, special assistant to the Reverend Jesse Jackson and a world history professor, were the lead teachers. One visiting teacher was Chuck Stone, who advised that violent acts were not always revolutionary and that all revolutionary acts must have political meaning. He further shared with us his reservations concerning black elected officials' support for Israel. Another visiting teacher was Dr. Nathan Hare, who had been at the NSA conference when NABS first called for reparations. Dr. Hare made it plain that wearing African attire did not make you revolutionary, nor would the revolution for black freedom occur overnight. He was critical of mainstream press that instantly created "black leaders" and of those who proclaimed themselves as "leaders" after reading their names in the press. Dr. Hare was insistent that we understand the various positions of black people in the world of work. Just because they worked in the government as a "typist III" did not make them enemies of the black movement for freedom. Dr. Hare had a deep respect for black women and their roles, including leadership, in the movement.

Our last visiting teacher was James Forman, who thereafter made many visits to the NABS houses for study sessions. At his first session he talked with the NABS collective as a "big brother." Forman had been SNCC's executive secretary. He was by now in his late thirties and had been a school teacher during a time when almost all of SNCC's organizers were college students. Forman cautioned against students considering themselves the vanguard of the movement as a special, elite cadre. He was working with the League of Revolutionary Black Workers in Detroit. His message struck home when he told the NABS collective, "There are about 375,000 black [college] students in the country whereas there are more than 375,000 black workers in Detroit alone." He impressed upon the NABS collective, especially those who were first-generation college-educated, to yield to the wisdom of black workers—their parents and family members—as the true leaders in our fight for freedom. One of his critical observations that struck home with NABS was: "Counterinsurgency goes on in the USA, foreign countries and in this very organization. It is ridiculous to think that the CIA is not interested in NABS. The FBI never stops harassing people who attend black conferences."

To complement the study-discussion sessions, NABS showed a series of films: *The Battle of Algiers* (1965), a significant political film that chronicles the 1950s Algerian wars to liberate the country from French colonialism; *Salt of the Earth* (1954), a docu-drama that depicts the strike of zinc mine workers against sexism and exploitation in New Mexico; *Time of the Locust* (1966), featuring archival footage of the Vietnam war; *No Vietnamese Ever Called Me Nigger* (1968), covers the anti-war march of black people from Harlem to the United Nations and features Muhammad Ali initiating the slogan, "No Viet Cong ever called me a nigger," among others.

NABS student groups, including the Students Organization for Black Unity (SOBU), visited the NABS House on Wednesdays to be a part of the study group. SOBU was founded after NABS began. The organization was comprised of mostly women but with a few male leaders. The women played obsequious and subordinate roles. They served more as a harem for the male leaders than as organizers to deal with students' concerns. SOBU, a black, cultural nationalist organization, which concentrated on Africa without a world view, took exception to NABS's approach to race and class analysis to assess black people's status in the USA and the diaspora. Nevertheless, some SOBU members, all males, were serious students in our Wednesday evenings study sessions; SOBU women were not permitted to attend. SOBU's real problem was with my leadership as a black woman. NABS had a mixture of black women and men as organizers with black men being in the majority and my leadership as a black woman. The antagonism escalated to a point that Mickey McGuire took it upon himself to be my personal bodyguard.

Kwame Ture was the mentor and titular head of SOBU. Kwame/Stokely was my friend though through the years we disagreed on our analysis and strategy for our race to secure freedom. To abate SOBU's conflict with NABS, and particularly with me, I engaged Kwame in a debate on the question: "Is it just race or is it race and class?"

The debate, attended by least 800 students, was held in the Blackburn Center on Howard University's campus. As students relaxed and were sitting on the floor, every space occupied, their intermittent applause indicated that I won the debate. Kwame was an admirer of Dr. Kwame Nkrumah, the president of Ghana. My major source for the debate was Nkrumah's *Revolutionary Notebook and Class Struggle in Africa*. Kwame graciously accepted losing the debate. As we embraced at the end, I whispered in his ear, "Please tell SOBU people to stop attacking NABS and me. We are all in the struggle to free our people." Thereafter, SOBU became friends to NABS.

NABS negotiated with the New York City-based Queen Booking Corporation, which had a stable of black entertainers, for 5 percent of the proceeds when acts performed on black college campuses and at concerts sponsored by black student unions on predominantly white campuses. The agency had a stable of black entertainers, including Ray Charles and Aretha Franklin, who was the rave at the time. I learned much as to who the partners were in the booking-entertainment industry. Soon afterwards, NABS established the Student Economic Development Corporation (SEDCO), with Patrick Rooney's business acumen guiding us in his role as a pro-bono consultant. The intent was to sell franchises to colleges that carried NABS collegiate paraphernalia. NABS published a newspaper, *Struggle!*, that covered student concerns and the efforts of black college workers, mainly in housekeeping and cafeteria work, to unionize.

NABS had gained a solid footing.

25

Vicissitudes of Life

Meanwhile, Jerry asked me on bended knee, with ring box in his hand, to marry him.

Jerry had moved from New York City and was now living with me in the NABS House. I had had a long day with NABS business and Jerry and I were in our bedroom. "I'm not marrying a dope fiend," I replied.

I had never seen Jerry shoot dope, but I knew he was a heroin addict. When he needed a fix, his face contorted and he looked like a devil. Once when he was in this state, I told him to go to the bathroom and look at his face and then tell me what he saw. Who was the man in the mirror?

He promised to kick his habit and asked for my help. "I need you to be with me. It won't be easy. But you are strong. I know you can handle it," he said.

In preparation, Jerry rented a starkly furnished kitchenette in the heart of Washington's ghetto. Or maybe it was already his hideaway; I didn't know. In any case, we retreated there. He bolted the lock from inside the flat and handed me the key. "Do not give me the key," he said. He unpacked the suitcase full of bed linens, a blanket, towels, facecloths, our pajamas, and toiletries. I plugged up a small color TV I had brought. After he made the bed, we went to a nearby restaurant.

He explained what would be in store for the next forty-eight hours. I was somewhat frightened and asked if he might become violent. He assured me he would be too weak for that, and besides, "I can never hurt you. I love you too much. You are a good woman. I really don't deserve you."

We returned to the flat and settled in. Jerry was watching TV and I was reading Walter Rodney's *The West and the Rest of Us*. Walter had visited the NABS House the day after Ralph Featherstone was blown up and killed in a strange car accident. Jamil Al-Amin, aka H. Rap Brown, still SNCC chairman and who had been with Featherstone, was in a Maryland jail under the "anti-riot act," a law especially designed to imprison Jamil and other black militants. Rebellions in black communities from Los Angeles to Detroit and Plainfield to Birmingham were rocking the nation. Rodney was assassinated two weeks later in Central America.

My thoughts drifted to James Brown. He was performing in Boston when Dr. King was assassinated in Memphis. We in SNCC had chastised Brown for his record, "I'm Black, But I'm Proud." After our friendly sit-down, Brown did a remake of the record with the title, "I'm Black *and* I'm Proud. "Black and Beautiful" had become the mantra for the movement. In Boston, Brown asked the audience not to riot as a response to Dr. King's murder. He asked the crowd, "What must I do to keep everybody calm?" His fans roared, "Dance, brother, dance!" Brown sang and danced nonstop for seven hours. He truly was the "hardest working man in show business."

By midnight, Jerry and I had drifted off to sleep. Two hours later, I was suddenly awakened. Jerry was shaking like a tree branch in a tornado. He curled himself into a fetal position and was crying and calling on the Lord to help him. I cradled his head on my breast. His shaking gave way to shivering and teeth-chattering. I wrapped the blanket snugly around him. Soon he was sweating. I soaked cloths in cold water and placed them on his forehead, with dry towels around his neck. He clung to me.

He hoarsely whispered, "Give me the key." But I had hidden it in the cast on my leg. Abruptly, he jolted out of bed and began to frantically empty drawers and cabinets and rummage under the mattresses. His eyes blazing, he demanded the key.

I replied that he needed to get the poison out of his system and implored him to come back to bed. Finally he limped back to the bed, fully spent from his fruitless search for the key. I smothered him with kisses. I pulled the ring box from my purse and opened it to display the matching gold bands. "Remember we are to get married after we beat this demon," I told him.

That seemed to calm him, though all through the night there were bouts of chills that quickly turned into cold and then hot sweats. When he left the bed to go to the bathroom, I followed to make certain that he had not stashed any drugs. He lay on the cool tile floor, pushed up the commode seat, and began to heave into the toilet. After this episode, I washed his haggard face with a cold facecloth and gave him a paper cup of mouthwash. He finally took the cup, gargled, and spat into the sink. "My mouth feels better," he said, trying to muster a smile. I smiled back and softly kissed him on the forehead. I helped him back to bed. He finally fell asleep. When I knew he was sound asleep, I closed my eyes, too.

That Saturday afternoon when I awoke, Jerry was already awake, propped up on a pillow and looking at television. As he leaned over to kiss me, I could see that some color had returned to his face.

I got dressed to go out for a few things and locked the door behind me. When I returned, Jerry had fallen asleep again and the television was watching him.

Sunday, mid-morning, Jerry seemed almost back to his old self. "I'm going to send your photo to *JET*," he joked—the magazine had a centerfold section featuring stunning black women.

"Pshaw. I have a cast on my leg."

"The photo doesn't have to show your legs."

Jerry was still weak. We sat at the cheap, 1950s kitchen set, drank chicken broth from styrofoam cups, read the paper, and engaged small talk. I had a speaking engagement the following Friday at the University of New Mexico in Santa Fe. Jerry agreed to go with me. It would be a celebration. He would have been drug-free for one week.

WHILE IN SANTA FE and being that far west, I decided that we should go to Las Vegas to visit my Aunt Samella, my father's sister and the oldest of the Patton children, and my Uncle Ernest, my father's youngest brother (in fact, he was a year younger than I). Jerry had never met my father's family. We had an exciting weekend in Vegas with the glitter of the "Strip" and the "cha-ching" of the casinos.

On the way back to the airport, Jerry instructed the cabdriver to stop at a "marriage chapel." I was surprised and reluctant. But he insisted, "I want to marry you, Gwen. I love you more than myself. You are good for me and I need you. I promise to be a good husband." He pulled out the ring box that I had used as an incentive to get him to stop his feverish searching for the key during his drug-withdrawal odyssey. I relented. When we returned to the NABS House in Washington, we were a married couple.

I soon went back to New York for a checkup with Dr. Robbins. Looking at the x-rays and nodding his head with a smile on his face, he said my cast could come off, that the bone graft had "adhered and it is as strong and as hard as your own bone." When he sawed off the cast, I saw my leg and foot for the first time in three and a half years.

He warned that I would have little motion in my foot. It is stabilized in a ninety-degree, acquiness angle. Do not ever try to walk on your mended foot without your built-up shoe." Dr. Robbins told me to stand without letting my foot touch the floor. I used a chair to steady myself while he measured from my hip bones to my knees on both sides to make certain they were aligned. He measured the circumferences of both legs from the ankles to below the knees. He told me to sit in the chair and place my good foot on the floor. Of course, my repaired foot could not touch the floor. Getting on his knees, he measured the varying distances from the floor to my toes, $1\frac{7}{8}$ inches, $2\frac{3}{4}$ inches from my sole and inner sole, and $3\frac{1}{2}$ inches from my heel.

I then hopped on my good foot back onto the treatment table, and Dr. Robbins fashioned a cast lining around my leg and foot, followed by wet strips of plaster, with a rubber sole in the cast's heel.

He had me draw a picture of shoes I would like. It was fall 1970, so I drew a calf-high, laced-up boot. Dr. Robbins said he would give my sketch and his measurements to the shoemaker and I should have shoes in two weeks.

Meanwhile, house shoes or other soft-soled shoes were out; I had to have solid support under my repaired leg.

ON MY RETURN to Washington, the two NABS houses were bustling with activity, including by the New Republic of Africa (NRA), founded by attorney Milton Henry and John Williams, brother to Robert Williams, who was now in exile in Cuba because he had dared defend his family and community in Monroeville, North Carolina, when the Ku Klux Klan came shooting and bullying the black community (read Williams's *Negroes with Guns*).

NRA's program called for reparations and secession; they wanted a section of the South set apart as a black nation. NRA had self-proclaimed the NABS houses as their embassies. Every fall for a week, they came from all over the country to conduct their international business and to visit African embassies.

NABS accepted NRA's platform for reparations, but not for a separate African nation within the U.S. We thought the "land concept" was impractical and untenable. The Civil War had already been fought. There was little interaction between NABS and NRA, though the crossing of our paths was friendly.

I shared with the NABS collective my thoughts that I should move on. I was convinced that NABS should be under the leadership of current college students. The collective thought that my leaving NABS was premature. Their insistence that I should stay only reinforced my decision to leave. Dependency and the possibility of "stardom" were finding roots.

MY NEW SHOES arrived. They were sharp and in vogue. The lift was inside the shoe, which gave the appearance that my legs and feet were even. The shoemaker had also designed a suede mule house shoe with a strap around the heel; the lift was visible, but I was more than pleased. And I was grateful that God had placed these men in my life.

When I strutted into the NABS house wearing my laced-up boots, escorted by Jerry, the collective gave a rousing cheer.

The Jerry situation, however, was not all cheers.

When I walked into the reception-conference area one day, "Big Shelia," a woman from Montgomery, was waiting on the sofa for me. She had been

Jerry's girlfriend before he met me. And today she had a black eye.

"What brings you here?" I asked. Shelia started crying and said Jerry had locked her out of the kitchenette flat. That was news to me.

She said, "I know you and Jerry are married, but Jerry and I still see each other." I sensed she was his drug companion.

Drawing on my mother's experiences as *the wife* who tolerated my father's outside women, I quietly said, "Well, you can stay here for the night. But tomorrow morning you will have to leave. Do you have any friends in D.C.?"

She didn't, but she said she would figure something out.

I asked if she was hungry and when she said no, I thawed a steak under the sink faucet for her black eye. I led her to the basement guest room. She lay on the bed as I placed the steak over her swollen eye. I turned on the television and warned her not to come upstairs—"If Jerry sees you here, your black eye will just be the beginning."

Jerry came home to the NABS house about 9 p.m. He worked late that night. As we were preparing for bed, I told him that "Big Shelia" had come looking for him. I did not tell him she was sleeping in the basement. If I had, I knew he would have bounded to the basement and then beat the stew out of her. Jerry had never raised a hand to me. He knew I was firm, but and in addition, my sickly experiences throughout our relationship gave him a sense to take care of me. On the other hand, "Big Shelia" was from a five-block community, "The Vineyard," in Montgomery, where weekend brawls were part of the culture.

Jerry cuddled up next to me in bed, but I told him that I was very tired. We caressed each other and I rocked him to sleep. He was tired, too, after working a twelve-hour shift.

The following morning while Jerry was still sleeping, I went to the basement. I woke Shelia and gave her $20 and advised her to leave before Jerry woke up, found her, and threw her down the front steps. She hurriedly left.

Jerry came downstairs for our breakfast. He did not have to be to work until 10 a.m. I matter-of-factly told him that Shelia had come by and had slept in the basement. "She had a black eye." Jerry sat motionless. "I didn't tell you because I didn't want any fighting in the NABS house. She's gone now."

We finished our breakfast in silence. Jerry, eating little after I told him that Shelia had spent the night, pushed his breakfast plate aside. He went upstairs and dressed. He returned to the kitchen, kissed me on the cheek, and said he would be home by 6.

After Jerry left for work, I packed his belongings in his Air Force duffel bag and placed it on the front porch. I was sitting there when he came home from work. He sat next to me on the porch swing and reminisced about our swinging together on Mommy and Poppa Washington's porch in Montgomery.

Spying his familiar duffel, stuffed to the hilt, he asked, "What's that?"

"Your belongings," I replied. "You don't live here anymore. I don't mind your having other women as long as it is not brought to my face and in our home. You should have made it clear to Shelia that she dared not even think about coming to our home. Something about your relationship with her made her comfortable to knock on this door."

"Can I stay for the night?"

"Nope." Jerry knew I could not be dissuaded. And Mickey McGuire was inside the NABS house. Mickey had made it clear through the years to all that he was my personal bodyguard. I left Jerry sitting on the front porch.

Despite the NABS collective's objection, I took the conference manager's position with Patrick Rooney's firm, the Golden Rule Insurance Company. Patrick and I for the past two years had had heartfelt dialogue about black students majoring in business, communications, and journalism. Patrick, a Lincoln Republican, was elated that at last black students were entering the white business world. I was concerned that these black students not abandon the black community. Though Patrick and I strongly differed on economic philosophies, the company's conferences served as mutual means for our different ends.

The conferences were quite lucrative as businesses were eager to pay the costly registration fees that covered the costs of black students' participation. Fifty per cent of the profits went to NABS. Corporations usually sent one of their vice presidents and someone from their personnel departments. Colleges sent their brightest students.

Patrick commissioned a communications expert to produce a slide show, set to appropriate music, that reflected the African and African American experience in the U.S., from slavery to the assassination of Dr. Martin Luther King Jr. It was a hard-hitting and heart-stirring presentation. Patrick wanted to sensitize the business community. I wanted to raise the consciousness of black students, lest they forget. Again, the means spoke to our separate ends.

The most insightful activity was the game "Star Power." The game involved three groups, each mixed with businessmen and students. The game was rigged so that one group ended up with all the power and had the authority to set the rules for the other two groups. I was shocked when the "power group" ended the game by going to a leisurely lunch in the hotel's restaurant, leaving the other two groups to stew in the conference room, awaiting directions from the "power group." Power is viciously intoxicating.

Patrick and I became extremely close. We often traveled together for our conferences. I served as his consultant when the Illinois State Insurance Regulatory Commission wanted to introduce a test for first-level insurance agents, those who visited homes to introduce term insurance and to collect premiums. The test was to be in English. What did this say about Spanish-speaking agents whose clients were Spanish-speaking families? Surely Spanish was friendlier language that would increase the insurance market. Patrick, a certified underwriter, and I opposed the test and won the argument for the day in 1971. I audited Patrick's economics class at the near-by Vincennes University in Indiana. I learned much about capitalist economies, but I was not persuaded.

I encouraged Patrick to take a fact-finding visit with me to Cairo, Illinois, which was not far from Lawrenceville, Illinois, the headquarters site of Patrick's insurance business and where I had moved after leaving NABS. Cairo was a plantation county only slightly above plantation counties in the Alabama Black Belt. Reverend Charles Koen, a black community leader, had been brutally beaten by the police. With their batons, the police broke all of Koen's fingers. His hands were wrapped in thick bandages when we visited him. I also urged Patrick to provide material support to the Vietnam veterans who were bringing truckloads of food, clothing and household items to Cairo's impoverished people, black and white.

Patrick's children, Christina and Patrick Jr., an expert horse trainer, visited me often in Lawrenceville. Patrick Jr. was with me when I bought my first car—a classic 1965 XK 150 Jaguar with a wide black belt across the hood.

Patrick and I were often together, and quiet talk began to spread through Lawrenceville that Patrick and I were in a relationship. Lawrenceville was a 99 percent white community with a small-town atmosphere. The leading black citizen, a charming woman, was named "America"; she was a fierce advocate of "the American Way: Love it or Leave It."

No doubt the quiet talk was a dismaying, roaring rumor to his wife's ears. She and Patrick were on the verge of a divorce.

Patrick suggested that I send for Jerry. I asked what in the world Jerry could do in Lawrenceville. Patrick owned practically all of the businesses in Lawrenceville. He was the major employer for the city. He suggested Jerry could work with Patrick Jr. in setting up a car-wash business.

I was separated from Jerry and contemplating divorce. However, I still had feelings for him. I weighed the situation. NABS was getting income from my work with the conferences. Black students were being reminded of their roots through the conferences. Jerry would have a managerial position. Perhaps there could be reconciliation.

I sent for Jerry.

At first we were happy together in Lawrenceville. But he soon became bored and irritable with the small town. Though Jerry came from a small village in British Honduras, he had left his home country to see the bright lights in the U.S. He was fascinated with the hustle and bustle of people in the urban ghettos of New York and Washington.

I was still traveling extensively with Patrick during the week to facilitate our conferences. On weekends, Jerry would sometimes hide my boots and house shoes to keep me from leaving the apartment so I would be with him exclusively. He waited on me hand and foot, cooked scrumptious Central American and West Indies dishes. He served my meals on a tray as we watched television.

I knew Jerry was holding me captive in the "name of love." I knew my independence was too much for him in terms of how he saw his manhood. For us to have a lasting relationship, I would have to be dependent upon him in every aspect, even our standard of living.

I finally concluded that I was not the "marrying kind."

After the year's last conference, I told Patrick that I was leaving Jerry. "I understand. He's been scouring the community, even driving to Vincennes, looking for heroin," Patrick concurred.

I told Jerry I had to go to St. Louis. Valerie Tucker, a NABS member and in its speakers' bureau, wanted me to facilitate a state-wide black students' union consortium. My stay would be about a month.

Jerry said he couldn't stay in Lawrenceville alone for that long. "I know," I said. "Why don't you go back to D.C. My work with Patrick is completed."

But I didn't want Jerry staying in the NABS house or around the NABS collective. I knew he had backslid and was again addicted to heroin. I suggested he draw money from our joint bank account for his travel expenses and to set up an apartment for us in D.C. Probably sullen, he withdrew the entire account.

In St. Louis I saw and visited for the first time my grand-uncle Robert, my Grandfather Patton's older brother. Now, I saw why MaDear named my father after Uncle Robert—they looked so alike. Uncle Robert and Aunt Christine had a son, Curry, who could have been my father's twin. Curry and his wife, Earnestine, owned a prosperous restaurant and a night club. Blacks in St. Louis still had a foot in the infrastructure, not only in entertainment and service businesses, but also in the construction industries. I ventured across the bridge to East St. Louis, which is in Illinois. It was practically an all black-governed city. Though it was more urban—and called the "redlight" city, it reminded me of my hometown, Inkster, Michigan.

My organizing travels took me to Kansas City, Missouri. At the first opportunity, I went to the corner of 12th Street and Vine, made popular by the late 1950s record, "I'm going to Kansas City." This tune was one of my favorite dancing songs. The sounds of jazz were everywhere. I pigged-out on plenty of Gates' barbeque.

After about a month in St. Louis, Jerry called me at Valerie's home. Nobody knew how to get in touch with me except Mommy. I had called her previously to let her know where I was and that I was leaving Jerry. Jerry had called Mommy and she gave him Valerie's number. I was furious with

Mommy for that. She was an independent woman and had divorced her first husband because he was an alcoholic. But then again, she knew that Jerry was loving, caring, and had been attentive during all of my episodes of sickness. But she did not know that the demon of alcohol had been usurped by dope.

26

Settling Crosswinds

Mickey McGuire came out from the NABS collective to help with the final organizing for the Midwest Regional Conference in March 1971. Two hundred students from Missouri, Kansas, Oklahoma, and Iowa had preregistered. There was a need for grassroots and working people to be a part of the conference, and Mickey was one of the best grassroots organizers. He had the gift of discernment to separate those who were serious about improving their stations in life from those who were hustlers and on the take. Mickey was in his early thirties, considered "old" at the time.

"Gwen, X is constantly creating confusion and conflict with the other NABS coordinators," Mickey informed me one day at a Catholic church's bingo parlor while we and some students passed out leaflets inviting grassroots people to the conference. Several people said they would attend.

Mickey went on to say that X was criticizing my leadership and also had allowed Progressive Labor Party (PLP) people to move into the NABS houses. This was definitely a no-no; notwithstanding the coziness with the New Republic of Africa, NABS was set up to be nonpartisan and ideology-free in terms of a party line.

I reflected on how X became a part of the NABS collective. From the outset, there were reservations regarding his participation. His college, the University of Pennsylvania at College Park, was thought within movement circles to be a training ground for FBI and CIA agents.

"PLP calls you a petit-bourgeois-capitalist." Bourgeois was a derisive term in the movement.

"Is PLP visiting or staying in the NABS Houses?" I asked for clarity.

"They live in the houses. Their toothbrushes are in the bathrooms."

The three PLPers were from New York City and previously lived in apartments. It dawned on me that they were generations of propertyless people and knew absolutely nothing about purchasing a home or owning property. Perhaps they had a subconscious resentment towards people who owned property. I wondered what they thought of Southern black farmers who through hard struggle held onto acres and acres of land.

I concluded that the PLPers were arrogant chauvinists, suffering with pent-up frustrations of a peasant mentality. Their glorifying China's reckless "cultural revolution" was an extension of this malady.

I resolved that after the conference I would return to the NABS collective. If the PLPers were FBI plants, their presence at least indicated that NABS was successful enough that J. Edgar Hoover thought he needed to destroy us.

THE 1971 CONFERENCE, convened by Valerie Tucker, University of Kansas student and NABS midwest regional director, was a great success. Interestingly, one of the major student concerns was the problems black people faced in the Catholic Church.

Afterward, Mickey returned to the NABS collective and I returned to Lawrenceville. Patrick and I were discussing the possibility of NABS purchasing a cable television station. After a meeting with people in the industry, I left for Washington. I knew driving up to the NABS houses in my Jaguar would blow the minds of the PLPers. I was very clear on driving nice cars. My father once admonished a movement person when he saw my father's Cadillac and made a whistling criticism. My father quickly replied, "We make the Cadillac. How come we can't drive what we make?" I was prepared to handle the PLPers.

I took a leisurely drive cross-country, stopping and visiting with key NABS contacts along the way. I suggested we call for our third national conference to assess our work and progress. Our first two-week national conference had been held in Detroit in conjunction with the Black Workers Congress and the League of Black Revolutionary Workers in 1970. The outgrowth of that conference was a NABS treatise, *From Student to Student-Worker to Worker Consciousness.*

NABS' 1971 conference had been held in Chicago. A NABS board delegation journeyed south to Lawrenceville to observe my work planning conferences with black students and corporations and other economic efforts that would financially sustain NABS, independent of begging foundations and donors for NABS' existence and livelihood. The board overwhelmingly approved my work and insisted that I move forward with the economic thrusts.

The NABS board also approved my travel to Santiago, Chile. I had been selected by the World Federation of Democratic Youth (WFDY) to tour Chile under the socialist president Salvador Allende's government. The first week I spent time in the countryside looking at parallels with Alabama's rural Black Belt. I spoke at several rallies with the campesinos and appreciated their struggles against the corporations that had usurped ownership of copper mines and farm lands. The second week, I lectured in Chilean high schools and universities. I was amazed that the Chilean youth spoke English, as a second language, better than many people in the U.S. I shared freedom songs of the Southern movement and the history of black people's movement throughout the country.

The students identified with our struggles. With support from the Chilean Parliament, President Allende ushered in policy reforms that the USA's black movement had only dreamed about. Upon the sudden and strange death of President Allende, I was not surprised when the U.S. government rushed to support military leader Pinochet, who later was described as a dictator. The deadly transfer of power to protect U.S. corporate and governmental interests at any cost was a classic military coup.

OUR UPCOMING THIRD conference was to take on the issues of non-ideological, non-partisanship, and the notion of "petit-bourgeois-capitalism." The crux of this discussion had to focus on ownership: as a private individual or the NABS Collective. I was contemplating that NABS could offer over-the-counter shares to students to buy stocks for the establishment of the cable television station and to enhance the Student Economic Development Corporation (SEDCO). I was disheartened that so many black men, in the name of "revolutionary blackness," could be duped by white men into a posture that kept our people dependent upon white philanthropy and largesse. Was there something in their unconscious psyches that bought into the racist whim of the "noble savage" and the "great white hope"?

While driving, my thoughts drifted to FBI and CIA agents. I surmised, as a student-scholar-activist at Tuskegee Institute, that black administrators collaborated with the FBI and provided information on our student organization, the Tuskegee Institute Advancement League (TIAL). I was informed by my progressive social worker that while I was a patient in the Hospital for Bone and Joint Disease the FBI had gained access to my medical records.

My father had also told me he had been visited in Inkster by an FBI agent who claimed he had alarming news about me: "Your daughter is a leading member in the violent black power movement."

"Good. It's a sign that I raised her right!" my father retorted as he slammed the door in the agent's face.

More recently, the FBI archives in Pennsylvania had been liberated. I learned that I was classified in the "security and agitator index files," with my photograph.

Earlier, I was convinced that a white supposed student at the 1969 National Student Association conference was an FBI agent, assigned to ingratiate himself with me and my friend Mae Jackson when reparations to establish NABS were placed on the agenda. He bugged us to no end with his presence. Finally, I relented and accepted his offer to "wine and dine" us in Juarez, Mexico, just across the border from El Paso, where the NSA conference was being held. After a day of shopping, buying us serapes and souvenirs, and an evening of entertainment, I said, "Thank you for the outing. I guess you'll put this day on your FBI expense account." He turned "whiter shades of pale."

When I later obtained my FBI and CIA dossiers under the Freedom of Information Act (FOIA), I read about one meeting that ". . . Patton was definitely the leading influence of the meetings, showed herself to be restrained, highly intelligent, with a clear grasp of objectives. At the same time she tried not to push herself to the front, and allowed as much free discussion as possible." That report had to have been written by a black informant because that particular meeting at the NSA conference was all-black.

Another report read:

> GWEN PATTON is not known to be a violent type individual and is not considered to be dangerous. She has never directly advocated violence of any kind, however, her past speeches and writings are directed toward attracting individuals into the movement by projecting herself as appearing to be very militant and somewhat prone to violence, although this is not the case at all.

I guess my seriousness for my people's freedom warranted FBI surveillance. The surveillance was relentless. FBI agents evidently detailed to me—what a waste of taxpayer dollars—knew when I traveled, who picked me up at the airports (by writing down license plate numbers and then researching the owners, who no doubt were added to the FBI "spy list"), and in what hotels I registered.

> Early on the morning of 5/3/1970, at about 4 a.m., Subject (GWEN PATTON) was visited in her room by six Negro male Americans and they were overhead discussing what will be happening on the campuses soon in a revolutionary context according to people who overheard the conversation from an adjoining room. No further details are available regarding the conversation or the persons who overhead the conversation.

How stupid. FBI agents listening through walls in a hotel room. And then sending a hearsay report that could not stand up even in the flawed U.S. justice system.

Even more ridiculous was a report to FBI Director J. Edgar Hoover:

> Referenced communication contained New York lead to verify Subject (GWEN PATTON) marriage to her present husband, JERRY WOODS. Marriage records in NYC are maintained on a chronological basis and

it would be physically impossible to review marriage records for the five counties in New York without some indication of the date of marriage. It is further noted that there is no evidence that the subjects were married in NYC at any time. Should WFO develop more specific information or be able to furnish New York with an approximate date of marriage, New York will initiate a search of Marriage Records for a record of such union."

Absurdly silly. All the FBI agent had to do was to call me on the phone, and I would gladly have told him that I was married in Las Vegas. My telephone number had always been listed. Indeed, I would not call friends, movement and otherwise, if their phone numbers were not listed. I reasoned that if the FBI can obtain your phone numbers, why can't I? I was proven wrong. The FBI did not have sense enough to consult the phone directory.

Again to J. Edgar Hoover:

The LHM classified 'CONFIDENTIAL' as it contains information from a confidential source, which if it became known could result in the identification of the source and negate his future value to the Bureau. New York is requested to conduct indices check and advise WFO if JERRY WOODS, who is reported to have married GWYN PATTON, has been active in militant activities in the area. If identified, furnish background information to WFO.

Meanwhile, an FBI agent was reporting that "he had not heard PATTON make any statement advocating violence; as a matter of fact, she had discouraged not only actual violence, but any statements advocating the same."

I apparently had become so popular with the FBI that the agency included in my dossier a Sunday *Washington Star* article on my 1970 speech at the National Education Association in Washington. Reporter Jackie Trescott fleshed out her article by interviewing me at the NABS Headquarters. Her article was favorable and positive. I still cannot fathom why the FBI would include such an article in the investigation on a dangerous revolutionary such as myself.

But, I have never been bent out of shape by FBI or CIA infiltration. I presumed these agents were in all movement organizations in some capacity. Whenever anyone in any discussion offered irrational, illogical and/or provocative input, I dismissed that person as an agent or a peanut-brain.

By the time I drove up to the NABS Houses, I was fortified and ready to deal with any conflict head-on. We had a SNCC-fashion "sit-down" discussion of personal introspection and a sharing of each other's lives for the past fifteen years. The meeting lasted ten hours as PLPers gradually slunk out. At the end of the meeting, I asked, "Who is the agent in our midst? Who wants to impede the freedom of our people by surreptitiously conveying information about NABS to the FBI?" No hands rose. But I knew an agent was still in our midst.

THE 1972 NABS conference in Washington was a success, with greater attendance than the previous two conferences. The board voted unanimously to reaffirm and for me to continue my leadership. Yet I knew an intense struggle was in the making that would determine not only the life of NABS but the righteous concerns of black students to make their education relevant to serve and to uplift our national community. The U.S. government and its FBI protectorate had made clear their intent to eliminate progressive leaders, if not by murdering them, by making it impossible for them to earn a quality living in capitalist America. The education of black students from elementary school onward would be dumbed down. Never again would there be conscious and critical-thinking masses of black people. If need be, the government would make plentiful the substances for black people to become dope fiends; would create social and economic circumstances that would force them into criminality, and in this process would criminalize and dehumanize, again, the race as a whole; would destroy the moral authority that had sustained them since slavery and had been an international thorn in imperialist U.S. foreign policy on the question of human rights.

All these ominous warnings had been foretold during our ten-hour NABS discussion. It all left me in no mood to entertain inane pronouncements about male leadership as superior to female leadership within the overwhelming context of the struggle of our people. Like Harriet Tubman, I was ready to aim my shotgun and tell the brothers to run on to freedom.

I was realizing that our movement for respectable survival was wherever you found yourself. NABS did not have to be my venue. The struggle was everywhere, on every level and in all circumstances. It mattered less, man or woman—if they had the trust of the community—who led the charge in our quest for human dignity and human rights. Such discussion on the "man-woman leadership" was a diversion. Those who persisted in such talk should ask J. Edgar Hoover to put them on the FBI payroll. He, too, did not favor women as equals, let alone as companions.

The hostility in the NABS houses was intense, with some directed at me. I harbored no hostility and my neutrality was felt by the collective. All staffers except one sought me for advice as to the next stages in their lives. I urged all students to return to the academies until they earned their diplomas and degrees. All but one staffer accepted my advice. My sister, Sandy, NABS' secretary, began in earnest to pursue her singing career. Mickey McGuire went to Houston to work with playwright Ernie MacMillan. The Hinsor family elected to stay in the NABS houses. I decided to move into an apartment one block south.

NABS was in its death throes. I was resigned to the reality that J. Edgar Hoover and the FBI were bent on destroying progressive black organizations via COINTELPRO.

The right-wing FBI had help from the left wing. It was abundantly clear that organized left groups were fanatically bent on recruiting black people to their political line at the expense of demolishing any democratic formation born out of struggle. The PLPers had leeched onto NABS, infected its organizational body by convincing a NABS staffer that "NABS is not a developed collective, but a developing cadre." The concept of a "cadre," with all of its intrigue, had provided the basis for SNCC's destruction by internal and external reactionary forces.

NABS was never to be a "cadre"; it was to be a network (collective), grounded in sound philosophy for critical thinking, to unite black students and to provide a forum from which they could articulate and resolve the problems they confronted in the academies. The intended second phase of NABS was to build consciousness for students so they would willingly return to our community to advance human rights and dignity.

After about two weeks, I walked from my apartment to the NABS houses. The main house/headquarters was open, abandoned, and ransacked. File drawers were pulled out and documents were strewn throughout the main floor. I did not go downstairs or upstairs. I simply left. (The NABS properties were ultimately foreclosed on and reverted back to the bank. Later, while at a Pride, Inc., staff retreat, I was informed that the NABS main headquarters (3418 17th Street, NW) had burned to the ground. Arson was suspected, but I never learned about the source of the fire. In fact, I had removed the demise of NABS from my consciousness.)

A later entry in my FBI file stated: "Gained entry into NABS Headquarters and informed that Subject (GWEN PATTON) is not with NABS." Collaboration with the right and left wings was at its height.

J. Edgar Hoover sent a memorandum to the Internal Revenue Service:

> We have separately furnished your Service with a communication dated December 17, 1971, entitled 'National Association of Black Students (NABS), Extremist Matter (Organization); Gwendolyn Marie Patton Woods, Extremist Matter – NABS'. Inasmuch as the communication contains information indicating captioned individual has used funds of the National Association of Black Students, a nonprofit organization chartered in Washington, D.C. for her personal use, we are calling this matter to your attention for whatever action your Service considers to be warranted. Woods, according to sources of this Bureau who have furnished reliable information in the past, is a former official of the Student National (sic) (Nonviolent) Coordinating Committee, a black revolutionary organization. We would appreciate receiving the results of any action taken by your Service in this matter.

Apparently no action was ever taken in that I never received a communication from the IRS. I have always had a professional accountant to prepare my income tax statements.

An April 6, 1972, memo to Hoover stated:

> As the Bureau is aware, the National Association of Black Students

(NABS), of which subject was the first National Coordinator, is no longer in existence. Mrs. WOODS is now working part-time at Pride, Incorporated and is attending Antioch School studying law. Her activities are not such that she should be included in ADEX (Agitator Index) at this time, accordingly WFO is placing this case in a closed status. In the event subject becomes active in a militant group this case will be reopened and the Bureau advised.

Yes, I was studying at Antioch College's Washington campus, but not in law. I was in the master's of education and the art of teaching program. Supposedly no longer under FBI scrutiny, my FOIA file nonetheless included a confidential note:

> Gwen Patton Woods attended a rally held at Meridian Hill Park, 16th and Euclid Streets, N.W., WDC, on June 5, 1972, in celebration of the acquittal of Angela Davis. At this rally Mrs. Woods (Gwen Patton) called upon those present to give more help and exert more effort to free poorer prisoners who are not celebrities, do not have funds, and therefore go unnoticed and are very often forgotten.

WHEN I LEFT the NABS collective, I moved into an apartment building one block south of the NABS houses. I later moved to a three-room apartment with a walk-in vestibule and closet, a living room, bedroom, and kitchen that comfortably accommodated a dinette set. The rooms were large, including the bathroom with its odd-shaped tub that was a precursor to the Jacuzzi.

Mount Pleasant Avenue, where my apartment building was located, was really an extension of 17th Street and was the commercial corridor for the Mount Pleasant neighborhood to the west. The avenue was picturesque with its 1920s architectural designs and structures.

This was my first residence where everything was conveniently within walking distance. A small but well-stocked grocery was next door; I could order by phone and for a nominal fee my groceries were delivered to my apartment, an absolute convenience since I lived on the second floor of a four-story walk-up apartment building. The beer and wine store was across the avenue, and this establishment also delivered. The drugstore, cater-corner from my apartment, had maintained its quaint 1950s décor with a soda fountain and round, vinyl-covered stools and a pharmacy that resembled an apothecary shop. This business also home-delivered its wares and medicines. The barbershop that kept my Afro neatly coiffeured was on the avenue. There was a "five and dime" store, several women's apparel and lingerie shops, and a newly opened washeteria and adjacent cleaners—more home delivery. Three restaurants provided Italian, Chinese, and Cuban dining. I wondered why there was no "soul food" or West Indies restaurant. Though the neighborhood was predominantly white, I believed restaurants with black cuisine would fare well.

Jerry was living very close to my apartment building in an efficiency, a step-up from the kitchenette, on the west side of 16th Street, the dividing line for urban Washington. To the west were the upper-working and middle classes. Further west was the Adams Morgan neighborhood of the upper-middle class. East of 16th Street was the black ghetto that was rapidly deteriorating from the 1968 rebellions in the aftermath of Dr. King's assassination. That was where Jerry had lived in his kitchenette after our first separation. Now, he was in an efficiency in the Chalfonte Apartments, a beautiful structure of ornate French architectural design. A large living room doubled as the bedroom, and there was a kitchen and a walk-in closet that opened into the bathroom. Though the apartment was lovely, I did not take to the combined living/bedroom. Such an arrangement made you a hostage to visiting company.

But the apartment layout was not my only reason for not living with Jerry. I needed solitude. I had given advice to the collective as to how they must go on with their lives after the demise of NABS. Now, it was time for me to go on with my life. I applied for the advertised position for curriculum specialist offered by PRIDE, Inc., enrolled in Antioch College's extension program to earn my master's degree, and continued my movement commitment to free Angela Davis and other political prisoners.

PRIDE, Inc. was a federally funded program for 18–26-year-old black males. The program was run by SNCC past president Marion Barry, and his first wife, Mary Treadwell, who was really in charge. I had known Marion through the years. When he became SNCC's Washington coordinator, I journeyed from Atlanta to join him and others in picketing Hecht's department store for fair employment practices. I met Mary Treadwell when Mary Richardson, a mutual and dear friend who was convinced that the movement should seek coalitions with the Philadelphia, New York, and New Jersey mob families, visited with me at the NABS houses while I was still a part of the NABS collective. Treadwell was thoroughly impressed with the houses and NABS work with high school and college students.

I was hired to be PRIDE's curriculum specialist supervisor, with two recent college graduates to assist. This experience brought home the truth of the NABS treatise, *From Student to Student-Worker to Worker Consciousness*, about the disconnect between the college training of the black middle class and their relationship, or the lack thereof, with the urban, inner-city masses of black males.

The service group for PRIDE was young black males, most of whom had criminal records. The goal was to turn them away from criminal activity and help them become responsible and productive citizens. There was hope for some, but many had inculcated a lifestyle of "getting over" by any means possible. And, it did not matter if this was at the expense or the detriment of the black community as a whole. Some of the incorrigibles rejected rehabilitation for positive reentry into their families and the black community.

My supervisor was a military retiree. He was extremely disciplined and clipped in his communications. I liked his no-nonsense managerial style. Together we designed a three-component module:

—Reinforcement Learning Laboratory (RELL) where the targeted population, whom we called "dudes," could earn their General Education Degree (GED) and receive counseling for values clarification;

—Continuing Education Learning Laboratory (CELL), which was similar to a high school-college preparatory curriculum; and,

—Higher Education Learning Laboratory (HELL), which had an articulation program with prestigious colleges, particularly American University, for dudes who excelled in the two previous components.

PRIDE, Inc. also had an intermediary training program in janitorial, maintenance, and building trades for dudes who did not graduate to the HELL component.

I asked one of my assistants, a first-generation fresh college graduate, to design a work schedule for a dude to sweep and dust the hallways and to clean the bathrooms of the three-story PRIDE headquarters building. When she submitted the schedule, I asked if she thought it was realistic.

She had the dude sweeping three flights of double stairs, each with a landing, and the hallways in one hour, dusting and polishing the ornate banisters for each flight of stairs in one hour, and cleaning the building's twelve bathrooms—cleaning the fixtures, mopping the floors, restocking paper towels, soap and bathroom tissue—in an hour and a half.

"Oh, yes. We need to keep dudes busy at all times," she responded with arrogant confidence.

I smiled and nodded my head. Then I asked her to check the time-frame by doing the work herself and reporting back to me on how the schedule was working out when she had reached three and a half hours.

When she reported back, her attitude was different, and she was nowhere near done with the tasks. I told her, "First of all, we have to respect janitors, those who clean. They are essential in any work environment, not only here at PRIDE, but in hospitals, schools and every environment where people congregate, including your home and church. Janitors are just as important and necessary as doctors, teachers, preachers, and any other professionals."

Her naivete graduated to sensitivity and conscious appreciation for workers on every plane. A college degree did not exempt her, nor did it provide her an escape to obliterate her roots. Ironically, her father had been a janitor who had worked hard to become a custodian supervisor to earn more money to send her to college.

In 1971, the curriculum and graphics departments had produced illustrated booklets on Dr. Martin Luther King Jr., Malcolm X, and Marcus Garvey. As head of the curriculum department in 1972, I received approval to produce booklets on black institutions. Since my youth, I had seen personalities overshadow the very organizations that made them leaders in the first place. Organizations sustain movements, not individuals. I selected Tuskegee Institute, with its historical curriculum in the building trades and mechanical industries that evolved into the professional training of architecture and engineering, as a natural fit for PRIDE's educational programs. Two others were Parks Sausage Company in Detroit and Madame C. J. Walker Hair Care Products Enterprise. The research to produce these booklets felt like the laborious research required to write doctoral dissertations.

I was earning $8,000 a year. However, I had set my worth at $200 a week. This calculated to $10,400 a year. My supervisor informed me that I had to discuss a raise directly with Mary Treadwell.

Mary was a high-strung, sometimes emotional woman. I once saw her throw a glass of water at a waitress while attending a PRIDE leadership retreat.

After I made my case for a raise, Mary asked, "Who is your hero?"

"My grandmother. I call her Mommy."

"I mean outside of your family."

"I have no heroes outside of my family. I admire some people, but I put my respect and emphasis on organizations. I don't believe in icons."

After a round of small talk, Mary said, "I don't think I can give you a raise."

I silently rose from the plush chair in front of her lavish desk and walked out. As I was halfway down the hallway, I heard her calling my name. I turned around and stood as Mary was approaching.

"Gwen, I decided to give you the raise," Mary said. "Anybody who has the nerve to walk out *on me* without being mad or not saying a word is a tough biddy. You've earned my respect."

Perhaps Mary had succumbed to conflict and confrontation as normal behavior. Friday paydays at PRIDE were like the wild West. Dudes stampeded the headquarters to pick up their checks. If checks were delayed one minute, some pulled out their guns. It was rumored that Mary, too, was packing. The dudes respected her rough and tough manner.

It was too much drama, or should I say, trauma, for me. I had no intention of modifying my behavior to accommodate an uncivil environment that could erupt into a shoot-out. Mary's decision to raise my salary because I walked out on her and not because of my merit and service to the organization never settled with me. I knew I was biding my time at PRIDE, Inc.

MY UNION ORGANIZING work when I was a patient at the Hospital for Bone and Joint Disease in New York City had trickled up to Leon Davis, president of Union 1199. The union was organizing hospital workers in Washington and needed organizers. I quietly left PRIDE, Inc. and became a paid 1199 union organizer with a $10,000 yearly salary.

Union organizing can be dangerous work, especially if you worked the 11 p.m. to 7 a.m. graveyard shift. Hospitals had armed security guards. One black 1199 organizer was shot by a security guard in a Philadelphia hospital. I observed that white male union organizers fared better than black organizers, and in particular black female organizers. The white organizer could don a white medical coat, put a stethoscope around his neck, and gain entry into a hospital at any time. Not so for black organizers. This institutional racism of "white-skin privilege" presented a dilemma for 1199. Most of the workers in housekeeping and in nonprofessional patient-care auxiliaries were black women. "Black is Beautiful" was embedded in the black psyche. Even the best and most sincere white organizer found difficulty in organizing black workers. They wanted to see someone who looked like them to gain trust and to talk about the benefits of joining the union.

Most of my work was outside the hospital, catching workers coming to and from the hospital during the morning and afternoon shifts. Sometimes I visited workers in their homes. I planned and facilitated outings for workers and their families. Union organizing was no different than my movement organizing in rural Alabama.

The major task was getting individual workers to sign cards that stated s/he wanted Union 1199 to be the representative to negotiate contracts and benefits. This was no easy task, given that workers to some extent were held captive for eight hours by hospital administrators, who were omnipresent in the cafeteria and breakrooms. If an organizer was able to convince a worker to get peers to sign cards inside the hospital, he/she did so at great risk of getting snitched on and fired. After getting more than a majority of the workers to sign cards, union representatives could request a formal meeting with the chief hospital administrator to present the cards and to ask for an election to include all workers to vote up or down for union representation.

I worked with a black male organizer, who was in charge, and a white male organizer, who was pleasantly bold in his organizing techniques.

We were jubilant when workers at Providence Hospital voted for 1199 to represent them.

Concurrent with my organizing, the union won the right to come under the jurisdiction of the National Labor Relations Board. This legislated public policy got its teeth from the Executive Order of President Harry S. Truman who established the Fair Employment Practices Commission. U.S. Representative Frank Thompson (D-NJ) shepherded the legislation to include 1199 Union hospital-care auxiliaries. Union 1199 President Leon Davis asked me to join him to visit Representative Thompson's office on Capitol Hill to personally thank him for his successful legislative effort. When it was time for the ritual photo-op, Leon quickly opened his briefcase, pulled out the 1199 hat, shaped like a child's folded-paper boat, and plopped it atop my Afro.

"Where's your 1199 hat?" I asked, surprised by the sudden gesture.

"Oh, I don't need one," Leon said. He then directed his attention to the photographer. "You can take our photo now." I was standing with the 1199 hat on my head between Leon and Representative Thompson.

After the photographer snapped our picture, I took the hat off and handed it back to Leon. I was incensed. Here, I thought, is the president of 1199, ashamed of wearing his own union hat. My role, I realized, was to portray a hospital housekeeping worker. I put in my letter of resignation.

27

Freedom Struggles in the African Diaspora

From its founding, Antioch College in Yellow Springs, Ohio, was known as a progressive college. Mrs. Coretta Scott King sat on its board of trustees. Antioch had a tradition of recruiting smart students of color and wanted to increase its enrollment of "color" even more. Matriculating black students recommended to the administration that they should take the college where the people are. In other words, take the mountain to Mohammed.

So, Antioch established satellite campuses in Texas, Vermont and Washington, D.C., affectionately known as "chocolate city." The D.C. campus was very popular. The Antioch collegiate experience was one where students and professors interacted as a family, similar to the sister- and brotherhood you found in a church. Students sensed that their professors were genuinely interested in their intellectual growth. Antioch was not threatened by competing ideologies and various world views. Some described the college as "the little white schoolhouse that was red on the inside." Mind you, Antioch's outreach to students of color and from different backgrounds was at least fifteen years before "affirmative action" and the noble call for "diversity" in all facets of U.S. culture and life.

The success of the undergraduate program gave rise to a graduate school in education and a school of law in Washington. I enrolled in the graduate school.

For the first time I was in a classroom with practicing teachers who were my peers. They, too, had enrolled to earn a master's degree in education and in the art of teaching. I registered for the standard courses in the education rubric. The highlight of my Antioch experience, however, was taking courses outside of the traditional educational fare. Antioch, under the able leadership of Tom Porter, offered "Political Economy," taught by the inimitable Dr. R. I. Rhodes; "World, Slave and Labor History," taught by the distinguished writer, Jack O'Dell; "Chinese History to the Modern Period," taught by attorney Mary Terrell; and "Methods of Thought," taught by the brilliant scholar Tony Monteiro.

I finally learned in my political economy class the "workings" of capitalism and the too-common downsides of inflation, stagflation, recession and the need for a permanent underclass to depress the wages of the working-class. How China became a communist nation was no longer a mystery, as I learned of that vast country's attempts to employ and to feed the billions of its people. At last I gained insight of the Crusades not simply as a religious movement to spread Christianity, but more importantly as imperialist wars to usurp lands and to subjugate peoples.

My favorite class was "Methods of Thought." The main text was Lev Vygotsky's *Thought and Language*. The light bulb that went off in my mind has been burning ever since: U.S. citizens are consciously taught (programmed?) throughout school to be unconscious and noncritical thinkers. The natural capacity for thought is deliberately stifled, stymied, and thwarted via an unnatural educational system.

I was a quick study. Antioch asked me to serve as an adjunct professor to teach labor history to undergraduates. The main text was *Labor's Untold Story* by Richard Boyer and Herbert Morais. I supplemented this text with Jimmy Boggs's *Racism and the Class Struggle: Further Pages from a Black Worker's Notebook*. Boggs was an Alabama transplant to the auto factories in Detroit. My other supplemental text was hot off the press: Hosea Hudson's *Black Worker in the Deep South*. Hudson was another Alabamian who was a critical part of the labor struggles of black workers as sharecroppers and steelworkers. For a class research project, I asked the students to approximate the number of maids—euphemistically called "domestic engineers"—and their ethnicity in the D.C. area. The primary source was the database of the District's Labor Department. The students were shocked that the U.S. Department of Labor had no records of maids working in private households.

Somehow my teaching labor history found its way to Local 800, Committee on Political Education (COPE). The local invited me as a paid consultant to conduct seminars for its members. I asked the local to look into the potential of organizing domestic servants into a union. I knew three maids and I was certain they could recruit thirty more to a conference to discuss the possibility of a union. Local 800 and Antioch students planned the conference. Seventy maids showed up for the Saturday conference.

Simultaneously, RAP, Inc., a residential drug rehabilitation program, patterned after the west coast Al-Anon Community, asked me to teach English, writing, and communication skills to the residents.

JERRY, MEANWHILE, REALIZED that I was not going to move in with him in the efficiency. He asked for another try. No doubt my work with RAP influenced me. I relented, and he moved in with me. It was another mistake.

I had an electric typewriter, but it still made noise when I typed into the night on my master's thesis. One night as I was typing in the living room

Jerry emerged from the bedroom to complain that he couldn't sleep because of the racket. "Gwen, are you gonna type all night? You already have one degree! Why do you need another?" he said as he got dressed and went to a neighbor's apartment for the remainder of the night.

I understood that it would never work with Jerry. I was not good for his ego nor his sense of manhood. He needed another type of woman to make him feel whole. And I struggled with the reality of class distinctions in my marriage while I fought against class distinctions in the black community as a whole. I have yet to resolve the contradiction.

MY SUPPORT OF Angela Davis, who had been on the FBI's "Most Wanted List" and was now languishing in a California prison while awaiting trial, brought me in contact with the Young Workers Liberation League (YWLL). Angela was charged with conspiracy related to the armed takeover of a California courtroom in a failed attempt to free several Black Panthers who were on trial. The presiding judge and three blacks were killed. Angela was not present.

YWLL was an intermediary organization of the Communist Party USA (CPUSA). I was neither a communist nor an anti-communist. While I was student body president at Tuskegee Institute, I had knowingly invited Gus Hall, the chair of CPUSA, and Dr. Herbert Aptheker, a well-known communist and a premiere scholar on U.S. slavery, as campus speakers for the lecture series.

As a YWLL member, I met two people who became my lifelong friends, Gracie Lewis and Jackie Metzner.

Gracie worked as a secretary for a government agency. She could type at least sixty words a minute and had phenomenal mastery of shorthand. Gracie was a firebrand and an ardent Angela Davis supporter. She had many run-ins with her supervisors because of her refusal to remove a framed "Free Angela Davis" leaflet from her desk. She was moved from one agency to another, carrying the framed leaflet from one desk to another. She stood her ground. Gracie, like me, believed that family was the basic foundation for the movement. Movement work and everyday life were the same. She was a strong advocate for public transportation vehicles that would accommodate physically challenged people, especially those in wheel-chairs. Every time I see a city bus with special mechanisms to lift wheelchair-bound passengers, I smilingly think of Gracie. She also fought the government up and down about cancer treatment. Her mother was suffering with throat cancer. The pharmaceutical companies had a firm grip on politicians via campaign contributions that were basically bribes. Cancer treatment then was strictly with a chemical regimen of drugs. Gracie, after a great deal of personal study and research, insisted that nutrition and diet were important components for cancer treatment. Today, nutrition and diet are considered essential to a cancer treatment regimen.

Jackie lived in the upscale northeast Washington area. She was a beautiful, ebony-hued woman from Birmingham. She met her husband, Eric, in Alabama during the 1960s when Eric came South from New York City to support the civil rights movement. Eric later became a part of the U.S. diplomatic corps, transplanting himself, Jackie, and their two sons to Nairobi, Kenya. Some twenty years later I was a guest in their lovely home with a spectacular second-floor veranda view of Mt. Kenya.

Though YWLL had a broad slogan, "Young Workers Should Have the Right to Learn and Earn," its action program was limited. I fought hard to expand the "free Angela" support to include other political prisoners, especially Ruchell Magee, who had been arrested with Angela. After much discussion, YWLL accepted my suggestion that we should be a part of the "D.C. Coalition for Statehood." Residents of D.C. could vote for the president, but they had no self-governance. The mayor was appointed by Southern U.S. congressmen, who had oversight (overseer?) prerogatives to govern (rule?) the predominantly black city. YWLL's joining the coalition broadened its base and drew in respected community organizers Jo Butler and Nia.

The CPUSA tried to recruit me into their political party, but I had too many reservations based upon my observations of their sectarian approach to community organizing. Several other YWLL members, however, did join the CPUSA.

During this period, Washington was electrified with city-wide political activity. What was dubbed the first "Black Power Convention" (really the first was in 1967 in Tuskegee and the second was in 1970 in Atlanta) was the matter of the day. The 1972 convention promised a massive and engaged turnout. To be a voting delegate, a person had to be elected by the community base. A formula based upon population determined the number of delegates for each city throughout the country. Certification papers had to be notarized to prove that the person was duly elected. The delegation and credentialing process was similar to how the Democratic and Republican parties peopled their national conventions. The Mississippi Freedom Democratic Party (MFDP) was the progenitor for black people in this new political foray. I was elected as a delegate from Washington.

As anticipated, thousands attended the convention, convened by the newly elected mayor of Gary, Indiana, Richard Hatcher, in that city's civic auditorium. The blossoming of the convention was soon nipped in the bud. The raging argument of "race vs. class," which during this period could bring fisticuffs between brothers, dominated the discussion. Black nationalist and cultural nationalist brothers took charge of the platform stage and controlled the plenary. Black workers, particularly union workers, had no central role, which was surprising because Gary was still a thriving steel-industry city. Surely, a black representative from the United Steelworkers Union (USW) should have addressed the convention. I became disappointed and disgusted. I dumbed out. I went to visit my one-year-older-than-I Uncle Marion and his wife, Gloria, in East Chicago, Indiana. Marion was a strong USW member, as his oldest brother—my father—was a strong United Auto Workers (UAW) unionist.

I returned to Washington somewhat disillusioned by the self-appointed leaders of the black movement. A strategy for a black agenda was yet to be forged.

UPON MY GRADUATION from Antioch College, Dean Tom Porter asked me to be a full-time undergraduate instructor for the Labor History course.

Charlene Mitchell with CPUSA visited several times in my Washington apartment. She was impressed with my library that boasted forty-five volumes of Lenin's work, four volumes of Marx's *Theories of Surplus Value* and other books by Engels, Adam Smith, Trotsky, Stalin, Rosa Luxemburg, C. L. R. James, and Jimmy Boggs, amidst an array of books on philosophy, American and European literature, African history, and black culture and literature. Since I was working with communists, I needed to understand their methods of thought and their analyses of capitalism.

On her last visit she asked me to come to New York City to work with the newly formed National Alliance Against Racist and Political Repression. Angela Davis, exonerated of the charge of conspiracy, was the national chair. I found solace that the CPUSA saw the need to fight for the freedom of other political prisoners.

I accepted and told Jerry I was moving to New York City to work with the Alliance. He said he wasn't going. As a dutiful wife, I reckoned that I should stay in D.C. with my husband. But I knew our differences could never be reconciled. I needed a mate who was as much married to the movement as I was to him. I asked if he would help pack my belongings and drive me to New York, leaving by the end of the week. He knew that I was not going to change my mind.

We motored to New York City in my Jaguar with a U-haul trailer behind, arriving in upscale Washington Heights, next to Columbia Presbyterian Hospital and satellite Columbia University schools. My new neighborhood was similar to the one I had just left in D.C. Within walking distance of my new apartment were a large supermarket, restaurants, bars and retail stores, a bank, post office, hospital, and elementary school. Broadway and 168th Street was the subway stop.

Maxine Orris, who had lovingly befriended me during my time in the Hospital for Bone and Joint Disease, had secured the apartment; we were to be roommates. When Jerry and I arrived, Maxine greeted us at the door with my crutches I gave her upon her request after I got my first pair of built-up shoes in 1970. When we finished unpacking my belongings, I gave Jerry the key and signed over title papers to the Jaguar. In his paid-for sports car, he headed back to D.C.

Apartment #41 at 600 West 169th Street at the corner of Broadway was huge. The well-bolted front door opened into a large vestibule that I transformed into a sitting parlor with a Sheraton sofa, a large Spanish globe that was a hidden bar, and a French provincial sofa table that held a Tiffany lamp and framed photographs. The parlor to the immediate right opened through an archway to the dining room. The living room with French doors was directly ahead. Adjacent to the dining room was the study with French doors. The short hallway to the kitchen was a pantry with many cabinets to store canned goods and staples. The hallway also served as the laundry area, with more cabinets for bed linens and towels. The kitchen, with its built-in cabinet with French doors (and an operative dumb waiter to draw up telephone-ordered excellent meals from the downstairs Italian restaurant) led to the well-bolted back door. Outside the door was a fire escape landing where we placed our grill for barbecue.

To the left of the kitchen was the maid's quarters, large enough for a double bed and a small table with two chairs, and a half-bathroom. We used this area as a guest room and for a breakfast area when we had no guest. Two bedrooms with a full-bath between them was to the left of the parlor. The apartment was larger than many homes in Alabama. The rent was an absolute steal at $289 a month.

Maxine was exceptionally resourceful. I did not know if she and her family were wealthy, nor could I tell from Maxine's behavior and low-key, self-effacing attitude. However, her father, Leo, was a doctor, and her mother, Trudie, was a homemaker. They owned a four-story home in the West Village. Maxine's only sibling, Peter, was a doctor in Chicago. She was about ten years younger than I and truly loved me as her "big sister" that she always wanted. Some would have judged her plain-looking, but I thought she was strikingly beautiful, with her wavy blonde hair plaited in a single long braid that reached to her waist. She thirsted for knowledge but was not quite sure what she wanted to do for the rest of her life. I suggested that Antioch's Washington campus would be a good place for her to earn her baccalaureate degree; she had the wherewithal to commute from NYC to D.C. We made arrangements with Maxine's parents and Antioch's administration to pay me adjunct fees as Maxine's resident instructor in labor history and political economy. Maxine eventually became a doctor, following in the tradition of her father and brother.

On weekends Maxine and I motored to upstate New York to her family's summer home, a few miles from the Massachusetts line. We frequented auctions to buy antique furniture to furnish our apartment. For pleasure, we crossed the state line to Tanglewood to listen to the Boston Pops Symphony under the stars.

IN OUR BUILDING, Dr. Moer and his family occupied the only apartment on the first floor. The apartment was twice as large as ours, but it also housed his medical practice. Dr. Moer became my resident primary doctor.

I was the only black resident of our building. I visited every tenant on the fourth floor. My neighbors, who became my friends, were a professional photographer and his family, and a holocaust survivor who as a child had been in a German concentration camp; both of her parents were exterminated by the Nazis. She sorrowfully showed me the Star of David and the identification numbers that the Nazis had permanently tattooed on her upper forearm. We had many discussions about Israel's aggression in expropriating Palestinian lands.

I suggested that as the Nazis had oppressed the Jews, so Israel had oppressed the Palestinian people. She replied that God had promised the Jews that they were the chosen people, the heirs to those lands. Yes, I replied, but the Old Testament required Jews "to be civil and caring to strangers and foreigners."

I did not want to raise the touchy belief that Jesus Christ's presence and crucifixion on earth, predicted by the Old Testament prophet, Isaiah, guaranteed that all believers were God's chosen people, Jews and Gentiles. As a result, we were under a new covenant and inheritance.

I told her, "I'm a Southern black woman who has suffered, and my people have been murdered, under the tyranny of Jim Crow racism. My historical reality is that my people were forced into slavery by Europeans, some of whom were Jews. The Star of David and identification numbers had to be embedded in your skin. Our skin color was the obvious sign for white Europeans to strip us of our human dignity and freedom as God's children. Moreover, it was Ralph Bunche, a black man, who negotiated the rights of Jews to return to Israel as their ancestral home, but not at the displacement nor annihilation of the Palestinian people."

She said nothing nor made a gesture.

After our many discussions in my Jewish neighbor's apartment, she would rap on my door to bring me home-baked cookies and to visit. One day she said, "I have become an anti-Zionist."

Movement work is about moving people, preferably in a neighborly fashion, and other times in a confrontational manner, depending on the tenor and order of the day. The purpose is to encourage people to appreciate new understandings and to transform their thoughts and consciousness where they still saw their own humanity in the transition. My neighbor was not only my friend. She became a participant at anti-Zionist rallies in NYC.

My thoughts of the movement as part and parcel of everyday work in my life, family, and community deepened. I knew during my childhood, youth and as a young adult in the South that the movement was not outside my daily existence. Such work gave profound meaning to my own humanity in relationship to the consciousness of those who were close and around me.

THE CPUSA HAD a tremendous and well-financed infrastructure. In NYC the party must have had at least a hundred people, including the staff of its intermediary organizations like the Alliance, on payroll. My salary was $75 a week, the same as it had been for SNCC organizers in the 1960s. However, the CPUSA as my employer paid their share of my social security and medicare taxes.

Three black women, including me, one white woman, and one white man were on the Alliance staff. The office at 150 West 5th Avenue was located near the old SNCC-NYC office. Except me, the staffers were all members of the CPUSA. My co-workers constantly asked me to join the party. I was hesitant. I could not accept their party line of uncritical support of white workers, and certainly not the fantastic notion that they will be the vanguard in the Revolution. I reflected on the accolades heaped upon a white male YWLL member in Washington. He was elected president of his all-white American Federation of Government Employees local. I thought that if he were not an outright racist, he at least accommodated racism by not raising the issue of racism within his local. He could only be respected in my eyes if he were a thorn in the side in his local.

White workers since slavery time were the most virulent racists. When the English, Germans, Irish, Scots, French, Greeks, and, to a lesser degree, the Italians, homogenized and nationalized themselves into the melting pot of the white race, the racist working class became the overseers on plantations and formed terrorist organizations like the Ku Klux Klan to murder, maim, and intimidate black people. White workers, called Reds, may have led the 1917 Revolution in Russia, but from my historical viewpoint it would never be replicated in the USA.

My first year with The Alliance went somewhat smoothly until it was time for me to travel to Montgomery for my annual family reunion on my mother's side. Charlene Mitchell, the day-to-day boss in the office, and Angela Davis, the Alliance president, had an extensive Eastern European (USSR) speaking tour. They wanted me to remain in the office in their absence.

"My umbilical cord has never been severed from my family," I said as a way to let them know I was definitely going to Montgomery. Whatever their motivation, they granted me "leave," as if I needed their permission.

It became clear that CPUSA members severed ties with their non-communist family members and friends if they were not communists. The "new family" was the party. They socialized together, married each other, and divorced only to marry another communist.

In my neighborhood I had many friends who did not have an inkling about communism. Nevertheless, they were righteous-thinking people who would join a movement with clarity in the struggle to fight injustice. My neighborhood bar, The Palmetto, across the street from my apartment building, was the watering hole for the few blacks who lived in Washington Heights and for the black members of the 1199 local who worked in the neighborhood's prestigious Columbia Presbyterian Hospital. Black people from Harlem would travel uptown just to be in the company of our community bar.

When I returned from Montgomery and Charlene returned from the USSR, office relations resumed as if there had never been a conflict in the first place.

The Alliance plate was full with black and Latino men being harassed and thrown in jail for their movement activities. The year 1972 was another "law and order" period, which swept Richard Nixon into the president's office for his second term. With his leadership, police power became more deadly than ever.

In February 1973, I was invited to join the 6th Contingent of the Venceremous Brigade to Cuba for a three-month stay. I accepted. I wanted to witness a communist country in action, from top to bottom. I had to journey to Philadelphia, where I met Rosemari Mealy who was in charge of the orientation workshops for participants before they traveled to Cuba.

Cuba was a beautiful island, just 90 miles from Miami. For over a century the Cubans had been fighting for their independence, first against the Spanish, and then against the U.S. when the U.S. in 1898, ostensibly supporting Jose Marti and Cuban revolutionaries to throw off Spanish colonialism, betrayed the people by seizing rich Cuban lands. U.S. capitalists gobbled up the mining properties of iron ore, manganese, chrome, copper and nickel and transformed cane and tobacco fields into *latifundias*. For all intents and purposes Cuba became a U.S. neo-colony. The U.S. government had made it clear since the 1897–1901 presidency of William McKinley that it was U.S. destiny to control Cuba.

After Cuba's first democratic election of the progressive President Tomas Estrada Palma in 1902, there came a succession of bad to ugly presidents supported by the U.S. government. According to Huberman and Sweezy in *Cuba: Anatomy of a Revolution*, Cuban presidential terms "were characterized by venality, nepotism, incompetence, and despotism" (p. 17).

In 1933, the Cuban people, led by university students, overthrew the presidency of General Gerardo Machado, known as "the Butcher." He was replaced by the forward-looking Dr. Ramón Grau San Martin. However, Grau was not supported by the U.S. and President Franklin D. Roosevelt did not recognize the Grau administration. Strongman Fulgencio Batista muscled himself into power by taking over the Cuban army in 1934. Batista ruled until 1944. In 1952, he led a bloody *coup d'etat* and reinstalled himself as president with U.S. capitalist backing.

In the 1950s, there were about 6.4 million Cubans. It was a relatively small number of people living on an island rich with natural resources, all of which was being cultivated and harvested by U.S. capitalists and a small Cuban elite. One would think the people would be well off, but most were woefully poor. The average yearly salary was $312. Rural people lived in thatched huts without running water, toilets, and electricity. Up to twelve family members lived in two-room huts. Health problems, especially for children, were horrific. Schooling for rural children was nil. A fourth of Cubans could not read or write.

Batista had done nothing to alleviate the devastation of the Cuban people. Instead, he permitted the mafia and unscrupulous capitalists to make the Island into a major center for drug trafficking, prostitution, child pornography, and gambling.

I wanted to see with my own eyes and hear with my own ears how President Fidel Castro, affectionately called "El Heje," and his compatriot ragamuffins—so labeled by the U.S. government—turned the island around to serve its people in the noblest tradition of human rights and dignity.

The U.S. after its fiasco at the Bay of Pigs had placed an embargo on Cuba. Thus, the 6th Venceremous Brigade had to fly to Mexico, which maintained its diplomatic relationship with Cuba. Cuba sent its planes to Mexico to ferry the brigadistas to Havana.

Arriving in the city in April 1973, it was like stepping back in time. Most of the cars were 1950s' U.S. models; the Cubans had become masters in restoring these cars and keeping them running in tip-top form. The popular music was from the 1950s black repertoire of Little Richard, the Coasters, the Teenagers, Little Anthony and the Imperials, Chuck Berry—especially his "School Day" ("up in the morning and off to school, the teacher is teaching the golden rule")—and other black singers of the period. White musical artists had little or no play in Havana. However, Ernest Hemingway was revered. The Havana apartment where he did much of his writing had been preserved as a museum showplace.

Havana was an art déco city in motion. Most of the buildings suffered from peeled paint as a result of neglect and the high humidity. Cubans compensated for the peeling paint inside the buildings with creative prints and folding designs of cloth received from Holland to cover the walls.

We arrived in Cuba during the *zafra* season when sugar cane is cut and sent to the sugar mills. We lived in large barracks centered between several cane fields. The simple bunk beds were covered with mosquito nets. There were a dining area, several showers, and a large room for study, reading, and socializing.

After an early breakfast, we loaded onto large trucks and went to the cane fields. We were paired with expert Cuban cutters who taught us how to cut sugar cane stalks with machetes. We worked from 6–9 a.m., had a break and then worked until 11:30 a.m. We were carried back to the barracks for lunch and a siesta rest until 2 p.m. Then we reloaded the trucks and returned to the field to continue our work with a 4:30 p.m. break and returned to the barracks at 6 p.m. for dinner and relaxation. Sometimes we had dances, reminiscent of old school dancing of the chicken, hulley-gulley, bop, and cha-cha-cha. We never stayed up late. We needed to rest to regain strength before returning to the fields the following morning. Some of us while in bed rubbed down in alcohol and liniment to loosen up the muscles in our forearms, now aching from swinging a machete. Though we were sore, the experience was exhilarating and comforting. We were providing an appreciated human service to uplift our brothers and sisters. Our immeasurable reward was that we were becoming more humane in the process.

After two weeks in the cane fields, my repaired leg could no longer withstand the stress. The Cubans reassigned me to the building-trades brigade to assist in building modest homes and school houses. My job was to recycle nails from the construction sites. I would sit atop a work table and hammer the bent nails until they were straight again.

After a month's work, the brigadistas had a week's vacation. We traveled by bus and plane all over the Island. We visited Pinar del Rio, Matanzas, Santa Clara, Camagüey, the Sierra Mountains, and Santiago de Cuba. The Cubans in each city embraced us with genuine, heartfelt love. They always made a distinction between the U.S. people and the U.S. government. I thought I saw pity in some Cubans' eyes, a sorrow that we lived under a rapacious government.

Visiting the community hollows of the Sierra Mountains was pure joy. The people were unadulterated and unpretentious. Every home had electricity, running water, toilets, and a pressure cooker on the stove. Chickens pranced through the homes like children. They were more like pets than farm animals. But all knew that they would soon be in the pressure cooker. Chicken was one of Cuba's favorite foods.

Our last stop was near the southern end of the Island, Santiago de Cuba in the Oriente Province, Castro's family home. His father was rich and successful in the sugar and lumber industries. Fort Moncada, the second-largest military fortress in Cuba, was located in Oriente. It was the first site that Castro and his 200 compatriots, including two women, attempted to liberate on July 26, 1953, from the despotic and deranged dictatorship of Batista. The revolutionary thrust failed.

In Santiago de Cuba, I met my *amore* companion, Eduardo. He traveled several times to Havana to court me when I returned to continue brigadista work. He proposed, but I could not accept; I was still married to Jerry.

Before we commenced our second month of work, our Cuban leaders/facilitators held a production meeting with us. They reported the pounds of cane we had cut, the pounds of stripped leaves, and the pounds of sugar that had been refined from the canes in the mills. They beamed with appreciation and congratulations that we had done a splendid job. Our facilitators did not ask us to raise the output. Instead, they cheered us on to "keep up the good work!"

After another month's of work, we had our second week-long vacation. This time we visited schools in the city, countryside, and the Isle of the Youth. The Isle was first called the Isle of the Pines and was the site of the jail where Castro, his brother, Raul, and a close compatriot, Juan Almeida, also from Oriente, along with others, were jailed for their failed attempts to liberate the Moncada Fortress.

School children were lovingly called "Young Pioneers." They wore different-colored neckerchiefs to denote their levels of schooling: elementary, middle, or high school. All Cuban youth went on to post-secondary schools, either at the university or technical colleges. Cuba achieved 100 percent literacy and 100 percent employment. There were no prostitution, drugs, gambling, and child pornography in Cuba.

City youth commuted from home to school or they could attend the countryside boarding schools. I was amazed by the brilliance of elementary school Young Pioneers in the countryside. In addition to mastering the rigorous academic subjects, they also had a comprehensive curriculum in agricultural production. From their science classes they learned soil agronomy and seed germination. At the beginning of the school term, the Young Pioneers determined a produce-production plan and anticipated yields. They grew tomatoes, watermelons and other vegetables and fruits. The surplus produce which was not needed for school consumption was sold to the state. The Young Pioneers met again to determine how they were to collectively spend their profits for school equipment, always in the sports arena to buy baseball bats and balls, basketballs and sports uniforms. Cuban people loved sports and baseball was their favorite pastime. These Young Pioneers no doubt could manage any U.S. agri-business corporation.

Our third month of work ended with a series of celebratory parades and informative, yet festive, gatherings in the Revolutionary Plaza in Havana. On one parade I was falling behind with my padded cushion in hand. A jeep near the front of the parade pulled out and was soon slowly driving alongside me. "Get in, sister," the voice said. It was Raul Castro, the number two man in the Revolution. I climbed onto the back seat of the jeep and sat next to a black Cuban brother. I was humbled when he told me his name, Juan Almeida, the number three man in the Revolution. I was given a prominent seat in the outside Revolution Plaza, but I preferred to sit with the U.S. brigadistas further up the concrete bleachers. I was escorted to that area.

Castro talked nonstop for six hours. We were never bored or restless. His address, loaded with statistics, gave the state of the nation. From where Cuba came in 1959 and now in 1973, the 14th year of the Revolution, we were without a doubt witnessing an utopia. The crowd cheered, stamped their feet, clapped their hands, and roared with laughter at Castro's analyses of the imperialist's follies to destroy Cuba. People had ample supplies of water, picnic baskets of snacks and cushion pads for their bottoms. They were prepared to listen and to respond in the black Baptist tradition all night to their chosen leader and elected officials who brought them out of living hell. As I looked out at the mass of caring and hopeful souls, silent tears cascaded down my cheeks.

We left Cuba by way of a small Holland ocean liner, which had an on-deck swimming pool and several bars stocked with Cuban rum and featuring live entertainment. Our destination was Montreal. Canada had maintained its diplomatic relations with Cuba. Thousands of Canadians vacationed in Cuba.

I spent most of the five-day cruise reading and talking with Jorge Gonzalez. I had met Jorge in Santiago, Chile, in 1971. We both laughed at our memory of the Alarcon son (I was guest of the Alarcon family) walking several feet behind us when Jorge took me to see and to hear the Quilapyon, a fabulous musical group who played wooden flutes. We had the same custom in Inkster, Michigan, where I grew up until my teens. My brother would walk several feet behind me and my date until he delivered me at home.

Jorge was carried to Miami by his family who opposed the Cuban Revolution. As soon as Jorge reached the age of twenty-one, college-trained, he repatriated to his birth country, joined the Communist Party, and soon was elected as a municipal official in Havana.

I told him I wanted to return to Cuba as soon as I could to visit the university, hospitals, factories, court system, and the prisons. He assured me that could be arranged, especially since I had made a positive impression on officials I had met. And, as he had in Chile, Jorge urged me to join the CPUSA. To that, I reminded him that I had strong philosophical differences with the party. "They are 'slaves' to the white working-class and cannot see that others, for example black workers and students, may be the leaders of the revolution in this historical period," I told him. I mentioned that Castro, a student and a lawyer, and Che, a doctor, worked with the peasants and brought about the Cuban Revolution. "In fact, I think I am more progressive than the CPUSA," I said.

We spent a great time of time talking about the possible impeachment of President Richard Nixon over the Watergate debacle. Jorge was very interested in learning about U.S. grand juries. He considered them a facist procedure where the accused did not have the right to hear allegations of witnesses, yet the "secret" accusations could be cause to indict and arrest the person. I knew a little bit about grand juries when my father was summoned to give information about his nemesis in the number business or he would be indicted. I never learned the outcome, except my father nor his nemesis never went to prison.

After some difficulty navigating the narrow Saint Lawrence River, we arrived at the Port of Montreal. The Montreal progressive community was there to greet us with applause. As I walked down the gangplank, I was surprised to hear voices calling my name. I knew no one in Montreal. I searched the faces of the welcomers and saw the tall, lanky Stokely Carmichael (later to be known as Kwame Ture) towering above the crowd, and Rosie Douglas, his West Indian compatriot. Rosie was out on bail. He was awaiting trial for his work in the Black Liberation Movement. If convicted, he was facing two to seven years in prison. I waved to acknowledge that I saw them. We rushed toward each other and hugged.

It turned out that Stokely wanted me to share a panel with him at the University of Montreal. I was taken aback and reminded him that we didn't agree on the strategy for black and African Liberation.

"I know," he said, "but we are abiding friends and have lovingly agreed to disagree."

"Will any of your comrades try to kill me?" I asked. Sometime earlier, while I was serving as co-convener for a Chicago conference in support of the African National Congress, a U.S. black nationalist aligned with Stokely had closed the auditorium doors, stuffed gasoline-soaked rags under the doors and set the rags afire. Fortunately, people outside the auditorium stomped out the fire.

Stokely said he was "sorry that the brother does not know your role in our long struggle and I was horrified by what he attempted to do. We call you our 'Harriet Tubman.' You can say whatever you wish on the panel. If there is disagreement, it will be food for discussion."

I knew he was sincere. He was a true friend and he always loved debates.

I had been an ANC supporter since my college days at Tuskegee Institute. ANC had a race *and* class analysis in their anti-apartheid struggle to free South Africa. Unionized black African workers were key leaders and a central base in the struggle. When the workers held union strikes, they paralyzed the nation. Nelson Mandela was in Robbins Island Prison for his revolutionary actions in the fight for self-determination of the African peoples to form a non-racialist society. ANC had white African members. But it was not a question about white membership, but about leadership. It was abundantly clear that black South Africans were the leadership of ANC.

Stokely and his compatriots supported the all-black Pan African Congress (PAC) and the all-black Azanian People's Organization (AZAPO). I saw the pitfalls of race minus a class analysis in Tuskegee, where the black middle class formed organizations that excluded black working-class and poor black people. Middle-class black Tuskegeans were not interested in helping blacks outside of their class to become registered voters. The middle class was safe, secure, and could elect their choice of officials with their limited number of voters.

On the other hand, I saw the limitations of race-only analysis in Uganda with Idi Amin and in the handwriting on the wall with Buthelezi, the South African Zulu leader.

I served on the panel with Stokely, but I had little to say and allowed the tenor of the panel to inform my remarks.

Michael X was also on the panel. He was Stokely's Trinadadian home boy. While Stokely spent much of his life in the U.S., Michael had lived mostly in London. He had a close relationship with Pakistani Muslims in London. He became a Muslim himself after serving as one of the escorts for Muhammad Ali's bout with, and defeat of, British heavyweight boxing champion Henry Cooper. Michael adopted "X" as his last name after meeting Malcolm X, who was invited to London to debate William Buckley, the famous, arrogant U.S. conservative.

Michael X was the founder of the Racial Adjustment Action Society (RASS), the first "Black Power!" organization in London. Michael was a spellbinding storyteller. Much of his narrative magic was in his mixture of West Indian sing-song punctuated with a clipped British accent. He had a manner of transposing statements into questions and then answering the questions. After he told a story, he would fall out laughing as if he was hearing it himself for the first time. It did not matter if you got the message. You fell out laughing, too. I could never discern if Michael was telling a tall tale or the truth.

AFTER CUBA, EXITING LaGuardia Airport in NYC with modern cars whizzing about, I was almost dizzy from cultural shock. As I entered my apartment, the phone rang. I quickly answered but could not believe my ears as I listened to the voice on the other end. I had not talked on a phone in three months. I told the caller that I had just returned from Cuba and Montreal and that I would have to call back. I turned on the radio. The disco music threw me for a loop. I quickly turned the dial to my favorite jazz station; jazz was always a steady rock for me.

Maxine finally came home. I was beside myself to tell her about my Cuban experiences. She had never been to Cuba. However, she was close to Ricardo Alarcon, the highest-ranking Cuban in the United Nations. Maxine frequented the Casa de la Cuba to learn Spanish and Cuban dance steps. Maxine was dating a Cuban, who worked in the UN's Interest Section with Ricardo. She arranged a lunch in a downtown Manhattan restaurant. Ricardo assured me that my return to Cuba would be no problem. The next time a special delegation of educators, journalists, lawyers and health professionals was assembled, I would be invited.

I counseled with Maxine about Jorge's request for me to join the CPUSA. She was elated. She assisted with my signing up to become a member. However, I still had reservations.

I RETURNED TO the Alliance office and to an overflowing plate. Anne Braden was in NYC with urgent concerns. Anne from Alabama was a spry woman with unlimited movement energy and compassion. Now living in Louisville, Kentucky, she could hold her bourbon like I could hold my beer. She and her husband and soulmate, Carl Braden, were movement legends. Former journalists, they co-edited the *Southern Patriot*, a first-class newspaper that had covered freedom movements in the South since the 1940s. Anne was a staunch anti-racist and was one of the few white supporters of SNCC's call for "Black Power!" She issued a corresponding call for "whites to organize in the white community" and formed the Southern Organizing Committee (SOC). She raised funds to hire white organizers to organize in the Appalachia communities of coal miners and poor whites. She always emphasized that organizing had to be in the self-interest of the community with the fight against racism as the central tenet.

Now, Anne was in a frenzy to save the life of a black brother accused of rape in Louisville. Of course, I had no trouble pulling together a defense committee for the brother. However, I had some anger as to why brothers would place themselves in circumstances where a white woman could yell "rape!" After sober thinking, I reached back to the "Scottsboro Boys" rape case in 1931. Nine brothers in their teens were accused of raping two white women who were hoboing in a railroad boxcar. I self-criticized myself. Brothers did not necessarily place themselves in such circumstances. Racists would flip any innocent situation as a cause to lynch blacks. No one better understood this racist mentally than Anne Braden, who grew up and lived all of her life in the South.

Anne's next concern was about the Louisville Black Panther Party. She agreed to share the Southern Conference Education Fund (SCEF) office with the BBP. SCEF had an admirable record of raising funds to support Southern freedom movements. The BBP had commandeered the front office of SCEF. Anne capitulated to this unreasonable demand. Soon the BBP issued an order that no white person could enter the front doors of the SCEF office. Anne accommodated this foolishness until the BBP issued an even more outrageous "missive": no white person could enter the SCEF office. Then there was a physical altercation between the BBP leader and his wife. Anne counseled the wife not to press criminal assault charges, but rather to prepare papers for her husband to be committed to a mental institution for a short-term therapy. Anne meant well. But in the 1970s, black men preferred prison over a mental institution.

I thanked Anne for her support of the black movement in which she saw that her own freedom could only be realized within the context of the black movement. Then I added, "There is no such thing as unconditional love and uncritical support without the bottom line of principles and expectations. Sometimes your fight against racism borders on liberalism and paternalism." From that day until her passing we became symbiotic sisters in constant consultation with each other. I went to Louisville as a facilitator to settle the conflict between BBP and SCEF.

On July 4, 1973, the Alliance sponsored an organizational fundraising celebration to honor Clarence Norris, one of the Scottsboro teens, who was living in Queens, New York. Clarence was now 61 years old. His pardon from the Alabama governor was imminent. There could be no better way to observe July 4th than to celebrate the freedom and independence of Clarence Norris.

In mid-July, Charlene and Michael took a vacation from the Alliance office and went to the USSR. The other two black and white female staffers were also due a vacation. Since I had been in Cuba for the past three months, I readily offered to staff the office in their absences. I had many friends who would gladly volunteer to work in the office to assist me. My co-workers agreed that to bring in volunteers would both broaden the Alliance's base and broaden the perspective of the volunteers.

While manning the office, I received an alarming message that Michael X had been extradited from Guyana to London. He had been convicted in 1972 by the Queen's Court for murder; how he escaped to Guyana is still a mystery. Michael was to be hanged in Port of Spain, Trinidad and Tobago. In response to this news, I quickly called progressive black, brown, yellow and predominantly white organizations, including Amnesty International (AI) to form a "Free Michael X Defense Coalition." We developed a strategy. First we had to set up another base of operations in Brooklyn where the largest Trinidadian and West Indies immigrant communities were located. We had to raise funds to underwrite the strategy. I received permission from the NYC Department of Social Services for the coalition to have a "Can Day" solicitation. Coalition members spread throughout the subway stations to solicit contributions.

An agreed-upon press release was printed in coalition members' respective organs and sent to major news sources. I called my friend and Tuskegee Institute graduate, Chester Higgins, who had transplanted to Roosevelt Island near NYC. Chester was a professional photographer with friends and relatives who worked for *Jet* magazine. Chester made certain that *Jet* covered the story. I had been a special correspondent to *Muhammad Speaks* in Chicago, covering black people's movements against the war in Vietnam, so I contacted it.

I called Dr. Carlos Russell, a progressive Panamanian who was dean of the School for Contemporary Studies at Brooklyn College, City University of

New York. Carlos, a drop-dead gorgeous brother, told me how to send letters of support and appeal via the diplomatic pouch through the international consulates in NYC. The final prong was for Amnesty International to alert its London affiliate to make haste to organize efforts to save Michael X's life.

On their return, Charlene and Michael came directly to the Alliance office from the airport. The urgent business could not wait a day for them to re-acclimate to NYC after five weeks in the USSR.

"Gwen, we need to have a 'criticism-self-criticism' session," Charlene said. She did not go into her inner office. She and Michael pulled up chairs to my desk. Charlene did all of the talking.

"You had no business organizing a defense committee for Michael X."

I replied, "The brother's life was in the balance. Surely, he was a political prisoner. I thought the Alliance mission was to fight against racist and political repression."

"And, you definitely had no business inviting Amnesty International to this office!"

Charlene had not heard a word I said.

When I asked why, she said it was because AI had not supported Angela's defense. And when I asked what that had to do with trying to save Michael X's life, she moved on to criticizing the fact that I held a workshop and taught twenty-five organizations how to conduct a "Can Day."

I excused myself at that point to go the restroom, and after some thought I left the building and went uptown to my apartment. When the phone began to ring, I did not answer it. When Maxine came home from school, I informed her that I was not answering the phone, and if Charlene or Michael called, to tell them I desired not to talk with them.

Maxine's loyalty to me was humbling. Because of her support, I decided not to withdraw my membership with the CPUSA. I had yet to go to a meeting. I was still in "New Members Orientation and Study." I was hoping that Maxine was representative of a rank and file membership that was above petty and sectarian politics.

The next morning I was in front of 150 Fifth Avenue, the building that housed the Alliance. I had a sign around my neck that said in large, bold letters, "Hire an Organizer for $15 a Day!" When Charlene and Michael came to work and saw my one-person demonstration, they rushed into the building.

I later took the subway to Brooklyn to the School of Contemporary Studies. Dressed appropriately, I entered the dean's office and told the secretary my name and that I didn't have an appointment but hoped to see Dr. Russell. The secretary buzzed the intercom. Within a few minutes, the dean came out and ushered me into his office.

I told him that I needed a job and gave him my credentials—I never talked about my educational background with movement people. Dean Russell seemed unsurprised that I had a master's in education and in the art of teaching. "I always suspected you had professional training. You're a helluva organizer," he said, with his signature twinkle in his eyes.

"I don't know about that," I replied. "I have been reprimanded as an organizer." I shared with him the "criticism-self-criticism" session with Charlene. He knew Charlene.

Though Carlos was a movement activist, I respected his position as a dean of an educational institution. He had no time to "shoot the breeze" about movement memories. He suggested that I apply for an English instructor's position, saying he had no doubt I would be hired.

On the subway ride back to my apartment, I thought about Northern notions that stereotyped Southern blacks as simple, uneducated, and poor. I recalled when Charlene had complimented a pants suit I wore to the office. "Who bought that for you?" she asked. She had no idea that I was a complex thinker, educated, and from a family of means who would unquestionably support my movement activities. Besides, I had my own means to sustain a quality life. Why else would I work as a movement organizer for $15 a day?

Thirty years later, Charlene and I reconciled at a Bannerman Fellowship Retreat in Laguna, California.

28

Back in the Classroom and the Church

I submitted my application to the School of Contemporary Studies (SCS) and within a week was informed that I had been hired to teach English for the Fall 1973 semester. The first week in October was the Fall/Harvest Festival for NYC public schools and colleges. This holiday week was also known as the Feast of the Tabernacle or the Feast of the Booths, celebrated by members of the Jewish faith. I took the week to go to Montgomery to visit family and Tuskegee Institute. I called Jerry in Washington and asked if he wanted to go to Montgomery with me. Without hesitation, he said, "Yes, let's see if we can straighten out our relationship." I took the Amtrak train to Washington and from there Jerry and I flew to Montgomery.

For the past five years I had wanted to meet again with Dr. Luther Foster, president of my beloved Tuskegee Institute. After a pleasant visit with family, Jerry and I took the Greyhound bus to Tuskegee. We checked into Dorothy Hall Guest House on campus for two nights. That afternoon I met with Dr. Foster. Mrs. Pauline Punch, his secretary, was still surly towards me when I arrived at the president's office.

Dr. Foster and I embraced warmly. As a gift, I had brought him a copy of the illustrated booklet on Tuskegee Institute I had done with Pride, Inc.

"Dr. Foster, I love Tuskegee. I cut many wisdom teeth here."

"And so have I," he laughed.

I told Dr. Foster I wanted to talk about the 1968 student rebellion, when students all over the world, including many at black Southern colleges, were trying to convey to administrators that the academy's mission should be to hone young minds to serve and to uplift the human community. Some of us were shot and killed by state-sanctioned police over our efforts to protest.

Such violence was averted at Tuskegee, but events there easily could have turned out tragically. Students had taken over the annual April trustee board meeting and barricaded the building, and Dr. Foster had invited the National Guard to take control of the campus. I genuinely wanted to know how he had allowed that in the face of joint student-administration policies negotiated during the 1966 campus-wide moratorium while I was student body president.

"The students should not have held hostage the board of trustees in Dorothy Hall," Dr. Foster replied.

"Students had followed proper protocol to arrange a meeting with the trustees, to no avail," I said. "Students wanted in-depth discussions with trustees who claimed that they did not have time. Thus, the students locked them up and gave them time. The students were organized and had a list of well-thought-out concerns and suggestions to overcome the impasse."

"Kidnapping is a federal crime," he said.

I reminded him that this was all taking place during the time of Dr. King's assassination. He was a scholar and an intellectual who refused to disconnect himself from poor and working-class black people, and his murder had compounded students' frustrations. "Teaching students to turn their backs on their families, communities, the human condition and to fight international wars is a crime against humanity. Calling out the National Guard exacerbated a situation you already considered untenable. This action could have led to carnage like what occurred at South Carolina State, Texas Southern, Jackson State, and Kent State. This action was irrational on the part of the administration."

He was silent.

I pressed on to say that I took all this personally, because it seemed that as soon as I left Tuskegee, he rescinded our 1966 agreements that, among other things, students would sit on policy-making committees, a student judiciary committee would complement administrative actions, a free student press would be respected, the theatre and speakers' bureau would be in compliance with the standards of academic freedom, and a general philosophy would be promulgated that a black university's mission was to train students to uplift the community.

I was laying the blame for the 1968 student rebellion at his feet. We talked on, and he heard me out. Finally, after another silence, he switched gears to talking about the coming Institute centennial celebration and capital campaign. He said he would need my support to connect with the alumni from my student cohort. We talked more about the university's mission, and our conversation drifted to the first Institute president, Dr. Booker T. Washingon, who was dedicated to the uplift of our people.

I said that I had reevaluated Washington's philosophy and concluded that he is truly the "father of black power."

As our meeting ended, Dr. Foster asked how much longer I would be in Tuskegee. I replied that the next day I would tour the campus and old haunts and visit with some of my professors and Sheriff Lucius Amerson, then the following day I had to return to Washington and on to New York City. He surprised me with the warm gesture of offering Institute transport back to Montgomery to say good-bye to my family and then take Jerry and me on to the airport.

We parted with smiles of deep respect. We had shared this experience in the past. I hoped that this time it would be genuine and lasting.

STROLLING THROUGH THE campus, hand in hand with Jerry, brought back memories of our innocent love when I was an undergraduate. We visited the goat and horse farms and marveled at the large blue turkey eggs in the high grass. We went to the campus cemetery and read the epitaphs on the graves of Dr. Booker T. Washington and Dr. George Washington Carver.

Thomas Reed, now an Alabama state representative—first elected as an independent candidate under the political symbol of the Black Panther—owned the main eatery on Campus Avenue. The Deep South cuisine of turnip greens, macaroni loaded with cheese, fried chicken seasoned to perfection, and corn muffins made from scratch put aside our need to talk about the state of our marriage as we snuggled together in the restaurant booth.

We visited with Sheriff Lucius Amerson in his office after lunch. Amerson was the first black sheriff elected in the Deep South since Reconstruction. He was elected in Macon County with the support of Tuskegee students.

I wanted to hear Amerson's version of how the National Guard had gotten called to the Institute in 1968. He said he wasn't responsible.

"The student-trustee standoff was within the jurisdiction of city government," Sheriff Amerson said solemnly. "President Foster called me from Dorothy Hall around 2 a.m. He asked me to bring whatever forces were necessary to rout and to arrest the students in Dorothy Hall, who I understood were still in intense discussions with the trustees. I with another deputy car drove up to Dorothy Hall. Hundreds of students were out front. Remember Dr. King had been assassinated. I understood the students' anger. The students immediately encircled our cars. We could have gotten out of our cars, guns drawn, but I refused to give the order. Soon Dean of Students P. B. Phillips was at my car door. He persuaded the students to open a way for my car and the deputy's car to leave the scene. I decided that this was a campus situation and was under the jurisdiction of the city. I was not about to call up the Alabama Guard; that could turn into a bloodbath. My loyalty has always been with the country people and the students. Not necessarily with city folks, black and white, who were determined to put students, and me, too, in what they thought were our 'proper places' to do their bidding."

Nevertheless, 300 guardsmen and 70 troopers, all white, in military jeeps and with fixed bayonets, had been called to Tuskegee. I sorely wanted to believe Sheriff Amerson, but I didn't. I knew he would abandon the students to curry favor with the black middle class and its political alliance, the Tuskegee Civic Association. Moreover, I strongly sensed that Amerson wanted to be accepted and to be invited into the inside of Tuskegee's social circle of black professionals and educated elites.

Now he told me, "Dr. Foster pressed charges of 'disturbing the peace' against several students. Your name was on the list."

Of course, I was in Queens, New York, with my friend, Vida Gaynor, when Dr. King was assassinated while the Institute students rebelled. But Amerson said the administration was convinced I was somewhere hiding in Tuskegee and orchestrating the student uprising.

I shook my head in disbelief.

Amerson said, "Because of the charges, I had to issue warrants for the students' arrests. Several were held in the county jail. We treated the students more like guests than as prisoners. Bail was set at $1,000, but it was lowered to $500. All of the students were released on bail, but they were *persona non grata* on campus. If they as much had put their big toes on campus, they would be charged with trespassing and re-arrested."

A legal defense fund had been established to fight for the re-admission

of fifty-four students who were expelled. When the case came to trial, U.S.
District Judge Frank Johnson revoked the expulsions on the ground that
the administration had unconstitutionally singled out a group of students
for expulsion while readmitting hundreds of other students who were also
a part of the rebellion.

I leaned back in my chair before Sheriff Amerson's roughly-hewn desk.
I took in all that he said. We both sat in deep thought for a few minutes.

He had been in his first term during the students' rebellion in 1968.
Now, he was in the swan years of his second term and was vying for a third
term. True to his word, he did not abandon the rural people. He served them
with fairness, dignity, justice and distinction. He never denied his roots as a
poor and rural Alabamian native son. The rural people loved him as one of
their own who had broken through the racial-class caste system in Macon
County. Sheriff Amerson would go on to serve for a total of twenty years
before his retirement in 1986.

"Thanks, Sheriff Amos, for talking with me and giving me your side of
the Tuskegee student rebellion." We stood and firmly shook hands across
his desk.

As promised, the Institute transport collected Jerry and me at Dorothy
Hall the following morning and drove us to Montgomery, where we caught
a plane back to Washington. Jerry and I continued sharing our courtship
memories, laughing at our past silly antics. I still was not ready to talk about
our future together. I spent the night with Jerry in his efficiency. The next
day I took the Amtrak train to New York City.

AT THE SCHOOL for Contemporary Studies (SCS), I was promoted as director
of SCS's Summer Outreach Program. Many of the students in the program
registered as freshmen for the fall semester. Dean Carlos Russell asked me
to serve as director of Evening School, tantamount to being "dean of night
school." After a year in this capacity, I requested a return to full-time teaching during the day. I was more than willing to take a cut in pay as a result
of being relieved of administrative duties.

Dean Russell had assembled a remarkable progressive and forward-
thinking faculty. The two-year school had automatic admission to Brooklyn

College and other four-year colleges in the city university system. SCS's rubric had four major modules: human studies, communication studies, field studies, and independent studies.

I taught in the communications studies module under the dynamic leadership of Director Edith Chevat. She was seventeen years my senior. Though she treated me as her daughter, she also recognized me as a peer and consulted me regarding my insights and advice on many departmental issues. I considered her my mentor. She was a master in teaching communications. She broadened the module beyond writing and critical thinking and research necessary for good writing to include arts, drama, rhetoric, and debate. I taught debate.

The highlight of my tenure at SCS was teaching, learning, and exchanging ideas with my students. The thesis titles of my first- and second-year students covered the political trial of Sacco-Vanzetti, application of socialism in Africa, mutagenic action of mitomycine (cancer arrest), the manifesto of Malcolm X, rehabilitation of criminals, critique of bilingual programs in NYC, the struggle for decent housing in NYC, seizure disorders in children, and the effects of Watergate in the political environment. Such titles were worthy of any Ph.D. dissertation. Yes, our movement had made an intellectual and conscious impact on contemporary youth.

In my debate classes, taught in a theater-style classroom, we debated the definition of political prisoners and the impending hanging of Michael X. Students on their own, especially students from Trinidad and the West Indies, organized "Save Michael X" defense committees. Several of my colleagues, including Dean Carlos Russell, visited their native countries' consulates in New York City and sent communications via diplomatic pouch to their respective governments, urging a reprieve for Michael X.

TWO OF MY brightest students confided that they were gay partners. I had never met a lesbian to know one. I had a gay male friend who lived in my Washington Heights community, and I had a beloved cousin-in-law who was gay and a U.S. Marine veteran. But I knew no lesbians up close. I had once witnessed a heavy-set lesbian, called a "butch" or "dyke" in my generation, fighting with a man over a woman in the Big Apple Bar on 7th

Avenue and 135th Street in Harlem. The lesbian, dressed like a man, kept circling the man as if in a wrestling match. She caught him off guard and threw him to the floor. She then grabbed the woman off the bar stool and they walked out arm-in-arm.

My gay students, an interracial couple, invited me to their neighborhood bar. I did not hesitate. My commitment has always been to young people and wherever I could to help them with their intellectual growth and their responsibilities to themselves and the greater community.

As we entered the lesbian bar, the somewhat oldie, "My Girl," was playing on the dj's turntable. Girls and women were dancing with each other. The white member of the couple introduced me to her mother, who had divorced her husband and come "out of the closet." I did not accept any offers to dance, but all in all it was a pleasant, learning experience.

Upon the couple's graduation from SCS, the black partner's mother hosted a pot-luck party. It was a fun event. The mother, a single parent, pulled me to the side for a discussion. She had accepted her daughter as a lesbian. But, now her son had declared that he was gay. She was perplexed. All I could say was, "You still have a daughter and a son. Love them. They are your children."

SINCE 1972, WHEN I relocated to New York City, Jerry came up from Washington every year to be with me on my birthday, October 14th. Usually around 6 p.m., he was at my door with a bouquet in his hand. He would take me to dinner, spend the night, and leave the following morning.

My 1974 birthday was different. I had a new beau who was a gourmet cook of Italian cuisine. While I was teaching, he and Maxine were in the apartment preparing a surprise birthday dinner. When I arrived home and unlocked the door, the fragrant aroma of Italian herbs greeted me. I hung my coat on the rack and laid my books and papers on the desk in my bedroom office and then proceeded to the kitchen.

"Surprise!" My beau, Maxine and her friend, and another friend couple leaped from the study with a shout. They wore party hats. My beau rushed to kiss me and placed a party hat on my head. "Happy birthday, Gwen!" I was truly surprised.

While we were sitting at the dining room table with practically a seven-course meal of veal, Italian-style bread dressing, zucchini, Roman tomatoes and red onions, seasoned-steamed shrimp, spinach salad with black olives, deviled eggs, cream cheese-pimento stuffed celery stalks, and garlic bread, our conversation was interrupted by the intercom buzzer in the kitchen. It was 6 p.m.

"I'll get it," I said, and went to the intercom. "Who is it?" I asked.

"Jerry."

I blanked out for a moment and then pushed the button that opened the downstairs vestibule door. Jerry was soon rapping on the apartment door, bouquet in hand. With a deep breath, I opened the door. We embraced and he said, "Happy birthday, Gwen."

I led him by the hand to the dining room and introduced him to my birthday guests. It took less than a moment for him to discern that the odd male was my beau. Someone scurried to pull up another chair to the dining room table. "No, that's okay. I'm not staying," Jerry said. He gave me the flower bouquet and said again, "Happy birthday." My roommate led him to the door.

About a month later, Jerry phoned me to say that if I wasn't back in D.C. by the weekend he would divorce me. I asked if he already had the papers drawn up and if I would owe attorney fees and have to come to court. He said yes, no, and no. I told him to send the papers and I would sign them.

In less than a week the divorce papers arrived. Jerry claimed "abandonment" as grounds for divorce. I signed the papers and returned them by certified mail.

I PLANNED MY own 1975 birthday party. I decided my celebration should have a cause. I invited my New York relatives and cross section of friends—students and colleagues from Brooklyn College and other surrounding universities; 1199 hospital workers at Columbia Presbyterian; neighborhood bar friends; Communist Party members and other friends from progressive organizations; friends in the music industry, including the 1950s Teenagers who could still croon "Why Do Fools Fall in Love" and their other hits; friends in the theatre, especially cinema actresses Gracie Carroll and Beatrice

Winde; Harlem Renaissance playwright Abe Hill and his wife, Ruth Mueller, who sat on the National Executive Committee of the Republican Party. I asked my friends to bring "spirits" and to bring checkbooks and contributions in lieu of birthday presents. Maxine and I made the party trays of finger foods. The cause was to support the African National Congress and the anti-apartheid movement in South Africa. Some 100 friends celebrated my birthday with a collective contribution of more than a thousand dollars.

I WAS NOW a card-carrying Communist Party member. However, I could not find my niche. The first group I was assigned to was consumed with sharing their sessions with their therapists. Psychoanalysis was then the in-thing in New York City, but I was not in nor desired to be in analysis.

Upon request I was reassigned to a group of renowned intellectual communists. I was in the company of Herbert Apetheker, author and labor historian Eric Foner, Dorothy Burnham, and to my surprise, a colleague who worked with me at the School for Contemporary Studies and the Department of Education Services of Brooklyn College. I became acquainted with the "Benjamin Rush" and the "Orton" societies and presented full-length papers at their conferences. I enjoyed the stimulating discussions and grew intellectually as a result.

Nevertheless, I was still uncomfortable with the CP's policies. The party's subtlety in supporting President Richard Nixon in 1972, though Angela Davis ran as a Communist Party candidate for the U.S. presidency, did not sit well with me. I wondered if Angela's candidacy was to siphon off progressive votes. Nixon was a "law and order" candidate who gave increased rise to the FBI-CIA counter-intelligence program (COINTELPRO) that destroyed and devastated progressive organizations, especially black organizations, and that maimed and killed progressives, especially black progressives.

The party's opportunistic rationale was that Nixon had initiated a détente with the USSR that might end the cold war. I was certain that such discussions would lead to a "one world order" of unbridled capitalism and international thugism. My other concern was the invasion of Czechoslovakia by the USSR to put down democratic reforms.

The Soviet Union had yet to resolve the ethnic and cultural differences of what was called the "National Question" (the disrespect of culture and governance in the northern provinces of the USSR) And the CPUSA still persisted with the unrealistic line that "white workers will be the vanguard of the USA revolution." When the party put forth a short treatise that "racism was a special problem of black people," I was done. Black people did not have a "special problem." The special and peculiar problem was white racism. I was not about to become a part of blaming the victim. I was not going to allow racism to hide behind my black skin. I stopped going to Communist Party meetings. The party knew there was no need to call me in for a "criticism-self-criticism session." For all intents and purposes I withdrew my membership, though I maintained close friendships with many communists.

ONE SUNDAY I walked through wide double doors of Harlem's Canaan Baptist Church of Christ. The massive lobby of the former Loews Theater at 132 West 116th Street still had its charm. The concession stand was now enclosed as a room with chairs and special furnishings. The outer wall facing the lobby had an inscription in bold letters: "Liberation Chapel."

I walked through another set of large double doors. A hostess in a long red dress with beautiful white silk corsage pinned on the right shoulder greeted me as she handed me a bulletin. I walked down the descending aisle and took a cushioned seat on the end of a row. The decor of the huge auditorium that could seat 1,000 people on the main floor still resembled a movie house, but it was abundantly clear that I was in a house of worship.

The white-robed members of the sanctuary choir were in rapt attention as they faced the music director. In perfect harmony, their hundred voices lifted the congregation to a higher spiritual level. The song of praise was Mary A. Baker and H. R. Palmer's "Peace! Be Still!" And a complete peace did envelope me physically, mentally, and spiritually. I sat transfixed and permitted the spirit to restore my being and soul. I had not been in church as a worshipper for ten years.

The minister in his pastoral robe entered the platform from a side curtain. He took his seat behind the pulpit and was no longer in view. After following the Missionary Baptist Church's protocol of services, the choir stood in unison upon the director's cue. They sang "I'll Do His Will."

While the choir sang, the minister rose to the pulpit. Though it was now 1976, he looked exactly as I remembered him from 1956 when he delivered a stirring sermon at the Holt Street Missionary Baptist Church in Montgomery during the bus boycott. The Virginia preacher, the Reverend Dr. Wyatt T. Walker, now transplanted to New York City, had not lost his zeal to "preach the Word."

Walker, a scholar in religious music, joined in singing with the choir. Before the song came to an end, he began to line out Charles Wesley and Hugh Wilson's hymn, "A Charge to Keep I Have." Since my childhood I had loved this plaintive call of commitment even more than Isaac Watts and Hugh Wilson's "Amazing Grace," which is considered the national Baptist anthem.

The "lining out" was significant. When black people were no longer held in bondage as slaves and were denied education to learn how to read and to write, the religious leader would "line out the hymn." The genius of the black congregation would quickly retain and then repeat the words in a transposed musical arrangement in a poignant and penetrating manner that fortified the commitment "to keep the charge." This was a testimony that we would continue our race to freedom.

Reverend Walker's sermon that day came from Luke 15:11–32, the return of the prodigal son. Though I had not wasted my money nor possessions, I had allowed my spiritual life to lie dormant, thus wasted, in the name of the movement. It was such a contradiction when the movement during my lifetime had grown out of the church's transformation to the social gospel. Jesus was a revolutionary. He committed his life on earth to serve and to save people. He was crucified because of his commitment and his belief that people will fight back the demons in life and make the choice to be free for all eternity.

Before Reverend Walker ended his message of the father welcoming his prodigal son with loving and opened arms, I was marching down the aisle with joy in my heart and tears cascading from my eyes. I joined Canaan Baptist Church of Christ that Sunday and remained a faithful member until I left New York City.

29

Expanding My Human Understanding

Administrative politics at SCS were hot and heavy. I have yet to fully understand why intrigue and power struggles in the academy are endemic. Thankfully, George West, past SNCC campus traveler and now teaching at Goddard College in Vermont, asked me to apply for a visiting faculty position in Goddard's Adult Degree Program. I did and was hired.

The picturesque train ride to Montpelier, Vermont, was relaxing. The pristine snow, untouched by human feet, glistened and sparkled under the bright sunshine and blanketed the land. George met me at the station and drove me to Plainfield where Goddard College was located.

I had known George since our college days at Tuskegee Institute. George worked hard at being enigmatic and mysterious. He exuded a non-verbal aura of fear. If you became fascinated by his manner, you came under his spell. George had an uncanny "tinkering obsession" with cult development, voodoo, and the yin-yang approach to life. I found George's antics amusing. Because I did not fear him, or anyone else, he engaged in mental struggle in his efforts to control me. I knew he respected me and my teaching abilities, thus his informing me of the faculty vacancy, but I sensed that George had other motives for wanting me to be in his circle at Goddard College.

He took me to the winter/summer home of Anne and Charles Johnson for a short visit. To George's surprise, I already knew the Johnsons from the New York City movement. We then went to visit Betty Carter, one of my favorite jazz vocalists, and Danny Mixon, her pianist up from New York City to work on new compositions and arrangements. George, again, was surprised that I already knew Danny from the jazz clubs where he performed in the Big Apple. We visited other notables who lived in Plainfield. One was the secretary to the late Ghanian President Kwame Nkrumah, who had been assassinated. Not knowing who I was, she cautioned me—or was she talking to George—not to "tinker" with African religions of antiquity.

I spent the night in the home of George and his wife, and their infant daughter, whose crib was a cushioned dresser drawer. I found the well-insulated clapboard cottage, with a full bathroom and two large rooms, a kitchen and a living room which doubled as a bedroom, rather quaint. The large pot-bellied stove, reminding me of the smaller stove in my grandmother's home during my childhood, adequately warmed the cottage. George and I spent the evening talking about the genius astronomer Carl Sagan and George's current project of constructing an igloo as a winter home for his family.

The following day I arrived on campus. Dean Dick Herrmann oriented me on the innovative program to earn a bachelor or master's degree or a teaching certificate. Students had to devote twenty hours per week for prescribed home study, two weeks at the start and two weeks at the end of each semester. Mid-terms required an in-progress research paper based upon readings and field work. Students had to be in regular communication via letters and with visitations if possible with the assigned faculty member—me. A final research paper with an annotated bibliography was one of the requirements to pass the semester.

My teaching-learning objective focused on educational development with underpinnings of philosophy, psychology, and communications. In my syllabus, I stated:

> My concern is with the development of the thought process and the complement of curriculum, methodology and instruction in activating the thought process to higher levels of concept formation for conflict resolution. My philosophy of education is interactionist (student/teacher, environment/ability) and is based upon an interdisciplinary/intersensory approach.
>
> This process is to learn how to think, how to analyze, how to refute, how to formulate and how to articulate, verbally and written, those ideas and concepts which when implemented can resolve conflicts. Therefore, the thought process needed to write the simple sentence, progressing to the complex sentence, the paragraph, the research paper, to the formulation of social policy (sic) demands skills and comfortability with language. The outcomes are self-assurance in understanding phenomena, self-confidence

in expressing this understanding and offering solutions/social policies to resolve conflicts.

The bottom line being communications, we will look at written, verbal and visual expressions as means to social change. My goal is that we become scholar activists.

Eight undergraduate and graduate students, the maximum, signed up for my seminar. My students hailed from Vermont, Tennessee, New Jersey, Texas, Connecticut, and Massachusetts. Their subject matter included codifying with descriptions and then evaluating the delivery of services of social agencies in the student's community; analyzing speeches in the political arena; methods of encouraging young pupils to love reading; instructional communication media; the theories and practices of educational philosophy, thought and language and the relationships that determined behavior; and, a biographical novella by my oldest student, a divorced mother.

During the second week of teaching, I fell and traumatized the knee on my impaired leg. I was ordered complete bed rest and could only ambulate with crutches to and from the bathroom in the small faculty residence quarters. The students were determined not to be denied of my teaching. The male students hoisted the twin bed with me in it upon their shoulders and carried me to the faculty parlor. As the students were carrying me in my bed, I mused about London's Queen Elizabeth and Uganda's President Idi Amin who were hoisted in their carriages by their "subjects" to seats of "power."

After an intense two weeks, I had to return to New York City. I was still on crutches and knew I needed someone to help me negotiate train and subway steps. Marty, a Goddard student who was not in my seminar but often sat in on the discussions, offered to accompany me. I was deeply moved and grateful. Marty had Williams Syndrome, a genetic condition which causes many debilitating physical problems. A first glance at Marty could be shocking. However, there was nothing wrong with Marty's thinking capacity. She was brilliant. The train ride with Marty will forever be a cherished memory. It deepened my love for the human condition and gave real meaning and understanding of why we are here—to uplift each other. Marty was my guest for three days before she returned to Vermont.

Some time later, another student visited and stayed with me for five days to observe alternative schools: Little Red School House, Manhattan Country School, and Harlem School for Children and Parents. His study was a critical comparison of the educational philosophies of Piaget, Vygotsky, Montessori, and Dewey. His reading list of twenty-three books ranged from Bruno to Erickson to Haimowitz to Vygotsky. He was a freshman—a sterling reaffirmation that our movement to understand human development had taken hold.

Another student requested a two-week residency with me. Terri was not my student though she was the twin to one of my students, Millicent. Terri was writing a paper on African women of antiquity and her core professor, George West, suggested she should talk and study with me. My expertise was not within this subject matter.

From my limited knowledge and in consultation with Terri, we developed a learning plan for her to visit and arrange workshops at the Yoruba Temple in Harlem; arrange an interview with Professor John Henrik Clarke, the foremost scholar in African history and cultures; visit and talk with primary sources in a Haitian church and community in Brooklyn; study African women warriors, e.g., Dinzinga and Sitou; read the Bible and do research on Zipporah, Moses's wife, and Bathsheba, David's wife.

After Terri had been in my home for a week, I confronted and asked her, "Why are you really in my home, Terri?"

She hesitated, gazed into space, then said, "I've been ordered to kill you."

"Terri, look at me." She faced me. I searched her eyes as windows to her heart and soul.

"Why would you want to do somebody else's bidding? Our movement, our struggle, was to free ourselves of doing someone else's bidding, to free ourselves of physical and mental slavery. Do you *want* to kill me?"

She looked down at her hands in her lap. "No, ma'am." Her Tennessee upbringing was kicking in. "This week with you has been one of the most important experiences in my life. You are the model of commitment, love and caring for our people. I've learned much from you."

Suddenly, she was hugging me, tears streaming down her face. I consoled her by responding to her hug and patting her back as if she were a baby.

She did not have to tell me who gave her the order. In due time, I knew I would handle him. My concern was whether Terri could remain strong and independent in his presence when she returned to Goddard. It was clear that West was abusing his authority as her professor.

The need for "control over others" was the underpinning motive of Jim Crow and racism. This need escalated in its raw and inhumane form when black people en-masse determined not to do the bidding of Jim Crow any longer. A variation of this pathology with the same deadly outcome is the root of domestic violence and male supremacy. People who had the need to control others usually got out of control when they could not. This need, often parading as superiority, was really a reflection of insecurity and low self-esteem. It is sad when someone has the need for others to be inferior in order to feel whole as a human being.

She smiled in surprise when I told her to stay another week to write an annotated bibliography of the books she had read and brief summaries of her interviews and observations. She grabbed up her notes from the sofa and went straight to the typewriter in the study.

I was back at Goddard College at the end of the semester. I wasted no time in confronting the wanna-be incognito perpetrator: "Don't you ever send someone to do your bidding. If you have this sick need to kill me, trust me, I'm quite capable of defending myself. I am not afraid of you. And, for God's sake, please stop imbuing our youth with your evil thoughts. The fact that you attempt to brainwash our kids instead of trying to convince your peers of your thoughts is a blatant manifestation of your weakness."

He stared at me with his arms folded across his chest, his head cocked to the right and saying nothing.

"Whatever your beef is with me, I'm more than willing to sit down with you to talk about it in a civil and rational manner," I said.

Squinting his eyes, he said, "I'll like that."

We never did meet, however.

ALL OF MY students passed the semester with flying colors, including Terri. My student evaluations were worthy of framing as plaques of appreciation and commendation. My most favorite evaluation came from my divorced-mother-student: "I cannot tell you how pleased I am that I was able to work with you. You made a tremendous impression on me. I found you supremely intelligent—a no bull-shit woman."

The Goddard administration asked me to become a full-time faculty member as head of the teacher-certification committee. I was not ready to make the commitment. The winters were just too brutal to consider permanent residency in Plainfield, Vermont.

I spent my remaining two days at Goddard in the archives, perusing John Dewey's collection. I beamed with pride when I read that Dewey considered Alabama State Teachers' College (ASTC), the black college in Montgomery, Alabama, one of the best teacher-training programs in the country. Dewey's observation confirmed my selection of an ASTC graduate to earn her doctorate at Rutgers University as a Reverend Doctor Samuel Proctor Fellow.

On a day some time later my phone rang. Since childhood, I have never liked the telephone. Most of my life when people called me it was always about a demand to get something from me or to complain about their current situation in life or about their health. It was exceptionally difficult for me to listen to people who complained about their health problems when I overcame tuberculosis and three years of surgeries to walk on my own two feet, and I very seldom if ever talked about my physical tribulations. I never engaged in a "pity-party" and would not allow others to draw me into their realm of self-pity.

When I finally picked up the receiver, the caller identified himself as Mr. Hurte. "Ms. Patton, my daughters have told me that you are a wonderful professor at Goddard." I immediately knew he was the father of my student, Millicent, her twin sister Terri, and their younger sibling, Cherri. I thought how refreshing to receive a phone call of good news and not of bad news.

But his conversation quickly changed. He went on to say that Millicent had called to inform him that Terri and Cherri were part of a cult led by one of their professors and were off in some remote Vermont woods exercising rites of exorcisms. They thought they were transforming themselves into all-powerful supernaturals and zombies who would never die. "Millicent is frightened. Her sisters were ordered to kill her, but they couldn't."

I gasped, though I should not have been surprised.

He said he was going to Vermont with a deprogrammer to get his daughters back. My heart sank. I was not about to get entangled with this deadly intrigue.

He wanted to talk with me before he went to Vermont, but I told him it would be better if he visited me when he returned with his daughters in tow. Then, I said, we could have a meal in my home and I could talk with his daughters. I told him I had broken the spell over Terri when she was a student-resident in my home and I could do it again as long as she was not under the influence of her professor.

Ten days later, Mr. Hurte, his three daughters, and the deprogrammer were in my home. We talked little as we ate the meal I had prepared. I did learn from Millicent that it was a harrowing experience to "kidnap" her sisters from the woods. The deprogrammer had made some inroads, but it was obvious that future therapy was needed for the entire family.

George relocated to Haiti and helped produce a television documentary on voodoo religion that was aired in the U.S.

Terri eventually called to thank me for the intervention. She had become a practicing attorney in Detroit. I wondered how she handled cases of murder and attempted murder.

THE SUMMER OF 1977 continued to be full of challenges. The Soweto youth in South Africa, led by Steve Biko, founder of the Black Consciousness Movement, had an uprising. They, like their African American counterparts, were opposing apartheid-Jim Crow education that had been institutionalized to perpetuate racism and classism. The apartheid government, like the U.S. Southern Jim Crow government, attempted to smash the movement, murdering hundreds of Soweto youth.

One day Mary, a CPUSA member with whom I had remained friends, called to ask to meet with me. I invited her to my home for a light dinner, and over baked orange pork chops and a pickled beet salad, she said the party wanted my help in organizing a rally in support of the Soweto youth.

"Why me?" I asked. She replied that first, I was a good organizer, and second, I knew lots of people in Harlem and the CPUSA wanted many black people to attend the rally. I was somewhat taken aback. Part of the reason I left the party was the criticism I had received for my organizing style.

The party wanted to hold the rally downtown at the Local 1199 auditorium. I suggested it should be held uptown, at a black church in Harlem. She said the Party had few contacts with black churches. That was true, but I had contacts.

Eventually I agreed to help provided the rally would be planned by a broad coalition and held in a black church. Mary evidently presented a persuasive argument before the Party. She was given the green light to work with me.

I contacted the pastor of Convent Avenue Baptist Church, centrally located in Harlem at the corner of 145th Street. The minister was elated that his church was chosen as the rally site. I asked if one of his choirs could provide music and if one of the boards would serve as ushers. I anticipated an overflow gathering in the large church.

The Party subsequently sent letters to every church in Harlem. I also had an exhaustive list of Harlem groups, from nationalist organizations to social clubs to youth groups.

When I suggested that Borough President Percy Sutton, the progressive owner of a popular radio station, should bring greetings, the Party's staffers balked. They relented when I reminded them that Benjamin J. Davis, elected as a communist city councilman to represent Harlem in 1943, was subsequently imprisoned on McCarthy-related charges and that Harlem had unequivocally supported a "free Ben Davis" campaign.

The successful main planning meeting was held in the famed Liberation Chapel of my church, Canaan Baptist Church of Christ. CPUSA's members were astounded to be in the company of so many everyday black people. There were some cultural disconnects. Later, when we were hanging anti-apartheid banners in Convent Avenue Baptist before the rally, a communist attempted to place political literature on the Communion Table. He was spooked when I admonished him not to desecrate the table. We put the CPUSA political literature on the tables in the church vestibule instead.

The program was planned to include black and white, young and old, with Convent Avenue Baptist's pastor presiding. As a black, Baptist, Southern woman, I fully understood black preachers. It would have been an insult to ask the minister to use his church and not to include him prominently. Thousands of leaflets announcing the rally were printed to give to ministers for dissemination among their congregations and to youth to distribute in their schools and neighborhoods.

More than 1,000 people attended the rally. The crowd was electrified when the choir sang "Keep Your Eyes on the Prize and Hold On!" Even the communists were on their feet, clapping to this black Baptist hymn of perseverance and resolve.

ULTIMATELY, THE SAVAGE apartheid-police regime in South Africa kidnapped Steve Biko from the Soweto ghetto and brutally murdered him seven hundred miles away on a lonely back road. The Botha regime, armed with tanks and other military weapons, had already murdered more than six hundred unarmed students during the June 1977 Soweto uprising. Thousands of youth had been maimed, tortured, and imprisoned. Tens of thousands of black youth said, in one resounding voice, "Never!" to being taught in Afrikaans, the oppressor's language. Franz Fanon's *Black Skin, White Face* had internalized in the consciousness of South African black youth and in black youth across the Africa diaspora. Youth were fighting for their own minds, now anchored in black consciousness. "Black is Beautiful" and "I'm Black and I'm Proud" were universal themes.

Racism is inherently ignorant. Its weaknesses will always be exposed in the courageous face of a great movement. The state-sanctioned goon squads, thinking that their murder of Steve Biko on a back road would never come to light, demonstrated the limited thought process of the apartheid regime. Moreover, the racist notion that a movement is sustained by a leader, and if you kill the leader, the movement will die, shored up the irrational thinking of the oppressive regime.

Biko's murder galvanized the international anti-apartheid movement. Great movements are based on universal principles of human dignity and self-evident human rights. Just as the black community in Montgomery waged its 1955–56 successful city bus boycott for human dignity and against

Jim Crow seating patterns, so had black South Africans in 1957 boycotted against unjust hikes in bus fares.

LEARNING OF STEVE Biko's horrific murder in September 1977, I began to plan another birthday party fundraiser to support the African Nationalist Congress to call for immediate and unconditional release of Nelson Mandela. My first birthday party fundraiser in 1975 had been to support the South African anti-apartheid movement, the ANC, and Nelson Mandela and other political prisoners, and as a tribute to Michael X, who was hanged on May 16, 1975.

This time, my Local 1199 union friends, who worked at Columbia Presbyterian Hospital next door to my apartment building, wanted me to have a heartier spread than finger sandwiches: they brought two huge, well-seasoned beef roasts. My neighborhood bar friends brought a large ham, covered with pineapple and cherries, and a most delicious Chinese roast pork. My actress friends, Carroll and Beatrice, asked if they could bring their tarot-card-reader friend. He wanted to read cards for my guests, for a fee. I had no problem with that if 10 percent of his fee went to the "anti-apartheid pot."

As news of my "anti-apartheid-birthday party" spread, friends from Chicago, Boston, Plainfield, Philadelphia, Washington, Detroit, and Newark called to tell me they were coming. Again, my hospital-worker friends responded with food for my out-of-town guests to have Sunday breakfast. Such is the wisdom of grass-roots people to be hospitable.

Over 300 friends came to the party. They danced in the living room and front parlor, sated their appetites with the spread in the dining room, and played chess and cards in the study—10 percent of the poker pot had to go to the anti-apartheid movement. Tarot card readings were done in privacy in the "maid's room" off the kitchen. My bedroom was the arena for "movement talks" on the revolutionary developments in South Africa with international implications of black people fighting for their freedom everywhere on earth.

In the midst of all this, someone peeped his head around my bedroom door to announce that Stokely Carmichael and about six of his friends were at the door.

Stokely/Kwame had expatriated to Conakry, the capital of Guinea on the coast of West Africa. He was back visiting in the U.S. and had heard about the party. Kwame was a staunch supporter of the South African Pan African Congress (PAC) that basically had a racial analysis, while I supported the ANC that had a racial *and* class analysis. I wondered whether Kwame had internationalized the revolutionary-class significance of the three-day general strike of black and colored (mixed races) in South Africa with the complementary support of black, colored, and white students. This strike after the youths' Soweto's uprising shook the anti-apartheid government to its knees when the workers withheld their labor to continue to add to the coffers of the oppressive government.

Kwame came straight to my bedroom while his friends joined in the dancing and eating.

We were eager to hear about Kwame's experiences in the awesome presence and wisdom of Kwame Nkrumah and Sekou Toure. He explained why he had chosen his new name: In Africa, all names have specific meanings. "Kwame," in the name of the president of Ghana who was forced into exile with U.S. assistance, meant "redeemer of the nation." *Sekou*, meaning "defender of the poor," is the Madinka name of the president of Guinea. *Ture* was not *Toure*, but it was close and the affinity was clear.

Kwame/Stokely regaled us with tales about his involvement with armed committees to defend revolutions on the continent and the revolutionary commitment to serve the people in the implacable face of U.S. imperialism and neo-colonialist lackeys' determination to destroy the people's movement for freedom and human dignity.

Kwame shared his vivid descriptions of African countries. In addition to his permanent residency in Guinea, he had been to Ghana, Ivory Coast, Tanzania, Kenya, Uganda, South Africa, Senegal, and Algeria. I resolved that I would someday visit some of these African nations. I specifically wanted to see the "slave castles" that Europeans had built to hold our people in kidnapped captivity, later to be exported as chattel slave labor to enrich the nascent capitalist-economic system in the so-called "new world."

Listening intently to all this, I suddenly had a revelation. And I blurted out, "I'm going home!"

"To the Motherland? To Africa?" Kwame asked with delight dancing in his eyes.

"No, to Montgomery, Alabama. I need to give my Movement Report to the elders, to the wise old men and women of our freedom struggle here at home."

I DECIDED TO have a light teaching load for the summer of 1978. The past six months had been a whirlwind with a full-time faculty position at the School for Contemporary Studies, Brooklyn College, and being a visiting seminar lecturer at Goddard College. Plus I was doing educational consulting with E. M. Green Associates, which had a program-evaluation contract with Model Cities in Hudson County, New Jersey, and Kings County (Brooklyn), New York. To catch a respite, I only accepted two-hour per week visiting positions at Seton Hall in South Orange, New Jersey, and Brooklyn College in New York City.

One morning on one of my off days, I was propped up against a fluffy pillow in my bed. With a bowl of cubed fresh cantaloupe, I turned on the television to watch the *Today Show*. I was pleasantly surprised to see Tuskegee Mayor Johnny Ford, the first black ever elected mayor in Tuskegee, and his wife, Frances "Taz" Rainer Ford. She was a white University of Alabama graduate from Union Springs, Alabama. That was the surprise: she was not a northern liberal but a Southern belle. When I left Alabama in 1966, interracial marriages were against the law. Had race relations in Alabama progressed to embrace the human right to marry whomever you love?

I became even more determined to return home. Though I was not certain to land a job, given that Alabama Governor Wallace had warned me in no uncertain terms—with his face red with hostility— that I would never land a job in Alabama. This was when I was protesting outside the high school graduation ceremony of the "whites-only" Macon County Academy. This school was financed with state taxes; the graduation was being held in a state armory. Governor Wallace was the graduation speaker.

I threw Governor Wallace's threat to the wind and decided to step out on faith. I knew I wanted to go home to Montgomery, especially to be with my grandparents and relatives.

I called my many, many New York City friends to plan a series of "packing parties." Mayflower movers delivered a slew of packing boxes, crates and wrapping paper for dishes, paintings, and small items. A late August 1978 date was set for the movers to come to load the packed boxes and furniture.

In the interim, Dr. Luther Foster called. When I had visited him during my 1973 visit to Alabama, he had said he would appreciate my help in communicating with alumni. Now he asked me to consider a position at my alma mater to help with the Tuskegee Institute Centennial Capital Campaign that was to culminate in 1981.

"Nobody could raise money from the activists-students-alumni like you can," Dr. Foster implored. "If you accept, we will underwrite your traveling and moving expenses."

Who says God does not have "a ram in the bush" when you need one? My strong faith stood on this promise. I immediately accepted Dr. Foster's offer.

I sent letters of resignation to all my employers and signed authorization papers to withdraw my pension funds from the TIAA-CREF. Tuskegee Institute arranged a pre-paid Delta Airlines ticket for my pickup at LaGuardia Airport.

I was all set, ready to go. However, my neighborhood Palmetto Bar friends wanted to host a farewell-toast party. I was overwhelmed when so many people attended: colleagues, students, hospital union local 1199 members, neighbors, my doctor, my lawyer, and everybody else who happened to drop in for a nightcap. The juke box rocked with two of my favorite selections: Duke Ellington's rendition of "Take the A Train" and "One O'Clock Jump" by Count Basie. It was a night of pure reverie and memories, especially when my students, particularly my Vietnam vet students, mimicked my teaching styles. It was a hoot. When the vets punched up Teddy Pendergrass singing "Wake Up Everybody" and "What's Going On" by Marvin Gaye, tears cascaded down my cheeks.

I knew I would miss them and promised that I would stay in touch. But I wanted to go home.

I had seen a lot in my quest for freedom, justice and peace. I had savored ethnic cuisine, learned about new cultures and languages that melded together in a vibrant New York City of nine million people, lived in a variety of abodes, traveled extensively, and participated in various organizations with different philosophies, tactics, and strategies. My experiences had shown me the fundamental differences between personal transactions that led to individualistic, rank opportunism—for example, racism hiding behind a black skin (Fanon's *Black Skin, White Mask*)—and personal transformations that gave rise to lifelong moral principles. It had been made clear to me that the movement is a mindset, a lifestyle in conducting one's life, a set of values that propelled purpose in all personal endeavors to uplift self, family, community, and the world where you live.

It had been twelve years since I left home. It seemed like a lifetime.

Yes, I wanted to go home. I wanted to give an account to my family, my mentors and elders who had shaped me since my infancy to continue the transformational legacy to uplift our people.

Epilogue

So in August 1978, I indeed did move back to Alabama.

The family gathering held in honor of my homecoming was heartwarming and reassuring that I had made the right decision to rejoin the fold. I was met by cousins at the Montgomery airport and whisked away to a welcome home dinner featuring traditional Southern foods—crispy fried chicken, collard greens boiled with ham hocks, steamed okra, "cha-cha" (chow-chow), hot buttered corn on the cob, macaroni and cheese, cornmeal hoe cakes, and fresh peach cobbler. I was definitely back home.

I bought a car and a house and settled in, and although I have traveled over the years to Canada, China, Mexico, Africa, the Caribbean, and Europe, I have not lived away from Montgomery again. Nor did I ever remarry. Before moving from New York, I had talked by phone with Jerry.

I told him not to call or visit me, that there would be no reconciliation. I have not heard from him since.

Shortly after Labor Day 1978, I started working on the Tuskegee Institute Centennial Campaign, which concluded with a great Gala Festival in 1981. Over the next 35 years, I kept food on the table with various teaching and administrative positions at Tuskegee (now University), Alabama State University, and Trenholm State Technical College. At Trenholm, my last institution, I became an archivist as well, creating an archives program unique for such two-year vocational colleges and now containing the valuable papers and documents of a number of significant Montgomery civil and voting rights activists such as Solomon S. Seay Sr., Rufus Lewis, Idessa Redden, Charles Conley, and Zecozy Williams. I retired from Trenholm in 2015, at age 72.

Of course, I had not put my own activism in a box on a shelf when I left New York in 1978. Between and sometimes during my academic appointments in Montgomery, I worked with the National Political Congress of Black Women to organize civil rights tours of the South to teach youth about their legacy; with Congressman John Conyers on low-income housing initiatives; with the Children's Defense Fund and United Church of Christ on programs for children of incarcerated mothers; as coordinator of the Southern Regional Anti-Apartheid Movement; as a consultant for the National Committee on Independent Political Action; as organizer for the Southern Rainbow Education Program, the Working Group on Electoral Democracy, and the Federation of Southern Cooperatives; among others. All of this work entailed building coalitions of grassroots organizations, unions, and church and community groups to encourage economic and social justice and more inclusive electoral participation. Some of it was effective, some less so. All of it felt worthwhile.

I also ran for political office several times. In 1986, after being denied tenure (for what I felt was political reasons) at Alabama State University, I challenged popular State Representative Alvin Holmes in my local House district. Alvin and I clashed to the point that my father flew down from Detroit to "straighten him out," and I lost, but since then Alvin and I have become good friends. My second campaign was in 1992 as an Independent challenger to incumbent U.S. Senator Richard Shelby (then masquerading as a Democrat). Unfortunately, I had to sue the Alabama Secretary of State's office to get on the ballot, and U.S. District Judge Robert Varner, never a friend of constitutional rights, ruled against me, so my campaign never got out of the starting gate. In 1994, I ran for a seat on the Montgomery County Commission. My father again supported me, but he was so disillusioned with politics that he was relieved when I lost. "Gwen," he said, "you cannot play the political game. Your principles will not allow you to compromise to an action that you think will harm the black community. Stay in and be a part of the community, the grassroots. Change comes from the bottom up."

I understood his feelings and shared them to some extent. After 1994, I gave up on politics as the vehicle for change, and I never sought political office again.

SOON AFTER I moved back to Montgomery, I joined Hutchinson Missionary Baptist Church. I was a fourth-generation member. My grandfather, Sam Patton, had been the general contractor for construction of a new sanctuary after eminent domain took the old church to make way for Interstate 85. Sam and Mary Jane (MaDear, the grandchildren called her) Patton were faithful members of the church and were well-known in the community.

Every Sunday after church services, I visited with my Patton grandparents for dinner. I was always amused when Granddaddy would put two scoops of ice cream in his and my dessert bowls and only one scoop in MaDear's bowl. When she complained, he reminded her that she had diabetes and he didn't. My greatest joy came while sitting at their large dining room table to make out checks for Granddaddy to sign. At last I had convinced my grandparents to move some of their savings account to a checking account. Gone was the day of my driving about the city to purchase money orders and then to various establishments to pay their bills.

My maternal grandmother, Mommy—Juanita Foster Bolden Washington—had welcomed me back to Montgomery with a round of elegant tea parties for the friends I had known when we were teenagers who were still living in Montgomery. Most were now college graduates and working. One of my special guests was Viola Bradford, who as a high school student had worked on the civil rights era newspaper, the *Southern Courier*, then interned for *Newsweek* while she was a college journalism student. When Mommy's tea party brought us back together, she was teaching at Alabama State University and producing "Harambee," an Alabama Public Television show; I happily accepted her offer to be a commentator.

Thankfully, I had come home when I did and was able to spend some precious time with my grandparents before they died. Granddaddy Patton passed in 1979 at age 79. MaDear lived another six years and passed in 1985 at age 82. Both are buried in our family plot in Montgomery's Oakwood Cemetery.

Poppa Washington died suddenly in 1980 while visiting his New York family, and Mommy and I agreed he should be buried there. Shortly after we held a memorial service for him in Montgomery, Mommy herself took ill. She died that fall, at age 76, and is buried in Kindle Cemetery in Montgomery.

Meanwhile, I was battling my own health problems. Ironically, given all the traumas I had suffered with my leg, the most serious leg- and foot-related challenge I have faced has been the difficulty of finding corrective shoes so I could walk evenly. Instead, this time I had a tumor in my breast. I was the same age as my mother when cancer killed her. However, I had a mastectomy and survived.

My father had visited me once a year when I lived in New York. Now that I was in Montgomery, he visited at least four times a year to do repairs in my home, wash my windows, oversee the care of my lawn, and of course to visit with our many relatives and his high school and college buddies.

His eventual divorce from Lois (she passed in 2005) had been inevitable, partly because she prevented their children from getting the upbringing Bob and I had when we spent entire summers in Montgomery during our childhoods and youth. My father deeply loved his extended family and saw the value in bonding with them to strengthen roots and continue their legacy.

My father became very ill in 1998. My brother Bob was his caregiver. While visiting them in Inkster, not long before his death, I asked my father if he wanted to be buried in the Patton family plot in Montgomery. He said, "No, bury me next to your mother in Westlawn Cemetery" [Wayne, Michigan]. He made his transition in 2000 at age 77.

My siblings are all living.

Brother Bob retired as a UAW union member from the Ford plant in 1999 and lives in our hometown of Inkster, Michigan.

Sister Sandy retired as voice instructor with the Swiss School of Jazz in Bern, Switzerland. She has had a spectacular career as a vocal artist and continues to record and to perform in jazz venues throughout Europe.

Brother Frank is a practicing anesthesiologist in the Atlanta area.

Brother Jeffery is a bank vice president in Ypsilanti, Michigan.

Though my grandparents and parents and my aunts and uncles now live only in our memories, I have many nieces, nephews, cousins, and in-laws who still live, albeit scattered around the country and globe.

Living and dead, my extended family members remain meaningful to me. As Dick Gregory said, "A man without knowledge of himself and his heritage is like a tree without roots."